Love and Violence in Sierra Leone

In the decades following the civil war that took place in Sierra Leone between 1991 and 2002, new laws were passed to rebuild the state and to prevent rape, teenage pregnancy, and domestic violence. In this ethnography, Luisa T. Schneider explores the intricate semantic, empirical, and socio-legal dynamics of love and violence in contemporary Sierra Leone, challenging the oversimplification of these phenomena. Schneider underscores the limitations of imposing singular interpretations on love and violence, advocating for a nuanced, phenomenological approach that reveals how state and institutional attempts to regulate violence and loving relationships without considering local lived experience and meaning-making can yield negative consequences. By analysing how love and violence are historically constituted, experienced, and (re)produced across personal, social, legal, and political levels, this book critiques the construction of violence within gendered sexual relationships by development agencies, lawmakers, and politicians, urging them to engage with local knowledge and experience.

Luisa T. Schneider is a sociocultural anthropologist specialising in intimacy, violence, and law. Schneider is Assistant Professor at VU Amsterdam, a published academic and public author, and advisor to policy-makers and practitioners. She has conducted ethnographic research that emphasises the importance of local knowledge for over ten years.

THE INTERNATIONAL AFRICAN LIBRARY

General Editors

LESLIE BANK, *Human Sciences Research Council, South Africa*
HARRI ENGLUND, *University of Cambridge*
DEBORAH JAMES, *London School of Economics and Political Science*
ADELINE MASQUELIER, *Tulane University, Louisiana*
HELENE NEVEU-KRINGELBACH, *University College London*
DAVID PRATTEN, *University of Oxford*

Managing Editor
STEPHANIE KITCHEN, *International African Institute, London*

The International African Library is a major monograph series from the International African Institute. Theoretically informed ethnographies, and studies of social relations 'on the ground' which are sensitive to local cultural forms, have long been central to the Institute's publications programme. The IAL maintains this strength and extends it into new areas of contemporary concern, both practical and intellectual. It includes works focussed on the linkages between local, national, and global levels of society; writings on political economy and power; studies at the interface of the sociocultural and the environmental; analyses of the roles of religion, cosmology, and ritual in social organisation; and historical studies, especially those of a social, cultural, or interdisciplinary character.

For a list of titles published in the series, please see the end of the book.

Love and Violence in Sierra Leone

Mediating Intimacy after Conflict

Luisa T. Schneider
Vrije Universiteit Amsterdam

CAMBRIDGE
UNIVERSITY PRESS

Shaftesbury Road, Cambridge CB2 8EA, United Kingdom

One Liberty Plaza, 20th Floor, New York, NY 10006, USA

477 Williamstown Road, Port Melbourne, VIC 3207, Australia

314–321, 3rd Floor, Plot 3, Splendor Forum, Jasola District Centre, New Delhi – 110025, India

103 Penang Road, #05–06/07, Visioncrest Commercial, Singapore 238467

Cambridge University Press is part of Cambridge University Press & Assessment, a department of the University of Cambridge.

We share the University's mission to contribute to society through the pursuit of education, learning and research at the highest international levels of excellence.

www.cambridge.org
Information on this title: www.cambridge.org/9781009533034

DOI: 10.1017/9781009532990

© Luisa T. Schneider 2025

This publication is in copyright. Subject to statutory exception and to the provisions of relevant collective licensing agreements, with the exception of the Creative Commons version the link for which is provided below, no reproduction of any part may take place without the written permission of Cambridge University Press & Assessment.

An online version of this work is published at doi.org/10.1017/9781009532990 under a Creative Commons Open Access license CC-BY-NC-ND 4.0 which permits re-use, distribution and reproduction in any medium for non-commercial purposes providing appropriate credit to the original work is given. You may not distribute derivative works without permission. To view a copy of this license, visit https://creativecommons.org/licenses/by-nc-nd/4.0.

When citing this work, please include a reference to the DOI 10.1017/9781009532990.

First published 2025

A catalogue record for this publication is available from the British Library.

Library of Congress Cataloging-in-Publication Data
Names: Schneider, Luisa T. (Luisa Theresia), 1991– author.
Title: Love and violence in Sierra Leone : mediating intimacy after conflict / Luisa T. Schneider.
Description: Cambridgef ; New York, NY : Cambridge University Press, 2024. | Series: The international African library | Includes bibliographical references and index.
Identifiers: LCCN 2024014457 (print) | LCCN 2024014458 (ebook) | ISBN 9781009533034 (hardback) | ISBN 9781009533003 (paperback) | ISBN 9781009532990 (epub)
Subjects: LCSH: Intimate partner violence–Sierra Leone. | Sexual assault–Law and legislation–Sierra Leone. | Sierra Leone–Social conditions–1961–
Classification: LCC HV6626.23.S44 S45 2024 (print) | LCC HV6626.23.S44 (ebook) | DDC 362.82/9209664–dc23/eng/20240520
LC record available at https://lccn.loc.gov/2024014457
LC ebook record available at https://lccn.loc.gov/2024014458

ISBN 978-1-009-53303-4 Hardback

Cambridge University Press & Assessment has no responsibility for the persistence or accuracy of URLs for external or third-party internet websites referred to in this publication and does not guarantee that any content on such websites is, or will remain, accurate or appropriate.

For you

Contents

List of Figures		*page* viii
Acknowledgements		ix
Glossary		xii
	Introduction	1
1	Access, Methodology, and Ethics	19
2	The Impact of Violence on Relationships	42
3	Loving and Living Relationships in Freetown Today	59
4	The Spectrum of Violence in Relationships	76
5	The Language of Violence	93
6	Household and Community Mediations of Violence	112
7	Invoking the State: When Adults Report Violence in Their Relationships to the Police	144
8	Minors before the Law: Building Futures, Policing Sex	169
9	Perpetrators? The Consequence of the Sexual Offences Act for Young Men	194
	Conclusion	212
	References	232
	Index	252

Figures

1.1	The logo of Eat As You Can	*page* 20
1.2	Aunty Watche's house	21
1.3	The compound I shared with 11 others at Allentown	24
5.1	Sharing food near 24	101
8.1	An example of the campaigning that accompanied the SOA. Poster by UN Women and UNFPA	176
8.2	Poster framing early sex as destructive	177
8.3	Then president Ernest Bai Koroma's poster under the cotton tree	180
8.4	President Ernest Bai Koroma as the guardian	181
C.1	Poster in Freetown	228

Acknowledgements

I thank the many Sierra Leoneans who made this book possible. My heart goes out to their incredible strength and resilience, to the love and warmth with which they strike back when hit by calamities, to the laughter with which they terminate palaver, and to their ability to embrace life with and not despite all its twists and turns. Amongst the many things you taught me, I am most thankful for learning to measure days not in hours but in interpersonal encounters and to be determined to find the ounce of gold in a seemingly endless morass of dirt.

To those who generously shared their life stories and entrusted me with sensitive and often painful aspects of their experiences, I am deeply indebted. I am equally grateful to those who allowed me to accompany them in their daily lives and attend hearings of deeply personal cases, and to those who conversed with me or welcomed my presence within prison walls. I sincerely hope that I have done justice to the faith you placed in me. You are the body and soul of this monograph. Many individuals remain unnamed in these pages due to potential risks associated with revealing their cases, while others have since passed away. My aspiration, however, is that this work will serve as a lasting tribute to your memory.

I thank the extended households at Allentown, Naimbana Street, and 24 for their hospitality and unwavering support. I owe a great debt to Darren, Mr. Mohamed, Aunty Eleanor, Papani, Aunty Kadie, Mariama, Isatu, small Isatu, small Kadie, small Eleanor, Josephus, Aunty Watche, and all EAUC members: thank you!

I am grateful to the Studienstiftung des deutschen Volkes, Oxford University, and the Distinguished Women Scientists Fund (LNVH) for funding fieldwork in Sierra Leone. I am grateful to Russel Martin for his careful editing and his keen eye for detail and to Eugene Jones for checking the Krio and for offering invaluable lessons that had me delve deeper into the etymology of certain words and their spelling. I thank the IAL and, in particular, Stephanie Kitchen and Deborah James for working so deeply with me on this manuscript. Not only did you think with me about framing and content, but you also offered practical support and answered my many questions. I am grateful to three anonymous reviewers for their careful reading and invaluable suggestions. I hope I did your suggestions justice. Any faults are my own.

I thank Hawa-Jane Bangura for her beautiful design of the book's cover. I am grateful to Ashlee Beazley, Maaike Matelski, and Rebekah King for their continuous emotional and linguistic support. I could not have hoped for better friends! Thank you David Pratten and Ramon Sarró for your academic mentorship and unwavering support. I am furthermore thankful to Elizabeth Ewart and Hélène Neveu Kringelbach for their careful reading of my work and for urging me to publish it. I thank them for their feedback and encouragement with regard to both publishing this work and pursuing academia with open eyes. I would also like to thank Michael Jackson for the brunch that reminded me why I want to continue the way I started and the many emails that meant the world.

Thanks also to those who read drafts of the proposal or chapters, sent resources, or had conversations with me that gave me ideas, including, but not limited to, Andrew Jefferson, Stephen Jensen, Amanda Hammar, Tomas Max Martin, Julienne Weegels, Alice Ievins, Rune Larsen, Bertram Turner, Bethany Schmidt, Anastasiia Omelianiuk, and Robbert Dillema. I am furthermore grateful to Freek Colombijn, Ellen Bal, and Marina de Regt for their academic friendship and support.

Thank you to Andrew Jefferson, Lotte Baelum Mortensen, and Amanda Hammar for opening their doors and sharing their homes with me and for making me feel like I belong when I had nowhere to turn. Thank you to DIGNITY, the Danish Institute Against Torture, and the Center for African Studies in Copenhagen for having me as a fellow and providing a simultaneously calm and stimulating environment to progress with my writing. I thank my colleagues at the Max Planck Institute for Social Anthropology for providing the space and support necessary to complete this work and for supporting its publication emotionally and financially. I am grateful to the Department of Law and Anthropology under Marie-Claire Foblets, which generously financed the Open Access publication of this work. Thank you to the Anthropology Department at Vrije Universiteit Amsterdam for providing an academic home and for supporting the final steps of this manuscript. Furthermore, I am grateful to the editors and publishers of articles where I first explored some of the ideas that have been more fully developed in this monograph. For further details, please refer to the following publications:

Schneider, Luisa T. 2020. 'Degrees of permeability: confinement, power and resistance in Freetown's Central Prison', *Cambridge Journal of Anthropology* 38 (1): 88–104.

Schneider, Luisa T. 2020. 'Elders and transactional relationships in Sierra Leone: rethinking synchronic approaches', *Africa: Journal of the International African Institute* 90 (4): 701–20.

Schneider, Luisa T. 2019. 'Partners as possession: a qualitative exploration of intimate partner sexual violence in Freetown, Sierra Leone', *Journal of Aggression, Maltreatment & Trauma* 28 (2): 127–45.

I am grateful to Marcin, Micha, Mailee, Laura, Rune, Lisa, Anna, Hanneke, and Youri for their love, feedback, and encouragement. Thank you for always bringing the sun back into my life and for helping me find my way after I got lost. To my parents, Karin and Roland, who never cease to inspire me: if I did it, I did it because of how you raised me!

I thank my family and loved ones for much more than words can contain.

Glossary

ansa bele	a practice regulating pregnancies out of wedlock by which a man accepts full social and financial responsibility for a pregnancy
ataya bes	a coffee place for men serving *ataya* tea, which is believed to provide energy; mostly young people gather there to drink and discuss politics and daily events
bambrus or *bambrusing*	treating someone or something roughly; can also be used to describe rough sex limited to penetration; can also indicate rape
bod ose	a wooden house
bossing	consensual sex where the man is dominant
chɛr am	to tear, to rip apart; here it is describing men's sexual conquest of attractive women
cober lappas	minors, 'girl lovers'
contract relationships	cohabiting partners who are not exclusive but may not bring other lovers home
cut	male orgasm
cut and play	sex that considers male and female pleasure
fala-fala	someone who loves to escort another person; here a love potion that leads a person to follow another person wherever they go; *fala* can also mean to have sex
faray	an addicted smoker; also used to describe a woman who is embedded in street life and who smokes but who does not engage in sex work

Glossary

financiers or providers	middle-aged men/elders who enjoy the (sexual) company of women and girls in exchange for financial support, often in the form of school/university fees or rent
fine boy	pretty boy; a physically attractive or sexually skilled person without the financial resources desired of a main partner
gbagba	black magic that prevents someone from urinating or going to the toilet; this spell is said to be often used against 'passers-by' (q.v.)
gɛt bɛlɛ	to be pregnant
gɛt-to gɛda or <u>*chillin*</u>	outing organised by social clubs in Freetown for club members and friends
ifohn or *swear medicines*	traditional medicines used in oath ceremonies as truth-determining devices in theft cases
kedi masta	someone who runs a brothel or gambling place and who takes a commission for services provided in exchange for a place, security, or introduction to customers; brothels are often run by women
ketch	to catch; also the name a female sex worker may use for a customer or a man to describe a new sexual partner
kongosa	gossip, backbiting
lɛk-lɛk	love potion mixed in substances, food, or ointments; used against a partner to prevent them from loving someone else; used against a stranger to make them fall hopelessly in love and surrender all control; the charmed person's free will is taken away
mami kɔs	calling someone's children bastards, thereby cursing someone's mother
mami kwin or *mammie queen*	female leader
mas am	to step on someone; also used to describe men or boys sexually penetrating women or girls, yet not necessarily in a violent way
na mi bɔs am	I am the one responsible for taking her virginity

Glossary

nak am	means to hit someone, but is also a slang term for having sex; for example, *Ar wan nak am* means I want to have sex with her
nɔr lɛf mi so	do not leave me like that
pan bɔdi	corrugated-iron house; zinc house
passer-by	a man who makes empty promises to a woman or who only takes when having sex and does not give the woman pleasure
pikin biznɛs	child's play; also used to indicate a physical relationship that involves kissing and touching but does not lead to sex
plaba	palaver, to quarrel or fight
play	female orgasm
playing in her garden	a man sexually pleasuring a woman; a man giving oral sex to a woman
pul di bɛlɛ or *pwɛl di bɛlɛ*	to have an abortion; to perform an abortion
pul na do	the naming ceremony for Muslim babies
put mɔt pan di fɛt or *putting mouth into the fight*	involving oneself in someone else's argument; talking to people while they are fighting
rare gal	female sex worker deeply involved in street life and sometimes in gangs
I nɔr ansa di bɛlɛ	to deny having caused a pregnancy
rɔb- rɔb	ointments that are believed to be magical and that people rub on their bodies either for protection from magic that could be used against them or as a charm to use against others for personal desires
sexing	consensual sexual act
show face	the father of a baby introduces himself to the family of the woman he impregnated, to confirm that the baby has a father without taking social or economic responsibility for the child or the mother
side-chick	a woman who is very attractive or sexually skilled but who is believed not to possess the qualities of a main partner and is therefore an intimate partner among others
snatching	stealing someone's partner

Glossary

sugar daddies	middle-aged men/elders, who enjoy the (sexual) company of girls and young women in exchange for money, mobile phone credit, clothes, or hair
swallow	apologise ritually at the end of informal community and household mediations and acknowledge that all issues have now been attended to
swear (n.)	an oath
tabulay (n.) or *tabule* (v.)	a drum or to drum; can also be a nickname for male or female sexual organs
tap to mi	cohabiting without being engaged or married
tay-tay	(mostly ropes) that are believed to be magical that people tie on their bodies, for example on the waist, ankle, wrist, or neck; this is done either for protection from magic used against them, or as a charm to use against others for personal desires
tɛdi bɔi	a gang member or young man engaged in the illicit economy who asks his girlfriend to make money for him (often through sex work and associated trickery)
tit ɛn tɔŋ mɔs jam or teeth and tongue jammed together	the quarrels that necessarily occur between people who are close (e.g. kin, lovers, or friends); it is used to describe the relationship between men and women
toma	namesake (i.e. someone with whom you share the same first name); a term especially used by the Mende people
wahala	conflict, trouble, or problem

Introduction

One Metaphor, Many Faces

Papani (55) leans back on his bench, so that his back rests against the coarse yellow stone wall of the two-room-house which we share with nine others in the hillside community of Allentown in the eastern part of Freetown. He closes his eyes to let the sun kiss his face or maybe to block out my anxious expression. He takes time to answer, and, while I observe him, I feel like one massive bundle of nerves.

After many years of research and countless conversations on this very bench, I had just explained to Papani once again how I aimed to write this ethnography of violence in relationships. This was the ninth time I offered a framing, and, at last, the sun seems to have penetrated the skin as his features turned to one big smile:

Madam Schneider, finally you have understood that all rests not within one interpretation against the other but in their simultaneous presence with all the hardship this entails. Mind you that this insight was always with you in the metaphor of the teeth and the tongue. You just needed time to see that all these different interpretations are like a microcosm for our world.

The metaphor of the teeth and tongue jammed together (*Tit ɛn tɔŋ mɔs jam*), which Papani refers to, says something valuable about the relationship between men (teeth) and women (tongue). During my research in Freetown, the teeth and the tongue were my constant companions. This notion was invoked again and again to express widely contrasting attitudes towards love and violence in Sierra Leone. These differing interpretations can also be found in development discourses, anthropological literature, and oral history. Gender studies read the teeth and the tongue as a metaphor for sex and for the female reproductive organs (Bledsoe 1980a). Development discourses tend to see in it a critique of physical violence against women, of men's sense of entitlement, and of gender inequality. Indeed, it was often referred to when I spoke with employees of international organisations (IOs) or non-governmental organisations (NGOs), development practitioners, policy-makers, and expats working in and on Sierra Leone. I was told that the tongue represents the woman, who is locked in and controlled by the teeth without the possibility of escape or independent existence, getting bitten whenever she makes a questionable move. The teeth stand for violent men ready to crush and grind anything that gets in their way. Many of my interlocutors invoked an individualistic, rights-, and empowerment-based narrative (see Abdullah and Fofana-Ibrahim 2010) when proposing their solution to this scenario of patriarchal oppression. In their view, women's empowerment should be achieved through awareness raising, education, a well-functioning legal and political system, and the implementation of universal human rights. These would ideally allow women to leave those men who maltreat them and, though this is hardly ever mentioned, men to leave those women who hurt them.

In contrast, local understandings hold that the metaphor of the teeth and the tongue highlights the complementarity of men and women. Without teeth and tongue, it becomes impossible to digest food and people will starve and eventually die. The teeth chew the food, while the tongue helps to move it around. Before swallowing, the tongue must move some of the chewed food towards the back of the throat and into the opening of the oesophagus. The teeth are responsible for the manual labour, while the tongue organises the processing and distribution of food and is also the organ of taste. Between themselves, teeth and tongue divide the labour necessary to nourish the body, but, while they agree on the overall goal and the need to cooperate, their relationship is not inherently harmonious. In relationships between men and women, teeth and tongue may collide or hurt each other. But the bottom line is that no matter their disputes, neither can nourish the body without the other. Hence, they are jammed together, not in the sense of something blocked or unworkable, but in the sense of codependency and reliance. I was often told that 'no matter how often the one hurts the other, they still stay together in one mouth. They need each other'. The men (the teeth) do the rough, independent work, while the women (the tongue) are the soft organs, the social connectors to family and community, and thus those who give taste and meaning to a relationship.[1]

---

[1] These are but two well-known interpretations. Metaphors are of course open to many readings and constantly reinterpreted. See, for example, the birdcage metaphor in feminist discourses or Ramon Sarró's (2005) work on differing notions of 'the throat and the belly' among the Baga. Sarró argues that teeth and throat open two different symbolic domains. Swallowing is constructive of personhood and community, while chewing is destructive. In many African languages, eating something that implies chewing with the teeth (such as meat) is expressed with a different verb from eating something for which the throat alone is necessary (such as rice).

These contrasting interpretations of the same metaphor show how different outlooks, experiences, and dispositions can give rise to a broad variety of understandings of the same process. This is true, too, of the function and significance of violence in relationships and of appropriate forms of mediation and punishment. Such variance in interpretation, which is based on the social positions of various actors, is crucial for the analysis to come in this book.

Indeed, love and violence are strong concepts, which have come to form doxa, in that many believe they know precisely what love and violence entail. Yet, these popular opinions are not necessarily epistemes, and people's beliefs often contradict not only each other but accepted practices, rules, and laws as well. This makes them particular analytical problems. The two seem to occupy polar opposites that are connected along lines of intention, purpose, and consequence. They are affective and emotional concepts and are seen as both intensely individual and at the same time connected to the making and breaking of personal, social, and societal bonds. Love and violence lie at the heart of social, economic, political, and legal fabrics. And they also trigger interventions. However, while policy-makers need simple narratives to frame social problems and justify intervention, just as lawmakers rely on them to defend legal prescriptions and sanctions, these narratives tend to collapse when they come up against lived experiences (for an analysis of such narratives, see Autesserre 2012). The resulting 'social struggles' around power, justice, rights, and violence – and the social, political, and institutional responses to them – reveal discrepancies between global (rights) epistemes and local lived experience (Cowan, Dembour, and Wilson 2001; Cowan 2006). They challenge us to find ways to reconcile competing claims and justifications, but also to accept the idea of incommensurability (Cowan, Dembour, and Wilson 2001; Cowan 2006). Uncovering the difficulty of imposing single words charged with strong connotations – like 'love' or 'violence' – to capture phenomena that are empirically diverse and complexly related, this phenomenological and critically feminist book deconstructs singular meanings and foregrounds the ways in which both love and violence are locally experienced and conceived.

Ethnographies that illuminate such discrepancies between local meanings and political, legal, or policy conceptions can help enhance the knowledge of policy-makers and improve social interventions. In particular, the anthropologist can penetrate below the surface to uncover those underlying nuances that otherwise remain invisible. During the two decades following the civil war in Sierra Leone (1991–2002), the country experienced rapid and fundamental legal changes. Laws were passed to rebuild the state and in particular to prevent rape and teenage pregnancy. These laws ended up severely impacting on relationship dynamics, triggering fundamental changes in the politics of intimacy and throwing the respective jurisdictions of households, communities, and criminal justice institutions into question. Yet we lack an analysis of the deeper context that goes beyond the current political moment. *Love and Violence* seeks to remedy this by providing a thorough analysis of the role and place of violence within intimate relationships and its mediation. In this way, I hope to unravel the changing role of the state and its component organisations and illuminate the relationships between the state, individuals, communities, and households.

In the course of this study, the metaphor of the teeth and the tongue offers a framework for understanding how my research collaborators,[2] the Sierra Leoneans with whom and alongside whom I conducted my research, execute, witness, or endure violence; how they make sense of their experiences; and how they navigate between household, community, and state systems to mediate violence. The metaphor furthermore helps us understand how these different systems conceptualise and mediate violence in terms of their respective ideals of gender relations, and how partnerships and individuals often become 'jammed' between these opposing ideals.

The Relationship between Love and Violence

This book is an ethnographic study of violence in intimate relationships in Sierra Leone. It explores how such violence is experienced, negotiated, and regulated in the context of often colliding domestic, local, international, and global forces. In this sense, it addresses two core concerns of our time: (1) the understanding and control of intimacy and sexual practices; and (2) the meaning and role of violence in relationships and the appropriate forms of its regulation. Violence and intimacy are becoming increasingly pressing issues in our contemporary world, shaping relations between states, institutions, and people. This is especially the case in sub-Saharan Africa, where a politico-legal discourse about the control of intimacy and sexual practices seeks to legitimise the expansion of state jurisdiction into spheres that are otherwise reserved for communities or households (see, for instance, Thomas 2003; Parikh 2004b; 2012; Lorway 2008; Tamale 2011; Steinberg 2013). A complicated history of international influence and exploitation weighs down on these states, which

---

[2] In this book, I use the term 'research collaborator' to refer to the people who let me into their lives and with and alongside whom I conducted research.

are being pressured to further international development agendas. In this book, I explore this trend in Freetown, focussing on what happens when state institutions and local communities fundamentally disagree on how to approach issues of intimacy and violence.

This ethnography first introduces the reader to contemporary relationship dynamics in Freetown and the diverse forms of violence within them. I examine the social significance of violence in intimate relationships and the gendered dimension of such violence. I show in which circumstances specific violent acts are tolerated or even expected, and when they are seen to cross a line. I then analyse how violence regarded as illegitimate is mediated and punished within a complex plural legal system by households, communities, and criminal justice institutions. The book combines a detailed examination of laws and policies around violence prevention and response with grassroots conceptions of violence in relationships in Sierra Leone. In this way, it contributes to the anthropological literature on the multiple, often contradictory pressures and influences exerted on persons and institutions as they enact, experience, and respond to violence.

An important precondition for a fuller and deeper understanding of this phenomenon, which is essential for developing social policies that actually work, is analysing what is considered to be violence and what is not and questioning prevailing interpretations and responses to violence. Scholarship that only localises or individualises violence neglects larger structural factors. Studies that shy away from including perspectives that complicate one-dimensional interpretations of violence and treat violence not as unequivocally negative prevent the development of a systematic analysis. Understanding violence requires an analysis that is both theoretically and empirically rigorous. It should also account not only for the way in which histories of oppression, global power, and the dynamics and structures of violence impact local lived experience, but also for how people themselves shape their conditions.

Knowledge production is political in nature. To be committed to emancipation and liberation, it must value and take seriously research collaborators' perspectives, consider a plurality of stories, engage with uncomfortable aspects when they appear, and allow them space within published work too. Forcing my data into a unifying narrative that describes violence as always bad would not do justice to the complexity and breadth of the phenomenon. This would only have served to elevate myself above my research collaborators and interpret or explain their narratives and experiences in ways other than their own framing ('this is what they really mean'). However, treating violence as multifaceted is not the same as condoning it. This book attempts to explain how violence is executed, perceived, and responded to. I consider how these perceptions came into being in the first place and which mechanisms strengthen them. In sum, the book moves beyond studying either structural factors or individual experiences in order to provide an encompassing, multi-layered perspective on violence.

The starting point for this analysis lies in rethinking pervasive assumptions about love and violence. This is a necessary first step if we are to engage with the subtleties of violence in intimate and familial contexts. It is already well known that the forms violence takes are historically contingent and that perceptions of violence are context-specific, but the assumption that love and violence are two opposite ends of a continuum remains widely held. In many of the love stories depicted in this book, these certainties become unsettled. I demonstrate that in some contexts, such as in post-war Sierra Leone, many forms of violence between partners are perceived as signs of an active struggle to maintain relationships and sustain genuine emotions. In the understanding of my research collaborators, violence, the fear of violence, the diverse messages it communicates, and the pain it can cause are valorised as necessary for a functional relationship. Within relationships, violence thereby becomes constitutive of the experience of affection and love – although careful distinctions are drawn between so-called acceptable violence and transgressive or unacceptable violence.

An important part in this negotiation between the accepted and the unaccepted is played by generational tensions and by people's social position within the urban community. Thus, different life stages allow for distinctive relationships and generate specific expectations and tolerances regarding violence. In fact, what forms of violence are accepted in a particular context and by whom has as much to do with life stage, seniority, and social capital as with gender. This effectively challenges a second widespread assumption that where intimate violence exists, women tend to be on the receiving end of it. The ethnographic account of love and violence that I present here disrupts common victim–perpetrator narratives. It nuances these fixed positions into relational ones and shows how the acceptability of a practice can change over the course of people's lives and depends on the relationship between the partners. In contemporary Sierra Leone, there is often an expectation on the part of younger women that love and care will be manifested through physical violence. Here, women are not simply passive victims. What is more, men can in fact feel under pressure to execute violence.

In addition, I show that violent practices are perceived to be gendered – but not with women as victims and men as perpetrators; rather, it is with men using violence mostly against bodies and women infiltrating and controlling minds. With these uncomfortable but important insights, I highlight the tension between the assumptions of global rights and local experiences and between simple narratives and messy day-to-day intimacy. This is necessary if we are to grasp the role and place of violence in intimate relationships and to comprehend why interventions fail if they simplify the intricacies of the contexts in which they operate.

These insights allow me to continue a strand of regional anthropology that started during the civil war and that has shaped the scholarly understanding of violence in conflict globally. Catherine Bolten's (2012) ethnography illustrates how Sierra Leoneans survived wartime violence by invoking love, a deeply compassionate relationship rooted in exchange and nurturing. At the time of the conflict, anthropologists working on gender and sexual violence sensitively moved analyses past simplistic male/perpetrator, female/victim dynamics by showing the various roles women and girls played during the war. Illustrative of this trend is Chris Coulter's (2005; 2009) work on bush wives and girl soldiers and Dara Kay Cohen's (2013) study of female fighters and women's perpetration of war-time violence. In this book, I attempt to move this work beyond the sphere of violent conflict and into that of everyday intimacy. By examining both male and female agency in respect of issues of everyday violence in sub-Saharan Africa, I seek to build a bridge over the perceived gendered gap between violent men and violated women.

What Laws Do: Community Continuity and State Rupture

This book also contributes to the anthropological study of policy, laws, and their impact at all levels of people's lives. While violence is not summarily condemned or even rejected in Freetown, its acceptability has clear limits. According to a moral economy of relationships, violence is accepted in these dynamics as a form of give and take so long as it does not cause excessive harm that cannot be undone (Burrill, Roberts, and Thornberry 2010). If it does, people turn to their family, their community, or the state to report it. In Chapters 4 to 8, I examine how transgressive violence is regulated by different institutions, ranging from households to state courts. I show that for both households and communities, violence constitutes a relationship between people that must be cooperatively mediated. Building on a rich history of female political leadership in the region, such mediations are female-led and can adjudicate both male and female forms of violence. The criminal justice system, on the other hand, is restricted to judging visible or traceable violence and thus to violence predominantly attributed to men. This means that, if only the data from criminal justice institutions are considered, they support the gendered dualism of victim–perpetrator. But if non-state cases are included, a whole other set of violent practices emerges that state institutions cannot consider and that collapses this neat dichotomy. This finding raises questions about the ways in which violence tends to be conceptualised globally.

During household and community mediations, violent acts are re-embedded in the larger social context in which they occur, and what is put on trial is a person's overall comportment, not specific acts. Mediation follows a processual format that has been observed for other forms of disputes (especially concerning murder and land conflicts) in various parts of Africa (see particularly Gibbs 1963). Sessions can be lengthy, as room is given to all those who wish to air their grievances before they are asked to 'swallow' them and move on. Because holding grudges is seen as an ineradicable part of the human condition, such mediations do not seek to overcome discord to achieve harmony (*pace* Gibbs 1963; Porter 2017). Instead, they attempt to reduce anger to a bearable limit and, through various closing rituals, trap grievances within individual bodies so as to maintain those social bonds that keep a household or community functioning. Given the relational perception of harm and the need to ensure continuity, no single wrongdoer is identified. Instead, punishment is apportioned between the parties involved in a dispute. This can mean, however, that the needs of individuals are subsumed under those of the social group.

By contrast, the criminal justice system presides over specific acts, not personhood. Passing definitive judgements on acts requires constructing specific types of subjects, such as victims and perpetrators, thereby narrowing down the 'complex range of perspectives involved in rights processes' to a bare minimum and 'eliding the inherent ambiguity of social life' (Hall 1996; Wilson and Mitchell 2003; Hunter 2010: 8–9; Richter 2016). Here, no intrinsic value is placed on continuity. Since, according to rights discourses, rights are inherent in everyone, they cannot be given partially or divided between persons so as to appease a particular social group. In a court setting, the person identified as the harmed party is therefore encouraged to leave the relationship so as to end the violence and claim their rights. Here, punishment and imprisonment have the aim and outcome of rupturing relationships and dissolving social bonds.

As I show, the intrinsic unshakeable value communities place on continuity must be understood not as a conscious attempt to limit the individual but as a defence mechanism that developed in response to a long history of rupture – through colonialism, slavery, violent interventions, and conflict – that sought to undermine and override community mechanisms. In this book, I examine how household and community processes seeking to maintain relationships collide with state practices that rupture them. These different approaches towards mediation and punishment mean that for individuals confronted with unbearable violence, reporting such violence involves choosing one's allegiances and cutting one's losses. Reporting to state institutions leads to the withdrawal of community and familial support – sometimes even to fines and punishment – while reporting to the household or community results in the prioritisation of the needs of the group over personal exigencies. These insights help us understand why despite campaigning, legal reforms, destigmatising efforts, and institutional support, only certain individuals will consider reporting violence to the police. These are usually minors – or adults on behalf of minors – who do so as a result of the intense political focus placed on them or adult women who have enough resources to leave their communities and start over if their lives collapse after reporting. These findings should make practitioners and policy-makers aware that only some facets of a phenomenon can be derived from reporting statistics so long as many people continue not to report instances of such a phenomenon in the first place.

The book is set in the aftermath of the civil war and the Truth and Reconciliation Commission (TRC),[3] when efforts were undertaken to address sexual and gender-based violence. This resulted in the 'gender justice laws', which include the Domestic Violence Act (Government of Sierra Leone 2007c) and the Devolution of Estates Act (Government of Sierra Leone 2007b), which were enacted on 26 July 2007, and the Registration of Customary Marriage and Divorce Act (Government of Sierra Leone 2009), which entered into force on 22 January 2009. Any conduct within an intimate relationship that brings about physical, psychological, economic, or sexual harm to either partner is rendered unlawful and liable to conviction and imprisonment by these laws (Mills et al. 2015). The laws also animate women to formally register religious and traditional matrimony, and they accord equal rights to both spouses over all assets, including land and property should they divorce. A particular focus of these laws was the protection of young girls from sexual harassment and grooming and the prevention of teenage pregnancy. One means involved raising the age of sexual consent for girls and boys from 14 to 18. This was formalised in the Sexual Offences

---

[3] The TRC was a product of the Lomé Peace Accord between the Government of Sierra Leone and the Revolutionary United Front (RUF). After the civil war, the TRC analysed the causes of the war, human rights violations, and the influence of foreign actors.

Act (SOA) of 2012, which rendered sexual relations with – and among – minors illegal and provided sentences for up to fifteen years. Consent is no longer a defence.

After political power changed hands in 2018, sexual violence, particularly against young girls, and teenage pregnancy continued to loom large on the national agenda. Grassroots organisations and activists campaigned untiringly for increased protection for girls. Early in 2019, President Maada Bio gave in to their demands. He declared a national emergency on rape and sexual violence with the intention of making sexual penetration of minors punishable by lengthy terms of imprisonment, including life. Though the emergency was later revoked, this goal was still achieved by the Sexual Offences Amendment Act, passed in September 2019. This provided for the possibility of life imprisonment for offenders and of sentencing twelve-year-old boys for sexual penetration (including sleeping with girlfriends). These legal changes became the subject of a global debate about consent and protection against violence. Sierra Leone emerged as the development movement's poster child – a place where the tireless efforts of grassroots activists and vernacular voices finally impacted on national politics and where effective steps were taken to establish zero tolerance for rape and sexual violence. However, while celebrated internationally as a milestone in the struggle against violence, from the outset these laws were ambiguous in their effects.

By documenting their impact in great ethnographic detail, this book provides an analysis of the unexpected effects of well-intentioned laws. While international organisations and transitional justice instruments have pushed for these laws to combat sexual violence, in practice these laws have often resulted in girls being forced to abandon their education and in boys and young men being incarcerated for up to fifteen years for having sexual intercourse in consensual relationships: 'Age-of-consent law is complex. If it is set too high, there's a risk that it will undercut young people's agency. If it is set too low, it does not offer enough protection for vulnerable young people' (Schneider 2019c). This is the quandary with which Sierra Leone has wrestled in the last decade. Sierra Leonean lawmakers have created some positive change: the Act protects children, particularly girls, who are abused by adults. Conjointly, however, it limits young people's liberty and criminalises not only violence but desire. Strangers are encouraged to report on each other, and stigmatisation and exclusion are common. For instance, a school ban carried out by invasive physical searches and tests has formalised a practice that had long been underway, namely barring visibly pregnant girls from going to regular schools and taking exams.

The outcome of these rape prevention efforts, which made worldwide headlines, is therefore far-reaching. They go far beyond the prevention of sexual violence and underage pregnancies and touch upon the very foundation of intimacy. At their base, these laws and regulations have created a new punitive regime that polices intimacy and criminalises the sexual behaviour of young people. These rigid laws operate, moreover, in a seriously overstretched criminal justice system that does not have the capacity for appropriate investigations and trials and where prison conditions constitute a human rights problem in themselves (Schneider 2019b). These shortcomings are reinforced by discriminatory regulations such as the school ban.

Illegalising sex between minors and stigmatising teenage pregnancy not only blurs the line between sex and rape but also shapes coming of age, affects the formation and livelihood strategies of families and households, and creates intense changes in the fabric of social organisation. In this book, I explore the paradox between people's valorisation of violence, which can – if internally monitored against excess – be a productive force, and attempts by the post-conflict state and international community to police it. I try to show the consequences of the state's focus on sex for love, intimacy, and violence. In doing so, I study how rigid laws rub against contingent social categories and how the criminalisation and policing of sexual relationships clash with the normalisation of violence in ordinary speech, acts, and relationships.

Homing in on the Young: Gendered Ideologies in a Gendered Social and Legal World

By tracing how young people fare as the full power of state attention is directed at them while they continue to shoulder the expectations of their communities and households, I hope to contribute to the literature on the 'crisis of youth' in Africa. This rich body of work has done much to counter studies that start with the continent's 'youth bulge' to explain violence, conflict, migration, and radical ruptures in intergenerational relations. Instead, it established the notion of 'youth' as a relational category rather than as an age group (e.g. Honwana and De Boeck 2005; Christiansen, Utas, and Vigh 2006; Honwana 2014). Standing on the shoulders of this work, *Love and Violence* offers a counter-narrative to the popular one of radical rupture in the wake of civil war by showing that families and communities remain the principal mediators of violence and of problems between partners, though this mainly applies to marriages or committed relationships. In this book, I examine what happens to those who find themselves 'in-between'. I uncover the plight of the many urban youths who, unable to build formal alliances between households through marriage (often because they cannot afford to), attempt to create relationships that bridge their families' expectations, their personal desires, and the constraints placed on them. Different demands are made on personhood when trying to realise individual choices regarding lovers and at the same time cultivating social relations (e.g. Piot 1999; Jackson 2012). Sierra Leoneans negotiate relationships (and violence within them) between the simultaneous but irreconcilable desires for freedom through individually directed lives and for security through familial and community ties (Bauman 2001: 5).

Young Freetonians navigate changing gender dynamics in circumstances of poverty and contrasting expectations by developing a broad variety of relationship forms – some consecutive, others overlapping – that are characterised by varying degrees of permanence and commitment (Chapter 3). These relationship practices add further variance to the ongoing efforts of scholars to complicate one-dimensional notions of romantic love in Africa (e.g. Cole and Thomas 2009; Hunter 2010; Vaughan 2011). These have shown that while economy and emotion are entangled worldwide and intimacy is always also political, the ways these dynamics are navigated are far richer than the tropes of romantic love, sexual desire, or transactional relationships can capture. But I also consider the dark shadows that follow some of these attempts at building bridges between want, need, and obligation. Many relationship forms in Freetown today are an attempt at reconciling individual desire, social responsibility, and legal restrictions. It is the impossibility of achieving this reconciliation that gives rise to violence. As this book shows, aiming to satisfy these differing and fluid demands of starting a household and living a committed relationship while fulfilling personal aspirations and carrying the burden of hardship and poverty often creates dynamics that foster violence.

Hence, this book is an urban ethnography of how youth – caught between state laws that criminalise their sexual behaviour and elders who expect them to marry and start families – are coping under the attack of irreconcilable demands without being able to make any acceptable moves. But it is also an ethnography of how adults and elders deal with violence in their relationships when they, unlike young people, are expected to have figured everything out. To them, carrying out too much or too little violence or reporting violence to the wrong institution may well lead to the collapse of their carefully built livelihoods, social networks, and families.

Precarity affects all generations and makes it difficult to realise expected roles. Violence between partners, as anthropologists have shown, is often the result of structural violence by economic, social, political, and institutional forces (Bourgois 2004; Farmer 2004; Scheper-Hughes and Bourgois 2004; Accomazzo 2012: 547). This makes it impossible for people to fulfil the gendered ideal of a male breadwinner and female dependant living together in marriage. Throughout the book, I show how in real life both men and women are actively engaged in making a living and how gendered demands and roles are often inverted. Economic constraints and the impossibility of fulfilling expected relationship roles lie at the heart of forms of violence in Freetown, and not only for men. Hence, this work challenges the notion of a 'crisis of masculinity' that is present in much Africanist literature. It shows instead that it is gender relations as a whole that people perceive to be under attack, rather than masculinity on its own.

In addition, the book offers a new angle to the classic debate on gender complementarity. I agree with scholars working in the region that gendered differences, alongside the need for cooperation, form the fabric with which the social world is woven. However, I seek to advance this classic literature in two ways. Firstly, instead of focussing on women (gender parallelism) or men ('crisis of masculinity'), I look instead at gender and at male and female perspectives. Secondly, I show that the road to achieving complementarity has become rocky and is full of obstacles. Existing studies that focus predominantly on rural areas have revealed the manifold ways in which the idea of neat gender parallelism can be upset by lived experiences. At the same time, deviations from the norm are carefully concealed and do not openly challenge the ideal of complementarity (e.g. Ferme 2001). By contrast, in contemporary urban Sierra Leone, as a result of people's diverse relationship practices and the corresponding legal changes, there is no longer one main model of gender relations. Instead, institutions and communities struggle to promote their respective ideal of gender dynamics against the opposing views of other systems. And partners find themselves caught between them. What is more, relationships are often visibly spiked with violence and pain. Indeed, exposing and displaying dissonances forms an important part of contemporary intimacy. My study therefore argues for a more nuanced interpretation of gender relations that allows for an analysis of friction. It shows how everyday practices differ from gender principles, but it also shows how the principles are nevertheless held in place because of the important role they play in shaping expectations and behaviours. What we can observe in Sierra Leone today are competing gender ideologies rather than one main model of parallelism.

Imagined Others, Human Rights, and the State's Attempts at Future Making through Legal Reform

The Sierra Leonean case demonstrates that the 'crisis of youth' in Africa is constructed by policies promoted by NGOs and multilateral organisations. In post-conflict Sierra Leone, 'youth' are viewed as a 'problem' that requires policy intervention (Chapter 3). Much as in countries like Kenya (Thomas 2003) and Uganda, the control over girls' sexual behaviour, reproductive capacities, and premarital pregnancies has become a central concern for the state and its performance of power in Sierra Leone. Here, the state's vision of a prosperous future relies on the need to control girls' sexual behaviour, which is seen as a threat to the national project. Development agencies, lawmakers, and politicians have discursively framed and justified new laws by depicting young people implicated in sexual offences cases and pregnant girls as 'imagined others' (Carlbom 2003), whose frivolous sexual behaviour poses a danger to society's well-being. This framing has reduced young people's diverse relationships to a single, static aspect: sex. Young men and boys who engage in sexual activities with underage girlfriends are portrayed as threatening perpetrators who must be excluded from the national community for society to thrive. Young girls in turn are depicted as victims, and their virginity in need of protection. Pregnant girls are considered carriers of the 'disease of desire', which can only be contained by social distancing mechanisms such as excluding them from school, thereby limiting their contact with other girls. By depicting young couples as unruly subjects and exerting control over them, the authorities aim to enforce nationwide sexual self-control.

Through the above-mentioned laws, the responsibility for overseeing and regulating intimacy, sex, and violence has largely been transferred from households and communities to the state. However, it is important to note that this transfer of responsibility is contingent upon Sierra Leoneans reporting on each other's sexual behaviour. This presents a challenge for state institutions, as discussing another person's private affairs is considered antisocial behaviour in Sierra Leone (Szanto 2018), and there is also a long-standing ambivalence towards state laws.

During colonialism, Sierra Leoneans experienced systematic structural abuse, as colonisers divided and governed them on the basis of locally obscure principles (Ferme 2004: 92). Sierra Leone was a central site of the transatlantic slave trade, and its people experienced the capture, trafficking, uprooting, killing, and death of individuals. There is a complicated history between families who were enslaved and those who took part in or benefited from the trade in human lives on domestic and international scales.

After independence, state practices continued to be indirectly influenced by foreigners through development aid and humanitarian intervention triggered by the civil war and health emergencies. This had drastic adverse consequences on the ground. These multifarious influences, alongside privatisation, made it increasingly difficult for Sierra Leoneans to understand who was responsible and what goals were driving actions. The state, as an ominous body, seemed to be everywhere and nowhere at the same time (Ferme 1998; 2004).

Today, state legal practices tend to be perceived as capricious in that 'the state can arbitrate, decide, or create situations in which competing interests or interpretations of the common good obscure the threshold between legality and illegality' (Ferme 2004: 83). National laws are often experienced by people as consistently disadvantaging them and appear to 'serve the interests of particular categories of people' (Ferme 2004: 83). In the face of this adversity, communities attempt to keep the state and its institutions at arm's length by mediating conflicts internally and preventing members from turning elsewhere for support.

Socio-legal organisation in West Africa continues to be shaped by the notion of harmony ideology, which Laura Nader identified many decades ago (Nader 1990; Pirie 2007; 2014: 35) in her analysis of how colonised groups seek to escape the influence of colonisers. Communities seek to evade unwanted foreign influence, neo-colonial patterns, and state domination by presenting a united front to outsiders, even if they may be riddled with conflict internally. This creates a problem for the state, however, which may rightfully intervene in communities only if called upon to do so.

Mediations of intimate relationships demonstrate significant continuities between pre- and post-war periods, as well as between the longer historical trajectory of colonialism and slavery, and the ongoing international influences in the region. The criminal justice system contradicts community norms about 'how, when and with whom' minors can have consensual sex (Tamale 2011: 3), thereby unsettling the lines between state and community jurisdiction. To encourage people to report cases to the state, state institutions needed to instil the idea that reporting is a social responsibility that ensures the greater good (Kierkegaard 1940). After the passage of the Sexual Offences Act (SOA) and later the Sexual Offences Amendment Act (SOAA), human rights became the country's socio-political 'ideoscape' (Appadurai 1990; Cowan 2006) and were used to justify informing practices. The message was clear: to create a future free of rape and teenage pregnancy, sex among young people must stop. Because young people were not trusted to do this independently, and communities might have other interests, adults – including uninvolved bystanders – were made responsible for reporting any cases of early sex to the authorities. The success of this campaign demonstrates the power of a human rights discourse to shape 'how the world is apprehended' (Kierkegaard 1940; Cowan, Dembour, and Wilson 2001;

Cowan 2006). These discourses are so powerful that they can undermine pervasive social norms and long-established practices.

While the carefully drawn boundaries between state and community could not be permanently redrawn by conflicts and health emergencies, they have become unsteady now that individuals move between them to report. This practice of informing on one another, alongside the unequal implementation of the law for the rich and the poor, deepens existing structural inequalities and creates imagined communities woven together by the exclusion of 'imagined others' (Carlbom 2003). What takes place in Sierra Leone is an example of the formation of an imagined community through othering (Anderson 1983). Some of the disputes documented in the book also highlight how families or individuals – usually from different socioeconomic backgrounds – may use the law as a tool to control young men and women. These state laws now enable individuals to perform the dramaturgy of structural violence that was historically executed by colonisers and ruling elites, thereby exposing a historical continuum of structural violence (Whitehead 2004; Scheper-Hughes and Robben 2008: 81).

To date, the negative effects of only one of these regulations – the school ban – have received global attention. This shows the selectivity of rights discourses in the process of constructing unambiguous scenarios necessary for rapid dissemination. The school ban for visibly pregnant girls has been widely criticised as discriminatory and for exacerbating risks and hardships associated with teenage pregnancy (Amnesty International 2015). Grassroots, feminist and empowerment groups not only campaigned against this ban, but also filed a case with the Economic Community of West African States (ECOWAS) court on behalf of the over ten thousand girls directly affected by it. In 2019, the court found that the ban was contrary to human rights and ordered Sierra Leone to lift it. This was celebrated as a landmark moment for girls' rights in Africa and beyond.

However, despite this global debate, the drastic effects of the consent laws for young couples, for adults, and for the relationship between communities and the state remain unseen, untold, and unchallenged. While these Acts are framed as mechanisms of female empowerment and instruments of protection, the unfolding story on the ground is one of increasing marginalisation and increasing restriction of girls' and boys' autonomy in respect of their bodies and sexual behaviours. The life sentences young men can now receive for sleeping with their romantic partners are a human rights violation that goes unreported. The situation is accepted pragmatically as a kind of collateral damage for the sake of bigger human rights goals and development discourses. Moreover, the focus on minors has caused a backlog of cases that paralyses the legal system to the extent that it is unable to deal with adult violence cases (Chapter 7). Adults who turn to the state are often met with long waits, pre-trial dismissal, and referrals back to communities. It is young bodies that absorb state resources, while mature bodies are encouraged to negotiate violence informally.

This book adds to scholarly efforts that investigate the harm of instrumentalising human rights as the sole benchmark for judging violence (Cowan, Dembour, and Wilson 2001; Hastrup 2003: 309; Cowan 2006; Englund 2006; Johnson 2018). When protective or empowering human rights language is used by politicians and policy-makers to justify laws and policing tactics that limit personal autonomy,[4] we should be concerned. This ethnography shows how developmental and policy-oriented work can become alienated from the realities in which it claims to operate. It also demonstrates how current local developments cannot be examined apart from histories of colonialism and ongoing international influences. International human rights interventions that emanate from a desire to assist but do not examine the global socio-political, economic, and material inequalities that have given rise to them in the first place can inadvertently become part of a global strategy to achieve social control, rehabilitate what are deemed to be defiant states, and reproduce conditions of domination (see Jefferson 2005).

On a global scale, the Sierra Leonean case highlights the problems with development and rights discourses that emphasise the need for a strong and vigorous state capable of addressing social issues through legislation. Many of the social issues can be traced back to the legacies of slavery and violent exploitation: these are often neglected by global agendas that prioritise future development rather than address the underlying causes of current problems.

Violence is often treated as a localised issue, while the structural violence of international political and economic arrangements is overlooked. This places additional pressure on African states to overcome their marginal position in the global economy. Some states even attempt to extend their regulatory reach into private spaces such as households and bedrooms, perpetuating neo-colonial dependencies.

---

[4] For an overall critique of human rights instrumentalisation, see Hastrup (2003: 309). For case studies, consider, for example, the ban on ethnicities in Rwanda and the subsequent policing of speech (Lacey 2004). Consider, also, the subjective (e.g. Porter 2017 on Uganda), the political (e.g. Thomas 2003 on Kenya; Parikh 2004a; 2004b; 2012 on Uganda; Tamale 2011), or the cultural (Steinberg 2013 on South Africa) angle of changing discourses around gender roles, sexual practices, and sexual violence in contemporary Africa.

These consequences call for an ethnography that addresses the reasons for the incompatibility of state legal dogmatism and empirical multifacetedness, and shows not only what laws set out to do but also their impact. It is an analysis that critically examines the implications of seemingly neutral rights discourses.

Road Map of the Book

In its structure, this book follows the negotiations that my research collaborators explained when experiencing violence. Part one is concerned with examining the influence of external violence and historical developments on relationship dynamics over time (Chapter 2); with showing how intimate relationships are lived in contemporary Freetown (Chapter 3); with developing a critique of the concepts of love and violence; and with showing how violence in relationships is perceived and practised (Chapters 4 and 5). Part two is concerned with the mediation and regulation of such violence by households and communities (Chapter 6), state courts for adult cases (Chapter 7), and state courts for cases involving minors (Chapter 8). I also trace the effects of the new laws for minors imprisoned in Pademba Road Prison and their girlfriends (Chapter 9).

1 Access, Methodology, and Ethics

This book builds on a decade of engagement with Sierra Leone. The largest amount of data was collected in 2016 and 2017 during fieldwork in which I aimed to grasp in a grounded way the various forms that violence can take in relationships and how it is negotiated, mediated, and punished. I used ethnographic methods, particularly direct and participant observation. I conducted multi-perspective interviews (narrative, semi-structured, and open) and focus group discussions. I also collected 'love' and life histories and included primary and secondary sources in the form of published work, case files, and statistics. I discussed findings with my research collaborators, who challenged my interpretations.

Initially, the aim of this research was to examine the process of reintegration of Ebola survivors in Freetown after the pandemic there. However, during the early stages of my fieldwork, I was raped by the leader of the group I was studying. For my own safety, I had to withdraw myself from that environment (Schneider 2020c; 2023). After experiencing this sexual violence, I was excluded from my previous site of research and, while my physical injuries were healing, I had to remain in the compound where I stayed. To allow readers to follow the process of this research, I want to be candid about the violence I experienced during my fieldwork and the consequences this had on my research direction, the data I was able to gather, and the relationships that developed between my research collaborators and me during our research.

The sexual violence that I had experienced and my time spent healing in the community led many people to open up to me about their relationships, about gender, intimacy, and violence, and so brought about a reorientation of my research. While I had previously relied heavily on interviews, my research process was now one of 'deep hanging out' (Geertz 1998: 69; see Ugelvik 2014: 472). I observed people's 'everyday practices' (Certeau 1984) and paid attention to the manner in which they acted, interacted, and positioned themselves in the social world that shapes them and which they help to shape. When writing up, I focussed on 'thick descriptions' (Geertz 1993): I wanted to capture as

Figure 1.1 The logo of Eat As You Can.

many details of observations and conversations as possible, even those that might at first seem unimportant (Geertz 1993: 5–10).

I concentrated on exploring existing social rhythms and structural conditions. I learnt to unlearn what I thought I had previously understood.[1] I learnt from the silences that permeate companionship. I learnt from the pauses between words, from gestures and facial expressions. I learnt what is spat out frankly in conversations, constantly breaking boundaries, and what is never mentioned, which lines are never crossed, and which hierarchies are never transcended. I learnt about social structures from the way people argue and fight and the ways in which issues are resolved, mediated, or ignored. I learnt from affective, embodied experiences (Anzaldúa 2015). With time, behavioural patterns took shape and the people around me, their actions, perceptions, and ways of giving their lives meaning, became more accessible and intelligible.

Accommodation with Eat As You Can and in Allentown

As for accommodation, I divided my weeks between staying in a room with 14 members of Eat As You Can (EAUC), a social club for young men and their changing partners in Naimbana Street in Freetown's Central District (see Figure 1.1), and staying in Allentown, a community in eastern Freetown. If I needed to sleep, while staying with EAUC, I could do so in a room in Aunty Watche's house close by. Aunty

---

[1] For a reflection on feminist, embodied (un)learning methodologies, see Fullagar et al. (2021).

Figure 1.2 Aunty Watche's house.

Watche, a stern woman in her late forties, runs her own household with two teenage children and the son of one of her sisters who had moved to the United States (see Figure 1.2). She is an extended family member of Aunty Kadie, the female head of the household of the family I lived with in Allentown.

The social club was formed in 2008 by a group of childhood friends who were disconnected from their families and started sharing food, a place to sleep, and strategies for getting by. Members' socioeconomic backgrounds differ, but most are without familial support and trying to make a living through informal means. Others have found sponsors – so-called adoptive parents – in their church or mosque who fund their education or apprenticeship. Only two members are formally employed. Three members are married, and all but two members are in one or several relationships, with slightly over half of the members having children. The club's slogan, 'More than a club', captures their aim of sharing whatever little they have with one another.

The division of daily routines, the communal use of food, and the combined effort to gather resources led to deep friendships between members. The clubhouse provides a place of residence for 14 key members of the total of 39 who are formally registered. This room where I stayed with these 14 members for three or four days each week is called 24. It is owned by a member called Pastor or Belly (31) because of his large stomach. It consists of a single room about 8 square metres in size, which is furnished with two worn-out couches, two broken chairs, a huge poster of the rapper 50 Cent (Curtis Jackson) next to a clock with a picture of Jesus on the wall, and a small TV.

The room has an adjacent storage space filled with mattresses. As its name indicates, 24 is open to its members 24 hours each day and most members meet there daily. It is located on a small dirt road off Naimbana Street which is a busy street next to the stream Highbay Brook in the Western Area of Freetown. Here young people from central Freetown meet and hang out in the evenings. Naimbana Ghetto is located here, and several illegal brothels are also found in this area. Traditional masquerades and parades usually pass through Naimbana Street. It is close to Kroo Bay and within walking distance of popular, free nightclubs and bars such as Ivan Hose or WhatsApp.[2]

The club's membership is organised into different positions, which include president and vice-president, executive members, and treasurers. The president calls weekly meetings during which efforts to 'become successful' are strategically planned, activities allocated, and conflicts debated. The social club, EAUC, organises so-called *chillins*. These are outings to a beach or a place to party that is rented for the day. Attendees must buy a ticket, which costs between SLL 100,000 and SLL 500,000 (GBP 9.10–55.11). The ticket includes the bus ride to and from the location of the *chillin*. The more expensive tickets – the VIP tickets – also include drinks, food, and sometimes a club T-shirt. These outings are an important part of the club's efforts to earn money and gain prestige. Whenever they go to one of the popular underground nightclubs in the area, members must wear the club T-shirt – a black T-shirt with the club logo on it – to demonstrate the sense of unity within the club and its importance in Freetown's nightlife.

In case of wrongdoing or failure to fulfil club activities, members may be fined, suspended, or in rare cases lose their membership. Except for

---

[2] Other nightclubs where I conducted research were Asis and Agal.

me and one other woman, membership is strictly reserved for men. Gas, the president (26), said:

> We can only have men because while it is women that bring us together, it is women that will draw us apart. You know how men are. The second a woman is present, the brotherhood's unity is in danger. Women bring gossip, and men get distracted, and then they fight. No. Our members' girlfriends and affairs and wives and baby-mamas are important to us and always invited. We respect them very much, but they can never be members if we want the club to survive.

Although fights with other clubs occur frequently, the club has a strict philosophy that allows for informal business but no money may be gained from underhand or illegal dealings (Mynster Christensen and Utas 2010). Members must not participate in organised crime and may not be affiliated with the flag movements, which are the most popular gangs with political affiliations in Sierra Leone today. Within universities, there are the black and the white flags; and in the city there are the bloods/the red flag (MOB or Movement of Blood), the blue flag (CCC, or Cent Coast Crips), and the black flag (So-So-Black) (see Mitton 2018). EAUC members may belong to any religion, may support any political party, and may be from any ethnic group, as long as they do not try to encourage one another to follow a particular movement.

Allentown is situated on the hills in the far east of Sierra Leone's capital city, Freetown, with Calaba Town to the west and Jui to the east. It is 238 metres above sea level. The family house I stayed in was located within the community of Upper Allentown, just off the 'pipeline' – the dirt road on the mountaintop. It is a stone house painted yellow with two rooms and a parlour, which housed 11 people besides me (see Figure 1.3). With its veranda reaching out in front, it allows a view across the community to Tagrin Bay, the swamps, and the Atlantic Ocean. On good nights, sitting on the narrow wall that separates the veranda from the dirt road, and the compound from the community, I could see what someone told me were the lights of the mines of Port Loko.

Staying in Allentown and Naimbana Street was possible because some of my research collaborators, whom I have known since I had first conducted research in Freetown in 2012, acted as guarantors and intermediaries for me (Gobo 2008: 122–3). In Allentown, the family I lived with had hosted me during several research stints previously,[3] and many of the members of EAUC have been associated with my work for years.[4]

---

[3] They previously lived at Kissy Road, and I stayed with them there during previous sojourns in Freetown.
[4] Some have close ties to the under-resourced communities of Kroo Bay and Susan's Bay, where I did research previously.

Figure 1.3 The compound I shared with 11 others at Allentown.

I went to parties and soccer games and on outings with EAUC. I experienced their struggles to make ends meet. I became familiar with the many different relationships that connect the young women and men in Naimbana Street, and the ebbs and flows of disagreements, fights, reunions, and ruptures that structure them. I became acquainted with the particularities of nightlife and saw members hustling in and around the clubs in Freetown.

In understanding my association with EAUC, Henrik Vigh's concept of 'rhizomatic fieldwork' becomes highly relevant. Vigh (2006a) explained how he followed his research collaborators around, his primary place of fieldwork being their meeting places rather than a traditionally localised setting. Fieldwork thus becomes 'an interconnected set of horizontal and vertical ... orderings' like a rhizome that 'doesn't begin and doesn't end, but is always in the middle, between things, interbeing, *intermezzo*' (Deleuze and Guattari 2002: 24–5 cited in Vigh 2006a: 18, original emphasis). While in Allentown my research was based in the community, and most research collaborators' lives were organised around that geographical location, other focus groups, especially EAUC, were 'all over the city', as Suge (34), their former leader, said.

Hence, their activities defined the localities of the fieldwork, and the interconnected webs spun by their movements constructed the site. As well as moving with EAUC through the city, I accompanied people involved in disputes or legal cases to the different places of their hearings: a market woman from her home to the shops where she bought her produce and then on to her stall; girlfriends when they tried to visit their imprisoned partners; and so on.

At Allentown, I engaged in chores with people; I observed how resources were distributed, who was controlling what, who was included, and who was left out. I attended community festivities, masquerades, funerals, and different *rites de passage*. I sat in on mediation processes when conflicts between neighbours arose (and they always did). I spent hours listening to life histories. I learnt about people's dreams and desires, their pains and failures. I collected their narrations of love and loss, of success and failure. And I listened to the community's stories about the fortunes of the local soccer team; disputes over resources; the disappearance of chickens; relationships that formed and dissolved; experiences of disaster, war, displacement, and sickness; and beauty pageants. The community opened its doors to me. I learnt how to braid hair, teach kids, cook, and do laundry. I learnt what 'masculine domination' (Bourdieu 2001) means and why in Allentown it is the women who secretly control the resources. In this manner, I learnt about violence in relationships and the various ways it is mediated by the criminal justice system and by household and community systems.

Focussing on research collaborators' interests and letting them participate in the process of my research allowed me to reach out to other groups and visit other areas with their support. In this way, it became much easier to develop fruitful networks. Within a few months, I had contacts with focus groups from diverse economic, social, cultural, ethnic, and professional backgrounds all over Freetown. I involved different age groups (from 14 to 88) and demographics, so as to be attentive to intergenerational changes and questions of intersectionality (Crenshaw 1991; see also hooks 1983; Collins and Bilge 2016), especially around gender and class. Among the research collaborators from households and communities were boys and men working at garages, welding shops, carpentry shops, and coffee shops; market women and girls; women and girls working in beauty salons; traders; caterers; drivers; businessmen and women; journalists; social and humanitarian workers; politicians; men and women belonging to social clubs; sex workers; elders; people frequenting the streets; families; high school and university students; members from the 'Ghetto'; imams; pastors; traditional people; and individual members of secret societies.

I followed court proceedings involving violence in relationships in the Magistrate's Court and occasionally the High Court. I also conducted research in Pademba Road Prison, and I visited the East End Police Station and the CID (Criminal Investigation Department). I interviewed policymakers, law enforcement officials (police, lawyers, judges, and prison staff), activists, and NGO and media personnel. I spoke with politicians and businessmen who were instrumental in designing, lobbying for, promoting, or opposing the 'gender justice laws', and those tasked with the handling and documentation of cases and their various repercussions. I interviewed 'Don Bosco' workers, who accompany survivors of sexual violence to court. The Salesians of Don Bosco are a Roman Catholic religious congregation and charity, founded by Saint John Don Bosco, an Italian priest, at the end of the nineteenth century, with the mission of supporting underprivileged children globally. In addition, I interviewed staff of the Rainbo Centres, where survivors of sexual violence receive free treatment and psychosocial and legal counselling, and where medical examinations are conducted that serve as the main form of evidence in court. Furthermore, I interviewed employees of Family Support Units (FSUs), which are independent units of the Sierra Leone Police that are attached to 42 police stations across the country. They are responsible for investigating cases of child abuse and gender-based and domestic violence and are specially trained to settle matters before they reach court. I visited NGOs and IOs, journalists, legal practitioners, and researchers and experts working on violence. In 13 months, I conducted 464 formal interviews, sampled case files, accumulated crime statistics, and analysed social media chats from 17 groups. These data accompanied my participant observation, the main foundation of my research. Interviews and conversations were sometimes in English, sometimes in Krio, the lingua franca in Sierra Leone, depending on the preference of the research collaborators.

Main Focus Groups

King George's Old Age Home

I have known King George's old age home in the Grafton area since I started conducting research in Freetown in 2012. Aunty Kadie (52), one of my closest friends and main research collaborators, works there, and during most of my research stays I spent several weeks living at King George's and participating in the home's activities. Whenever I was at King George's, I was struck by the depth of the residents' perspectives and by how much their experiences and insights could add value to an otherwise fragmented picture. I therefore started to systematically include their perspectives in my research. I collected the life and love histories of 23 elders – 15 men and 8 women – between the ages of 51 and 88 who lived at King George's.

The Garage Focus Group

A second focus group was located at Star Motors Garage in the Cline Town area in constituency 103, East II, Freetown. Led by 'Boss Kay' (53), the chairman of the garage, it specialises in panel beating and spraying, automatic transmission, and electricals. According to the secretary, Mr Tennyson Saidu Momoh (42), the garage employs 73 men and boys: 12 specialised bosses, 23 senior boys, and 38 junior boys. Even though seniority is based on the level of experience attained, the bosses are usually between 45 and 60 years, senior boys between 30 and 40, and junior boys between 12 and 20. To become a member, a fee must be paid, and each apprentice must bring with him a few tools and have a guarantor vouching for them. Young boys often sleep in cars in the garage. Garage workers engage daily with girls who sell goods from the baskets they carry on their heads. Relationships often develop and, not infrequently, customer and seller disappear into one of the cars at the back of the garage – sex in exchange for purchasing the 'entire market', which means all the items the woman or girl carries in the basket on her head.

The Market Focus Group

The Kennedy Street market is located in constituency 104, East II, Freetown, and is commonly referred to as Upgun Market because it is believed to have started somewhere in the Upgun area before moving to its present location. According to a plaque on the wall, it was opened on 14 November 1995. The market consists of about 500 stalls, tables, and trays. Ownership of a stall or table is obtained by registering with the Freetown City Council. The daily market fee amounts to SLL 500 (GBP 0.05) per table or tray. Goods commonly for sale include rice, vegetables, spices, fish, and meat, as well as building materials and household electricals. Unlike the garage with its purely male membership, the market is predominantly run by women. Street markets are usually run and stalls usually owned by women, while regular stores located within buildings are often owned by men. Most of the businesswomen are between the ages of 20 and 60, and many are assisted by children aged 6 and older. Children sell goods by going around with small trays, or they sit by the tables of their parents or guardians. Some of them do not attend school, while others sell before or after they go to school, depending on whether they go to school in the morning shift, which starts at eight, or the afternoon shift, which starts at two. Most of the women who manage their stalls have not gone to school; the few who did go had dropped out after two or three years.

I also spent time with street traders around the intersection of Ecowas and Lightfoot Boston streets in Freetown's business district. Here, I observed the exchange relationships that formed between businessmen and the women and girls selling foodstuffs, snacks, and drinks to them.

A third market focus group drew on girls and women between the ages of 14 and 29 who carry goods for sale on their heads. They are usually given a specific quantity of groundnuts, boiled eggs, yoghurt, ice, or water at the beginning of each day, which they carry in buckets or baskets on their heads. They walk around offering their goods to passers-by, drivers-by, and garage workers. Once they have sold everything they had brought with them, they return home. I followed these girls and women mainly around the Upgun Turntable (roundabout), in Abacha Street (central Freetown), and in Calaba Town (east Freetown, next to Allentown).

Puku's Ataya Bes

Another important focus group consisted of *ataya bases*. In an article in *The Economist* entitled 'Caffeine overload: Sierra Leone is worried that its young people are becoming addicted to tea', the author stated: '*Ataya bases* are to Sierra Leone what Starbucks and its ilk are to Western countries. The makeshift cafés are everywhere on the dusty streets of Freetown, Sierra Leone's capital. They serve *ataya*, or strong, hot tea, to a mainly young and male clientele' (T.T. 2013; see also Kamara 2011). Originating in Senegalese tea culture (*ataya* is a Wolof word), *ataya bases* have become popular but controversial hang-out spots for men and boys across Freetown and throughout Sierra Leone. At these places, *ataya*, a Chinese green tea, is served. This 'gunpowder tea' is brewed together with mint leaves over a charcoal stove, becoming bitter and strong. It is then poured into small glasses, mixed with sugar, and poured again from glass to thermos and back to produce a foam. The higher up the mix is poured from, and the thicker the foam, the better the tea.[5] *Ataya* is customarily brewed and drunk by men, and *ataya bases* are male spaces.

---

[5] See Saveur editors (2017) for an explanation of the Senegalese *ataya* ceremony, which has similar characteristics.

Except for market women who occasionally pass by selling groundnuts, women and girls stay away from these spaces. Many men and boys spend several hours daily at an *ataya base*, where they meet their friends, drink *ataya*, chew groundnuts, and discuss politics, football, family life, or whatever else comes to mind. The number of *ataya bases* has reportedly been growing in conjunction with increasing unemployment in Sierra Leone (Remoe 2013; T.T. 2013). At King George's old age home in Freetown, *ataya* tea has been criticised for leading to addiction and psychosis (Remoe 2013; T.T. 2013). My female research collaborators, who often wait for hours until their partners return from an *ataya bes*, said that they are 'worsening idleness'.

For my research, these *bases* were interesting, because it was here where men and boys spoke freely and openly about their world views, the pleasures and pains of their lives, their relationships, and their aspirations. I was welcomed at an *ataya bes* owned by and named after Puku, a Fula man in his late fifties, because (in the words of a regular) I was considered a 'researcher not woman'. After having visited four other *bases*, I was drawn back to Puku's because it was here that the liveliest debates took place.

Hair and Beauty Salons

I also conducted research in hair and beauty salons, for instance at Aleksal/Alexsal Beauty Salon, near Upgun Turntable, and Sannish Favour Beauty Salon, located on Fourah Bay Road towards the Savage Square junction. Both salons have predominantly female customers and offer hairstyles ranging from Afro-kinky to Brazilian hair and dreadlocks. While *ataya bases* are by and large male spaces, beauty and hair salons are predominantly female spaces, where women and girls meet and talk. Early in the morning, I often joined the women and girls who met under the mango tree in front of the house in which I stayed in Allentown to braid hair and discuss news. Another female space that was important during my research was the catering apprenticeship school in central Freetown, where I participated in several baking classes.

The University Focus Group

The campus of Fourah Bay College (FBC) is located at Mount Aureol, Freetown, in East II of the Western Area. After I secured permission from Professor Alfred A. Jarrett, former Head of Department of the Social Work Programme, several focus group discussions took place in the course of seminars with first-year students (they numbered 277 in all). Afterwards, some of the students opened a group on WhatsApp called 'Oxford PhD Research', where 30 or 35 students aged 19 to 25 discussed questions around violence in relationships.

Kroo Bay

I also conducted many interviews and observations in Kroo Bay, an informal settlement located on a swampy piece of land on the coast in front of old, run-down but nevertheless majestic colonial houses. The settlement of Kroo Bay is home to about 11,000 dwellers (Shack Dwellers International 1992; Winnebah, Brewah, and Francis 2006). Kroo Bay is the product of a process of artificial land creation. In their search for a place to live, socio-economically marginalised people began reclaiming parts of the foreshore of Freetown by dumping garbage into the sea, thereby adding to the collections of the city's waste that filled the waterfront. They then converted the trash beds into land by fencing them off with dirt, sticks, raw garbage, and cloth. Time and water turned the materials into a rotting mass on which shacks made of corrugated sheets (so-called *pan bodies*), cloth, plastic and the like were built. The settlement was born in colonial days. At the beginning of the twentieth century, 'crews from ships of the Kroo tribe settled there' (Shack Dwellers International 1992). Today, there is a Temne majority, but the settlement houses various groups from different ethnic, political, and social backgrounds, many of whom either fought on different sides during the civil war or were captured during the insurgency. Occupants lack adequate access to sanitation and health services, and there are little or no economic prospects. Various gangs have established themselves along the lines of previous civil war groups. The social club EAUC plays football against teams from Kroo Bay more or less weekly, and on almost every occasion one or two knife fights can be observed between dwellers.

The Court and Police Focus Groups

Here, I focussed on cases involving violence in relationships (such as domestic violence, sexual offences, battery) at Magistrate's Court no. 1, where Abu Bakarr Binneh-Kamara (Dr Binneh) was the magistrate, and at the High Court. To protect people's anonymity, I refrain from referring to names when writing about the High Court.

I concentrated on the Eastern Police Station, the Calaba Town Police, and the FSU of the CID. I spoke to police officers and was able to observe when reports were made and statements collected.

Other focus groups included the Old School Ghetto in Black Hall Road, the Kissi Municipal Senior Secondary School, Culture Radio, BBC Media Action, and Galaxy Radio. I also included commercial sex workers from a brothel around Peace Market, where they spend the day before they make their moves to the nightclubs in search for customers. Nightclubs like Ivan Hose or WhatsApp were other locations. In Naimbana Street, I also spent much time with the girlfriends and lovers of EAUC members.

Data Collection

Informal Discussions and Life Histories

I sought to reach an understanding of my subject cooperatively with my research collaborators, taking seriously the myriad imaginative ways in which they reflected upon their actions, desires, emotions and affects (Hendriks 2016: 231). Because I lived with them, I could often discuss my findings, challenge my own understanding of them, and find answers to my many questions. The places where I stayed, Allentown and Naimbana Street (no. 24), were the key centres where I could think through the data with my main research collaborators. In the evening, it was there that I reflected on and digested the happenings of a day of fieldwork, and it was they who helped me to process and fine-tune my research methods, questions, and approaches. Discussing my research with them helped ensure that I thought *with* my research collaborators, rather than *about* them, just as I did not aspire to study them from an (arguably impossible) objective stance (Hendriks 2016: 231). I believe in a vulnerable, engaged ethnography that prioritises lived experiences and aims to reach an understanding by thinking with research collaborators through the fieldwork process and the findings. When I drafted explanations of certain processes or procedures, I shared and discussed these drafts especially with Darren (29), Issa (33), Eleanor (43), Mammie Zainab (64), a community elder from Allentown, Papani (55), the elder from the compound at Allentown in which I stayed, and Oki (37) from EAUC. Sometimes, I also presented my thoughts to EAUC members, who then gave me feedback and additional explanations.

My research assistant was Mr Mohamed (35), whom I had met in 2012 when he was studying at Fourah Bay College; he lived partly in Allentown and partly in the city centre. Our work together consisted in me teaching him about qualitative (especially anthropological) research methods and him sometimes accompanying me to a new site. Mr Mohamed, who was deeply interested in relationship dynamics, kept a diary in which he noted down all things connected to intimacy and violence. His notes were the basis of deep discussions between us. Later on, he also led focus group discussions at some sites, including Star Motors Garage, Fourah Bay College, Puku's *ataya bes*, and Aleksal/Alexsal Beauty Salon, where he took extensive notes. These findings, as well as our dissection and analysis of them, helped illuminate the dynamics around gender, age, class, and race. As I remunerated him for his work and also offered him tutorials on research methodologies, data collection, and analysis, he was able to continue his studies and secure an additional income for his wider family too.

Life and Love Histories and Focus Group Discussions

To understand the significance of violence in relationships against the personal historical, and biographical background of each research collaborator, I conducted retrospective narrative interviews and collected 'life' and 'love' histories from them. This helped me to understand how research collaborators had come to be where they were, how practices had changed over time, and 'to situate the living present within myriad references to the past' (Sarró 2009: 10). According to David Pratten, 'to account for the contingencies of life trajectories requires ethnography bent to the biographical'. Adapting C. Wright Mills's phrase, he argues that 'these perspectives place ethnography at the intersection of biography and history' (Cooper and Pratten 2015: 13). Through their focus on 'the making of social life through time' (Connell 2005: 80), life histories allow an investigation into social change. According to Raewyn Connell, they provide insights into 'personal experience, ideology and subjectivity ... But life histories also, paradoxically, document social structures, social movements and institutions. That is to say, they give rich evidence about impersonal and collective processes as well as about subjectivity' (Connell 2005: 89). 'Love histories' (Porter 2017), on the other hand, focus specifically on a person's relationships and romantic experiences. Focus group discussions on love, relationships, and violence and its mediation further enhanced my understanding of the way various positions, narratives, actions and opinions generate a meta-story.

Everyday practices do not just burst into existence and insert themselves into the world. Rather, they are formed and shaped, and can be better understood as lingering repercussions of the past as well as symbols of aspirations that manifest themselves in the present (Geschiere and Jackson 2006; Sarró 2009: 11). Sherry Ortner (1984; 1989: 12) and Holly Wardlow (2006) view people's actions as being influenced by cultural norms, social relationships, and historical events while also being a part of shaping these aspects of society. Using the lens of everyday practices, and following an approach of integrating observation, participation, life histories, and discussions, I sought to take seriously people's perspectives and make visible important and often neglected aspects of how they operate and position themselves in their encounters with social realities. This process does not understand structure and agency as opposites but pays attention to their constitutive relationships.

Police Stations, Courts, and Pademba Road Prison

As the research progressed and I was confronted more and more with what anthropologists call 'weak legal pluralism' (Griffiths 1986; Sezgin 2004) – different dispute mediation systems which exist under the umbrella of state law including, in the Sierra Leonean case, household and community mediation systems, religious systems (sharia and church), and state laws – I started to include research in police stations, courts, and prisons. By this means, I sought to understand how citizens' informal mediations and the state's legalistic practices influence and shape each other, and how violence is mediated and responded to by state institutions. I followed cases from the time of their reporting at the police stations to conviction or dismissal, I heard them at the Magistrate's Court and sometimes at the High Court, and I conducted research with people imprisoned at Pademba Road Prison. Furthermore, I viewed statistics and case files that have been assembled by Don Bosco. These case files and the ones I viewed in court were seldom complete and often inconsistent. I was told that no reporting statistics were available before 2011, and I had to rely on the interpretations of legal enforcement officials. From 2011 until 2015, only an aggregate number of reported cases was available. The outcome of the cases as well as the age of the alleged perpetrators and victims were unknown. After 2015 (because of the Ebola pandemic), more detailed statistics became the norm. Yet, individual case files were still hard to track down, and those I accessed were full of missing data. Together with additional research I conducted involving journalists as well as numerous organisations and institutions, these different sources allowed me to combine an analysis of legal, institutional, and governmental frameworks with lived realities and mediation strategies at the local level.

This study is thus a 'project ethnography' in a double sense. It shows how laws 'enter into existing life worlds and both shape and are shaped by them' (Evans and Lambert cited in Parikh 2012: 1776). It also shows how the legal reforms were enabled by specific historical processes and gendered practices and perceptions, even if they are now in friction with them, and how they were perceived by research collaborators. Following Shanti Parikh, I used a 'dialectical framework' which 'moved between analysis of the macro-level' legal reform, 'critical investigations of everyday experiences with the law', and mediation practices that took place away from state law (Parikh 2012: 1776). Courts, police stations, and prisons are highly controlled and formalised environments. For practical, analytical, and ethical reasons, they require a different set of methods from those for households and communities. The people who move within these places are either professionals, or they are implicated in cases and thus in a vulnerable position.

Observations, Shadowing, and 'Going Along' with Research Collaborators

To be able to follow what litigants and legal personnel 'do' (Bierschenk and de Sardan 2014), I applied the tactic of 'shadowing' (Czarniawska 2007) – following people who navigate highly formalised and complex settings. Barbara Czarniawska emphasises that shadowing requires an attitude in which the ethnographer keeps in mind their outsidedness in relation to the field of study. This is for ethical reasons; it is also a constructive method to discover things which research collaborators may consider irrelevant and which might not be the topic of an interview (Czarniawska 2007: 20–2). The presence of a single, white woman in a police station, a male prison, or a courtroom – especially during sexual offences cases, which are held in private chambers – is not a 'natural' presence. It proved impossible for me to 'hang out' there. Rather than trying to 'blend in', I became a visible 'shadow' who observed (Czarniawska 2007). I found it important to clarify my specific position and limitations in order to minimise trigger reactions, trauma, and the nurturing of false hopes, both for research collaborators and for myself.

In my focus on alleged victims of violence, I supplemented the method of shadowing with go-along interviews. I accompanied them from their homes or shelters to police stations, court hearings and medical examinations, workplaces or schools, and their households. Margarethe Kusenbach (2003: 463) has argued that the value of the go-along interview 'is that ethnographers are able to observe research collaborators' spatial practices in situ while accessing their experiences and interpretations at the same time'. Sometimes, informal discussions took place while I accompanied people; sometimes silence prevailed. While movement was part of these processes, 'waiting' and 'returning' played a much bigger role. I would wait in hospital waiting rooms, courtrooms, and cramped busses stuck in traffic or at bus stops. After accompanying somebody to an appointment and waiting for them to be attended to – such as a court hearing, a medical examination, or a visitation – we were often turned away and told to return another time. After experiencing this several times, it was almost as though there was a certain routine, a circular movement of ever-repeating 'almost happenings'.

I also spoke to lawyers from the Legal Aid Board – an organisation offering free legal assistance to people experiencing poverty – in particular to Cecilia Tucker (30s), who usually handled over 20 cases at any given time. Many of the imprisoned people I spoke with at Pademba Road Prison had been represented by her. She detailed her movements between holding cells, court hearings, and her office and discussed the intensity of her workload. Workload was also the leading theme in my interviews with two police officers at Eastern Police Station who worked through piles and piles of reports daily.

Interviews in Courts, Police Stations, and the Prison

To record what litigants and legal personnel 'say' (Bierschenk and de Sardan 2014), I used various forms of interview. At the shelters of Don Bosco and at the FSU, I spoke mainly to women and girls who were survivors of (sexual) abuse or trafficking. In prison, I spoke to men and boys who were alleged to have committed sexual or domestic violence or had been convicted for this. They had been sentenced to between five years in prison and life imprisonment. Such interactions require one to critically examine potential repercussions for research collaborators, both practically and emotionally (see Enria 2015).

In the prison, I was subject to restrictions imposed by prison officials. I was permitted to enter the building between one and four in the afternoon. I was instructed not to speak about incidents of torture, maltreatment, or sexual violence in the holding cells and the prison more generally. On any given day, I had one hour to speak with one research collaborator. But after the first few days, I usually spoke to three or four people who were imprisoned. It was always unclear whether and under what circumstances I might see a prisoner again.

Being confronted with a stranger from outside the prison walls and being encouraged to speak about one's case and about one's experiences of violence (both committed and endured) can trigger difficult emotions. Many of these research collaborators were extremely traumatised, and quite often they were also violent. To give them as much control of the process as possible, I started interviews only after a rigorous consent procedure. I explained my research, gave an overview of the questions I would ask, and explained that the interview could be ended or paused at any point, and that consent to use the information given could be withdrawn up to two months past the interview. I told them that I intended to write about them and publish my results. I discussed anonymity. I also stated that my presence would not have any direct benefit for them. I was transparent about the restrictions imposed upon me by prison staff, and I explained that I would not appear as a witness, would not contact kin or loved ones, and not take sides or interfere in their case in any way.

Only after gaining oral consent for each of these points would I start interviews. Sometimes interviews did not take place, sometimes they were stopped prematurely, and occasionally consent to use the interview was later withdrawn. It was difficult to adhere to this rigid procedure, but I never wavered because my situation was uncertain. I wanted research collaborators to speak to me on their own terms rather than because there was the possibility of an added benefit. Never knowing whether I would be allowed to return for the next hearing or prison visit, I found it unethical to try to influence cases, and I tried not to nurture hopes which might later be crushed. Unlike informal discussions, this tactic created a barrier between me and the research collaborators, which led to interviews being stiffer than they would be in the fluid settings of the city. But it also was meant to limit false hopes, at least as far as possible, and minimise adverse effects on both sides.

During the interview, I asked the imprisoned person a few open questions about their case and then left them to direct the conversation. Some 25, 15, and 10 minutes before the hour was over, I indicated how much time was left so that they could prepare appropriately. While I conducted semi-structured, problem-centred, and structured interviews in these settings, I did not push research collaborators to speak about their life histories, their backgrounds, or their families if they did not initiate these topics. While speaking about the life they had prior to prison can be positive, asking about loved ones can also cause distress. Hence, it was they, not I, who made such choices. My ability to provide background stories for many of the research collaborators in this book has therefore been determined by their willingness to disclose such information to me. Often, simply discussing their cases and their circumstances was enough.

I interviewed 53 men and boys in Pademba Road Prison accused of or convicted for sexual and gender-based violence. These interviews shed light on the perspectives of the alleged perpetrators and complemented the data on men and boys who were never officially accused or whose cases were settled informally.

When speaking to women and girls who were alleged victims, I was often able to stay with them after the interview, if they wanted my company, or to visit them frequently. For those research collaborators – such as young girls – for whom there are support structures in place in Freetown, I also had referral and information forms with me, which helped direct them to appropriate sources of support. While psychosocial services for men and boys are almost non-existent, there are several organisations which cater to women and girls who have experienced violence and who need emotional, psychosocial, or medical support.[6] I had reached out to these organisations prior to starting interviews to make sure that they would be able to accommodate my referrals.

Partiality and Mosaics

Because court cases often take years to pass through the entire system, it was not possible to follow all state cases from beginning to end. I therefore applied a mixed-methods approach, combining case studies, analyses of court records, and ethnographic fieldwork with those involved. I gathered in-depth information on 98 cases, interviewing the alleged victim, the legal representative (if any), and the judge, and I was present during the course of several court hearings. In over 100 additional cases, I was present during only one hearing. For ethical reasons, as well as conditions of availability and access, it was often not possible to interview both the victim and the perpetrator. For these cases, I gathered information and interpretations from law enforcement officials, media personnel, and involved actors (sometimes from communities, sometimes from NGOs).

With the household and community cases, however, I either followed only the proceedings and conducted no interviews, or I conducted interviews with those directly involved who took the stand but did not follow the proceedings closely. Each approach depended on the specificity of the case. In some cases involving accusations of infidelity, talking outside the official sittings is considered an offence, so I could not conduct any interviews without interfering in the case.

Personal Consequences, Safety, and Ethics

Fieldwork and theory-generation can never be complete, straightforward, uncontested, or neutral. They are always partial, controversial, and shaped by the presuppositions, assumptions, political motivations, world views, and choices of the researchers, research collaborators,

---

[6] This emphasises the embeddedness of gendered victim–perpetrator perceptions.

universities, funding bodies, publishing standards, and reviewers. The process is also affected by gender, age, class, origin, socioeconomic background, profession, and framework of reference as well as 'the influence of prejudice, conditioned by historical circumstances, on interpretive stances' (Kinsella 2006). And as Elizabeth Kinsella, drawing on Sandra Harding (1991), said: 'Within such a view, we are called to account, to the extent that we are able, for the situated location of our subjectivity' (Kinsella 2006). In fact, 'emancipatory social science can only be achieved through analyses that contain an element of autocritique, which attempt to examine how the conditions of research defined in the widest sense determine the research conclusion' (Karp 1986: 135).

In her work on solitary confinement, Lisa Guenther said that 'access to the written word, as well as access to interview opportunities or any other form of interaction, is shaped by race, class, gender, and geographic location' (Guenther 2013: xiv). The intersectionality of identity and subject positions shaped my positioning in the field, my access, and certainly also my analysis and interpretation. My gender, for example, allowed me to gain access to both male and female research collaborators, while my relationship status – not married – meant that on occasion I had difficulties speaking to those who were married and experienced harassment with others. In other situations – for example, when speaking to elders – I was considered, because of my unmarried status, to be insufficiently knowledgeable to say anything about marriage. Interestingly, these conversations generated rich material because elders then explained everything to me in detail, starting with the basics, much as if teaching a child.

I was deeply affected by the research topics, and by the precarious circumstances in which many research collaborators found themselves. These conditions also influenced my approach to analysing the data. At times, life and love histories were emotionally challenging to listen to, and hearing how families were separated, relationships broken, and people violated often left me feeling helpless and in pain. Moreover, it was difficult to hear about the research collaborators' encounters with violence. I lack the training of a qualified psychologist to provide the emotional support that many of them were seeking, and I had difficulty listening to stories of violence without being personally impacted (Schneider 2017). It took me about one month to establish a referral network through which I could connect vulnerable research collaborators with qualified people and institutions available to assist them. It has taken me several years to process my own experiences, and I am still actively working on this (Schneider 2017).

When speaking to those involved in a court case, as well as to imprisoned people and alleged victims, I aimed to keep what Luisa Enria termed an 'empathetic distance' (Enria 2015; Schneider 2023b). Such research requires empathy as well as a recognition of difference. In some ways, my research collaborators and I shared experiences of hardship, violence, and pain. In her work on rape and its aftermath in Uganda, Holly Porter reiterates this point by saying:

> When I talk of a shared experience, I mean one that we experienced together and yet, not in the same way. Put in more anthropological language, what I mean by shared experience is that I engaged in 'interexperience'; I explicitly do not claim that the empathy that I feel for my informants has in any way qualified me to talk as if I 'relived the experiences of the human beings who were being studied'. Rather, this fieldwork, and the intersubjective encounters that it has involved allow me to hear stories of rape and not just hear a tragic event, which happened to a stranger, but to hear it as a part of this rhythm of life that I participate in and observe. It allows for an existential interpretation of the phenomena. (Porter 2013: 29)

Empathy does not mean categorising research collaborators simplistically as victims or perpetrators (Enria 2015). Rather, it is an attempt to appreciate the complexity and multi-sidedness of experiences and reactions while carefully reflecting upon 'the incompleteness of intersubjective understanding' (Enria 2015: 41). And it was also an attempt at protecting myself. While I sought to put research collaborators in control and made every effort not to cause them further harm, I also needed to be attentive to my own well-being. Anthropological research does not allow for an examination of violence from a position of safety. As I wrote elsewhere: 'Research on sensitive topics in precarious environments is often accompanied with a complex and demanding appendage. Researching violence can lead to experiencing various forms of violence' (Schneider 2017: 36). While many research collaborators and friends went out of their way to accommodate and protect me, and most of my experiences were positive, certain vulnerabilities remained. Challenges came from the sites of my research, especially ghettos, settlements, and nightclubs, as well as prison, my living circumstances with EAUC, and my research topic. On several occasions, I had difficult experiences. In prison, there were no protective mechanisms. Nothing could safeguard me from the secondary trauma which followed from hearing some stories of unspeakable violence and suffering repeatedly, first personally, then in recordings or in my notes and, later, on paper. These stories became uneasy companions and a part of me.

As I have indicated, I used an adaptable methodology. Hence, the choice of conversation, whether an informal discussion or open or structured interview, was dependent on the conditions of the field setting, the research collaborator in question, and the ethical and moral requirements of the encounter. Making these elements visible allows for an enhanced contextualisation of the data (Bosire 2012: 55–6).

Many of the people I conducted research with and the communities I frequented were familiar to me from 2012, when I did my first stretch of research. They are now key research collaborators of mine as well as close friends. In addition to openly stating my role as an anthropologist and rendering visible my standpoint, motivations, and struggles as much as possible, my positioning was a matter of continuous critical reflection. The different places my research collaborators and I occupy on the socioeconomic, racial, and structural spectrum called for great sensitivity, as did the fact that other people's lived experiences and stories were serving as the foundations of my career.

Most of the research collaborators included in this research come from vulnerable communities and low socioeconomic backgrounds. Throughout my ten years of engagement in Freetown, I tried to mitigate the exploitation that occurs when researchers 'collect' information and then disappear, by discussing my research with the research collaborators, by sharing my research findings, and by building stable relationships with them. While this rendered my research more reciprocal, it also meant that I needed to be very careful to separate interviews from private conversations. I felt that neither my curiosity nor my access justified that I make all narratives the subject of my research. At Allentown and in Naimbana Street, I lived in households which kept very few secrets from me. I hope that I can honour this trust by writing only about events which I was given permission to describe and to do so in a respectful manner. However, in courts, police stations, and the prison, this kind of relationship building is impossible. When speaking with litigants and criminal justice personnel, I encountered research collaborators in that specific subject position. Often it was impossible to ask about their backgrounds, families, or life histories without transgressing rules I was given to follow. Police officers, lawyers, and judges had to be treated in their professional capacity. When I was talking to them, they shared their professional and sometimes their personal opinions, but I could not blur the boundary between these and other roles they occupied – for example, a police officer I interviewed later appeared at a party as the husband of someone I knew.

The field research was approved by the University of Oxford's Ethics Committee and the School of Anthropology and Museum Ethnography at the University of Oxford (Ref. No SSH_SAME_C1A_16_006). I was granted a research permit in Sierra Leone and was affiliated with the Department of Sociology and Social Work of Fourah Bay College in Freetown. All participants learnt of the aims and objectives of the research and gave oral consent. When asked, I removed the identifying characteristics of research collaborators to protect their identity, and often they chose pseudonyms for themselves. This is also the reason why some research collaborators are referred to by their forenames only, while others appear with both their names. Anonymising certain political and legal figures is close to impossible, and so I do not refer to them unless they gave me permission to do so. To protect research collaborators and make them unidentifiable, in several cases I also had to change certain details.

2 The Impact of Violence on Relationships

Violence plays a central role in the production and reproduction of social relations. An analysis of intimacy and violence therefore requires examining the influence of violence on relationships over time. Relationship dynamics are influenced by complex pasts as well as by the particularities of contemporary life. This chapter first considers how, even though relationship dynamics and routes to adulthood have always been multifaceted and messy, historical models of marriage paint pictures of a simpler, more linear past. In urban areas, Sierra Leoneans perceive these historical models of marriage, in which achieving social adulthood and financial stability were prerequisites, to have been disrupted by the civil war (1991–2002). Violent experiences during that period reconfigured prevailing gender positions involving a strong husband and a protected wife, and deconstructed marriage as the main relationship form. The chapter reflects on the impact of such violence on men and women, and then moves on to analyse how young people deal with these changed relationship dynamics in Freetown today.

In contemporary Freetown, where conventional pathways towards social adulthood are blocked by the structural violence of socioeconomic marginalisation, those confined to the youth stage of their lives employ an elaborate system of doing favours and collecting debts to navigate everyday life and build possibilities for adulthood. This also affects intergenerational dynamics. Especially among other generations, the complexities of the present lead to a longing for an idealised, simpler past that has never truly existed.

Today's changing social landscapes reveal two contradictory trends. On the one hand, urban dynamics foster diverse relationship practices, which are carefully labelled with various pidgin terms. In Sierra Leone's urban centres, (transactional) relationship forms that had to be kept hidden in rural communities can now be lived openly. Urban life encourages the formation of social alliances through the exchange of gifts, goods, or services that contribute to a reciprocal economy of desire. In the gap that has opened between previous models and what may be, people can experiment with desire more openly, as women are no longer solely accessible to married individuals.

On the other hand, although the protective association of the family suffered during the war, households and communities continue to be the main informal institutions that mediate unbearable violence or problems between partners. However, their protection, recognition, and support are extended only to committed relationships. Youth who are unable to build formal alliances between households through marriage create relationship forms that traverse easily between such expectations, their personal desires, and the constraints weighing on them. Examining their tactics allows me to ask what relationship expectations and practices are 'doing' in the lives of young people and in their relationships. In this chapter, I tease out how relationships are lived and negotiated between the residues of the past and the constraints of the present with regard to underlying aspirations and various expectations.

In doing so, I also portray the underbelly of such creative navigation skills by showing that the bridging systems do not offer the same security as marriage. I also show how, in situations characterised by economic scarcity, attempts to satisfy these differing demands of starting a household and sustaining a committed relationship while fulfilling personal aspirations often create dynamics that foster violence. Understanding violence in relationships therefore requires an understanding of the complex factors weighing on relationships.

The Social Achievement of Marriage and the Desire for Others

In Sierra Leone, ideals of viable partners historically revolve around gender parallelism, in which there are differing but complementary roles for men and women (e.g. Ferme 2001). Within this frame, spouses are those who hold together a social fabric that incorporates previously separated households. Getting married is therefore a social responsibility that requires having achieved social adulthood. This is echoed in older ethnographies, where marriage practices were at the core of analysing Sierra Leone's social, political, and economic fabrics. In works such as Eberl-Elber's *Westafrika's letztes Rätsel* (Eberl-Elber 1936) or Bledsoe's *Women and Marriage in Kpelle Society* (Bledsoe 1980a), youth appear as an analytical category to explain larger organising principles and (power) dynamics relating to kinship, social organisation, and generation. At that stage, youthhood was mainly analysed as a transitional phase of coming of age, which was passed during initiation periods that lasted between several weeks and a few months (Little 1965; 1966; Jedrej 1976; Bosire

2012). Indeed, before the civil war, when over 90 per cent of Sierra Leoneans were still members of a sodality, the 'youth' period of life was short. Before initiation, a person belonged to the household of their parents. After initiation, a person completed the transition from child to adult by marrying and starting a household, thereby becoming a big man or big woman. According to William Murphy, it was the 'secret' connected to sodality membership that used to 'separate elders from youth' and supported 'the elders' political and economic control of the youth' (Murphy 1980: 193).

Marriage is therefore at the heart of adulthood. Marriage, in turn, is enabled by the exchange of capital, which serves as the physical manifestation of the symbolic, social, political, and economic ties binding individuals and households together. In Sierra Leone, the groom visits the bride's family to officially voice his intention of marrying and to distribute money or goods to her family. The closer the kin relation, the more money is given. However, important members of the community, such as neighbours, pastors, or – in village settings – the chief, are also included in the distribution of money.

Completing bride price payments symbolises that the bride's affection has been earned and that she is now a full part of the groom's household.[1] This is reflected in marriage terminology, which revolves around sexual possession and gendered positionality. Mabinti (64) from Allentown told me: 'When a Mende man asks for a woman's hand in marriage, he says *nya longua nyahin gi sorvah*, which means "I want this woman for sex", or "I want this woman for possession" ... The parent of a man says *inyahin majuah*, "he possesses a woman". For a woman, the parents say *ihindui majua*, "she possesses a man"'. Mabinti also explained the Limba and Temne marriage terms to me: 'In Limba, a man says *yama dennyeh ni/ yando kai ka dennya*, "I am the one sitting or placing her/a woman down". A woman says *dehnah dennyeh ya ma*, which means "he is the one marrying me". However, the interpretation is rather that it is him [sic] who sat me down, or *donah dennyo yan*, meaning "it is here, I am seated or placed down"'. When a Temne man asks for a woman's hand in marriage, he says *iyaima nintei*, 'I want to see something', and a woman agrees by saying *ipobaal*, 'I am obeying'.

---

[1] In 2009, with the Registration of Customary Marriages and Divorce Act, the Sierra Leonean state urged all spouses to register their marriages to legally share equal access to land and property and to be protected in case of divorce and to be recognised in inheritance cases. Marriages can occur in a church or mosque (religious marriages), in the community (traditional marriages), or at the city council (registered marriages).

These exchanges establish a union not just between two persons, but between two families. Teeth and tongue are firmly placed in the mouth. They are part of the larger structure of cells, tissues, systems, and organs that make up the human body. Marriage is thus about social relations and symbolises a person's relationship with society. It enables the building, rebuilding, and maintenance of households, lineages, and social unions (Eberl-Elber 1936; Bledsoe 1980a; see also Radcliffe-Brown 1950). Because marriage is part and parcel of kinship and alliance structures, kin groups continue to exert considerable power after the wedding (Wardlow 2006).[2] The union provides a safety net for kin groups, who will be supported by the newly formed household in old age. In turn, kin groups form a protective association supporting spouses when they experience problems within their marriage (Chapter 6).

Yet, unsurprisingly, my research collaborators made it clear that marriage was never the only conjugal form. As everywhere in the world, people may be attracted to or fall in love with someone who is not their spouse. However, before the civil war such relationships were severely constrained in Sierra Leone. Owing to the financial security needed on the groom's side, young men found it difficult to raise the bride price required to marry. Instead, older men married young girls who had just completed their sodality initiation and included them in polygynous households (Richards 2005). Nevertheless, some girls and young women were drawn to boys or men of their own age (Leach 1994; Ferme 2001). Marina Temudo (2019) argues that because in Guinea-Bissau such love affairs are common but not tolerated in village settings, designated spaces for agreed love outings were created that provided time away during which women could have extramarital affairs before returning to their spouses. In Sierra Leonean village settings, such arrangements were never openly accepted and extramarital relationships needed to be carefully concealed (Schneider 2020b).[3] Indeed, the fines and hardship attached to being found out – the 'women trouble' – was chiefly responsible for men 'running away' to the city (Richards 1998). However, when the civil war commenced, marriage patterns and secret love affairs were irrevocably transformed. The conflict also interrupted initiations and therefore the 'smooth' transition from childhood to adulthood. Moreover, it brought changes to the governance of elders over youth,

---

[2] Families also influence the choice of marriage partner.
[3] Bledsoe (1980a), who compared women's lives in rural and urban areas, found that women in urban areas tended to live more autonomously from their families, married later, and had more access to wealth and property. Now, almost 40 years later, relationship practices in Freetown are constantly renegotiated.

with the result that marriages outside warring factions came to a near halt. The extensive violence that led up to and accompanied the civil war and its aftermath continue to affect relationship practices today.

Residues of a Violent Past Continue to Linger

This destabilisation and encroachment of violence on everyday lives did not begin with the civil war, nor did it end thereafter. The civil war can be located within a much larger history of violence, rupture, and transformation. Colonialism and slavery had ensured the perpetuation of violence for centuries beforehand. Yet, research collaborators never mentioned colonialism and slavery when they spoke about interpersonal relationships. They referred to history in terms of 'before the war' and 'after the war'. The silences around centuries of colonial violence, during which women and girls – and men and boys – were uprooted, trafficked, subjected to extreme forms of violence, killed, or left to die, point to collective, ongoing trauma, which is transmitted from generation to generation (see Rothberg 2008: 226, 230; Craps 2010: 53). These traumas persist but defy language partly because of the severity of injuries caused, partly because little acknowledgement followed (e.g. Schneider 2023a; for analyses of such traumas, see, e.g. Nkrumah 1974; Erikson 1994; Lascelles 2020). This raises the question of how one accounts for the pain and violence of prolonged exploitation that is not mentioned. After the civil war, there were apologies, reparations, and regrets. After slavery and colonialism, however, there was hardly an acknowledgement of wrongdoing, let alone a real apology. The violence of empire and racism continue to linger, now taking shape in seemingly benevolent development and rights discourses in which 'white people know best' and 'have come to help'. There is therefore no before and after. Time and global paradigms of colonial exploitation do not pass; they accumulate (Baucom 2001). Silences may thus not be absences but presences of what Viviane Saleh-Hanna brings to the fore in her conceptualisation of a black feminist hauntology (Saleh-Hanna 2015). They simultaneously indicate a coping mechanism and a resistance to being defined by – and perceiving the world through – colonial logics, such as the reductive binary of 'coloniser' and 'colonised'.[4]

---

[4] Saleh-Hanna married Toni Morrison's (1987) concept of 'rememory' with Jacques Derrida's (1993) 'hauntology' to show how structural racism permeates and constructs race and class, gender and sexuality, place and space, and life and death as binary conceptions that enable conquest and suppression.

The civil war was a response to pre-existing social, political, and economic conditions of inequality that continued into the neo-colonial post-independence era (Abdullah 1998). At this time, gerontocratic exploitation increased. In response, youth from the 'former slave classes' opposed the prevailing 'labour exploitation and lack of freedom of opportunity' (Richards 2005: 586). They fought against the common notion of 'having wealth in people' (Bledsoe 1980a) and thus the control of young men's labour and of women by a few elite men or elders through the institutions of slavery and polygynous marriage. They also resented the constraints resulting from 'women trouble', when monetary fines and free labour were imposed on them for having relationships with women and girls who were married to these elite men or elders (Ferme 2001; Diggins 2015). Their main aim, according to Paul Richards, was to escape dependency and patriarchy, and construct a different future for themselves.

During the war, brutal atrocities were committed by fighting factions consisting in large part of 'girls, boys, young men and women' (Human Rights Watch 1998; Ellis 1999; TRC 2004a: 2 n.41; Coulter 2009: 54). It is estimated that, taken together, all fighting factions systematically subjected up to 250,000 women and girls of all demographics to sexual violence. Violence was often accompanied by abuses against family and community: 'Relationship practices and values were deliberately undermined in that child combatants raped women who were old enough to be their grandmothers, rebels raped pregnant and breastfeeding mothers, and fathers were forced to watch their daughters being raped' (Human Rights Watch 2003: 4). It is estimated that between 10,000 and 20,000 women were part of the Revolutionary United Front (RUF)[5] (Friedman Rudovsky 2013). Some women and girls joined of their own accord, but many were abducted. They were fighters, 'bush wives' through forced marriage, domestic workers, or slaves (Human Rights Watch 1998; 2003; Human Rights and Dufka 1999; Coulter 2009: 51; Cohen 2013; Marks 2014). Many women and girls remained with the RUF for long periods and in that time gave birth to children (Coulter 2009: 51).[6]

The literature on the civil war has done important work in focussing on women and girls not only as victims of, but also as participants in violence. However, it engages mainly with the activities of fighting factions (e.g. Coulter 2009; Cohen 2013; Marks 2014). Significantly less

---

[5] The RUF fought and eventually lost the 11-year civil war in Sierra Leone.
[6] Even though about 30 per cent of under-age fighters were female, 'only 506 girls, compared with 6,952 boys, went through the DDR' (Friedman Rudovsky 2013; see Shaw, Waldorf, and Hazan 2010).

attention has been given to experiences of violence among the civilian population, those who 'remained at home'. Yet these experiences featured most heavily in the stories of my research collaborators, who described how the civil war changed relationships and violence within them. *Love and Violence* thus carries scholarship on violence during conflict beyond fighting factions and into households. It shows the ways in which the violence of the civil war impacted on domestic relationship dynamics, gender roles, and ideals of partnership. At the same time, it draws connections between larger histories of structural violence and the recent history of conflict. It is therefore imperative to read this analysis of shame, emasculation, and disintegration in light of the country's and the region's wider history.

Mr Chernor Barrie (86), who lives at King George's old age home, explained:

Before the war, sex outside of marriage and even teenage pregnancy was not so common. But violence in marriage and between spouses and children was normal and expected. We had no law in place that punished men for violence against their wives ... We have this long tradition, this norm of beating the woman with a belt or with objects and having the woman go sit down and be silent and the man to force her to sex. The Temne even say that if your husband does not beat you, he does not love you.

During the war the violence escalated, and men felt like they can just have any woman. Not only the rebels and the army men participated in the violence. For example, when there was a coup, many times the families scattered. Then girls, instead of being raped by everyone, were looking for one guy who could give them food and shelter and that guy could do to them whatever he wanted. He could beat them and *bambrus* [here, rape] them many times every night.

One experience foregrounded in many interviews was the helplessness that men and boys experienced when witnessing how their wives, daughters, and sisters were abducted, raped, and killed. Mr Mohamed (35), my research assistant in Allentown, explained:

During the war, it was very common for the women to be abducted. The girl I told you about, my main girlfriend, the one who punched me with an electric cord when she found out that I was cheating; the beautiful one. When the rebels came to Freetown, they abducted her and took her to the bush. And then she was with one of the rebels, and she became pregnant. Then one day, he was beating her and kicking her in the stomach, and that is when she started bleeding and died. That is how I lost her.

I was told repeatedly that losing partners and daughters to rebels was emasculating for men. They felt unable to protect their families and loved ones. Referring to Mr Mohamed, Rafieu (37), his brother-in-law, explained:

You know what is common here? Like Mr Mohamed now, he has loved this one woman so much, like so, so much. You know how he always talks about this. But then the rebels came and took her, they just took her, and he could do nothing. He has never loved since. But it happened to many. They just came and took our women, or we had to allow our women trading their bodies for foodstuffs to neighbours and police and ... everybody. It is shameful, like what kind of men were we, you know? It has really, really impacted [us].

Rafieu's description of the experience of shame during the conflict and its effect on men's lives was echoed in many conversations. Bonnie Mann shows how 'shame taps into the memory of a deep, bodily incapacity to *live* without engaging the regard and the embodied agency of someone else' (Mann 2014: 122, original emphasis). Shame is therefore 'an impotence-making experience' (Kaufman 1980: 9 cited in Mann 2014: 122) that negates independence and creates a state of feeling 'very weak and very powerless toward things of the greatest importance' (Nussbaum 2004: 177 cited in Mann 2014: 122). Papa Jones (87), from King George's old age home, illustrated this emotion by describing how 'during the war it became common that you can just have any woman, just like that, not only your wife. By now, it is habit and it will hardly ever change. But also, your wives and daughters were not under your hand anymore. Others can just come and take them. You are completely powerless'.

Papa Jones clarifies the effect of the civil war in negating previous boundaries because it became common to just 'take women'. Access to women was no longer dependent on the approval of kin and community or on a woman's affection and her willingness to transgress limits. Indeed, the protective shield of the household was rendered entirely ineffective. It became nearly impossible for men to guard their mothers, wives, and daughters from the grasp of others. Women and girls who stayed at home were consequently subjected to extreme forms of violence.

Rachel Kalish and Michael Kimmel developed the notion of 'aggrieved entitlement' (Kalish and Kimmel 2010: 452) to analyse men's use of violence 'to avenge a perceived challenge to their masculine identity'. 'For many men', Kalish and Kimmel stated, 'humiliation is emasculation', which 'must be avenged, or you cease to be a man. ... Aggrieved entitlement is a gendered emotion, a fusion of that humiliating loss of manhood and the moral obligation to get it back' (Kalish and Kimmel 2010: 454; see also Mann 2014: 121). In Sierra Leone, marital rules and responsibilities that designated belonging and positionality became meaningless. Wives could no longer be 'placed down' safely in a man's home, and men could not live up to the demands of heading a household. The humiliation and shame that men felt when they could not prevent their loved ones from being subjected to violence undermined the ideal of strong and protective masculinity. Because aggrieved men were unable to avenge such violence, some became increasingly violent towards those loved ones they could not protect. Consequently, as Fatima (79), who lives at King George's, stated:

> Women were not safe anymore from nobody. During the war, violence came from all sides. Our men were traumatised or afraid, so they would become very angry. Then they beat, and they forced us without mercy. Even those who were never violent before. To be protected, we had to trade sex for foodstuffs, or for not being exposed. Then, our men became even angrier. They knew they cannot protect us, and we must sex others, but they hated us then, and then we would be beaten by both: the neighbour and the husband.

What Fatima's portrayal also shows is that women officially and visibly became the main breadwinners, while men's failure to provide and protect was exposed. To return to the metaphor of teeth and tongue, these experiences of paralysis in the face of violent encroachments on male authority and against those whom men are supposed to protect, the subsequent impossibility of embodying and enacting expected roles, and the resulting shame are like teeth that have been knocked out of the mouth (war) or have fallen out after decades of malnourishment (structural violence, colonialism) and that now lie outside the mouth in a place where they can no longer perform their role. They can still be recognised as teeth, are preserved as teeth, but they cannot be put back into the mouth. While the tongue may be burnt, swell, or be hurt, it will always remain in the mouth. By contrast, teeth do not retain their role forever, unless they successfully perform it. They will eventually be replaced by other teeth, and, even if they are not, it will become more difficult though not impossible to eat. This symbolic knocking out of healthy teeth, the falling out of teeth that have become loose or rotten, or the pulling of teeth that have become infected, and that have thereby hurt the entire mouth, all lead to reactions and counter-manifestations. Men (the teeth) seek to demonstrate how securely placed they are, how steadfast and how essential they are for the mouth. One such means of doing this is violence.

In many interviews, violence seemed to be the result of an inability to adhere to gender ideals and expectations. Darren (29), who was a child during the war and who hid with his extended family in the Naimbana Street mosque, pointed out:

> Outsiders don't ever understand the real issues, the real consequences of the war. Everyone was inside. People were tense. There was much fighting and disagreement among adults ... Space was limited, so we saw what they do to themselves in marriage. Family members everyone, but we could never ask because the bigger problem was outside.

Without a doubt, these experiences led to a reconfiguration of relationships. Despite the declaration of peace in 2002, the trauma of war has 'left scars which run through the fabric of households, families and communities' (Mills et al. 2018). Consider the explanation of Amadu (40), a mechanic at Star Motors garage: 'Because men became useless during the war, after the war they had to prove themselves. They were very harsh and violent to establish control in the house again. Also, they probably violated others during the war. That stayed with them. For women as well. Then, children are raised the same way again. It becomes a system'. The problems Darren described, which were buried below 'the problem outside', were not a focus of post-conflict recovery. This has led to the prevalent notion, here illustrated by Eleanor (43), a mother from Allentown and Mr Mohamed's wife, that

> everybody suffered but sometimes I think that those who actually fought and those who were abducted had it better you know, because later on they got money and support through the DDR [Disarmament, Demobilization, and Reintegration programme].[7] For us here, we got nothing. We were raped by friends, uncles, neighbours. We had to do unspeakable things to put food on the table. We were always in one room, so, so many of us. Trust really suffered because everyone exploited everyone because we had to, and you learnt that deep down people are black. That attitude stayed with us.

Scholars analysing the reintegration process have pointed out its shortcomings in attending to fighters and victims alike (Shaw 2007; 2014; Shaw, Waldorf, and Hazan 2010; Ainley, Friedman, and Mahony 2015). Similarly, Sierra Leonean officials such as Charles Vandi, the director of the Gender Desk at the Ministry of Social Welfare, Gender and Children's Affairs (MSWGCA), disclosed that

> many of the fighters from all groups did not go through the DDR process. Especially problematic are not the actual fighters but civilians who engaged in violent practices but slipped through the net as they were never targeted by the DDR in the first place. Still, violent practices had been the norm and are now normalised both by men and women. People who lived through the war are now starting new families, and these children grow up with the same practices in the household and learn to see them as normal and common. This leads to a vicious spiral of violence.

---

[7] The DDR was implemented by the Government of Sierra Leone and supported by the World Bank and other international institutions and NGOs. It marked the official end of the civil war in Sierra Leone. The DDR is considered a success story: 'A total of 72,490 combatants were disarmed and 71,043 demobilised, and 63,545 former combatants participated in the reintegration segment, including 6,845 child soldiers' (Solomon and Ginifer 2008). However, its impact on households and individuals is less clear and is seen more critically (Solomon and Ginifer 2008).

As we can see, peace-time violence is related to war-time violence; current violence to past violence; and future aspirations to imaginaries of the past. The 'system of violence' that research collaborators described has tainted the 'moral economy of relationships' (Burrill, Roberts, and Thornberry 2010), and, as a result, many forms of violence are now perceived as normal aspects of any relationship (see Chapter 4). Relationship dynamics have thus been deeply influenced by Sierra Leone's (recent) violent history. As the ethnographic material has revealed, after the war the security previously attached to marriages could not be restored in the capital city, the authority of the family was diminished, gender relations were transformed, and relationship practices changed considerably. Those coming of age today are deeply affected by these ruptures. They are unable to return to previous ways of reaching adulthood. At the same time, the expectations that elders have of them remain largely unchanged, and gender ideals of a male provider and female dependant are still strong. This leads youth to break away from traditional relationship ideals and try instead to live and love in new ways.

Youthful Loving in Freetown Today

In the hastily transforming hub of post-pandemic Freetown, there is a disconnect between relationship practices, on the one hand, and ideals of marriage and gender parallelism, on the other. In the post-war landscape, people's lives are determined not only by family ties and kin hierarchies. People do not switch neatly from their family home to their own home (see Eberl-Elber 1936; Ferme 2001). Rather, as has been observed across sub-Saharan Africa, families are often scattered across the country and people grow up with distant relatives, often also with friends (e.g. Newell 2012; Stasik 2016). The hold of elders over youth continues to loosen. But past ideals still linger, and partners continue to demand economic and social protection. This leads to complex discussions about what love and relationships mean in Sierra Leone today and how relationships should be lived and negotiated between these competing and contradictory forces.

Because predetermined pathways from sodality initiation to marriage have become unwalkable, the 'youth' stage of life is no longer brief but extensive. This trend is not only observable in Sierra Leone. After the civil war, the concept of a 'crisis of youth' gained currency in Sierra Leone as well as beyond its borders. While it was 'initially used to explain the involvement of young people in armed conflict', scholars came to see that 'the inability of young people to attain social adulthood because of continuing gerontocratic and patrimonial control of resources' was being 'experienced much more widely among youths' and for a much longer period (Peters 2011: 129; see also Moyi 2013; Diggins 2014; Enria 2015). Concurrently, the category of youth began to subsume vastly different groups for widely different purposes (Schlegel and Barry 1991; Durham 2000: 116; Christiansen, Utas, and Vigh 2006; see Mead 1929).[8] In Sierra Leone, for example, the National Youth Policy 'defines "youth" as anyone from 15 to 35'; a youth is 'someone who is no longer a child, but not yet a "big man" or "big woman"' (Shepler 2004: 10). Many of the men I spoke to stretched this category until well into the forties while the women I spoke to had often referred to themselves as 'big women' as soon as they had had their first child or had undergone *ansa bele*, which is when a man accepts responsibility for a woman's pregnancy.

Economic constraints must, of course, be taken into proper consideration as a dominant pressure upon all such concerns. Oki of EAUC explained:

If I don't have [money], I must stay off you. When I see them [girlfriends], they say they want to eat and then I am ashamed. So, I just lay down with her and otherwise I keep to myself. Sierra Leone bothers today. The women ask for much because they themselves have nothing. We have nothing, and they have nothing. It is really not easy. Only when I have something small, when I have like SLL 5,000 [GBP 0.45] or SLL 10,000 [GBP 0.89], then I call a bike (motorcycle taxi) to take me to her, but when I don't have anything, I keep to myself.

Oki experiences shame because he is unable to provide for the basic needs of girlfriends and lovers. This ties in with the work of Bonnie Mann, who showed how experiencing shame 'makes gender very heavy' (Mann 2014: 2). The condition of urban poverty makes it impossible for many individuals to pay bride price and to re-establish previous roles of male supporter or female dependant. Oki's inability to embody the masculine ideal of the provider leads him to 'keep to himself'. These constraints have been noticed by various scholars (see Masquelier 2005; Grant 2006). For Sierra Leone, Michael Jackson (2011) described how, in a world of limited means but unlimited desires, the possibility to live and love can be thwarted for men by the impossibility to provide and protect. In his work on the ambivalence between popular 'love music' and economic constraints in Freetown, Michael Stasik analysed how the latter become traps confining people to youthhood (Stasik 2016: 223).

---

[8] In fact, Foucault already suggested in 1979 that 'youth as they become defined as a concrete category of social analysis become increasingly a socially problematic category, and studies of youth are too often studies of deviance or of problems needing programmatic intervention' (Foucault 1979 cited in Durham 2000: 116).

However, some research collaborators have embraced changing social and gendered ways. Amadu (24) of EAUC explained this in the following way:

A wife needs to be maintained financially. Well, even a girlfriend needs to be maintained. That is why you can only get married once you have become a big man, secured a job, and so on. For us, it is far too early. Maybe end of thirties or later. For now, girlfriends are hard to keep; they demand a lot. This is why we often have fast-fast relationships. But the things are shifting somehow, and girlfriends also often find ways to gain something maybe through other lovers or through some work.

In Freetown today, women are better able to achieve social adulthood than men. In a country where the labour market is gendered, they can find employment in the informal sector more easily than men and are often able to gain some resources from partners and lovers (Leach 1994). Women are therefore usually the main breadwinners in their homes, irrespective of the nature of their marriage or relationship (Pessima et al. 2009).

Not only are both partners actively engaged in making a living, thereby turning traditional dependency models on their head, but economic constraints also foster a multitude of informal and alternative relationship arrangements. Multiple, transitory, transactional, and rapidly developing relationships are employed in people's efforts to make a living in constrained environments (see Stasik 2016 for Sierra Leone or Lewinson 2006 for Tanzania). Young people in particular live various relationship forms. Stasik observed that '(love) lives and relationships ... are often characterized by chronic states of emotional uncertainty and dissatisfaction. Severe economic struggles and disparities lead to an increasing monetization of young people's relationships, driving them either into a fragile flux of multiple partners or out of intimate engagements altogether' (Stasik 2016: 215).

My fieldwork revealed, however, that research collaborators were not *driven*; they were the *drivers*. Their lives were not characterised by 'a fragile flux', nor did they give up on relationships. On the contrary, they tried to negotiate a situation where they could simultaneously live their desired relationships and adhere to the expectations of elders. To manoeuvre between experimentation and expectations, young people inventively used the staged exceptionalism in which the category of youth placed them. To understand these tactics, it is therefore important to trace what happened to the notion of youth in Sierra Leone.

Tactically Employing the Social Construct 'Youth'

Today, youth are described as 'the coming generation', who aspire, manoeuvre, or strategise (Christiansen, Utas, and Vigh 2006; Vigh

2006b). As such, they are the main target of development aid, socioeconomic restructuring strategies, and the state's attempts to build the foundations for a prosperous future. Youth are those people who are responsible for addressing and solving the problems and struggles that older people face in contemporary Sierra Leone. Simultaneously, they are said to constitute the biggest threat to these aspirations (Chapters 8 and 9). Youth are stuck in a stage of 'waithood' (Singerman 2007: 6; Masquelier 2013: 475; Honwana 2014), and in many ways they are the people whom one should be worried about (Restless Development Sierra Leone 2012).[9] Current media reporting in Sierra Leone, for example, uses the term 'youth' predominantly for those citizens with 'issues' (Campbell 2017). Students are simply described as students until forms of protest or deviant behaviour turn them into youth. 'Youth' therefore goes together with distinctive tags that cover a broad range of often contradictory characteristics.[10] Youth in Sierra Leone are said to be the embodiment of the 'angry, disenfranchised' (Thomas 2016), or the 'lost generation' (O'Brian 1996). Reference is often made to (remobilised) ex-combatants, unemployed youth, and members of gangs (for critical discussions, see Christensen and Utas 2008; 2010; Shepler 2010; Utas and Christensen 2016). We have read about 'militant', 'evil', and 'massacring'[11] 'mobs' (Lupick 2012) of youth. With reference especially to urban areas, youth are described as 'runaways' who aim to 'escape' the patriarchal structures of elders (Diggins 2014). In Freetown, they are given tags such as 'idle' (World Bank 2013: 8), 'inactive', or 'floating'. In their aim to make a living, they are said to be 'chaotic' and 'dysfunctional' (Pratt 2012). Consequently, youth are simultaneously 'dangerous' and 'endangered' (Scheper-Hughes 2004: 16, 45), destructive and destroyed, 'prone to violent behaviour' (World Bank 2013: iv), 'fragile', and 'vulnerable' (Scheper-Hughes 2004: 16, 45). They are, as Deborah Durham said, a '"social shifter" fuelling generational debates and constructions, engaging the social imagination, and challenging our thinking about agency' (Durham 2000: 113). These notions of youth as 'the problem' have also been picked up by policy-makers (see Chapter 8).

---

[9] For a critical analysis of the problems of the connections that the 'crisis of youth' literature draws with war and conflict in Sierra Leone, see Peters (2011).

[10] This language even extends to incidents where severe police violence is used against young people, such as when, in Kabala, police forces shot and injured several young men who were protesting the government's decision to relocate a youth village that had been promised to them since 2014, thereby killing two (Thomas 2016). In Thomas's article, the language shifts between youth (those who protest), boys (those who are shot), and students (those who are injured).

[11] See Peters and Richards (1998) for a critical discussion.

Young people in Freetown react creatively to these extreme expectations and contradictory classifications. Far from succumbing to these tags, many of those research collaborators who classify themselves as youth use this staged exceptionalism to their own benefit. Based on the realisation that 'as youth we can do nothing right anyways', as Barrie (32), a self-proclaimed hustler, said, they connect certain characteristics to the category. They see it as a fluid stage before settling down that involves the temporary rejection of formal employment and marriage and the absence of dependants. Their status as youth allows them to find informal means of gaining income, which would no longer be socially acceptable once they are big men or big women. The anonymity of such labour allows them to keep their income to themselves or share it with friends and girlfriends rather than family. Hence, youthhood becomes a way to manoeuvre around kinship reciprocity.

Only two members of EAUC are formally employed, and many of them reject such employment at the youth stage of their lives. Suge describes this sentiment:

You see, we in Africa we have this extended family. As soon as you started working, all relatives will send children to you so that you pay for their upkeep and schooling. You can't refuse that because you would go against the tradition. It is strain-ful. So, work can be a burden actually, and you will be in debt at the end of the day. When you are a man, yes, you work, but now as youth we are still free somehow, you know?

Suge's sentiment was widely shared. It seems that what counts for most young people in Freetown is not the distant future – for example, marriage and having children – but rather the present or the near future. Recognising personal and economic limits and making 'the best' of the present are the tactics they employ. Members of EAUC seem not to focus on longing for a future, which they cannot reach currently, but on negotiating possibilities for securing and spending income (for themselves and their lovers) from day to day. Sabrina (24), a scholar, who often sleeps at '24', explained this attitude in the following way:

The future is always tomorrow, but for us now, the security only lies in today. Me, I am not thinking about how I can be married or successful later, I am just thinking about how I can make most of today and maybe accumulate something, you see? The country is broken. So, no need to look for job or change or something like that. But people, friends, and neighbours, they are stuck with you, so you rely on them.

Instead of searching for formal employment or looking for a spouse, young people try to secure daily life through the strategic employment of social resources, attract informal jobs, extend networks of friends, and raise their status in society. Through skilled manoeuvres, a youth can become the popular 'go-to person' for any situation – whether it is to seek relationship advice, fix a phone, or make a business connection – and resources can usually be gained in one way or another from such exchanges.

However, the distant future is not ignored entirely, as young people try to 'prepare' themselves for coping with future hardship and mobilising resources quickly. In fact, a closer look reveals that the tactics of today are built on a strategy aimed at creating possibilities for tomorrow. Research collaborators collect 'debts' from friends and relatives by assisting them, and thereby build a network of people who 'owe them' and will be ready to help when necessary. This leads to the creation of webs of power, with the aim of ensuring the dependency of social networks.

When I asked people why they rarely refuse when they are asked for favours and go the extra mile to help even if it is not convenient for them, I was usually told that this is because it will go straight into their 'debt bank'. A negative balance is what is desired here. Through helping as many people as possible, favours are accumulated that serve as provisions for the future. Debts have interest rates and become progressively heavier throughout the course of life. Mr Twin (79) from Allentown explained this in the following way:

When we are both in school, maybe you will always ask me for help with homework or something and I will always help you. But then later when you have a successful job in maybe a bank or in politics, then I will come and say: 'Listen friend, I will need a job here, or my son needs fees for college'. Before, there wasn't much to give, but now the stakes are high. So, it is good to collect as much as possible early on and then cash in when the earnings are high.

Alima (25), one of Amadu's girlfriends, elucidated that 'you never know what the future holds, so it is worthless to worry about it. But if you know you can give something today, you should always do that because you don't know what you may need tomorrow. If you give, they must give back in the future'. Alima's idea chimes with that of Marcel Mauss (1970; also Anthrobase 2016) about how gift economies involve the obligation to give, the obligation to receive, and the obligation to provide a return gift (Strathern 1988). If gifts are not returned, equality and respect between the parties is unbalanced. In their interviews, older research collaborators in particular described in detail the time that elapsed between receiving and returning goods or favours. They depicted the growing chains of connection accumulated through the passing of time and the frequency of the trading. The 'debts' they collected when they were young were now helping them to get by.

While market economies foreground the object of exchange, gift economies create a bond between exchanging parties in the *longue durée*. Over time and through reciprocal gifts, multifaceted moral bonds are created between the exchanging parties. Gifts in Mauss's sense are more than things changing hands; they encapsulate the very fabric of every society (Anthrobase 2016). Favours, gifts, and debts are therefore a way in which youth try to erect bridges between scarcity and aspirations to traverse the social world from day to day. At the same time, they try to 'prepare' themselves to fulfil the demands that will accompany big-manhood and big-womanhood. The bonds these exchanges establish are intended to create a solid foundation on which one can later erect an adult life. This relates to Henrik Vigh's finding that in Bissau young people adhere to a praxis they call *Dubriagem*, which relates to 'immediate survival as well as to gaining a perspective on changing social possibilities and possible trajectories. It is both the praxis of navigating a road through shifting ... circumstances as well as the process of plotting it' (Vigh 2006b: 52).

This form of 'social navigation' (Vigh 2006a) is the basis for how young people live their relationships in Freetown. Youth engage in tactical considerations of the near future embedded in their immediate relations with the world. At the same time, they are careful not to venture too far beyond acceptable limits, so that they do not undermine the strategic considerations of a long-term future based on community-sanctioned practices and obligations. In a dynamic and imaginary way, people who classify themselves as 'youth' therefore 'situate themselves in a social landscape of power, rights, expectations, and relationships – indexing both themselves and the topology of that social landscape' (Durham 2000: 116; see also Shepler 2004; Enria 2015). They are sensitive to their position within 'fields of power, knowledge, rights, notions of agency and personhood' (Durham 2000: 117). And it is within this fabric that relationships are lived.

3 Loving and Living Relationships in Freetown Today

To understand love and violence, we need to analyse the various influences weighing on people as they enter into, live, and leave relationships. Relationships occur between two people (teeth and tongue), but they are embedded in kin and social relations (the mouth) and take place in sociocultural settings with their own rules and regulations (the body). The last-mentioned are in turn influenced by systems far beyond the borders of a relationship and by histories that long outlive its duration. To successfully negotiate various relationships, careful distinctions are drawn between diverse relationship forms and the respective roles and responsibilities of partners. Based on a careful analysis of 464 interviews and numerous additional conversations, I was able to tease out the fine terminological differences of local vocabularies of pleasure and relationship forms. Understanding these terms is like knowing the code that allows access to diverse rooms within a vast building. Here, the building stands for sex or for relationships, but understanding the individual terms enables one to appreciate not only the structure but the interior design, thereby giving meaning to diverse scenarios and arrangements.

Relationships, Reputation, and 'the Gamble'

Research collaborators differentiate between mamas and papas, who are partners that are significantly older, and *cober lappas* (girl lovers) or lover boys, who are partners that, according to numerical understandings of age, are often minors and always much younger than oneself. Age mates have no distinctive term. A 'side-chick' or a 'fine boy' is a person who is very attractive or sexually skilled, but who does not have either the resources (men) or the qualities (women) desired of a main partner. Side-chicks and fine boys are aware of their status and know that somebody else takes the position of main partner. 'Affairs', on the other hand, are sexual partners who may not know that their partner has other partners as well. Then there are 'contract relationships' for partners who live under the same roof or near each other. Having a contract means that both partners may see other people so long as they do not bring them to the shared space (see Chapter 6). Affairs, side-chicks, and fine boys all fall under the category of lovers. Main girlfriends and main boyfriends are the primary partners of a romantic relationship. They are the ones predominantly responsible for caring for each other. This includes providing money (for men) and chores, such as cooking and doing the laundry (for women). The research collaborator Darren explains: 'It also means being the partner your friends know for you and sometimes also the one your family knows for you. As a man, you must always be available, and you must care about the family, all the difficulties the other person is facing. As a fine boy or side-chick you just enjoy together'.

While fluidity within relationships has increased and the terminologies used to differentiate between partners have changed, older ethnographies are useful in shedding light on complex relationship dynamics as well. Mariane Ferme's ethnography, for instance, reveals careful distinctions between favourite wives, co-wives, first wives, separated wives, and jealous wives (Ferme 2001: 93, 157). Additionally, women often had children from various men, and distinguished husbands from lovers (Ferme 2001: 92–3, 104, 215). More recently, Jennifer Diggins differentiated between 'casual love affairs' (Diggins 2014: 91), (in)formal marriages (Diggins 2014: 105, 131), difficult marriages (Diggins 2014: 131), and various agreements held together through the exchange of raw (men) and cooked (women) fish. It becomes clear in these studies of rural areas that marriage is the main relationship, whereas other secondary relationships are based on careful camouflaging strategies. Ferme's study depicts the situation prior to the civil war, while Diggins's analysis in post-war Tissana shows that, although adulthood and marriage are increasingly difficult to achieve, people still view their various relationships in the light of that ideal. Drawing on my ethnographic material as well, it seems that, while marriage remains the main relationship in rural Sierra Leone, other relationships have gained the upper hand in Freetown today. There is no longer one relationship form against which all others are measured: there are instead many.

Life history interviews taught me that many EAUC members see relationships as ways to survive and gain status and temporary pleasure rather than to achieve long-term stability and what Mark Hunter termed 'provider love' (Hunter 2010). As it is no longer possible to follow predetermined pathways, the foundation of loving, much like living, has become strategy. Oki explains: 'For us here, love is something like a gamble. You win and lose, win and lose, win and lose. You get something, give something, and lose it. Maybe you win once, but next time surely you will lose'. When speaking of this 'gamble', Oki refers to the number of lovers a person is able to attract. Mariama (18), a student at Fourah Bay College, explains:

The more lovers you have, the higher your status. But not any lovers. Some of these men, they get one-night stands, but almost never side-chicks. The ones who have main girlfriends and then others, they are respected most because they have much to offer and plus they are honest (*laughs*). Affairs count least because they are the ones that are lied to. They think they are main lovers. For us, the women, it is much easier. We usually have many different partners. We don't need to lie, except maybe if we want to have more than one main man (*laughs*).

As Mariama's description shows, young people create reputations through relationships. Such engagements are no longer concealed, as they were in Ferme's (2001) or Diggins's (2014) ethnographies. Instead, (changing) partners, sex, love, and friendship occupy a central place in the daily routines of Freetonians. Many men and women spend hours daily strategising about how to win partners and how to keep them. They search for the balance between enjoying themselves and gaining something without making themselves vulnerable.

At the centre of these negotiations are friends. They take the lead in defining what and who is desired, comfort those who get hurt, and put them back on their feet. Friends punish deviations from expected norms, celebrate winners, and mock attempts that have gone wrong. Relationships come and go at quite a rapid pace. Friendships, on the other hand, are lasting pillars.

The role of friendships can be seen in EAUC. Here members jointly plan their social activities.[1] Like their peers in Côte d'Ivoire, as Sasha Newell (2012) has described, EAUC members go out on the streets, attend clubs and shows, and go on outings together. These are well-planned activities. Beforehand, members distribute clothes, accessories, and body-spray among themselves to make everyone look fashionable and smell good. This gives each an individual aura of popularity, which helps them to attract the interest of women. To court a woman, one needs a 'friend', who can be male or female. Women and girls may be approached either directly, on the street, or at parties, or even virtually via the phone (see Archambault 2013; 2018). In both instances, the 'friend' acts as the matchmaker. In the first instance, they introduce the

---

[1] This study thus continues a scholarly tradition of analysing social interest groups and societies in Freetown. See Abner Cohen's analysis of the Freemasons (Cohen 1981), John Nunley's study of Odelay masquerades (Nunley 1987), and Michael Banton's work on savings clubs and burial associations established by Temne migrants in Freetown (Banton 1956; 1957).

man or boy to the desired partner by approaching her independently and singing his praises. Issa explains the process:

> The quality of a man can be discerned from his friends. A man who comes to you on his own has nothing to offer. He must be disregarded immediately.
> Now, a man must send his best friend or at least a good friend who vouches for him. That man will then tell you about the guy, saying things like 'You see my friend over there? He is falling deeply in love with you! Let me tell you he is the most passionate lover, and he takes care of his girlfriends'.
> He then becomes the negotiating party. Then you can ask the friend whether the guy has a main girl. If you just want to be a side-chick, a main girl is OK. But if you want to become the main, you then should do some investigations into the guy with your girlfriends. Like is he a passer-by [see below], is he poor, is he a liar? Like that.
> Only once you [have] decided that either maybe he is poor, but he is too fine [pretty] or maybe he has some finances or maybe you are interested in being the main, then you allow the friend to introduce you.
> Also, very important[ly] that friend will always be the one you go to when any problem arises in the relationship. He is your advocate. And, in turn, you know that he will only praise his friend if he is serious. Otherwise, it is too much hassle.

If potential partners are approached via social media or on the phone, the matchmaker shares the picture and contact details of the woman and starts chatting with her to introduce his friend in ways very similar to those described above. Hence, before entering any relationship, people typically start an investigation into the relationship history of the man or boy in question. Just as kin groups used to investigate a potential spouse's history, people in Freetown today research a person's 'social CV' by asking a candidate's social network about his character, reliability, history, and prospects. Here, sexual behaviour is an important part of courtship.

During my fieldwork, conversations around sex took place daily. In the course of the discussions, people used exact terms to define practices and offer a picture of the situations under discussion and of the persons whose actions were being evaluated. Deflowering a woman is called 'virginating', and, if it was initiated and dominated by the man or boy, he may say *na mi bɔs am* (I am the one who deflowered her). Sex was understood in a myriad ways. 'Sexing' involves mutual agreement to the sexual act. Here both partners are equally engaged in pleasing each other, and foreplay is an important aspect. 'Bossing' means that a man dominates, while *bambrusing* is the term used to describe the situation where the man is not only dominant but rough and sex is limited to penetration. *Mas am, chɛr am* (describing a man thrusting his hips between a woman's widely opened legs) and *scatter am* (scatter her) are terms denoting men's sexual conquest of attractive women and the male penetration of women and girls (such as in the Sierra Leonean trio LXG's 2017 song 'Cher Am'). These terms are usually used by younger people. Older people tend to use more traditional terms such as *mek* or *yu de mek* (to make) or *tabulay*, which refers to a drum or to drumming but can also mean having sex (do you want to have sex?). Hence the terms with which sex is described reflect the age of the speaker. Popular songs marry traditional descriptions with contemporary definitions. Take, for example, Rich Blink's 2018 song 'Tabulay'. He sings: 'If you give me the *tabulay ... na for let me tamper de*. Give me, I want, I want for *nak am* [If you give me the drum, I want to play around with it. Give it to me, I want to beat it/hit it. *Tabulay- alaw mi mek ar tɔch am* means "allow me to touch or play with your genitals"]'. For people who are in casual relationships or who have a one-night stand, two main terms describe the encounter: 'cut and pass' and 'cut and play'. Overall, 'cut' refers to the man's orgasm and 'play' to the female orgasm. Albert (32) from EAUC sheds light on this terminology in the following way:

For we the men, it is just penetration, penetration and then, *pam*, we come in an explosion and then we have enough and move on. That's why we say cut. Before it is pleasure and with the orgasm, it cuts and then we are done.

For women it is play because you need to properly play with her entire body for her to come into the mood and for her to have an orgasm, and then after the orgasm she is really wet and hot, so then she is better ready for sex.

But cut and pass now means that you go, you penetrate her, and then you pull your pants up and go, leaving her high and dry.

Cut and play, that requires a patient professional.

'Cut and pass' means that a person engages in a sexual encounter predominantly to please himself, while 'cut and play' includes mutual pleasure, usually progressing from pleasing the woman to penetration, which is said to be mostly for a man's pleasure. Oki, who mainly sleeps with sex workers, has this to say: 'I try to cut and pass, but nowadays with most women you will not be allowed anywhere near cutting. Before they allow you to penetrate them, you must play around her garden, so you must suck their bobbies and you must suck them [oral pleasure]. If you do that well, then they allow you; if not, they just kick you off'. 'Playing around her garden' or 'in her garden' was usually used when men discussed strategies to please and pleasure women. If a person only 'cuts', but does not play, he quickly becomes a 'passer-by'. A passer-by is a man who selfishly follows his own desires and needs and who tricks women into giving him what he desires without giving anything in return. Passers-by can be men who promise a woman a lasting relationship, marriage, and children if she sleeps with them, but then try to abandon her after they have had sex, or who 'think only of themselves during sex', as I was told by Kadi (31), a hairdresser. Such men not only open themselves to female revenge, but they also ruin their social position. Sexual activities are talked about openly, and egoism can quickly ruin one's reputation as a good and generous lover. Consequently, over time passers-by find it harder and harder to interest new sexual partners. Sabrina (19) from Allentown says: 'Nobody likes a selfish lover. A selfish lover is a selfish man. Now we women, we talk. Everybody knows that. So, you cannot expect not to please one of us and then go on like that to another one. With our mouths, we will punish you'.

In a similar vein, Amina (27), a journalist from Naimbana Street, said: 'As women, we want to be pampered'. 'To pamper someone', she explains, 'means making them comfortable by doing things for them or giving them expensive or luxurious things. It is spoiling someone but in a good, caring way, also sexually like spoiling with pleasure'. This has a bearing on Megan Vaughan's observation in her analysis of histories of love in Africa that 'women's complaints about marriage largely revolved around the lack of generosity of their husbands' (Vaughan 2011: 22). 'Love', she explains, drawing on Epstein (1981: 118), 'meant being cared for and provided for materially, shown respect and being endowed with children' (Epstein 1981: 118). My research collaborator Suge added that 'men want to be good lovers. We want that image. So, we will be extra careful to try to cut and play so that the woman is pleased and will talk highly about our performance to our friends'.

Women are protected in uncommitted relationships in two ways. One is the fear of retaliation in case of abuse, especially from women in the form of magic (Groes-Green 2013; Chapter 4). The other is the power of gossip, the fact that 'words move fast' – they are, as Mark Schindler called it, the 'black market of information' (Schindler 2007: 6; White 2008). This notion of 'punishing with one's mouth' (see Chapter 4) was often talked about as a powerful form of female violence. One can therefore not expect to enter further advantageous unions if one has exploited former partners. Moreover, people who cut and pass, just like people who withhold sex, may lose their relationship or may be accused in front of the household or community (Chapter 6).

How Not to Break Up

With EAUC, I witnessed triumphant success, but also pain and failure, in the game of love. Whenever I sat with them, I heard that someone had just 'snatched a girlfriend' from another man, had lost a lover to another man, had been caught lying or caught someone in a lie, and was now strategising with his friends about what to do next in order not to lose face and to 'own the story'. Snatching girlfriends may take place between friends. It was not uncommon for EAUC members to try to snatch each other's lovers. However, snatching is restricted to side-chicks and affairs; main partners are 'off limits'. Snatching is a skill that requires a network of friends who are willing to advocate on one's behalf and attract the desired woman. In this way, it is related to the accumulation of debts and favours I have described above (Chapter 2) in that it requires money or a large credit in one's social debt bank to 'buy things and take the woman out like a queen', as Albert stated. For women and girls, the 'snatching strategy' depends on the desired goal. If a woman wants to become a side-chick, then signalling availability through a female friend is often enough. The friend then goes to the man and introduces the woman and explains her intentions while she waits 'in a nice dress, somewhere close by, but not looking desperate, looking too sweet and nice', according to Fatu (23), a baker from central Freetown. 'Men', Alima says, 'are too easily convinced. You shake your bum like that and immediately he will follow you. For the sexing, they almost never need much convincing. Only if you want some commitment'. If the desired goal is to become the main girlfriend, a woman – and here there was general consensus among the people I spoke to – needs to do the following in Darren's words: 'Become close to his friends. Be modest and caring. Cook for him and be available always'.

But it is not only attracting lovers that requires tactics and manoeuvring. Preserving one's image after having lost a lover is equally important. 'Owning the story' or 'keeping face' means finding a way of not appearing to have lost a lover to a friend or to another man or woman, but rather of having decided not to want that partner anymore. 'The trick', elucidates Mamadu (19) from EAUC,

> is to be very, very sensitive to what is happening. When you realise your partner is about to run away to someone else, then you must win her over so that she stays, even if you maybe don't really want her. If you know that you lost, you have to make it seem like this was all your idea from the beginning and like you just did not want to hurt the person's feeling[s] but actually want that person to be someone else's responsibility. Then everybody will think you are the real champion of the story.

Uncommitted couples seldom break up. When I asked how relationships end, I usually received answers such as 'they don't' or 'what do you mean?' At one point, I sat down with EAUC and voiced my confusion. 'It is simple', explained Gas willingly: 'We do not break up because we never know what will happen in the future. Maybe you are tired of somebody now, but who knows? Maybe you want to see them again in the future. And also breaking up is very strain-ful. Maybe you have to tell someone you don't want them anymore. Who would want to hear that?' This recalls Susan Reynolds Whyte's analysis of how people in contemporary East Africa negotiate social experience in the 'subjunctive mode' (Whyte 1997: 24). Relationships, as Gas's explanation shows, are not terminated because of what *is*; rather, they are kept in flux to accommodate what *may be*. The relationship between uncertainty, hope, and people's navigational strategies has been explored by various scholars (e.g. Whyte 1997; Crapanzano 2004; Jenkins, Jessen, and Steffen 2005; Zigon 2009; Parish 2010; Berthomé, Bonhomme and Delaplace 2012; Niehaus 2013; Cooper and Pratten 2015; Enria 2015). These writers have shown that a key element of managing uncertainty is mobility. Mobility requires one to be constantly on the move both spatially and socially. It depends upon a readiness to embrace new possibilities and to experiment, but also on a refusal to lock the door to opportunities. Through this, a space is created that might make what is impossible today possible tomorrow. This also requires one not to hurt or reject people, as they may be a lifeline in the future. When I asked how couples then know when a relationship is over, I was met with laughter:

Ah, you. You always have to know everything. For us, we don't. It is just open. When somebody does not call or see you anymore, you know they lost interest, but they never tell you that they don't want you anymore. Out of respect, you know. Maybe you would ask and cause palaver (*laughs*), but for us, after some days' silence, we are free. We can go with another one or do what we like. And if the person calls again, we can decide if we are interested or not.

However, there is a difference between ceasing to prolong the relationship (passive, personal), as illustrated by Darren in the quote above, and practising neglect (active, social) (see Chapter 4). The latter can lead to an immediate and public break-up. This often involves a declaration by the person who initiated the break-up that they were wronged. Moreover, it may involve a call for others to get involved to fix the relationship. Nevertheless, threatening to terminate a relationship occurs frequently and is a common part of lovers' arguments (Chapter 4). Memunatu (24), a Fourah Bay College student, explains:

If you say you don't want somebody anymore in front of everybody, it is a huge embarrassment for that person. So, either you do it as a threat when that person is maltreating you, [or], if you are serious, you do it either because you want to punish that person or because you actually do not want to break up, so you are looking for his friends to come and beg you to take him back.

With married couples, separations without divorce occur frequently. This means that spouses live separately and have new partners while remaining married to each other. Divorce for a 'registered marriage' is the formal process by which a marriage is dissolved and assets divided. In traditional marriages, a declaration by both partners that they do not want to continue their marriage suffices to terminate it. With registered marriages, both partners need to undergo a period of counselling before they can divorce, while traditional and religious marriages may be terminated immediately as long as the community consents.

Trading Sex and Shaping the Economy of Desire

Transactional relationships are often lived in parallel with other relationships, sometimes openly and sometimes in disguise. While many transactional relationships foreground social rather than economic connections at the heart of the encounter, those more strongly focussed on monetary exchange are typically one-night stands, sexual relationships with sex workers, and relationships with 'financiers' and 'sugar daddies'. These relationships usually occur between youth and big men or big women. Research collaborators distinguish between two types of sex workers: 'scholars' and *rare gal*s. A scholar is a sex worker who is said to be 'educated', 'well-behaved', and often 'shy'. These may be single mothers or daughters who engage in sex work to support their families. Others are without family or social networks and use sex as a means of getting by. A *rare gal* is somebody who is deeply embedded in street life.[2] As Michael Stasik noted: 'Freetown's rarray girls [*sic*] are reputed to be sexually promiscuous, to ignore social norms and to "use" men to pay for what is seen as a dissolute lifestyle. The term ... is used frequently in reference to "troublesome girls" who are said to engage in relationships only for the "love of money"' (Stasik 2016: 226–7).

*Rare gal*s often smoke and drink. They are frequently said to cause palaver (conflict) and to curse when arguing. *Rare gal*s sometimes fight (*beat*). While scholars usually work alone, *rare gal*s are attached either to a brothel and a *kedi masta*, which is usually an older woman who runs a brothel, or to a *tɛdi bɔi*. *Tɛdi bɔi*s are gang members or young men engaged in the illicit economy who send their girlfriends out to do sex work. *Rare gal*s then live with these *tɛdi bɔi*s, handing over most of – if not all – their money to them. The *rare gal–tɛdi bɔi* tie-up has become more common because, when *rare gal*s are taken to a customer's place to have

---

[2] They are called girls irrespective of their age or social status (e.g. mother, wife, widow), simply because they are said to behave irresponsibly and to have the characteristics of girls rather than women or big women. A woman who is embedded in street life but not engaged in sex work is called *faray*. *Rare gal*s bear a similarity to the *godrap girls* that Newell (2012) wrote about in Abidjan or the *ashawo*s in Accra discussed in John Chernoff's (2003) work.

sex, they wait until their customer falls asleep and then steal his possessions. Alternatively, they spy out the lie of the land and possible alarm systems so that their *tɛdi bɔi*s can later rob the place with their gang. This has been done so often that many men and boys now prefer to pay the extra SLL 30,000 (GBP 2.76) to go with a *rare gal* to a brothel or have sex with her in public rather than take her home.

*Rare gal*s always ask for payment before having sex, while scholars may agree to be paid after. Scholars are frequently taken home. Sometimes customers refuse to pay them. In these instances, there is very little a scholar can do. If she calls the police, she will be arrested for loitering and will have to pay a fine or, occasionally, sleep with an officer in exchange for her freedom (Mahtani and O'Gorman 2018).

'Financiers/providers' and 'sugar daddies' are middle-aged men, sometimes elders, who enjoy the (sexual) company of girls and young women in exchange for financial support. With sugar daddies, the relationship is clearly sexual, while financiers may also give financial support in exchange for company. Furthermore, sugar daddies usually give women and girls money, or buy things for them, such as top-up (mobile phone credit), clothes, or hair. Financiers/providers, on the other hand, are frequently involved in paying school or university fees as well as rent.

Agreement Relationships

In Freetown, one form of transactional relationship is the so-called agreement relationship.[3] These are partnerships aimed at gaining economic or social acceptance and mobility. Sex and keeping company are important for the partners, and romantic emotions are commonplace, but a permanent relationship or marriage is excluded. These agreements are understood as such by both partners and are often negotiated openly.

Agreement relationships coexist with other relationship types with spouses, main partners, one-night stands, and providers, and they demonstrate a pragmatic approach to dealing with want and scarcity. As I discussed elsewhere (Schneider 2020b), agreement relationships are not only employed by young people in their struggles to make a living in uprooted and constantly shifting social landscapes, but are equally important among elders. Most of my data on agreement relationships were gathered at King George's old age home, where I met many residents who had navigated and are navigating their social and economic lives in this way. Such relationships are the kind that brought men and

---

[3] This section is taken from Schneider (2020b).

women fleeing from 'women trouble' in the rural areas to the city. The exchange may involve food in return for access to education, accommodation in Freetown for household chores, and so on. Far from being a new phenomenon, such relationships are marked by historical, social, and cultural continuations that draw on notions of personhood, gift economies, and social and economic mobility.

Agreement relationships entail much more than a transaction of sex in exchange for gifts, goods, or money. Rather, they cultivate intricate and often lasting emotional engagements. Agreement relationships are based upon social navigation by means of favours and debts, as I have described above. The fabric of society is not made up of individuals who interact at random, but of engagements between people who get to know one another and then make choices based on that knowledge. The parties to agreement relationships are not interchangeable, as it is their unique subjectivity and the individual 'thing' – such as education, access, skills, or networks – they have to offer that allows two people to be matched together at a particular time. The transaction at its core helps develop social capital (Bourdieu and Wacquant 1992) while sustaining the very notion of such capital by keeping social and professional networks alive, and at the same time ensuring that they are restrictive and specific.

Agreement relationships are entered into by women and men alike throughout their lives, and continue well into old age. Particularly for women, such agreements provide a powerful means to turn gendered ideologies on their head and enjoy a certain freedom in the spaces between set gender roles. Women prioritise their individual choices and desires for mobility, economic security, specific career choices, or financial independence from kin and husbands above those of their kin, who often expect them to stay close by, marry, and raise children. Through the 'things' partners in agreements offer each other, they simultaneously contribute to a shared economy of desire and enable others to satisfy their material, emotional, and sexual needs. In this way, agreement relationships speak to Zygmunt Bauman's notion that the desires for both freedom – autonomously directing one's life – and security – living in a community – are essential, simultaneous, and irreconcilable parts of personhood, which influence relationship practices (Bauman 2001: 5; see Piot 1999; Jackson 2012: 3).

Committed Relationships and Their Marriage to Expectations

Notwithstanding the temporary freedom that youth – and certain big women and big men – negotiate for themselves in contemporary

Freetown, relationships are still married to expectations. Social status continues to be a crucial factor in Sierra Leonean society, where a hierarchical organisation privileges elders over younger individuals, married people over those who are unmarried, and employed individuals over those who are unemployed (Oyěwùmí 2005; Jackson 2017). The lives of women and men are still organised into distinct stages, with varying degrees of respect accorded to each; and it is to committed relationships between adults that the respect, assistance, and social protection of family and community are tied. Consequently, people cannot remain in the youth stage forever. Pregnancy – described as *get bele*, which literally means 'to have a stomach' – or growing in age increase the pressure on people to make the transition from youth to full-fledged adults. If a pregnancy is carried to term, the stage of youth must be left and youths must become big men and big women.[4] Furthermore, economic precarity does not affect only young people. Parents and grandparents still expect to be taken care of in old age and wish for their lineages to continue. Moreover, children are said to need more than their parents to be properly socialised. Contemporary demands thus require one to provide for one's family in old age, to bring children into the world, and to establish a household. Although the relationship forms I have discussed can be lived openly and are acceptable for youth, living them and at the same time becoming big men and big women is impossible. And yet marriage remains financially unachievable for many.

To reach adulthood, relationship forms have been established that enable young men and women to commit publicly and bindingly to another person and their family, and to legitimise children. In this way, attempts are made to weave two families together in webs of mutual dependence. Hence, there is a great amount of investment in bridging the different demands and aspirations presented by social pressures, changing relationship forms, and economic realities. Three practices highlight these tendencies particularly well: 'show face', *ansa bele*, and 'engagements'.

Show face is the process by which the father of a baby introduces himself to the family of the woman he impregnated, to confirm that the baby has a father. Often the father agrees to have the child take his last name to clearly show that it is not illegitimate. However, the father takes no definite social or economic responsibility for the child or the mother. Furthermore, the man or boy does not have to be in a current relationship with the woman

---

[4] Abortions, called *pul di bele* (to pull the stomach) or *pwel di bele* (to spoil the stomach), are either conducted at hospitals in exchange for a fee (usually SLL 200,000 or GBP 20.34) or traditionally. In the latter instance, women and girls are given strong herbs to drink.

or girl in question. If no pregnancy exists, show face can also simply mean the first official visit a person makes to the family of their partner.

Ansa bɛlɛ is a practice that has become influential in recent years. It aims to destigmatise and legitimise pregnancies out of wedlock. It literally means 'answering to the stomach' and openly declaring that 'I have impregnated that woman and fathered that child', as Chernor (34), a carpenter from Allentown, explains. Through the process, a boy or man accepts the pregnancy and takes full financial responsibility for the child born out of wedlock. The family of the woman or girl will customarily visit the family of the man or boy and explain that their daughter is expecting a child. Then, the family of the man will agree to answer to the pregnancy and take over the responsibilities of fatherhood. He and his family financially compensate the family of the woman or girl through processes that bear a strong resemblance to exchanges of bride price. As a result, the child becomes part of the lineage of the father and adopts his surname. While *ansa bɛlɛ* requires a father to provide financially for the child, he is not made to do the same for the mother. Consequently, pregnant women and girls or their families might restrict access to the child pending an engagement or marriage. If couples undergo *ansa bɛlɛ* but do not continue their relationship, the man may describe the woman as 'born for me'.

Ansa bɛlɛ can take place between the families of couples who love each other and are in consenting relationships. In recent years, however, it has been used by kin and elders as a process that follows an unwanted pregnancy or an assault. Many research collaborators stated further that marriages resulting from an *ansa bɛlɛ* procedure, where those involved did not consciously choose the union, led to maltreatment and violence. Such marriages may be perceived as traps.[5] *Ansa bɛlɛ* also comes with the full financial responsibility for *pul na do*, which is the naming ceremony for Muslims, or the Christian 'christening ceremony' or baptism. Moreover, children are not automatically assigned to the biological parents. Indeed, when the biological parents are seen as too young or unfit to take care of a child by their families, a grandparent of the child may symbolically marry the child. Here a ceremony is held, and the child is given a ring. It then belongs to the grandparent, who raises and provides for the child. This form of committed relationship focusses mainly on children and elders. It weaves together at least three generations: the partners, their children, and their (grand)parents.

---

[5] This is especially true if they follow the forced acceptance of a pregnancy through swearing; see Chapter 4.

The third type of commitment is the one that is closest to marriage, namely engagement. Engagement is the ceremony in which two partners publicly formalise their intention to marry. Often engagement rings are exchanged. The family of the man or boy gives donations of money to the family of the woman or girl. These donations are often confined to the nuclear family and not extended to the entire household, as in marriages. They are furthermore less expensive than marriage donations. Male research collaborators describe engagement as a way to 'close the door' to any other suitor (lɔk di do). Foday (36) explains: 'If I am loving that girl and I want to marry that girl, I will call the engagement, pay, and ensure her for me. This means that I reserved her for me forever'. For women and girls, engagement was usually seen as proof that a partner is serious and will support them. However, engagements often do not lead to marriage, but are in themselves accepted as a serious commitment, albeit not one on equal terms with marriage.

Another way through which people try to formalise a relationship is through cohabitation. *Tap to mi* means cohabitation without being engaged or married. Today, according to law, after five years of cohabiting, partners have equal rights to the joint property in case of separation or death. After concluding such rituals of commitment, a couple who are unable to build their own home usually move in with the family of the man, where they live patrilocally. If a man stays with the family of his wife, he is never considered head of the house and risks never achieving a position of great authority. Nevertheless, many such couples do not live together but continue to stay with their kin. Often, one partner's job leads them to travel frequently or to live in another part of Freetown or another town altogether, and to come and visit occasionally. Lovers and people in agreement or contract relationships, on the other hand, frequently cohabit. However, such habitation patterns are fluid and not accepted as a sign of commitment.

Marriage to 'Be for Somebody' and Lovers to 'Feel with Somebody'

As we have seen, in Freetown relationships extend beyond the two people involved and include additional actors such as kin, community, or religious groups (Jackson 2012; 2017). Most research collaborators have several relationships that are governed by underlying principles with different roles and responsibilities for each relationship form. Partners are categorised as lovers, side-chicks, people in agreement relationships, main girlfriends, spouses, and so on. These structures dictate the relationship – while a side-chick is for sex, and a lover for sex and company, a main girlfriend is expected to also attend to social and organisational needs, such as public engagements, the maintenance of familial relationships, and household chores. But, in addition, they give form to the interaction with (or restriction of access to) a partner's friends and family through procedures, such as show face, *ansa bɛlɛ*, engagement, and marriage, that come with different economic and social responsibilities.

The dynamics developed to build these kinds of bridges between aspirations, economic constraints, and expectations are creative forms of present and future making. However, their shiny upside has a dark underbelly. Seeking to satisfy the demands of one's family and live one's own aspirations may create dynamics that enable violence, such as when couples who do not want to be together are made to commit to each other because of a pregnancy.[6] According to Mr Saidu, a teacher from Western Freetown (in his forties), one of the main causes of violence within committed relationships is that many people do not enter them because they love each other but because the woman got pregnant and her family asked for *ansa bɛlɛ*. 'Most of these relations are built on this foundation, which can then lead to the men being absent most of the time or living somewhere else and cause frequent quarrels and problems within the family', he says. Many men explain their reasons for doing *ansa bɛlɛ*, getting engaged, or attempting to marry in exactly this way. Said (46), a social worker, explained to me that

to be a big man, you must be committed. I am a married man and thereby more valuable than a non-married man. I have reproduced. That's why we get engaged because society expects us to settle and reproduce to be 'somebody'. So, we choose who would make a good wife. But mostly love is not there. Love is with our girlfriends. Now, violence comes to both, the girlfriend because of jealousy, the fiancé because we don't communicate, don't 'fit'.

This statement, that violence comes to both, is one I often heard. It relates to Viviana Zelizer's observation that the very condition of intimacy is a convergence of vulnerabilities, a web of information about each other that could be harmful if revealed (Zelizer 2000). In view of their elaborate structures, it might seem as if the various relationships young people are engaged in are less tainted by inequality and exploitation than some rural marriages. But just as marriage in rural areas was often accompanied by patriarchal, gerontocratic structures of inequality (Richards 1998), and collided with other desire-based relations, the manifold relationships forming Freetown's emotional economy today are not without their problems. Indeed, fluid relationship forms are

---

[6] For a discussion of these difficulties, see Chapters 4 and 6.

not built on reliable bases and may collapse at any point, leaving individuals without the support of family or community. Additionally, problems and violence in such relationships must be dealt with interpersonally. Friends or peers can be called upon to mediate, but they do not have the same power to punish and enforce regulations as family or community. Hence, the freedom of such relationships goes hand in hand with the absence of elaborate social protection. Moreover, as Mauss (1970) shows, indebtedness and manipulation are the underbelly of benign relationships within gift economies. The economy of favours and debts involves a complex nexus of power relations with regard to how much is given and how much accumulated. This also relates to the debt bank that my research collaborators have created and to the strategies of 'snatching', 'owning the story', and 'keeping face'. By giving more than they receive, a giver establishes a power imbalance and ensures that the receiver stays in their debt. This is why people told me that it is of the utmost importance to stay free. How? Papani answered: 'You ... never take more than was agreed. Otherwise, you can be owned'.

In love histories, young people often differentiated between the person they loved and the person they decided to marry. Among EAUC members, it was very common for them to describe being madly in love with a woman but regard an eventual break-up as unavoidable. For those who come from families who can afford to pay for a marriage, such as Gas, this is even more the case. At the outset of my fieldwork, Gas explained: 'I love Isatu more than anything. It has been almost five years now, but I will never marry her. I must marry who my family is happy with'. About two months ago, Gas got married to a woman he hardly knew. As we have seen, in a marriage the relationship between spouses does not have a higher importance than the status reached through the marriage, and the approval or disapproval of family and community matters greatly. Many men do not marry women they love or had relationships with before. They often have many rapidly changing and overlapping relationships until they decide that it is time to marry. Women one could potentially 'place down' are not the same as the women one has relationships with. Such women need to be accepted by one's family and community. And often love is outsourced to other partnerships. This creates a dualism in which marriages and committed relationships are largely lived for the outside world, while extramarital affairs involve the more private feelings and negotiations between individuals. When my research collaborators describe with nostalgia how many love marriages were characterised by genuine affection before the civil war (see also Stasik 2016: 22), they yearn for an invented past. But they also highlight the importance placed on loving marriages and the remorse felt over how the affective aspect of marriage seems to have lost much of its power in Freetown today.

In a marriage, partners may have very little to share and to discuss. They talk to friends and family about their issues but rarely to their partners. At the same time, the new relationship forms do not offer the same stability as marriage. In marriages, spouses choose a patron from their consanguine family members, usually an elder woman. If problems arise, this patron then negotiates with both spouse and family to reach the most favourable solution (Chapters 6 and 7). If a person does not get married or enters a relationship that is based on economic exchanges between the families of the partners (e.g. *ansa bɛlɛ* or engagement), the family members are almost never invited to mediate if issues arise. Consequently, separations are much more difficult because those involved are not in a position to lean on a strong social network or fall back on an alternative living space.

In today's complicated landscape, where different gendered perceptions and ideals are in constant competition, people therefore juggle diverse roles, balancing those relationships that are driven by emotion with those that help them achieve a different position within society and those that ensure security. It is difficult to know whether people's relationship practices are defined by emotions or largely by society's approval or disapproval of the union. How people feel personally is just as important as the views of their family, community, or society overall. Partners are chosen because of emotional factors such as attachment or love. Equally, relationships are entered into for practical reasons, such as availability of sex, access to a certain social circle, or the inducement of an exchange. And partners are chosen because of suitability in the long run, respectability, social standing, and so on. In relationships, sociocentric and egocentric notions of personhood are continuously weighed against each other (Bauman 2001; Jackson 2012). The dynamic in relationships between the private and the public is constantly and awkwardly entangled. In these complex dynamics, acts of violence can be executed as a result of a sense of ownership or entitlement but also out of fear of losing somebody, or for the desire to maintain or regain emotions, authority, or status. Often enough, affection and violence are entangled, as the next chapter shows.

4 The Spectrum of Violence in Relationships

Gendered Agency and the Moral Economy of Violence in Relationships

Despite the important contributions of anthropology to nuanced and multi-layered interpretations of love and violence, the two are not often analysed as interwoven phenomena. But complex dynamics connect love, personal desire, social responsibility, and violence. These conditions challenge us to find ways to understand the acceptance of violence within intimate relationships without excusing or justifying it, and without leaning too heavily on overarching explanatory narratives that rely on history, structure, culture, socialisation, or pathology. Notwithstanding the intellectual schemes that have sought to make sense of violence, we should take seriously 'the ontological priority of social existence', which, as Michael Jackson says, 'affirms that truth must not be seen as an unmasking which eclipses the appearance of the thing unmasked, but a form of disclosure which does it justice' (Jackson 1996: 4). This requires a phenomenological and empiricist perspective that leaves classification and interpretation in the hands of the research collaborators and examines how violence is conceived locally (Bourdieu and Wacquant 1992).

This chapter is therefore concerned with the lived experiences of violence. It examines how Sierra Leoneans think through violence in their relationships, how they assess violent acts, and how they assign meaning to them. Violence, as we shall see, is perceived as an ineradicable part of human relationships. It is one that provides both a risk and a chance, a way to love and a way to hurt, one which must be controlled so as not to exceed acceptable and bearable limits. Research collaborators' insights into the place, role, and meaning of violence paint a picture of a social world where love and violence are not separate and opposed entities but can be co-constitutive of relationships. In Freetown, many women demand that their partners use certain forms of violence, and their absence is seen as a sign of lack of love. Many men, in turn, are worried that they will lose a partner if they are not violent. Consequently, men may beat their girlfriends because they love them, and women themselves may use violence against those they love.

This chapter pays attention to gendered expectations and experiences of violence. It thereby contributes to scholarly efforts to rethink the absolute framing of agency–victimhood in research on sex and violence (see, e.g. Jewkes and Morrell 2012; Campbell and Mannell 2016; Mannell, Umutoni, and Jackson 2016; Pells, Wilson, and Hang 2016; Fielding-Miller and Dunkle 2017). It shows that agency exists in a web of factors that shape lived experience; that it is embedded. Whether and to what extent people can exercise agency is affected by historical, sociocultural, political, economic, and legal factors. These shape the actions of people from all genders when it comes to executing, receiving, and responding to violence. To counter the prevalence of violence and develop real exit strategies, policy and law must consider how women, men, and people of other genders interpret their own actions, and shed light on the constraints within which they operate. These constraints must be accounted for in the development of policy.

According to my research participants, violence communicates emotions in relationships where feelings are not openly discussed. It serves as a mirror reflecting the state of a relationship. While some forms of violence demonstrate infatuation and love, others indicate falling out of love or lack of emotion altogether. Violence in relationships may be triggered by the pressure to uphold certain gender roles publicly or to fend off a threat to these roles. In enacting, witnessing, and enduring violence, gendered bodies thus become 'sites of individual agency and instruments of social control' (Masquelier 2009: 278). Violence allows individuals to (re)produce, resist, subvert, or embrace certain norms, values, laws, and practices (Masquelier 2009: 246). Accordingly, my analysis of what violence is, what it does, and how different acts are conceptualised and interpreted accepts that the many forms of violence described here are not necessarily of the kind that may be condemned or even rejected. Violence is not only about acts but about forms of becoming, remaking, and unmaking personal and social expectations. Violence is thus a way of acting upon and affecting the very systems that shape behaviour (see also Wardlow 2006).

To develop a situated analysis and understand the embedded nature of agency, I use the concept of the moral economy of relationships (Burrill, Roberts, and Thornberry 2010). A moral economy is a framework for analysing systems of exploitation in which certain forms of exploitation are consciously accepted, within limits, for the sake of protection and subsistence. Early approaches to moral economy were concerned above all with land and labour, but more recent studies like Burrill, Roberts, and Thornberry's 2010 volume *Domestic Violence and the Law in Colonial and Postcolonial Africa* have enlarged the concept. Viewing the moral economy as 'a governing network of obligations, entitlement, and provisions ... at the societal level', they extend it to analyse gendered and generational household hierarchies in 'contexts of unequal power distribution' (Burrill, Roberts, and Thornberry 2010: 106). What underlies the formation of households and marriages is a moral economy that oversees rules, responsibilities, and acceptable limits of transgression and exploitation. In such an economy, the breaking point

> is the incident or pattern of domestic violence. As such, domestic violence signals the breach in the system of obligations and reciprocity governing a set of relations. It is not simply an act of hitting, withholding food, forcing extra work, or leaving the home that causes the breach; it is when these acts exceed the limits of acceptability and threaten the mutuality of interdependence and obligation. (Burrill, Roberts, and Thornberry 2010: 106)

Within this domestic moral economy, there is an 'ongoing debate over the appropriate exercise of violence' (Burrill, Roberts, and Thornberry 2010: 72). Hence whether teeth and tongue are interdependent or create friction or destruction is determined by a web of lines of correlative expectation and obligation that must be held in place. The moral economy integrates historical forces and their influence on interpersonal relationships, and also adapts itself to current sociopolitical dynamics. In Sierra Leone, the experiences of violence during the civil war and the post-war process certainly contributed towards the present understanding and acceptance of violence within relationships (Chapter 2). So, of course, did the violence of colonialism and slavery. In this context, the moral economy is therefore not merely the result of a static 'prevailing culture of patriarchy' that 'helped define the place of husbands and wives in a hierarchical but mutually dependent moral economy of marriage' (Burrill, Roberts, and Thornberry 2010: 106). In addition, it is a dynamic mesh influenced by social, political, economic, and legal factors, and within it the levels and limits of acceptability are constantly renegotiated. In this way, 'normative limitations on domestic violence' are produced. The transgression of these limitations is socially condemned and punished. Consequently, the moral economy serves as a form of protection against 'outright abuse' (Burrill, Roberts, and Thornberry 2010: 98).[1]

---

[1] In assigning social and economic roles, the model of the moral economy of relationships encapsulates other theoretical approaches to violence, such as resource theories and family systems theories, which aim to 'understand individuals within their interconnected family roles and their (re-)negotiations of positions of power' (Johnson and Ferraro 2000; see Ofei-Aboagye 1994; see also Browning 2002 for social disorganisation theory), as well as ecological models that look at the interplay of these models (like Heise 1998).

In Sierra Leone, this moral economy extends beyond households and marriages. Indeed, various forms of local moral economies bind partners in different relationship forms together. The acceptable limits of exploitation and the existence of violence, as we will see, are dependent upon the particular relationship form and the level of commitment between partners. As we observed in the previous chapter, these relationship forms encompass a wide range of sexual interactions and dynamics. Violence in relationships, as I learnt, is a widespread concern and a central theme that permeates all of these different models. While many forms of violence are perceived as problematic, they are still considered integral to relationships and demanding of ongoing negotiation, rather than being treated as problems that need to be surmounted or solved. Within the diverse moral economies that form between different partnerships, the levels of acceptable violence and exploitation are constantly renegotiated. Moreover, intersectional parameters such as gender, age, class, and power are influential forces in determining how people endure, expect, and accept violent acts.

Local Perceptions of Violence

Unacceptable Violence: Of Warm Hearts and Warm Persons

As the metaphor of the teeth and tongue indicates, violence is only acceptable if it facilitates continued coexistence. Violence is unacceptable if its intent is to cause harm and if there is no possibility of restoring what has been undone. Harm is assessed in physical and social rather than psychological terms. Thus, forcibly taking a woman's or girl's virginity or impregnating her causes an irreversible harm, as does killing, mutilating, or otherwise inflicting impairment on another.

In Sierra Leone, where, as Jackson (2017) notes, moderation is regarded as an attribute of strength, unacceptable violence is seen as a demonstration of weakness and a shortcoming that reveals a person's inability to temper emotions and find a controlled outlet for them. This is expressed in the way unacceptable violence is described. Here, words such as 'wild', 'crazy', or 'uncontrolled' are frequently applied. Consider the following statement made by a driver about his brother who uses violence frequently: 'His heart is hot too much. He cannot control himself. Imagine the smallest fly in front of his face ... *ssss* and *zum*, he will explode like dynamite'. Or consider this statement by a cook describing his neighbour's temper: 'This woman is crazy. She is wild like a tiger, her heart is ... it is not even warm, it is hot'. Violent persons have a 'warm', sometimes even a 'hot' heart, meaning that they are easily angered, unable to restrain their temper or moderate their actions. This is in stark opposition to 'cool' hearts and 'cool' tempers, which belong to people who think through possible consequences before they act.[2]

There is, however, a significant difference between a person whose heart becomes warm or hot in specific circumstances and a person who has a warm or hot heart. While lapses of moderation can happen to anyone and are then weighed against the incident or emotion that led to the lapse, people who have a warm or hot heart are said to act in a manner disproportionate to the incident. They thereby destroy the equilibrium that communities try to achieve, and they let loose around them an inescapable vortex of ruptures. The question of the nature of one's heart therefore determines whether a person acted badly in certain circumstances or is a bad person. While the actions of people who behaved badly can be punished by households and communities themselves, conflicts involving persons who are in themselves 'bad' break the moral economy of any relationship, and their mediation requires state intervention (see Chapters 7 and 8).

Violence to Help and Protect

The intention with which violence is executed is another important factor when communities determine its level of acceptability. If violent acts are executed to help somebody – for example, to punish a partner for wrongdoing, to teach good behaviour, or to prevent further violence – and not therefore performed without good reason or intention – for example, rape, torture, or cruelty to children – they are usually accepted. If violence has the purpose of helping or protecting an 'innocent', it enters a grey area and may be condoned. We can see this in cases of violence against children (Bledsoe 1990a). According to Murray Last (2000), in Nigeria violence against children is often carried out to educate and protect. In Sierra Leone, the well-known proverbs 'spare the rod, spoil the child' and 'if you don't beat your child today, they will stone the thief tomorrow' have a similar meaning. Moreover, it is commonly understood that violence carried out by known persons is better than violence inflicted by strangers or state institutions, in which cases punishment is usually harsher. If a partner or elders learn of the behaviour of a loved one that is unacceptable, they may punish them as a corrective measure. Research collaborators often explained that they beat

---

[2] See the discussion of warm and cold hearts in relation to gender in Chapter 7. There is a vast cultural archive on this in (West) Africa; for a summary, see Thompson R.F (1979).

their partners, not because they believe in the value of beating, but because they want them to be protected from the beatings of others. The rationale is that if a person fears being beaten for certain behaviour, they will stop behaving in this way. As a result, they will never have to fear being punished for their transgressions publicly: this would shame not only the individual but their entire family and kin network.

Violence along Intersectional Lines of Proximity, Gender, and Power

The moral economy of relationships adheres to gendered notions of power asymmetries. These hold that men have control over women, but also that they must provide for and protect their partners. To be acceptable, violence must uphold, not break, this framework.

In relationships, a physical act is only considered as unacceptable violence if the victim is held down and forced. Coercion, intimidation, and manipulation are mainly speech acts and thus do not fall within the spectrum of unacceptable violence even if they make it possible. Michael (46), a teacher from central Freetown, said:

> If I go home and tell my wife to lie down and beat her, it is against human rights maybe and you know the beating is violence, but because she accepts, she lies down, it is still somewhat acceptable. It is between me and her. Only if she refuses or runs from me and then I make her, then that is unacceptable, and others must come intervene.

What Michael's statement shows is that others will only engage if the socially sanctioned line of acceptability is crossed. Consequently, what matters is not that violence occurs but why and how, and who was involved both on the executing and the receiving end (Chapter 6). Teeth and tongue constantly touch each other and interact with each other. Depending on gender, positions of power, and the relationship between those involved, similar acts can have entirely different outcomes. In her book *Masculinities*, Raewyn Connell illustrates 'two patterns of violence … First, many members of the privileged group use violence to sustain their dominance. Second, violence becomes important in gender politics among men' (Connell 2005: 83). These patterns are evident in Sierra Leone as well. If, for example, a young man beats his girlfriend out of jealousy after she goes to a party without asking for his consent, the likely interpretation is that both acted immaturely and irresponsibly. The acts in themselves, however, will not be condemned (Chapter 6). But if the male head of the house beats his wife after returning home from work because he is frustrated with his day, he is believed to have acted irresponsibly for a man in such an important position. If he returns home and finds that there is no food prepared for him, again the fault lies with both partners. Generally, acts of violence are tolerated more when they are executed by a senior against their junior (see Connell 2005). If an elder beats their junior, this will most likely be called disciplining or educating, maybe punishing, depending on its severity. If a young person beats an elder, such an act is a form of extreme violence.

Whether violence is acceptable or unacceptable also depends upon the demographics and relationship between the person who executes and the person who experiences the violence. Violence by strangers is always unacceptable, while within a family relationship certain forms of violence are acceptable, such as those committed by elders against the young, by parents against their children, by husbands against their wives, and by senior against junior wives. Hence, violence should stay between the teeth and tongue, which fill one mouth (symbolising an intimate or familial relationship). The line between acceptable and unacceptable forms is crossed when the violence committed permits no return to the previous state of the relationship. Hence, no physical injury or irreparable rupture of the relationship is justifiable. If it does occur, a person is considered irresponsible, angry, and destructive and loses respect and authority.

Violence as a Demand and an Act of Giving

Among my research collaborators, it was also commonly held that violence – both in its execution and its expectation – is learnt behaviour. Darren explained:

Women who have had bad experiences with an ex start to think that the best way to be treated when doing things wrong and if he cares is to be beaten. They believe that instead of discussing, beating is the main procedure of love. And that becomes the expectation. Women who have experienced violence might push for more violence: 'Why don't you beat me, don't you care for me? Why don't you always call me, tell me how to dress, where to go, check my phone to see who I talk with, never ask me where I am going?' Women's expectations might lead men to go through with physical violence.

The perspective of Adama (34), who works at the Rainbo Centre, underscores this:

Violence is not only the responsibility of those who use it but also of those that have been assaulted. If you have a partner who says that he cannot accommodate cheating but then you go on and cheat, then the man will say 'OK, it is done with us' and then you say 'I don't think this should be the end of the relationship. There must be something else that you can do'. Then violence can occur as punishment.

The notion of violence as learnt behaviour and expectation points to a persisting system of patriarchy that 'creates an environment that normalizes ... violence, simultaneously infantilizing women and reinforcing their subordination (alongside children)' (Namy et al. 2017: 40). Such patriarchal structures are not just local phenomena. Instead, argues Roseline Njogu, conceptions of sexual and intimate relationships have been 'transplanted through colonialism' and the 'internationalization of English monogamy'. These 'morph and merge with analogous indigenous conceptions to entrench and formalize the continued subjugation of the female body' (Njogu 2016: 16). One of the coping strategies within this larger, historically constructed system of male domination and violence is the offer by women to be subjected to violence in order to hold on to a relationship.

At the same time, these explanations shed light on Connell's notion that 'gender politics' (Connell 2005: 83) goes beyond men. It is shared between men and women. Within the moral economy, it seems that violence as punishment becomes an act of giving rather than imposing. This reciprocity of love and violence, in particular the notion that through punishment equality can be restored, is interpreted as an attempt to rebalance the moral economy. Here, the person executing the violence makes a conscious effort to restore equilibrium. Nevertheless, this moral economy also establishes limits that may not be crossed, and it is these limits that contain the severity of violence within relationships (Burrill, Roberts, and Thornberry 2010).

Violence is accepted less in temporary and fluid relationships than in lasting partnerships. Its acceptability also increases with the amount of genuine love and affection present in a relationship. In some ways, the more people love each other, the more they may also hurt each other by using violence without terminating the relationship. Hence, the more teeth and tongue sustain the body together, the more the tongue may push against the teeth and the more the teeth can bite the tongue. Punishing a partner for misbehaving is often viewed as a necessary component for a respectful and successful relationship. In their desire to live together, research collaborators who care deeply about their partners are overwhelmingly willing to use and suffer some violence to avoid breaking up their relationships (see also García Moreno, Jewkes, and Sen 2002; Burrill 2007). This ties in with the findings of scholars like Deniz Kandiyoti (1988), Saba Mahmood (2001), and Adeline

Masquelier (2009) that women may contribute to the continuation of practices that seem to lock them into marginal positions because of pragmatic considerations (Chapter 7).

The Pressure to Uphold Gendered Ideals

In their study on how to end gender-based violence in Sierra Leone, Mills et al. (2015) point to the important role men can play as role models who champion inclusive forms of masculinity. My research highlights another aspect. It shows that men can come under pressure from their partners and families to use violence and to be 'dominant'. Local gendered notions of manliness require men to be 'in control' over their partners. That it was close to impossible to embody these ideals during colonial rule and the civil war, and continues to be difficult in contemporary Freetown, especially in conditions of poverty, does not diminish the significance of these concepts. Each person is embedded in different moral economies. Male research collaborators often described the social pressure to beat their partners as 'heavy', stressing that trying to solve a dispute with their partner through discussion would make them the 'laughing stock' of the whole community. Consequently, the gendered ideals woven into the fabric of the moral economy of relationships can cut into a person's flesh when trying to transgress them. The visible marks it leaves can easily be decoded by a person's social network and can involve a repositioning of that person within the moral economy of the household or community. Hence, the social pressures accompanying their roles within a relationship, household, and community bear down on both men and women. If within the moral economy certain forms of violence are symbolically tied to love, partners do not automatically appreciate their absence. Such an absence can be interpreted as a form of emotional violence on the part of a partner, who may then share their pain with the community, thereby threatening the gendered identity of the other partner. Certain acts of violence are therefore understood as part of what constitutes a relationship.

Violence as a Form of Communicating Emotions and Preserving Relationships

As a result of gender parallelism, in which men and women have distinct yet complementary roles, many research collaborators believe that women and men are fundamentally different and cannot be friends (with the exception of the partner of one's best friend). Any contact between men and women has sexual implications and is fraught with misunderstanding and disagreement. Even within a relationship, men and women primarily speak to and spend time with individuals of their own gender whom they describe as 'their own kind' rather than with each other. Similar findings have been recorded in other ethnographies of Sierra Leone. Mariane Ferme's (2001) ethnography of the Mende, for example, describes distinct male and female spheres, activities, and gendered material worlds, which are complementary but hardly overlapping. Even in marriage, Mende men and women seldom cohabit, and their daily routines are firmly organised around people of their own gender.

In Freetown, gender can form a dividing line, which is said to hinder mutual understanding. Sab (33), from Goderich, said: 'Men don't talk, and they don't understand much of my sufferness. I keep them yes, but I rely on my friends. With the women you find understanding; with the men you find company'. And MSaw (29), from EAUC, added: 'You see, me and this woman now, we have been loving for many years, but still I don't understand her. At all, at all not. All the women, their mind is different from us. It is complicating. You can only communicate with heart, body, hands'. Amidst these struggles, violence is often interpreted as a form of communication and a demonstration of emotions. This communication of the heart, the body, and the hands, as MSaw said, serves to indicate emotions between women's and men's worlds, thereby building one of the pillars of the moral economy. Normal, even desirable, signals of a partner's affection include social monitoring, the isolation of a partner, tying the gift of money to certain conditions, and other forms of manipulation and emotional violence.

Here we can refer to the role of the mobile phone. Its importance as a tool by which 'virtual spaces of intimacy' (Archambault 2018: 22) are found, relationships are created and fostered, and authorship over personal life is sought was analysed by Julie Archambault (2018) as well as others. She shows how young people in Mozambique create elaborate profiles of their selves, characterised simultaneously by the 'display and disguise' of various relationships, social status, and (multiple) identities. This game of pretence and self-making is present in Freetown as well. Here, as Michael Stasik points out, 'elaborate monitoring systems' (Stasik 2016: 228) allow people to navigate their relationships. During my research, I observed that the phone was a constant source of anxiety and mistrust. Handing over one's phone to a lover for 'checks' was the only way in which truthfulness could be ensured. People unwilling to surrender their phone at a moment's notice were, without exception, understood to value intimate relationships through the phone over the one with the partner making the demand. These demands were made by men and women equally. In fact, the failure to insist on phone checks or other monitoring practices often caused pain and raised questions about the partner's fidelity or interest in continuing the relationship. The violence of these monitoring practices represents efforts to preserve a relationship and to hold on to somebody.

On the other hand, partners often perform 'partial disguise' (Archambault 2018). They may conceal their devotion to a partner and, through invoking jealousy, try to maintain or revitalise the desire of a lover. There are many ways in which violence is interpreted as demonstrating passion. Diamond (32), a builder from Allentown, explained: 'Real love must come with passion and passion is also jealousy. When you are jealous, your heart will become warm too much. Then there is some slapping or some beating. But it is part of the love'. Furthermore, if the possibility of loss is performed, a relationship that had been taken for granted may be reinvigorated. In this sense, violence in relationships can be understood as serving not only a disruptive but also a 'restorative' function. It has come to demonstrate the stability of a relationship and to prevent its dissolution. In certain situations, violence between partners can be executed, endured, and even expected as a means of expressing affection. The conversation I had with Sabrina (19) from Allentown shows this:

SABRINA: You know my story, my sufferness. You saw it right here. That man is not good. He was always out, no providing for me anymore. He stopped caring, and he must be loving somebody else.
ME: How do you know that?
SABRINA: Well for one, he stopped buying things for me. He doesn't buy top-up [credit for her cell phone] and doesn't call me first thing in the morning. He does not care where I go and what I wear. Last week, I dressed in super short clothes and went out. I walked past his friend's place. I made sure that they see me. Normally, he would have called immediately, he would have been so suspicious. Before his heart got very warm, he would have fought me so much and then he would have sexed me all night (*laughs*). But now I am free to go wherever and do whatever. I even took money from a man and left it lying openly, and he did not even investigate where it is from. No interrogation. It is horrible.[3]

Violence as Neglect

Neglect, as Sabrina demonstrates, is the opposite of caring and involves the public performance of lack of affection. It includes neglecting to spend time

---

[3] This statement reiterates the connection between genuine affection and the provision of money or goods.

with a partner, neglecting to put a partner's needs first and show respect to a partner's desires, but also omitting to show signs of possessiveness such as jealousy. Consider an excerpt from my fieldnotes (from October 2016) that describes the reason why Amina (26), the main girlfriend of Suge, the former leader of EAUC, publicly ended their relationship.

Two days ago, Amina terminated her complicated on-and-off relationship with Suge again. Like always, club members – myself included – visit her at her house to 'beg her' to take Suge back. It is my fourth time 'begging' at Amina's house. I expect to observe Amina to be angry at first but then flattered. The fact that Suge's friends come to beg her is a sign that they respect and value her and that they do not want to lose her. Previously, these visits were then followed by Amina's revenge – usually some other lover with whom she would attend an EAUC event – Suge's outbreak of jealousy, and then a reconciliation. Normally, these stages occurred in monthly cycles. Initial ruptures were usually due to infidelity, Suge's inadequate monetary provisions, lack of respect, or time. But this situation is different.

When Amina finally steps out of her house to greet us after letting us wait for almost an hour, what we meet with is a woman who feels deeply humiliated and maltreated. Amina's eyes flash dangerously at the small crowd and immediately the laughter collapses into giggles that ebb away and make room for suspenseful anticipation as she straightens her back, walks down the stairs, and sits up tall on one of the makeshift benches, fixing us with her stare and her silence.

The previous day, Amina had been unable to reach Suge. After repeatedly calling him, she made her way to 24. There, she met him with other EAUC members and Hellen (28), a former girlfriend of Suge, watching a football match on television. Hellen and Suge were immersed in conversation. Amina walked over to Suge and attempted to sit on his lap. However, Suge refused to let her sit down, remarking that he was having a conversation and attempting to see the match. Furious, Amina started to argue with Suge, who then grabbed her, carried her outside and shut the door on her. The fact that Suge had not allowed her – his girlfriend – to sit on his lap and had rejected her in front of his friends, led Amina to believe that there was no way to continue the relationship without losing face.

Now, one after another her visitors vouch for Suge, beg her to forgive him and assure to have her back and advocate for her in the future. Interchangeably, they praise Suge and condemn his wrongdoing. But Amina's mood does not change. She does not even look at the gifts of clothes and food they brought for her. After all arguments have been exhausted, Amina says: 'This man has no respect for me at all. Suge does not care ... neglecting me like that, me? Leave it. Let me go my way and let him go his way'.

As this case shows, neglect is linked to selfishness. It constitutes a form of violence that can lead to an immediate and public break-up in a social world where partners usually see no value in severing ties completely (Chapter 3).

In another case of neglect, Effe (23) left Amadu (24) from EAUC after more than three years because he refused to remove earrings that she did not like. After asking him repeatedly to change the earrings, she reiterated her demand in front of his friends during an outing. When he objected, she publicly broke up with him and left with another man whom she is now dating. The couple never reunited. Referring to this incident, Said (31) of EAUC, Amadu's best friend, told me: 'Amadu should have just taken out the earrings. It would not have mattered to him. Because, you see, if I love you and something is very important to me and does not make any difference to you and then you don't do it just because you are stubborn, then that shows that you have no care in the world for the other person. This selfishness cost him his woman'.

Alima (29), one of Effe's friends, reiterated: 'In a relationship, sometimes there is violence. But it depends. Fighting or arguing can be tough and beating may hurt, but all these things show that you care about each other, maybe even too much, so much that your emotions sometimes escalate. But if you don't do anything and refuse to even pay attention, that is like a declaration that the love has ended'. This shows that in a partnership it is expected that one partner will have access to the other person's body and will have a say in how that person dresses and styles their body. These expectations and questions of physical proximity – whether holding hands, hugging, kissing, or sitting on someone's lap – are not individual choices but mutual ones. The other members of EAUC unanimously agreed that both Amadu and Suge were wrong and that the neglect they displayed was unacceptable. Hence, while the acceptance of physical violence is often dependent on circumstance, failure to adapt one's behaviour even slightly and to show care and respect openly for a partner rips the fabric of the moral economy apart.

Sex and the Sharing of Bodies

Another, more private form of violence is sexual violence. Sexual violence was perceived to be intrinsic to romantic relationships. When, in a relationship, two bodies melt into one, one partner has the right to do what they please with the other's body. Withholding or claiming ownership over one's body easily incites violence. Research collaborators would often explain that sexual availability is part of traditional marriage terminology, in which both partners are described as possessions (Chapter 3). These terms are read as signs of a purposeful declaration of marriage, which regulate the interaction between a man and a woman. Consider Mr Mohamed's explanation: 'You know men and women; they are *very, very* different. Some yes, we keep for the company, but really we are all in it for the sex. I think also in your society, in every society. Men and women, why would they be together if not for the sex? So, if you withhold the sex, that is not correct'.

Forcing or coercing a partner into sex is seen to be the consequence of an unwillingness to meet one's duties in marriage, which is only acceptable when someone is ill. In that case, forced intercourse is ungentlemanly behaviour but was still described to me as 'acceptable' violence. Effie (41), a hairdresser from central Freetown, told me: 'Ah, Luisa, I am telling you, if maybe one time he says no [to sex] I will accept, but more than once, *no*. I will leave him or lay complaint'. When men or women report their spouses for withholding sex, communities usually heavily sanction them. However, among unmarried couples such cases are harder to win because there has been no official binding or public agreement about sexual availability. In that situation, women are said to have more power than men. One story that I heard in many different versions concerned young women withholding sex from young men, thereby embarrassing them in front of family or friends. Consider the story of Gas:

I don't know what it is about this woman. We have been together for three years now, but I desire her so much. Even when we are right done with sexing and she is only close to me, I want to sex her again immediately. But she, she will violence me too much. When I do something she does not like, she will just withhold the sex, yes. Imagine, then she calls me, and I go to her house and sit there in the parlour next to her family all excited to sex and she will not even let me into her room. No! She will not even come out. So, I will sit there, maybe with her sisters or her mother. It is a great embarrassment. I want to sex, why else am I here? Then she texts me and tells me to go and come back another day. They make us useless, these women. But I cannot stop it, I want her. I want her too much.

Gas's explanation, as well as his general attitude towards sex in relationships, creates a paradox. Like many research collaborators, Gas exclaims without hesitation: 'She is my girlfriend. I own her body for now. Can I not do to my own body whatever I want? We are in a relationship, so that means that she becomes my body as well'. Such statements can be interpreted as displays of systemic patriarchy that lead men to regard a woman's body as an extension of their territory to which they are entitled. Yet, the important consideration here relates to 'being in a relationship' rather than 'being a woman'. Gas refers to the implications of an emotional metamorphosis of two bodies into one which creates mutual physical entitlements. However, this notion has severe limitations in that without having access to a woman's body men cannot exercise any degree of control. In a marriage, withdrawal breaks binding obligations and can therefore be reported. In other relationships, the same expectation meets with the practical impossibility of enforcement and the absence of enforcing institutions.

Additionally, agreeing to sex but then withdrawing consent during the process was widely considered unacceptable. Said explained this in the following way: 'When you say yes to sex, you cannot stop in the middle. That we consider violence. You already promised'. According to these conversations, violence often occurs when one partner is seen to deviate from expectations. Darren elucidates: 'When you are in a relationship, you are entitled to that particular person, so if you refuse or withdraw in the middle, that becomes a suspicious thing. Now that you are refusing this, then I believe that you are seeing someone else. That can become a sexual violence'. Darren states further that withholding sex will provoke the suspicion of infidelity, loss of interest, or alternative motives for having entered the relationship (such as to gain status, increase one's circle of friends, or obtain money). Sabrina shed light on the reasons why women may attempt to 'stop in the middle'. She said:

> Some of the men, they try to trick you and say 'just some playing in your garden', which is the soft kind with kissing and everything and then when they start they want to try different positions and *bambrusing*, and maybe you don't agree at all anymore, but since you said yes to the sex it would be violence to stop now. That is why you need to negotiate terms *before* you start, because then when he breaks them, he is in the wrong.

Regarding sex, what is and is not acceptable is very clearly defined. Within the moral economy, give and take is paramount. If, according to the terminology around sex described in the last chapter – 'cut' for men and 'play' for women – a person only 'cuts' but does not 'play', they quickly become a passer-by (Chapter 3). Such men open themselves not only to female revenge, but they may also ruin their social position. Moreover, people who cut and pass, thereby withholding oral pleasure, just like people who withhold sex, may be accused in front of the household or community.

Pornography, Re-enactments, and the Economy of Naked Pictures

Another alleged cause of sexual violence was related to watching pornographic films and then wanting to re-enact scenes with a person who was not willing. When I spent time at EAUC, hardly an evening went by without members sharing, watching, or asking for naked pictures of girls and women they were interested in. Among these friends alone, several groups were opened on WhatsApp, such as 'MaturedMinds' or 'SexStuffs', dedicated to sharing and watching pornography. Alie (17) from EAUC was convinced that

> one actual violence factor is pornography. With WhatsApp now, we watch all these films, and we send sex videos around or film women when they shower, and we want to try the techniques we see. Sometimes, the women they don't, but then we make them ... and we the men we always ask for naked photos and videos and then we share them. But the women they cannot refuse; otherwise, you will go to somebody else.

Bockare (38), a journalist, told me that the

> stimulation of men and women is different. A man can view a porn movie and then get something out of that. The possibility for a woman to get something out of that is somehow slim. That can lead to unwanted sex ... We will say 'please baby do that for me, I want you to', especially oral sex or anal sex and when she hesitates, either we just take her, or we go to another one. So, mostly she will just shut up and do it because even if she leaves, her next man will surely want the same.

While I also met women who shared similar images and found watching pornography desirable, they did so privately since it was not considered 'natural' or desirable for them to do this openly. They were supposed to be the providers of such materials, not the consumers. The bigger problem, however, was not with pornography itself, which was considered a matter of personal taste, but with the actions inspired by pornography. When I spent time with women under the age of 30, they would usually share stories about those they sent their pictures to and what they had been asked to do sexually in the past few days. The question was not whether one wanted to share naked photos or engage in re-enactments of scenes from pornographic videos, but rather with whom one decided to do so. Many women and girls were less than keen but felt that, if they did not strategically choose one of their partners to do the things men wanted of them, they might be forced or their partners might leave them. Mabinti (24), a catering student, told me that 'there is no way around it, really'. Between lovers, the re-enactment of pornographic material has somehow become part of the reciprocity underlying the moral economy. A genuine lover must please a sexual partner. This pleasing requires men to ensure they attend to women's sexual needs and women to engage in practices important for men. Similarly, men who had no interest in these images still felt the need to ask their sexual partners for them so as not to show up empty-handed at the next meeting with their peers. However, because naked photos and videos do not stay within the confines of the moral economy but are shared with others, they breach the foundation of reciprocity. As the next chapter reveals, the involvement of others often constitutes the breaking point of the moral economy and the moment when violence becomes unacceptable.

5 The Language of Violence

Language, says Lynn Tirell, is

> a structure of significances that governs our lives. It contains and conveys the categories through which we understand ourselves and others, and through which we become who and what we are. Our linguistic practices are constituted largely by inferences which in turn constitute or contribute to our understanding of the connections (causal and otherwise) between things. These inferential roles and patterns, which are normatively inscribed, give order and significance to the categories. Once we realize that our linguistic categories reflect and are reflected by our social categories, and once we see that our discursive practices are normative, it is a short step to see language as an arena of political struggle. (Tirrell 2017: 137)

Language is a powerful and multi-layered symbolic system that articulates, forms, and reproduces normativity. What matters, however, is not just what is said, but who says it, who listens, and to what effect. The way we listen, how we listen, and to whom we listen is as important for understanding phenomena as language itself (Boyce-Davies 1994; Gibbon 1999; Spivak 2003). Language holds the key to understanding how violence and oppression are forged, how they operate, and how they are reinforced. But it also offers a road map for deconstructing harmful logics. Analysing language, as I do in this chapter, is therefore crucial for understanding the role and place of love and violence as well as their relations to each other in a given context.

The moral economy of relationships is erected on linguistic foundations. The terms describing acts of violence in development policies and in Sierra Leonean legal documents are either very broad or their meaning differs significantly from local interpretations. In Freetown, irrespective of age, class, gender, or socioeconomic background, research collaborators used the term 'violence' or 'violence in relationships'. This includes all forms of violence inflicted, endured, or regulated between sexual partners, irrespective of the nature of their relationship – be it married, dating, or cohabiting.[1] This umbrella term is a floating signifier,

---

[1] They thereby include forms of violence that are referred to as intimate partner violence (IPV), domestic violence (DV), and sexual and gender-based violence (SGBV) in the

however, in that it reveals no information about specific acts or their context. It is therefore of little use in everyday interactions. Instead, Sierra Leoneans carefully differentiate, through terminology, between expected and 'normal' acts and those which are deemed unacceptable and which demand correction. They assign meanings and messages to a broad range of violent acts. The term used to describe an act thereby offers the code to unlock its underlying meaning and the level of its social acceptability. Taken together, these terms produce a language of violence that communicates three layers of meaning: the description of the act, the meaning of the act, and the judgement of the act. This terminological assessment of a broad variety of acts reveals how Sierra Leoneans judge violence in a setting where global dynamics, national politics, and daily local lived experiences intersect.

The use of as well as the need for these terminologies is at least partially inspired by historical forces, public discourse, and legal reform. Many research collaborators explained that discussion of forms of violence within relationships and their acceptability is a post-war phenomenon. Consider this explanation by Umu (64), a market woman from Abacha Street:

Well before the war, what went on inside a relationship or house was personal. If someone complained, then they would call members of the family or elders and then they would describe the activity like 'he beat me with a belt' or 'she was having a relation [an affair]'. A word was not necessary. But after the war, with the TRC [Truth and Reconciliation Commission] and now with the laws and civil society – since it goes outside, we need to classify somehow – so this is how the word[s] 'violence in relationships' came in.

Umu sheds light on how post-war reconciliation processes and subsequent legal changes impacted on the way relationships are spoken about and to whom. To understand the effects of law and policy on concrete behaviour, one needs to analyse how terminologies change over time. Such ethnography becomes relevant for development workers and policy-makers, and for those who are themselves not in a position to explore how laws affect relationship dynamics.

As Umu claims, relationships used to be private matters. Today, in contrast, violence in relationships is the subject of a multi-layered public discourse influenced by state institutions and non-state actors alike (e.g. IOs, NGOs, civil society, and faith-based institutions). Actions deemed

---

literature. SGBV focusses on gender dynamics in the execution of violence, DV on violence between people who are in a familial relationship – in Sierra Leone this includes persons living in the same house, sharing meals in common, or being engaged in intimate relationships – and it pays attention to forms of violence that are often considered to be private and only seldom punished. IPV is confined to sexual partners.

illegal are no longer considered private even if they occur between spouses within the confines of their home. Since the introduction of the Gender Acts in 2007 and the Sexual Offences Act (SOA) of 2012 as well as the Sexual Offences Amendment Act (SOAA) of 2019, any behaviour within such a relationship that causes physical, psychological, economic, social, or sexual harm to those involved constitutes violence. Hence, Sierra Leonean state institutions, the criminal justice system, state laws and IOs, as well as NGOs apply the concept of rights and ideas of risk (Abrahams, Jewkes, and Laubscher 1999; García Moreno, Jewkes, and Sen 2002; also Chapters 7 and 8). In this official discourse, violence within relationships is analysed in relation to '(a) contextual characteristics of partners (demographic, neighbourhood, community and school factors), (b) developmental characteristics and behaviours of the partners (e.g. family, peer, psychological/behavioural, and cognitive factors), and (c) relationship influences and interactional patterns' (Capaldi et al. 2012).

But the official views on gender and violence often differ from local perceptions. As we have seen, within the overarching framework of the moral economy, research collaborators distinguish between 'normal and acceptable' and 'unacceptable' types of violence by evaluating intent, outcome, and the possibility of restoring the relationship. Moreover, through elaborate linguistic differentiations, the popular language of violence gives nuance to the understanding of various acts of both accepted and unaccepted violence. In addition, specific terms are assigned to acts that make classification and comparison possible. While the extensive local use of the terms 'normal', 'acceptable', and 'unacceptable', which are the meta-categories within which forms and acts of violence are clustered, points to the influence of ideas of risk and legal language on household and community perceptions, it also indicates how these are locally transformed and appropriated.

The most important differentiation is made between male and female violence. During my research, I never came across a research collaborator who would describe violence as a purely male or, for that matter, a purely female phenomenon. It was always said that men and women both use violence against each other, though not in the same way. But, as I show below, there is a distinction arising from the data between the acts of violence predominantly committed by men and those by women: men use violence mainly against bodies and women use violence mainly against minds.

(Male) Violence against Bodies

There is a whole vocabulary of terms used to describe (male) violence against bodies. Whereas *wahala* and 'palaver' are used to refer to conflict overall, other, more specific terms are used to describe the actions that occur. When somebody says 'they are having an argument', it means that after a scene was caused those involved have not resolved their issues (have not 'aired their grievances') but have resorted instead to avoiding each other. Yet they maintain the basic niceties such as general greetings. While arguments are largely tolerated so long as they do not last for too long, 'malicing' is usually unacceptable. Malicing involves avoiding somebody to the extent of refusing to be in the same room, refusing to greet them, and refusing to prepare food (women) or accept and eat food (men). In a society where love travels through the stomach (see Diggins 2014), rejecting food makes a strong statement. Malicing involves punishment through withdrawal. Prolonged malicing can turn into 'insulting', when malicing practices of avoidance or disciplining become visible to others. 'Quarrelling' is restricted to vocal arguments and includes shouting, insulting, screaming, and sometimes even cursing others.

While quarrelling is limited to non-physical confrontations, 'fighting' is the umbrella term for all physical acts, which, apart from 'slapping', are mainly carried out by men. Research collaborators distinguish carefully between these various acts. Take, for instance, Said's response to my question about the status of his relationship.

SAID: Well, mostly we are ok, sometimes we can quarrel, and then I can malice her or she can malice me. Only *sometimes* we fight.
ME: Do both of you fight, or does one fight the other?
SAID: Oh, we can both fight (*laughs*). Well, let me say, she is better at slapping, and me, I am better at beating (*laughs*).

A market woman from Abacha Street (in her fifties) explained her relationship like this:

ME: Are you in a relationship?
HER: Oh yes, I have a man.
ME: How is it?
HER: I tap to him [I live with him]. He likes me because I am a market woman. I bring home the money. But it is like they say: 'if you are with an Abacha woman you must bear the noise' (*laughs*). I like shouting. Sometimes fighting can come inside.
ME: Who can fight?
HER: We both can fight (*laughs*), but that is how we keep the love going.

Beating means repeated and forceful punishment with the fist or with objects. Here sticks, belts, and the like can be used. Beating, I was told, is most commonly used by men. However, if a man tells his partner that he will beat her, and she does not object or try to resist, it is referred to as a 'joint beating'. Then violence is not only carried out by one partner against the other, but the person who is beaten acknowledges the possibility of being beaten and accepts it. The level of acceptability further depends on where the beating takes place, the object that is used, the severity of the injuries, and the part of the body that is beaten. So-called private beatings in secluded rooms were considered less harmful than public ones in front of family or community. Beating a partner on the street was described as the most severe form of violence. The longer that injuries took to heal, the less acceptable was the beating. Moreover, beating parts of the body that are usually hidden, such as the back, was more acceptable than beating the face. Beating particularly sensitive parts, such as the soles of the feet, the hands, the inner elbow, or the thighs, was condemned unless it followed serious wrongdoing.

What these levels of acceptability show is that, whenever violence becomes visible to others, its acceptability decreases. A relationship is a bond between two partners, and its inner nature or quality is mostly invisible to others. Hence, public displays of violence or lasting injuries expose imbalances within the relationship to the scrutiny of households and communities. These public acts of physical violence often attract shame and are accompanied by symbolic violence because they tacitly invite others to judge the relationship. The beating of the face, for instance, is an act that displays a sense of ownership and also fear of losing a partner. Men who were sure their girlfriend had a lover told me that they 'beat in her face' to make her unattractive for the other man. In response to having beaten his girlfriend after he caught her cheating, Twin (45), a businessman from Naimbana Street, said: 'Loving is so many feelings you know, and they are very, very stressful. When you catch your person with somebody, you beat her because she is yours and you need to prove that you want her. At the same time, you realise that others want her, which means that you mean more because she is with you'.

A woman's beaten face can thus be read as a public code for her relationship status and for the insecurity of her partner. And yet it is also often interpreted as symbolising a desire to continue the relationship. When I asked a group of young women, all students of law or social work at Fourah Bay College in Freetown, about the beating of the face, Darina (23), a mother from Coal Farm, said: 'Yes, beating can hurt, but it shows his effort. Ask yourself, sister, is it this short pain that you want or the long one when he is gone?'

While beating in a relationship is almost exclusively a male form of violence, 'slapping' is female. The term 'slapping' refers to hitting or striking a person with the palm of the bare hand, never with the fist. Slapping is usually aimed at someone's face and is described as an act mainly carried out by women. Unlike beating, slapping rarely follows a threat to slap. Slapping does not cause lasting injuries and only occasionally does it involve severe pain. However, many men describe slapping, which is usually executed in public, as a form of violence aimed at undermining their masculine selves. Hassan (23), from Kroo Bay, explained that

> slapping is something you do with a misbehaving child without beating it. It comes quickly when somebody acts out of their character, so when a child is very rude to elders, for example. A woman slapping a man is like ... you do that in public to shame him because he did something that a real man won't do. People won't know what he did, but the slapping will tell everyone that he misbehaved.

If done publicly, slapping therefore negates the authority of a person. It is children who are slapped, not adults. Bonnie Mann analyses the ways in which a masculine self can be undone 'by an experience of "feeling like a woman"' (Mann 2014: 85). Such instances, Mann says, 'are structured around disruptions of the "I can" body, which is at the center of perceptual and kinesthetic experience. These disruptions ... have the power to terrorize as well as to mobilize the subject' (Mann 2014: 86). Similarly, being treated like a child can be seen as an attack on masculinity.

And yet slapping, if executed by men, was interpreted by my research collaborators as reinforcing affection and demonstrating love. Meadow (23), from EAUC, comments that 'slapping is something you do without thinking when you really, really love somebody and then that somebody becomes a question, like when they lie to you or ignore you or hide something'. Furthermore, slapping by men was described with words such as 'quick' and 'irrational', and was said to be done out of 'jealousy' or 'hurt'. Here slapping occurs on the spur of the moment as an irrational and affective reaction to jealousy, protectiveness, and the fear of loss. Female research collaborators in particular often shared strategies to 'provoke men to slap them' if they feared that the men would lose interest. Mariama (19), trying to educate me on how to act this way, said:

> OK, it is simple really. If you suspect him, maybe if you're lucky you can get his phone and do checks, but if you can't, you need to test, always test, if he has not been calling you in the morning and in the evening and he is not sexing you. So where does it go, ha? Surely someone must get it. So, you must find out. The best way is for you to totally ignore him and go out and start amusing with someone. If this does not become a case, if there is no beating or slapping or force, my sister, I am telling you, you are wasting your time.

The presence or absence of male slapping can be used to determine the level of 'heated' emotions between partners: if present, it is a sign of the health of the relationship and of a high level of affection between partners. Slapping is also used to draw boundaries or to punish overstepping without causing further problems. It can be an act of jealousy, a demand for attention, or a statement that there is a problem that needs to be dealt with.

These different interpretations of male and female slapping pose an interesting puzzle. Is it the specific act that is supposedly reserved for children that causes men to feel threatened? Might it be possible, as Mann argues, that women implicitly accept their 'abject social status' (Mann 2014: 84)? Put differently, experiences of physical violence committed by the opposite sex may perhaps be perceived as a potential part of a woman's world, while on the other hand they are excluded from the masculine imaginary. From my experience in Freetown, I get a different sense, namely that women do not question their femininity as easily as men imagine their masculinity to be under attack. This may also be the reason why female violence is mostly unseen, while men rely on acts of visible physical force.

Men's hands-on approach can also be seen in 'grabbing', which involves a firm grip, usually around the upper arm or waist, with the intention of dragging or pulling someone away or preventing them from leaving. Grabbing a woman's bottom was common but was conceived as a compliment rather than a form of violence. Grabbing was also often described as a form of 'foreplay' (see also Porter 2017 on Uganda). Grabbing a partner, throwing her over the shoulder, and carrying her off was sometimes described as 'manly' and 'admirable'. Consider Kiss Daniel's 2015 single 'Woju', which was a huge hit in Sierra Leone. In this love song, the text begins: *na you I wan for carry you go* [It is you that I want to carry to go]. Kiss Daniel's words not only imply as was explained to me by Eugene, an IT specialist in his thirties, that his protagonist is leaving with a girl he did not arrive with: 'Say for instance, I went to a party with my girlfriend, but meet this other girl that sweeps me off my feet so much that I don't mind leaving my girlfriend for her'. It also suggests the physical practice of carrying her away. However, if it occurs as a punishment, grabbing can precede a beating or coerced sex. It is often accompanied by a vocal threat or conditional statement: 'If you do not do that, I will not let you go'. It can often bring an end to quarrelling. Albert (32) explained to me: 'When she is arguing with me and I get tired and need this to be finished, I just grab her, throw her in the other room, and close the door. It is like a warning. She will know that if she continues, I will come back and beat her'.

Besides these physical acts between partners, there are acts that the law considers to be violence but that are interpreted differently by research collaborators. Whether or not such an act constitutes a wrong depends on the perception of the person it is done to and the relationship between the person who carries out and the person who endures the act. For instance, 'harassment' was described, almost jokingly, as touching the clothed breast, waist, or genitals of a woman. This can be done to a friend, co-worker, or a woman one knows, and was described as a compliment about her sexual attractiveness, a 'play', or a 'norm'. Foday (47), a businessman, states that 'there is a common play, a joke like a friendship thing, like touching the boobs or waist of a woman who is not connected to me or with me, that is a common sexual harassment'.

Statements like Foday's were common among the men with whom I conducted research. When I asked how they thought women felt if they were touched in this way, I was told that it makes them feel good. Collaborators qualified this statement by explaining that they only touched women whose implicit consent they had, that such touching constitutes a compliment, that it is fleeting and that, given its joking nature, it does not contain a sexual element. Women, on the other hand, stated that only men they trusted were allowed to harass them in this way. If harassment was intended as a friendly compliment, I was told, it takes the form of a short touch with an open hand, never a grab or a hold. A lasting touch is considered sexual and therefore disrespectful and inappropriate. While some described taking issue with a friend's and co-worker's touching, they denied that all harassment is off limits or that harassment always constitutes sexism. 'Friendships', Mariama said, 'are also physical but not physical like sexual relationships'. And Amina further explained that 'it is this idea people have about Africa where they say the women are oppressed and the men are sexist. Many men are sexist, not just the ones here, but many of the men here would not dare harass us if we would not somehow tolerate it. We have power too, and men do fear us'.

Harassing one's sexual partner is always acceptable. It usually means signalling arousal and wanting to have sex. I often witnessed this at 24 (see Figure 5.1). After one of the members touched his girlfriend or lover in that way, they would usually go next door to have sex. If she ignored him, turned away, or even slapped his hand, this would usually result in grabbing. Slapping one's partner after harassment is unacceptable but doing so after 'reaching' (described below) is commonly accepted and then leads to negotiating about whether the couple will have sex.

'Reaching' means moving one's hand down under the skirt or pants of one's partner in front of other people. Though often tried, reaching is unacceptable if unwanted by a woman. Such transgressions would lead to the slapping of a man's hand and to its withdrawal. Often, men and boys then start to beg by saying 'Please, baby, I want you now' or something similar. I often witnessed how women and girls would savour

Figure 5.1 Sharing food near 24.

these situations and hold a man back for some time before giving in to his request. If he does not stop reaching, however, his partner may start arguing and often others then step in and chide him.

Hence, violence perpetrated by men is characterised by physical manifestations of power and possessiveness, or at least attempts at (re-)creating such positions of power and possession. Furthermore, the various types of male violence carry specific meanings, which in turn complicate the way we are to understand physical violence within Sierra Leonean relationships. However, it is not only physical violence that plays a role within the moral economy of relationships. The next section reveals how female agency, in terms of violence, is equally acknowledged, albeit within a different realm: that of social reputation.

(Female) Immaterial Violence

According to the metaphor of the teeth and tongue, women are more talkative and are embedded in wider social networks than men. Men often cite women's 'tongues' (gossip) as a feared instrument of violence. Gossip involves 'sharing other people's secrets' to gain attention, create unnecessary 'heat', spread information that was shared in confidence, or make false claims. Women are often referred to as having 'loose tongues'. 'Women's talk' and its ability to completely ruin a man's reputation – to punish him with the mouth – was presented as a powerful way to keep men in check. That 'words move fast' was one of the most common phrases used when men explained why they would not dare to abandon a girlfriend or decided against engaging in other romances without their main girlfriend's consent.

However, whether men and boys fear that a woman may use her tongue to punish transgressions depends on the woman in question. As we have seen in a previous chapter, Suge is not worried that Amina will use revenge. As a born-again Christian, Amina is a 'God-fearing woman' for whom revenge is out of the question. Suge comments on women's violence as 'revenge' or 'sweet revenge' in the following way:

The women have killed so many men in Sierra Leone. At times, we are very afraid, very afraid. Because some women when you are with them and then you want to move on, they say 'don't leave me like this' [nɔr lɛf mi so] and then you have to fear for your life. They will put a spell on you or give you a sickness. And if you don't find a traditional doctor to heal you, you will die. Then you can try to find her and beg her, but many times you will not see her until you are dead. She will just disappear, fade away.

When Suge explained this at 24, the others murmured approvingly. *Nɔr lɛf mi so* was a strong concern among EAUC members when they weighed the possible repercussions of leaving a girlfriend. 'It means', as Anna (17), one of the sex workers from Naimbana Street, readily explained, 'that they cannot just break off the relationship before fulfilling at least some of their promises'. Said quickly added:

The problem for us here is that when we want a woman we will tell her whatever she wants to hear. We will promise her that at the end we will give something like marriage or children. Then when we try to move on they don't let us go, but they make us remember the promise. This is how they trap us.

Revenge is thus a corrective measure when male promises are not kept. Referring to the reasons why he remains faithful to his long-term girlfriend, Gas said:

The reason why I do not cheat is simple. I have been having this girlfriend for many years. Now I am slowly making my way through university. Almost every day, there are women who want to get with me because they know that one day I will be a successful somebody. But it is not worth risking my health and my life for that because now, if I go with another one, the first one who has been by my side patiently for all the years when I could offer her nothing ... will get really angry. It is too risky.

Hence, the possibility of revenge leads men to consider the long-term repercussions of giving into momentary desire. Albert, who himself uses this tactic of empty promises – he is currently dating two market women – explained:

> Also, many men who do not have money will seek to enter a relationship with market women or women who are otherwise engaged in businesses. These women will support the men, hoping that later they will take care of them. But often men leave the women when they are successful or move on to other women. There is not much women can do formally, but they can seek revenge by using traditional medicines. Several love potions are used, and there is also a medicine to harm the bowel movement of the men by collecting the semen and taking it to a traditional doctor. If it is buried, the man will get sick but can be cured ... if it is thrown in the water, the man will die. This is how women can seek redress.

What Albert was talking about here is *gbagba*, a spell that is mostly used against 'passers-by', which will block the bowel movement of the men, leading to a slow and painful death. *Gbagba* can be purchased from traditional doctors for as little as SLL 25,000–50,000 (GBP 2.40–4.80). The explanation of Oki, that women in Sierra Leone are dangerous and that they will kill you 'fast fast' if they think you have treated them wrongly, was echoed in many conversations. Some men, such as Oki, cited this as the main reason why they do not enter long-term relationships with women before they feel ready to keep their promises and are able to support a partner financially. When I first asked Oki whether he was in a relationship, he replied quickly: 'Me? Ah no, I stay away from that risk. It is dangerous for men like me. I am not crazy'. Instead, Oki, who goes to nightclubs almost daily, lives his sexuality with sex workers whom he knows well. Referring to these women, he said:

> I know them well because I am popular on the streets, but most of them I never meet [for sex] more than once because I don't want any relationship to develop that could potentially result in the women expecting something, getting disappointments, and harming me ... today we come together, today we leave each other [*wi mit tide wi lef tide*].

This 'cut and play' tactic is easier for him in view of his low income. Michael Jackson recorded similar attitudes. Many years after conducting his first stretch of fieldwork, Jackson returned to Sierra Leone with his son. There, he reconnected with Kaimah, a man in his late thirties whom he had known for many years. When asked about his relationship, Kaimah replied bluntly: 'You can't expect love when you have nothing to give but love' (Jackson 2011: 10). Kaimah's former partner Aisetta had left him for another man because he was unable to provide her with security, income, and prospects. In my research, men not only feared being left, but also being punished, as Albert's response to Oki's statement confirms: 'Exactly! There is a social mechanism that connects expectations and actions to deliveries. If you do not deliver, women might sanction you'.

Another form of violence women can use against men is that of 'trapping'. Ousman (32), a labourer from Kroo Bay, explained trapping in the following way: 'When they [women] get pregnant, they will not tell you until maybe four or five months in until it is too late to pull the pregnancy [get an abortion] and then men have to fear. They hate her, but sometimes they cannot run because otherwise the woman will use her power and the man can easily die'. Ousman's gloomy depiction is underscored by Mabinty (27), a mother from Kroo Bay, who said that 'women have much more power than the men here. For a man he will never use this traditional stuff, never. Only they, the women. They do that. Pregnancy or spell'. Jenneh (19), a hairdresser from Kroo Bay, added: 'The women, they know everything about protection methods now, so they will only get pregnant if they want to trap these men'. Indeed, women and girls who want to get an abortion usually ask their partners to pay. For EAUC members, abortion fees constituted a huge problem. Amadu explained:

Sometimes we only sleep with one once and then they come and say that they are pregnant, and we need to pay for the abortion. It can be two or even more women per month. But if we don't find that money, then they will make us responsible for all the costs with the child. It is the most wicked violence right now. How can we know if she is even pregnant? Maybe she just wants that money. But it is too risky not to give her [the money], and they know that.

When confronted, men may accept (*ansa bɛlɛ*) or reject a pregnancy (*I nɔr ansa di bɛlɛ*). If they refuse to acknowledge that they have caused the pregnancy, they may be asked to take an oath. This practice is informed by the Mende *hale*, which, as Charles Jedrej describes, 'is used to represent the relationship between the world of humans and the world of spirits. The relationships are manipulated by the people for their benefit by a variety of ritual techniques and objects, notably those commonly referred to as medicines, fetishes, masks, and institutions such as secret societies' (Jedrej 1986: 513).

Taking an oath can involve 'scratching matches during daylight', which means that a woman or girl points to the man who impregnated her. In these scenarios, men and boys are called and asked to swear an oath, not as to whether they are responsible for a pregnancy, but whether they ever had sex with the woman or girl in question. If they did, they are subsequently forced to accept responsibility for the pregnancy. This is a common practice in Freetown today in cases of pregnancy out of wedlock or infidelity within marriages. In the latter case, the practice is called 'call name', which means that a woman must call the name of her lover in front of her family and her husband. The lover is subsequently made to take an oath that he never had sex with her. Unmarried girls often choose a man, whom the family then asks to take an oath, on the basis of his likeability or his ability to provide. In the case of married women, a husband is thereby forced to accept other children as his own and take over the full financial responsibility of raising them. Mr Mohamed explained this process in the following way:

So, the man might know that he cannot be the father because he has had sex with her two months ago, but you have been found to be two weeks pregnant, so how will that be possible? It can be as far as three or four years back. But because the man has gone with her at some point or is married to her, he is now trapped. If the parents take an oath on them [the men] and they lie, they will die. That will force the men to take the responsibility of accepting the child of another. If they are in a relationship, this is how violence enters the relationship because they [the men] will know that it is not their child and they will always be angry and frustrated with the woman. Some they will not even touch her or have sex with her ever and will always quarrel and fight with her. When the man knows it is his child *and* if he wants the pregnancy, then he will appreciate and cherish her, but when he does not want it, it will be very hard for the woman and she will be exposed to so much violence.

In her work on Kpelle fatherhood, Caroline Bledsoe highlighted how 'claiming fatherhood adds expenses that might be spared by leaving paternity ambiguous until children reach an age at which they may be useful' (Bledsoe 1980b: 40). My data confirm this in that children under the age of 7 are legally assigned to their mothers. However, oath-taking and the resulting responsibilities make such postponements impossible. 'Scratching matches on the face' means that a woman or girl really does not know, or claims not to know, who impregnated her. In that case, all the lovers she calls are asked to assemble and to either agree on the 'one who must accept the pregnancy' or take an oath one after another. Then the family chooses the person who is to be held responsible for the pregnancy.

In both cases, men and boys swear an oath on the Qur'an or the Bible (depending on their faith), on some money, usually SLL 2,000 (GBP 0.18) or SLL 5,000 (GBP 0.45), and on a bowl of water. They take an oath that says: 'I swear to the Holy Bible/the Qur'an and the ancestors that I never lay with that girl'. After taking the oath, they are asked to drink the water and give the money to their father or mother. Through the oath, the power of religious deities and that of the ancestors are invoked simultaneously. Much as Elizabeth Tonkin described for Liberia, 'they [the gods and ancestors] are trusted as autonomous, unlike fallible human judgments' (Tonkin 2000: 366).[2] Annang concepts of oaths (*mbiam*) and ordeals (*ukang*) in Nigeria – which are very similar to the Mende *hale* in Freetown – have been described by David Pratten as 'truth-determining performative devices' (Pratten 2006: 726). This has also been observed in the Sierra Leonean fishing town of Tissana by Jennifer Diggins, who described the use of *ifohn*, or 'swear medicines', as truth-determining devices in theft cases (Diggins 2014: 218–27).

In Freetown, if the man or boy never had sex with the girl in question, he has nothing to fear and he remains unharmed (see Tonkin 2000). If he did, he must fear that the '*swear* catches him', which may result in illness or even death because, after taking the oath, he drinks the water, which now carries the oath. By giving the money to one of his parents, he further implicates them, and the oath may also 'catch them', leading to their sickness and possible death. If a man or boy has had intercourse with the woman or girl whose parents are initiating the oath, he usually admits to it in order to avoid the oath. If he admits to having had intercourse, he simultaneously accepts responsibility for the pregnancy. Usually, *ansa bɛlɛ* is initiated thereafter.

Another powerful form of violence women may use is temptation. Temptation is the manipulation of the 'power of female eroticism' (Groes-Green 2013: 103). It can be invoked with the use of love potions like *fala-fala*, *tay-tay*, *rɔb-rɔb*, or the *lɛk-lɛk*. Popular songs, like Emmerson's 2016 song 'Love Potion', describe how a man falls madly in love with a woman he never noticed before after she mixes a love potion in his food. Small portions of *fala-fala* or *lɛk-lɛk* can be purchased from apprentices of traditional doctors on Freetown's public transport. For strong potions and lasting spells, a traditional doctor must be consulted in person. *Fala-fala* and *lɛk-lɛk* can be absorbed by a man via his digestive tract or through his sperm. One evening, when members of EAUC explained the dangers of women to me, Lamin (20) summarised the preceding conversation:

> It is because of *lɛk-lɛk* and *fala-fala* that many men have started using condoms or why they do not let women leave the room straight after sex or want to watch her clean herself in front of them rather than in a bathroom because they are afraid that she might capture the sperm in a bottle and take it to a traditional doctor to possess him and make him fall madly in love with her and do anything she says. With *fala-fala*, a man will follow a woman wherever she goes, and she can send him to do whatever she needs. With *lɛk-lɛk*, he likes her so much that nothing else matters besides her.

---

[2] For a discussion of sasswood poison ordeals in south-eastern Liberia, see Tonkin (2000), who compares these to practices in medieval Europe, explores changes over time, and analyses their dramaturgy and political significance.

That such spells can be transferred through food can make difficult demands on people. 'Eating together is a sign of love and trust. If you refuse someone's food, not only are you showing that you are malicing that person, but you are also suspicious of their activity and afraid that they may cause you harm', Mammie Zainab explained (see Figure 5.1).

Understanding Male and Female Forms of Violence

How can the differences between female and male forms of violence be understood? Men's descriptions of female violence as 'worse' than male violence could be interpreted as an attempt to justify the violence they exert against women. But if we take seriously men's fear of temptation, revenge, and trapping, another interpretation arises. In this case, men fully recognise and fear female power. In Sierra Leone, it is women rather than men that are the pillars of society. Consider women's positions within households, where they form the nucleus, and their socioeconomic position often as the main breadwinner. They are the ones who nourish relationships within their families and maintain social relations. Furthermore, women can bring life into this world (Scubla 2016). This is paramount in a country where forming a household and having 'wealth in people' (Bledsoe 1980a) determine social status. Male violence may therefore be understood as an attempt to control this gift over life, to diminish women's superiority, and to 'put women in their place', as Rafieu and many others said. Thus, women and girls may be exposed to unacceptable male violence, not because they are marginalised, but rather because they are strong and powerful. Accordingly, accusing women of temptation may be an attempt to turn on its head the power that women exert over men. Rather than accepting that they are attracted to women or submit to the female power of seduction (see Groes-Green 2013 for Mozambique), men depict this attraction not as a natural emotion, but as a female construction to control them. These trends are captured by the literature on changing economies and the crisis of masculinity (see, e.g. Morrell 2001). It speaks about the specific struggles men face as household, marriage, and employment systems change. It analyses male violence to regain control over their livelihoods, families, and partners, and sees it as an attempt to regain and renegotiate the 'upper hand'. My research, too, suggests that the construction of female 'powerlessness' is a response to women's actual power and not to its absence.

Another interpretation is that women hold the power over life but are subjected to patriarchal authority and thus live within its bounds. The violence they execute ensures that, while men are officially and politically in power, women remain socially so. Their violence is both unacceptable and necessary. It is unacceptable because it scares men as a possibility and a threat; even the most extreme forms of protection, such as not leaving sperm behind or never accepting food, do not guarantee one will be completely safe from it. At the same time, it is necessary as it keeps men's behaviour in check and ensures that women remain in control over the gift of life and the direction of households.

If we take male and female forms of violence seriously and accept them as real, we can see that within a dynamic moral economy of relationships there are different forms of power and different forms of violence, which are enacted in constant negotiations between individuals involved in intimate relations and communities at large. The lines between them are blurred as positions are constantly negotiated and renegotiated. But, overall, men exert violence to punish, while women attempt to hold on to relationships. In a society where men are said to 'be for themselves' (Gas) and to 'easily break away', women try to bind partners to themselves. Whether it is temptation, trapping, or revenge, the main aim seems to be to show partners, who usually have a lot of power over relationships, that they should not try to just leave. A popular adage, that 'women are the honey and men are the bees', captures this sentiment. 'It means', explained Mammie Fatu (73), who lives at King George's old age home,

that women are the sweetest and most irresistible juice. So, men, who are the bees, want to do nothing more but taste, or even better bathe in that honey. But they underestimate the binding power behind the sweetness. No sooner they touch the honey, the honey sticks to them, and in their attempt to free themselves, they may sting, but once they exhaust stinging, they may well die. That is why men need to be wary of what they taste.

While the binding power of honey, however, is difficult to detect, the violence predominantly executed by men is traceable and provable. Showing marks or injuries and calling witnesses is enough. Darren commented:

Our compounds here are very small, and almost every activity is seen out in the open. Almost nobody has a private room, and usually we only have curtains not doors, and the children sleep with the parents in the room. When you lie in a room, you hear every word the neighbours say. No, we all know everything that goes on as long as it is spoken out loud.

At the compounds where I stayed, every conversation, even if spoken in hushed voices, was heard and commented upon. Whether desired or not residents became involved in all the ups and downs, the fights and reconciliations, the expressions of friendship, love, desire, anger, pain, and hate of others. I was in everyone's relationships, and they were in mine.

In my fieldwork, I have never encountered a household or community case in which it was impossible to find a witness to testify about the conversations or quarrels that took place between those implicated. In contrast, female violence happens in the invisible realm and only its effects are visible. Unless a woman acknowledges that she executed such violence or agrees to see a traditional healer, her involvement cannot be proven. Furthermore, it is mostly men who speak about and exchange stories regarding unacceptable female violence. Women usually make general comments such as 'Yes, we are very powerful, you will not see it coming'. This nourishes the power that is said to underlie such violence. Therefore, while household and community can, in theory, mediate male and female forms of violence (apart from temptation), it is predominantly visible forms of violence that are reported to households and community, as we will see in the next chapter.

Languages of Past and Present Structure Assessments of Violence

Moral economies develop between partners and build a framework for the ways in which partners behave towards each other. The terminology used to describe forms of violence and acts of violence shows how the moral economy bridges long-standing local perceptions and new influences by linguistic means. Anthropologists such as Mariane Ferme (2001) and Michael Jackson (2017) have revealed how speech is used to cloud or withhold information in Sierra Leone. Ferme notes that 'ambivalence is prized' (Ferme 2001: 7) among the Mende of Sierra Leone. 'Great value is attached to verbal artistry that couches meaning in puns, riddles, and cautionary tales and to unusual powers of understanding that enable people to both produce and unmask highly ambiguous meanings' (Ferme 2001: 7). Indeed, fine terminological differences between relationship forms and between different acts of violence carry worlds of meaning that are 'provided in encoded form, rather than withheld' (Ferme 2001: 230). In contemporary Freetown, this clouded, metaphorical communication, which seems elusive to outsiders but which is full of meaning for those it addresses, can be found in descriptions of violence. Ferme underlines the local importance of such clouded communication by showing that people who use direct speech and committed statements are 'considered idiotic or no better than children' (Ferme 2001: 7). If this insight is applied to the different ways women speak about and practise violence, it strengthens the perception of women as subtle yet self-controlled leaders. In contrast, legal language is direct and unambiguous.

When we compare how Sierra Leoneans themselves use the languages of love and violence with the language of law and justice instruments (including the risk-oriented language in which development discourses and practical interventions are phrased), we can see the potential for misunderstanding. This can have consequences for how laws and interventions are received and how effective they are. Moreover, local practices can be misunderstood if meaning is not carefully translated between these different systems of communication. As we have seen, the term 'violence', on its own, is meaningless. It tells no story and consequently allows no judgement. Hence, statements such as 'violence against women is wrong' or, as former President Koroma stated, 'violence against women is violence against the state' (see Chapter 8) find their way into local parlance as floating signifiers. They 'represent an undetermined quantity of signification, in itself void of meaning and thus apt to receive any meaning' (Mehlman 1972: 23; see Lévi-Strauss 1950: 63–4). Social campaigns consequently miss their goals if they use these unstable concepts to address social issues. As they travel down, they attract meanings and interpretations but fail to capture and communicate any specific message. Indeed, only a few Sierra Leoneans feel addressed by such campaigns at all. Apart from sweeping generalisations, people tend to avoid the word 'violence', except to make a broad, undifferentiated claim. When research collaborators explained their love histories to me, often within the first minutes they would issue a statement like 'Men are violent too much', or 'Women are very, very wicked; that is their violence'. Immediately thereafter, however, they would contextualise this statement by describing how and in which ways they experienced violence in their relationships. Hence, they relied not on overall claims but instead on specific terminologies. These form a language of violence that carries a message that can be read and decoded by others. What this shows is that, besides love, violence is an analytical problem, rather than a universal category, which must be solved by understanding its emotional embeddedness in 'historically situated words, cultural practices, and material conditions' (Cole and Thomas 2009: 3).

In Freetown today, people draw on all three influences: metaphors, specific acts, and legal language. Indeed, direct speech and metaphorical speech exist side by side and must be used and combined in specific ways. When violence is described or adjudged, the evaluation of individuals and of the relationship they have with each other follows the language of metaphors, while the specific acts of violence are described by referring directly to the act that occurred. However, as we have seen, specific terms for acts are firmly tied to their social evaluation. To understand how violence is spoken about, understood, practised, and perceived at different levels of society and to unravel misunderstandings, we must consider 'not what words mean in essence, but what they are made to mean in the contexts of everyday life' (Jackson 2019: 60). These nuances in language and performance render intelligible complex sets of emotions and help us understand how the same act can change from a desired moment of communicated affection to an instance of hurtful violent expression. Giving someone the cold shoulder, for instance, can turn to neglect when performed openly and then becomes a form of unacceptable violence. However, if it occurs in private or is not noticed by a partner, it constitutes a common form of moving on. What is perceived as violence is therefore dynamic, constantly evolving, and influenced by the presence of others. Hence, while teeth and tongue unquestionably need each other, the way in which they relate to each other, engage with each other, and may hurt each other is a point of ongoing contestation. It is through the language of violence and careful analysis of social relations that we are able to capture a phenomenon as complex as interpersonal violence in its context.

Within the moral economy, the overall situation – including the persons involved and the acts committed – is evaluated by recourse to the words 'acceptable' or 'unacceptable'. While acceptable violence is mediated interpersonally and almost never openly discussed with others, occurrences of unacceptable violence break the bonds of the moral economy and thus the confidentiality of the partnership. Hence, revelation and disguise play an important role in negotiations over acceptability. Burrill, Roberts, and Thornberry observed that, if the limits of the moral economy are transgressed, those who were harmed report to 'various forums for dispute resolution, whether informal kinship meetings or formal courts, often invoking this very idea of inappropriate violence' (Burrill, Roberts, and Thornberry 2010: 66). Similarly, the reporting that follows acts of unacceptable violence in Sierra Leone is built on the involvement of others, who then become the judges of persons, forms, and acts, as we will see in the next chapters.

6 Household and Community Mediations of Violence

Unacceptable violence is not always negotiated internally between partners; it sometimes involves various other parties. Non-state dispute mediations range from informal conversations with confidants to household arbitration and extensive community hearings. When Sierra Leoneans turn to their household or community to arbitrate violence they find unbearable, the process of such mediations follows a format that has been observed for other forms of disputes (especially concerning murder and land conflicts)[1] in various parts of Africa (see, for instance, Comaroff and Roberts 1981). Its features resemble the Kpelle moot, which Gibbs (1963) documented in Liberia. In Sierra Leone, a household or a community cooperatively presides over cases brought before it. Aiming at resolution, households and communities seek to maintain, not rupture, relationships. Violent acts are re-embedded into the larger social context in which they occurred, and what is on trial is not specific acts but a person's overall comportment. Various eyewitnesses and character witnesses are called, before the elders pass judgement. In these mediations, there is never a single wrongdoer, and punishment tends to be issued to those on both sides of a dispute, albeit unevenly. This highlights a distinct approach to justice, assigning shared responsibility for the violence committed and seeing the obligation to contain grievances and conflicts as relational (see Gibbs 1963; Comaroff and Roberts 1981).

Cases of household or community mediation in Sierra Leone can be distinguished from what has been observed elsewhere (see, for instance, Porter 2017 for Uganda or Gibbs 1963 for Liberia) in several respects. Here, the aim is not to preserve or generate social harmony. Instead, the hearings often force painful compromises, which are seen as necessary to maintain functioning social groups. Communities and households do not

---

[1] Take, for instance, Max Gluckman's study of the Lozi court processes of the Barotse. Here, judges considered contextual factors, locality, and litigants' lifestyles in their decision-making processes rather than focus mainly on acts committed (Gluckman 1963).

presume to resolve grievances, which to them constitute an unavoidable part of the human experience, but rather believe that they must be contained. Through various rituals such as 'swallowing' (see below), grievances are trapped in the bodies of individuals. This prevents those who bear grudges from acting on their hard feelings directly or releasing them into the wider community where they could infiltrate other bodies, cause bad blood, and eat away at the fabric of the community.

Kinship and gender dynamics further individualise solutions in that the weight of a witness's testimony varies greatly, depending on their relationship to those directly affected and to the community at large. This renders mediation outcomes highly case-dependent, and similar cases can lead to widely different assessments. Despite the prominence of women in the hearings, they are punished harder, both because the expectations of their behaviour are higher and because they are seen to be better able to bear and live with injustices. Moreover, younger litigants may suffer when the presiding elders act in the interest of community and custom while the young may be driven by needs and desires that diverge from these very customs.

Finally, such mediation processes are not only political in seeking to maintain functioning households and communities, but they are also greatly concerned with cultivating a relationship to state courts that is characterised by friendly distance. The aim is to be able to invoke the state if necessary, but to keep the state from finding its way into communities without the explicit invitation of the elders.[2] Scholars interested in legal pluralism have examined such manoeuvres elsewhere and have helped us to understand these as sociopolitical tactics, a performance of internal harmony vis-à-vis an external power – here the Sierra Leonean state – to keep state interference to a minimum (Gibbs 1963; Nader 1990; Pirie 2007; Porter 2017).[3]

Informal Ways of Reporting Unacceptable Violence

Research collaborators from the Allentown, Naimbana, and Kroo Bay communities use several tactics to respond to violence that they find unbearable. Apart from causing ruptures by breaking off relationships, avoiding persons, or spreading rumours (Ferme 2001; Rasmussen

---

[2] If cases are handed over to the state, they usually leave the locality of the community and enter the arena of formal state offices.

[3] This relationship distinguished the truth and reconciliation processes from war-crime tribunals (Shaw 2007; Shaw, Waldorf, and Hazan 2010; Ainley, Friedman, and Mahony 2015) and now shapes the difference between community and household mediations and the criminal justice process in Sierra Leone.

2001), such responses are usually geared towards resolving issues and maintaining relationships (Gibbs 1963).[4] An important part of mediation is sharing the emotions one harbours. Experiences of violence are negotiated in conversations with friends, neighbours, or other confidants. Such discussions are considered informal and do not initiate an official case. It is, for example, very common for women and girls to show injuries and marks to one another. Friends and acquaintances may offer advice on their treatment and listen attentively to descriptions of how they were inflicted, but they do not make authoritative comments about the relationship.

Consider how Issa (33), a woman from Allentown whose case I describe below, was treated by loved ones and acquaintances. Issa's boyfriend was physically violent towards her and often left her with deep and open injuries, some of which became infected. Her friends and neighbours visited with gifts of ointments for her injuries and provided tips on how she could treat and conceal them. What mattered was supporting her, not expressing personal opinions. Alhaji (30), an Okada bike-rider and one of her closest friends, once told her after a particularly harmful altercation with her boyfriend: 'Baby, use this cream, it will help you. That's how life is. One must just find a way to bear'. After she left to apply the cream, he turned to me and whispered: 'These injuries are very deep. They will leave scars. This man is wicked. She should leave him and find another'. When I asked him why he shared this opinion with me and not with her, he just shook his head at my ignorance and said:

> You don't know what is under and what is in it, and gossip is very bad. If you advise against [him], and then they reunite, you are the black monkey. If you stay outside, you are a better friend, and no matter what, she can come to you because you will not judge. It is not your business. She must make such decisions on her own.

In these situations, being a friend means providing the emotional support needed without presuming to know what is best. People appreciate that outsiders never see the full picture. They therefore differentiate between what is visible and apparent (such as Issa's injuries) and the emotional worlds that may exist but that are concealed (the intricacies of her relationship). Respecting those concealments and refraining from trying to penetrate them against a person's will is paramount for a true friend.

---

[4] In Freetown, a community is a group of people who live in a given area and who practise common ownership over that area. From any given house, these communities usually extend up to the next river, road, water tap, or big house that separates areas by means of high cement fences. In the absence of chiefs, authority is convened through elders.

Careful distinctions are drawn between someone who is 'sharing', someone who is seeking 'advice', and someone who is 'making a report'. Someone who shares must be met with an open ear to listen rather than with moving lips to voice personal opinions, pass judgement, or seek to influence the person who shares in any way. By contrast, advising takes the form of a subjective analysis of the pertinent situation. Finally, reporting is the only form of mediation that initiates an official case – a structured hearing of a matter presided over by community or religious institutions, with direct and often severe consequences for those involved.

Reporting to the Religious Community

It is common for a woman to report to religious institutions and confide in a pastor or imam, who is then asked to mediate a relationship on her behalf. However, with the exception of one case where an imam urged a woman to file for divorce because her husband had kicked her stomach when she was seven months pregnant, causing her to miscarry, women were told to 'bear' their partners in all 23 cases of reporting that I followed. Here, one can cite the example of Mariama (30), one of my main research collaborators from the informal settlement of Susan's Bay, whom I have known for eight years. She met her boyfriend shortly after we were introduced by Sabrina, a mutual friend, in 2012. 'Back then he catered to her every need', said Sabrina (28), beginning to explain Mariama's love story:

Because she was serious about the guy, she took him to her church and introduced him to her pastor, which is what Christians in Freetown do. A couple of months later, she found out that the boyfriend has another girlfriend who is staying in the US. When she confronted him, he admitted it and explained that he has been with this woman for many years, but that she should not be jealous because the woman is not here. Mariama felt that this put her in the situation of only a time-filler, rather than a girlfriend whom he would consider marrying, and consulted her pastor. The pastor told her to be patient with the man.

A couple of weeks later, the guy stopped contacting her and providing for her. After trying to reach him for several weeks, she went to his house only to catch him in the room with another woman. He introduced this other woman as his girlfriend, leaving her in shock. Now she told the pastor that she wants to cut off the relationship, but the pastor told her that it is not a woman's choice when a relationship should be terminated and that she should be patient with him and try to win him back rather than make things difficult for him.

Later that day, the girl was invited to a party by a male friend and decided to attend. The boyfriend, who had not spoken to her in weeks, heard of this. Furiously, he showed up at the party, created a huge scene, and took her home. At home, he dragged her into his room, shut the door, and locked it with the key, which he then threw under the bed. He gave her a serious, serious beating and raped her because he believed that she had cheated on him by going to the party. When she went to the pastor with a bruised face, telling the pastor that she had been raped and beaten, asking the pastor to please allow her to terminate the relationship, the pastor got very upset with her and her behaviour, explaining in rage that women need to be modest and cater to their man's needs and that she should have never gone somewhere where she would anger her man that much.

There were echoes of Mariama's story in other examples where women had turned to their church in search of support in what to them was a painful situation. Instead, they were told that they had misbehaved by questioning their partners, being overly demanding or putting their needs for attention, fidelity, or affection before those of the relationship. Overall, the church was often described to me as an institution that promotes a specific relationship – that of a married couple with a male breadwinner and a female dependant – whose maintaining requires 'patience and bearing'.[5] Women are said to shoulder great responsibility in that they are tasked with making sure that relationships last. Marriages may only be ended in the rarest and severest cases. Pastor Michael (54) said:

We [the church] do not allow people to just get married. First, they must undergo counselling for months and months during which they learn about the roles and responsibilities of lifelong marriage. Otherwise, we do not bless and do not allow the marriage. So, when they are married, we do not encourage people to separate. And in relationships, it is the same. Only after careful evaluation should you enter, and you should always find the fault with you and change yourself, not the other person. Yes, maybe there is some violence involved, but if you have the patience, you can have a successful and happy relationship.

Here, church and community share a similar goal. Both try to prevent separations that would lead to the dissolution of households, affinities, and carefully spun webs of reciprocity developed through exchanges of goods, people and money. However, while communities attempt to enable such continuity by punishing those who harmed others so as to manage grievances, keep people in line, and prevent resentment from becoming an insurmountable obstacle to stability, churches seem to ask their members to 'bear'. Finding fault with yourself rather than your partner is the quintessence of the practice of bearing. Isatu (27), Papani's daughter, exclaimed in response to a radio broadcast that stated that far more women go to church than men:

Of course! They have so much more to pray for and little options. Here, women can hardly get active against injustice. Only with these traditional stuffs, but the God-fearing woman must choose to sit in silence and pray. If she truly believes in

---

[5] For studies on gender and Pentecostalism, see Meyer 2004; Gilbert 2016.

God, she will accept whatever comes her way. They [such women] leave everything in the hands of God and pray for their husband to be less wicked, their aunt to treat them better, and their children to respect them. So, the more goes wrong, the more they must go to church.

The difference between 'sweet revenge' (Chapter 5) and 'God-fearing persons' was an undercurrent of many interviews.[6] Research collaborators spoke especially about the passivity of the Christian approach to resolution, as opposed to the active approach of more traditional variants. Prayer was often pitted against 'sweet revenge', the feminine form of violence described in the last chapter, which is marked by proactive avenging.[7] Different forms of reporting provide a middle ground between taking direct counteraction in the form of revenge and passive bearing through prayer.

Keeping It in the House: Household Mediations

When partners report violence that they find unbearable to their household or community, the first decision to be reached is whether the offended party wants to keep the issue 'in their house' and therefore private or involve other parties and thus 'carry it to their porch', as the local terminology has it. Carrying it to the porch does not necessarily mean that it will become public. Rather, it means that people who do not usually eat and sleep under the same roof will become part of the mediation process.

If people decide to keep the issue in the house, they call upon the elder(s) of the house to mediate. Every household has a male and a female elder. These are the oldest consanguine or affinal relatives who live in the household. The elders then consider the different sides of the grievance before they decide how it should be resolved. Another option is to report violence in relationships to the patrons who were chosen upon entering the relationship – usually a senior consanguine female family member, very often one's mother, grandmother, or eldest sister. These mediators then convene a meeting with all parties involved, discuss the issue at hand, and decide on the appropriate course of action. Whichever

---

[6] These ideas also underpin the dialogue between personal autonomy, rights, and protection. The 'guardian function' of (human) rights may restrict personal autonomy in the interest of empowering or protecting marginal groups (see Chapters 8 and 9). In Sierra Leone, we see similar dynamics in households, schools, courts, and prisons (see Chapters 3, 4, 5, 8, and 9).

[7] The question remains whether leaving things to God is equal to forgoing revenge or merely postponing it. Believers may find comfort in leaving the possibility of punishment to God, who will surely judge everyone.

form is chosen, the mediators' decision must be adhered to. Since what is at stake goes beyond the particular conflict and concerns the overall stability of the household. The elders' or patrons' decision marks the end of the case. Reopening it by discussing it with others is an offence. Mr Bah (in his seventies), one elder of the Naimbana community, elucidated:

> We do not encourage *kongosa* [gossip]. During a case, you should let out all the things that are in your heart so that they can be aired out once and for all. If you hold it in and let it out later, you act childish and stupid, and you will destroy the solution that was found. If you start gossiping about the matter later after you should have swallowed it, we will surely punish you for that.

Grudges, even irrationally severe ones, can and should be disclosed while the case is being discussed. Here litigants are encouraged to call each other every name in the book if that is necessary to vent their anger. Those presiding over cases make sure that all those involved can share and take as much time as they need to express whatever feelings they have been harbouring. However, once all testimonies have been heard, the time to vent is over and litigants must now let their anger go or hold their tongue. This is why cases end with swallowing. Whatever has not been said or openly felt at that time must now be swallowed and silently lived with.

Taking It to the Porch: Palaver and the Structures of Community Mediations

'Taking it to the porch' can be accomplished in two ways. The first approach, typically utilised by women, is to 'make palaver'. Women create a commotion by shouting at or insulting the perpetrator, stepping in front of their house, banging pots and pans together, in order to garner the attention of others, who then come and intervene. This strategy is usually chosen in response to physical or sexual violence and only rarely results in a community mediation.

When someone makes a report to community elders, usually within a few days a group of kinsmen, neighbours, and community members, which varies in size depending on the case, gathers to preside over the issue and decide cooperatively on the way forward. These mediations are like those practised by chiefs (male leaders) or mammie queens (*mami kwins*) (female leaders) in village settings (see Coulter 2005: 36).[8]

---

[8] For studies of chiefs' mediation practices beyond Sierra Leone, see E. E. Evans-Pritchard's (1940: 162) work on 'leopard-skin chiefs' or Isaac Schapera's (1994) on Tswana chiefs.

However, while chiefs usually have sole decision-making power, these urban community mediations are much more democratic in that they include all those implicated as well as trusted character witnesses. Those attending are supposed to form an organic whole focussed on finding a solution so as to move past the conflict rather than create further ruptures.

The opening of such sittings is marked by Christian and Muslim prayers, the pronouncement of blessings, and a reminder to maintain respect for all persons involved – *Lɛh wi lɛk wi sɛf. Lɛh wi tray fɔ setul di mata wantɛm. Lɛh wi nɔ mek plaba* (Let us like/love each other. Let us try to solve this issue now. Let us not fight or quarrel). These blessings are a reminder that the task is to solve a problem, not to create harm.

The case commences with the account of the claimant. After they have finished, an interrogation may follow, and questions can be asked by anyone present. Afterwards, the accused testifies and is subjected to questioning by those present. Then the two parties may engage in direct cross-examination and involve other attendees (see also Gibbs 1963 for Liberia). Subsequently, witness statements are heard. These can be of two categories. First, people who were either present or directly consulted by the litigants give their accounts. Then community members, neighbours, and kin are called upon to give an evaluation of the litigants' character, social standing, and responsibility. While accounts and questionings are energetic, nobody loses sight of the seriousness of the assembly and proceedings usually remain orderly. People who speak out of turn or spread *kongosa*, which includes all speculations and unproven comments, and those who make palaver may be fined or excluded from the proceedings. After all statements are made, the elders weigh the differing views against each other and then assign responsibility, fines, and punishment. The proceedings are held orally. They are not transcribed, and no written statements or summaries are issued at any stage. Instead, at the outset of any proceeding, one elder summarises what had happened till then.

Rarely is the blame for wrongdoing placed on one side only. Instead, it is usually shared, though unequally. The verdict reached includes penalties for both parties, and it is expected that all involved will comply with it. Before sentencing, the elders ask if there is any other issue, worry, or statement that needs to be considered. If attendees remain silent, no appeal is subsequently allowed. Consequently, no archive of any kind exists. Once a case is closed, it is closed forever unless a new case is opened. Before proceedings end, those found to be at fault are made to apologise publicly. All grievances must from now on be kept to oneself. This ritualised apology at the end and the public acknowledgement that all issues have now been attended are what is called 'swallowing'. Thereafter, gifts and tokens of appreciation exchange hands. These are brought by all sides involved in a dispute and handed to those who preside over the case and to the side found least guilty. Those who are found to be 'most wrong' must contribute the biggest share. Here again, we see the importance of exchanges and gifts in creating binding obligations. Before the crowd disperses, food and beverages are consumed together. This can lead to a social gathering with songs and dances that may carry on into the night, the intention being to restore or increase community cohesion. The litigants may participate or go their way.

It is almost always women who are assigned as community elders and who preside over such cases. In her critical study of gendered dynamics in Africa, Oyèrónkẹ́ Oyěwùmí foregrounds the importance of seniority over gender (Oyěwùmí 2005). Similarly, Caroline Bledsoe, writing about women and marriage among the Kpelle, notes that 'the distinction between the old and young may ... be more important in understanding people's ... strategies in many African societies than the distinction between men and women' (Bledsoe 1980a: 186). However, when it comes to community mediations of violence in Sierra Leone, age and gender reinforce each other (Chapters 3 and 4). Female elders are the mediators of and main decision-makers in cases of violence for historical, practical, and ideological reasons. Historically, this builds on the role of mammie queens, who were responsible for conflict mediation (Coulter 2009). Practically, women are responsible for directing and managing family affairs and hence for looking after younger people. Furthermore, it is women who run their business from home or are at least at home daily and who are confidantes in relationship matters. Hence, they are the ones who are called upon in the event of pregnancies, and it is usually they who initiate *ansa bele* and marriage and who work on deepening the ties between different families. Men's role, on the other hand, becomes important much later when the formal ceremonies occur. Moreover, if a person is sick or harmed, it is the women who accompany them to the hospital or the court. But women are not only influential in supporting others; they are also the key persons when it comes to evaluating social behaviour and to disciplining wrongdoers. Men are often absent and said to 'not really know' what goes on in a home. They are perceived to be too selfish, hot-tempered, and short-sighted to preside over complex cases. Furthermore, as regards emotions and desire, the conduct of men is commonly seen as consisting of responses to women's behaviour.

Finally, in terms of ideology, women are described as better able to put the needs of a household before their own and more able to understand the needs of all those involved. Hence, it is mainly women who facilitate and oversee community mediations, and the elder women of each compound are the main mediators of violence in relationships and in the home. The teeth (male) are the independent grinders and the tongue (female) the social connector to other parts of the (social) body.

Ethnographic Accounts of Cases

Josephus and Issa: Violence against the Body and by the Tongue

The 33-year-old Issa stays with her son, Lamin (11), in a one-room self-contained space attached to Josephus's compound in Allentown, the hillside community in eastern Freetown where I lived. Josephus, one of Papani's sons, owns the compound to the left of our house. He is Issa's boyfriend and her landlord at the same time. Issa's husband, the father of her child, lives elsewhere. He pays her rent and occasionally visits unannounced to check on her fidelity. Josephus and Issa have a complicated relationship. Issa told Josephus at the outset that she had left her husband because he was very violent but did not divorce him (a process known as 'seizing to continue'). Issa and Josephus entered a contract relationship, which is one in which both parties may see other people so long as they do not bring another sexual partner to the shared compound (Chapter 3). Issa cooks and cleans for Josephus, takes care of his children, and tries to build a relationship with his family. One morning while I kept her company as she was braiding the hair of Josephus's daughter, Issa told me:

> I went into the relationship without any expectation, but Josephus told me to try to be serious with him. He gave me the hope of a bright future. He always tells me sweet words like 'I love you so much. I never feel for anyone like I feel for you. I want you to be the mama of my children ... I want to marry you'. He sleeps at mine on most nights. When he is out, he always calls me and sends for me ... but, ah, that man is not serious. All lies!

As she said this, laughing all the while, she rubbed her hands against each other as if to wipe dirt off her palms. Lansana (38), Josephus's cousin, remarked:

> Josephus is what we call a 'passer-by', a man who creates a vacuum of hope around a relationship by telling a woman that he loves her and wants to marry her, so the woman feels that this is serious and goes all in. Then once she realises that there is a vacuum, he tries to fill that with company or compensation or promises or excuses for some time, until it all collapses and the man moves on to another woman, repeating the same actions again.

But Josephus is not the only one who has a box full of tricks. Issa, who grew up in the informal settlement of Kroo Bay and later supported herself through relationships with men in the Naimbana Street ghetto, describes herself as 'a real devil who can trick men into doing circus tricks'. She tests Josephus to judge the veracity of his promises. She explains: 'You know I used to have many boyfriends who took care of me. Yes, I am well known. I have a police officer, even a minister. Josephus, he is not serious if he expects me to only keep him; he needs to provide'.

Consequently, their relationship is a constant dance of needs, demands, conflicts, and compromises. To give just one example: when, after months of unemployment, Josephus got a job at a construction firm, he suddenly had an income and started spending most nights away. For a few weeks, Issa took care of his children and his compound. Then she decided that she had had enough. She left and stayed with friends in a different part of Freetown. On the nights Josephus came home, he found her missing. On two Saturdays in a row, a disgruntled Josephus had to wash his own laundry, with the mocking sounds of the women from neighbouring compounds in his ear. When Issa visited after that, he beat her with a belt until her back and arms were bleeding, and the neighbours intervened and told him to stop. But Issa would not be beaten into submission. When he realised that the beatings were not going to make her stay, he decided to give her some money to help her start a business. She then began to sell fishballs to the community. However, as Josephus was mostly absent and she sought to enjoy her newly gained financial independence, Issa went out more and more. Once Josephus learnt about this from his friends who reported on her moves, the violence escalated. Josephus explained:

When I have a woman, I expect her to be available and to give me sex always. She needs to be around whenever I am in need; otherwise, she cannot expect nothing. But Issa now, she is wild. She just goes out like that, and then my friends who see her call me and tell me where she was passing with so-and-so dress and so-and-so person. My women don't pass like that, I am telling you. When I ask her now, if she lies, *bam*, I will beat her like a plastic bag in the wind. Even if she tells me the truth, I have to punish her before it becomes a habit. When they [women] are like that, I cannot accept it.

Aunty Kadie, Josephus's mother, added: 'Josephus will never compromise. He is known for becoming very physical and very violent when it comes to sex'. Over time, Josephus and Issa's conflicts escalated. After Issa aborted her third unwanted pregnancy, which occurred after being sexually assaulted by Josephus, she suffered from abdominal cramps, fatigue, and bleeding. When she threatened to leave him, he started to 'beat in' her face to make her unattractive for other suitors. When I asked him about this, he told me:

For us men, it is very easy to get women. In a day, you can get one. Easy! But women are wicked; they do things to you to make you feel for them and not another one. Issa now, she is mine. Let her dare go out and try to find someone with that face. I marked her. Everyone will see that she has a main man already.

Here, Josephus describes possession as mutual. Because Issa possesses him emotionally, he retaliates by physically possessing Issa through the 'mark' and through his economic contributions. This relates to the 'female' violence described in Chapter 5, where women can tie men to them emotionally and men attempt to retaliate through economic or physical violence (see also Scubla 2016).

Even though neighbours secretly condemn this violence, they do not intervene because Issa is officially married to another man. Here, a quote shared by Jaydee to EAUC's WhatsApp group on 29 July 2018 is telling. It reads: 'In Sierra Leone most girls have two boyfriends. The one they are deceiving and the one who is deceiving them'. Although separations without divorce and the commencement of new relationships are common, they are still transgressions. While families, neighbours, and the community accept such couples in their midst, they usually 'stay out of the relationship'. Bintu (56) from Allentown says that 'everybody now has these relationships. But still they are based on deceiving other partners you know. We don't mind such relationships, but we want to stay out of it. Because if you now get involved in something that is built on lies and then it collapses, you will be buried under it'.

While staying out of other people's business is motivated by respect for privacy and intimacy and a deep hatred of the destructive qualities of gossip, it is also partly a residue of previous forms of social organisation. In the past, marriage was the official relationship form. Because marriages built lasting relations between families, kin had a strong interest in the success of the union and mediated problems when they arose. While more individual and fluid relationships certainly existed, they were not lived openly, and others did not publicly involve themselves in them. While non-marital relationships can now be lived openly, they do not offer the same security as marriages because today, when people are not married, or at least have not undergone *ansa bɛlɛ*, family and community have no official responsibilities. There is no expectation of intervention. Those who think about becoming involved enter unregulated territory and risk being blamed or punished when their mediation backfires. Issa and Josephus's case is one such example. It is also complicated by the fact that Issa is in fact married and that her family and the guardian she chose on getting married could at any moment decide to get involved too. Here, neighbours must consider not only whether they want to start mediating an unregulated relationship but also whether they are willing to run the risk of undermining the authority of people who are strangers to them. However, in Issa's case the neighbours' non-engagement changed because of the event that I will now describe.

The Incidents Leading to the Community Case

One evening in December 2016, I was sitting in my usual spot on the small wall that surrounds the veranda in front of the compound I share with others, my knees drawn up to my stomach, trying to capture the events of the day in the small notebook balanced on my knees. My thoughts were interrupted when Aunty Eleanor approached and explained in a hushed voice that Uncle Josephus had brought a lady home. Snapping out of my reverie, I realised how tense the atmosphere was. Issa was indoors in the room adjacent to Josephus while he was inside with another woman 'sexing her', as Aunty Eleanor repeatedly said, while five children slept in the adjacent room, separated only by a curtain. The news spreads quickly. The men of the neighbourhood gather at Papani's bar and the women at our veranda: everyone holds their breath. At first, Issa does not create a scene. Rather, she retreats to her room and calls upon her girlfriends. Giggling women hurry through the night purchasing alcohol, cigarettes, and marijuana from Papani, who runs a store from his bedroom window, to drown their sorrows; quietly complaining about the 'senselessness' of men. However, at some point during the evening the woman Josephus brought home comes outside and sits openly on the veranda. While she is probably unaware that the man she had sex with is sharing this house with his girlfriend, who is in the next room, her presence is a public insult to Issa. Everyone knew about her presence, but it was somewhat hidden, and it would have stayed that way had she remained inside. Now, the secret is out.

The woman sitting outside in the open and the sense of shame that seems to waft through the community leads Issa to complain loudly. When she does so, Josephus kicks down her door, plants himself threateningly in front of her, and commands her to stop accusing him. Seconds later, beating and wailing sounds cut through the silence of the night. The neighbours eventually force their way into the room after hearing the beatings for some time and pull Josephus away from Issa. He tells her that as a married woman she is being unfaithful to start with and therefore is not in a position to make any demands or to be upset. He then returns to his room. Some of the men provisionally fix the lock on Issa's door so that she can sleep safely, while Josephus spends the night next door with the new woman.

The next morning Josephus's *nyu ketch* – the term used to describe a new sexual partner – is still there. During the night, Issa started cursing. When I visit her the next day, she says that she heard Josephus "sexing" the woman, and that is when she started to *kɔs mami kɔs*, meaning that she started to call Josephus and his children bastards, a serious offence.⁹ The half-naked Josephus forces his way into Issa's room, grabs her by the hair, and drags her out of the compound. He beats and kicks her and threatens to either kill her or take her to CID headquarters in Freetown. This time, Issa's cries for help fall on deaf ears. The neighbours who had previously tried to pull him away retreat into their compounds and close their doors behind them. They lost all sympathy for Issa when she started to curse Josephus's mother, who, as an elder working in a government-run old age home, is one of the only women in the community with a steady income and has helped countless families in the neighbourhood in times of need. Eventually, Issa bites his finger, seizes his phone, and escapes to a neighbouring compound.¹⁰ In view of this commotion, a growing number of people gather around the compound and start to *put mɔt pan di fɛt* (to talk to people while they were fighting) while the doors of the immediately neighbouring huts remain shut. Whereas the night before they were disappointed with Josephus, their sympathies now lie with him. Mr Twin put it this way: 'Before we take Issa's side, because you know she takes care of the house and the children and Josephus should not bring his *kɛtch* home. But after the *mami kɔs*, ah, with her street background and such behaviours, she is only a dangerous *rare gal*'.

The Community Case Proceedings

Because the community peace has been disrupted and 'everyone's mouth is in the case', the community decided to intervene. The next day, they gathered to reach a decision about what should be done. Members of all neighbouring compounds were present. Mammie Zainab (64), the community elder, started proceedings by inviting two members of the community, one Christian, the other Muslim, to lead the opening prayers. In her calm voice, she stated: 'We have been called here because *wahala* has come to our community and has disturbed some of us. Let us take this time to settle the matter at once'. Mammie Zainab has been elected as community elder because she has lived in the community all her life. She is known by all and is deeply involved in the day-to-day affairs of most

---

⁹ Josephus has two children born out of wedlock from different women. The children were adopted by his mother, Aunty Kadie, who provides for them. Josephus was conceived when Aunty Kadie and Papani were not yet married. They married when she was in the third trimester of her pregnancy.

¹⁰ In numerous cases I recorded, women seized their partner's phone when they suspected or knew of infidelity and when their relationship status was insecure. By holding on to his contacts to other women, 'his numbers', they force their partner to reach an agreement in exchange for the phone and they protect themselves from a possible beating.

households as she goes around listening to people's concerns. She does not belong to a sodality, a church, or a mosque, and is therefore seen as able to represent the best interests of the community without bias or favour. The other elders were appointed, so that every ethnic, religious, and interest group had a representative. Mammie Zainab, the main elder, is described as patient and caring, but also as principled and rigorous.

After the opening statements, she called upon those who reported the incident to make their statements and then invited each member in turn to describe their side of the story. The attendees listened attentively to the proceedings, adding hisses, murmurs of agreement or disapproval, and signs of acknowledgement after each statement.

In the first session, Josephus's and Issa's accounts were heard. Josephus said that he did not invite the woman to come with him to his house, but that she simply followed him. Issa explained that Josephus beat her and that she had no defence other than to use words. She apologised for cursing and said that she should have never done that, and she should have known better how to control her emotions. She said she hoped that Josephus's family would forgive her and not hold a grudge. She added that she treated Josephus's children like her own and that she hoped that the community would judge her by these commitments instead. Then the elders decided that, because the curse was directed against her, Josephus's mother should be summoned and involved in the decision-making process.

On the second day, all the witnesses were called to report on the activities as well as generally on the relationship between Issa and Josephus. The first group described Josephus's disrespect not only towards Issa, but also towards his children and his parents and the community, when bringing a stranger to the compound for sex. They argued that Josephus should be made to take an oath on the Qur'an that he did not cause Issa's abortions.

The elders inspected Issa's injuries in private before listening to members of the second group. They stated that Issa was to blame because as a married woman she should never have entered the relationship in the first place. Josephus's frustration was understandable in the circumstances because the relationship could never lead to serious commitment and was therefore 'a waste of time'. This group pointed to Issa's bad manners and claimed that she had a warm heart and was easily angered. They explained that Josephus was from a good family with long relations with the community while Issa was almost a stranger. They agreed that Josephus used to be a 'useless man' without any job but pointed out that he had recently started to work. They further explained that Issa was known for keeping many men and that this behaviour was not good for the children in the house or the community, as she could easily provoke fighting between different suitors. They stated that it was sinful for her to have aborted children because children are a gift, and that Josephus could not be blamed for this because it was not even known whether he was responsible for the pregnancies. Afterwards, Josephus's mother, Aunty Kadie, and her family were invited to pass judgement, but they abstained.

According to the final judgement on the third day, while Josephus and Issa's relationship was not formal, their hearts chose each other. However, Josephus should either break off the relationship to Issa or abstain from bringing other lovers to the same house; such behaviour was a disgrace to the community and set a bad example for his children. Issa was obliged to pay a fine to Josephus's mother, which had to be paid in fishball deliveries to the old age home where she stays and works. She also had to publicly apologise, and, if she ever cursed or caused *wahala* in the community again, she would be expelled. Josephus should stop beating Issa with belts and sticks but should rather only slap with his hand if there was a significant disagreement. All members of the community were warned no longer to speak of this incident and to forgive and accept one another. Mammie Zainab's final conclusion was:

> We say that the heart has no bone; no matter what people do to each other, through love one can act irrationally and stupidly. When emotions are involved, people totally lose the ability to be consequent. That is why we all must ask ourselves what we are doing and whether it is right, *before*, and not *after*, we act. As adults, we need to comport ourselves responsibly and not like children.

Josephus then publicly 'begged' Issa for her forgiveness and she in turn 'begged' him and all those she had cursed. After deleting all his female contacts, she returned his phone to him. Food and drinks were distributed to all those present; these had been paid for jointly by Josephus and Issa. Issa and Josephus continue to be in a relationship and to live in the same compound.

Resolution through Contextualisation

What regulates behaviour and constitutes rules in these instances is shared social norms and social control rather than institutions of government. The offence of beating, for example, is not analysed apart from the circumstances in which it was committed. However, although personhood and context are distinguishing factors, there is a hierarchy of offences, in which cursing elders is worse than acts of physical violence in relationships (Chapter 4). More important than individual acts are one's general attitudes, behaviour, and social standing.

In this case, the physical and sexual violence to which Josephus subjected Issa as well as his infidelity was weighed against Issa's comportment, her marital status, and her cursing of Josephus's mother and children. Through their contributions, individual members at the hearing provided an assemblage of anecdotes detailing 'what kind of persons Issa and Josephus are'. This then served as a system of checks and balances against which the specific incidents were weighed. For example, Josephus's general hot-temperedness was balanced against his successful development from a 'useless man' into a 'responsible man' who was employed and who provided for his children and partners.

Furthermore, connection to the community matters. The woman Josephus brought home was unknown and was therefore considered a stranger. 'A stranger', explained Papani, 'is somebody we have no connections with. We don't know their business, we do not want to know their business, and we will never take their side'. A stranger is somebody from 'outside', somebody who belongs to another community. Because Issa used to live elsewhere, her husband and parents lived elsewhere, and she came and went; she was still considered 'almost a stranger'. Had she moved to the community with her extended family or at least with her husband, her membership would have been more quickly accomplished, because then her 'roots', as research collaborators explained, would have been 'replanted there', whereas now her roots were 'all over the place'. The longer one lives within a given community, the more one is considered to have secured one's belonging. This belonging is accompanied by knowledge about the strengths and weaknesses of the community and its members, and by the responsibility to safeguard them. It includes the possibility of harming others, but also of protecting others and contributing to the wealth of the community by contributing one's skills and participating in community life. As Mammie Zainab explained: 'The longer you stay, the more we know about you, and that ties you to us forever. We know your secrets and you know ours'.

Issa's belonging came mostly from the way in which she engaged with Josephus's family, especially with his children, and through the friends she made. She also started selling fishballs and thus became an important link in the chain of relations of exchange. However, being married to another man, Issa clearly has neither the status nor the responsibility of a spouse. Her actions were weighed against that subject position as were those of Josephus. Having a contract relationship, as Issa's landlord and as her boyfriend, he knows that she will never be 'his'. At the same time, he is asked to respect her and provide for her. Issa and Josephus both have children. Josephus is employed and has built a house, and Issa is married. Consequently, as discussed in Chapter 3, they are expected to comport themselves like big men and big women. Finally, once the community entered the case, headed by the elders, it was they who decided how the couple's relationship should be lived and the incidents evaluated, not Josephus or Issa. This case illustrates a form of mediation that is regarded as ideal by community elders because nobody is prioritised and the common good is put first.

Ester: Social Age, Desire, and the Preservation of Ideals

The next case vividly describes the differences between community and household mediation systems and the criminal justice approach. Ester is 17 years old, which legally makes her unable to consent to sex or marriage. In a state case, she would have been treated as a victim in need of the state's protection. However, within the community Ester's age is dependent on social rather than on numerical factors, and she is treated as a mother and wife.

Ester lives with her two sisters and Zainab, her twin, in the *pan bɔdi* or corrugated-iron house next to our compound. Originally from the rural areas, these young women are now staying with several aunts and their grandmother, a strict Mende woman, who is head of the house. Ester is married and is the mother of three. Because she refused to accompany him, her husband, who found work in Waterloo, 20 miles away, only rarely visits.[11]

The Incidents Leading to the Case: Inter-Family Mediations

While staying at Allentown, Ester started having affairs with other men and eventually became pregnant by one of her boyfriends, a young man who lives nearby. Once the pregnancy became known, the families of Ester and her husband gathered to discuss the issue. Ester's family was represented by her grandmother, whose aim was to preserve the family image and ensure that her granddaughter continued to be married and that she and her children were provided for. For his part, the family of the husband felt wronged by Ester's infidelity and sought to be recompensed for her transgressions. After heated negotiations, which lasted for several hours, an agreement was reached. Ester's family were to host and provide for two teenage sons of the husband's family in exchange for a continued marriage. Ester, her husband, and her boyfriend were not consulted.

To ensure that the husband adhered to this decision, Ester's grandmother invited him and asked him to accept the pregnancy (*ansa bɛlɛ*).

---

[11] Waterloo is the capital city of the Western Area Rural District. By car, the city is about an hour away from Freetown.

When he told her that he had not visited Ester for several months, that he knew that she had started seeing somebody else, and that they were having marital problems, Ester's grandmother made him 'scratch his matches during the daylight', which means that she forced him to accept the pregnancy by 'swearing' (taking an oath) (see Chapter 5).

The agreement led to an added financial burden for Ester's family, who now had to feed and care for two additional people. Consequently, Ester's position in the family deteriorated considerably. As the oldest sister and a married woman, she would normally not be asked to contribute to household chores and could just 'send' her younger siblings and the children living in the house to do tasks for her. Additionally, she would normally receive large portions of the best meat and fish. This status notwithstanding, she was now made to contribute extensively to household work because of the burden she had caused. Her grandmother started to beat her for 'the problems she caused the family'. On many days, she came to our compound to eat because no food was reserved or prepared for her at her place. As time went by, she started spending most of her days at our compound. There, she cleaned and cooked for Papani, who in turn provided her with food and occasionally also a place to sleep in our parlour.

Informal Community Involvement

The second part of the case involved the two compounds in the first instance and was later taken to the community. It escalated on 13 January 2017. As on numerous nights before, my sleep was ended abruptly by the ear-piercing sounds of metal banging against metal, underscored by the screams of a woman. Immediately, the three children who share my mattress start crying and a few seconds later sound clouds approach from different sides: the neighbours are coming. I peel the covers off me, rock small Eleanor, who is still a baby, back to sleep, push the curtain to the side, which separates my room from the parlour, and make my way through the labyrinth of limbs on the parlour floor, which features as a sleeping room for seven children, teenagers, and Aunty Eleanor at night. When my naked feet bang against a cooking pot, two of the older children, who had their eyes pressed against holes in the wall, jump up and race back to their sleeping spot. Everyone is awake, and excited eyes stare at me through the twilight, but nobody dares to move; the children know very well that this is a matter for adults.

Papani is already outside, his tenor mixing in with the other voices, and Aunty Eleanor is right in front of me. I stop at the veranda, ready to prevent any child from running outside, which would lead to significant sanctions from Papani. Hidden by the cloak of the night, I observe.

A crowd of maybe 15–20 people has assembled in front of the neighbour's *pan bɔdi*. Everybody is screaming and shouting. The crowd seems to form a circle around somebody, forcing that person away from the house. After some time, I recognise his voice: it is the biological father of Kadi, the baby girl Ester gave birth to a few weeks ago. He was intending to visit his daughter and probably her mother in the shadow of the night but was caught by Ester's grandmother, who immediately started to make palaver to wake up the neighbourhood to come and intervene. With sticks, the crowd is forcing the young man to step away, lashing at him whenever he opens his mouth. He cries in pain when he is hit, eventually breaks through the crowd, and disappears into the darkness. In the doorway of the *pan bɔdi* stands Ester, her daughter on her arm, observing the scene. After a few minutes, the crowd disperses, everybody retreats to their compound, and the silence thickens again.

When the events of the night are digested through conversation the next day among the younger women who in groups braid hair or wash clothes, the older women who clean fish, and the men who sit on Papani's benches smoking ties (marijuana) and drinking gin out of 4 cl plastic packages, I am surprised to hear that everybody seems to sympathise with Ester's former boyfriend. In their eyes, he was wronged by Ester, who had an affair with him while being married, and by her family, who stripped him of the possibility of fatherhood. And still, whenever he tries to see his child or Ester and whenever Ester's grandmother starts her palaver, they are ready to intervene and force him to retreat by beating him away from the compound. Here, beating functions as a tool to prevent greater harm (violence 'for your own good'). The beating hindered him from reconnecting with his child and causing the oath, which separated him and his child and tied the child to Ester's husband, to kill the boyfriend or the child. Mr Mohmo (in his sixties), the elder of the compound below us, explained it like this:

These are our rules. You know we say neighbours are your best family? Real family may be far, but your neighbours they live with you every day. In here we spend most times with our neighbours, and it is strong social bonds. If I need them tomorrow, they will also be here. That man is suffering because his daughter is now out of his hands, but the mammie [Ester's grandmother] forced the child and the other man together through the *swear* [oath]. This thing is powerful. If he tries to fend the child off the father now, the *swear* can easily hit him. Nobody can intervene with that. He should have brought a case immediately, but even then he would have most probably lost. It is not your child when you lie down with a married woman.

As time passed, Ester's husband, who was made to take over full responsibility for the child, visited less and less and sent steadily smaller allowances for the upkeep of both his children. Consequently, Ester increasingly struggled to provide for them. On the days when he did visit, he shouted at Ester and beat her and the children. On many occasions he called the children and sent them to break a branch off a tree and bring it to him. He instructed them to sit and observe while he peeled the bark off the branch and then started beating them, shouting: 'You are not my children. You are all bastards. Your mother is a witch, a useless woman ...' Papani explained: 'That man is angry that he was forced to accept the child, so now he is hating his own children. The mammie [Ester's grandmother] should not have forced him to *ansa* [the pregnancy].' This makes clear that personal opinions are secondary to accepting community structures and relationships of authority.

Another case of 'making palaver' involved Ester, who on a number of occasions would scream when her husband started to lash her. The screams drew the neighbours, who then tried to separate the two and reasoned with the husband to be patient with his wife. They often took him to Papani's bar, placed him on one of the wooden benches, and provided him with alcohol and marijuana until his complaint became slurred and he fell asleep on his bench. As a result, he would return to his compound only in the morning when Ester was already up.

At this time, Papani started intervening more and more to protect Ester from these severe beatings. Rather than taking care of the husband, he started ordering others to do so. He invited Ester into our compound and made Aunty Eleanor, who shook her head in discomfort at this unheard-of intervention, attend to her injuries. Ester now slept in the parlour several nights per week. But while Aunty Eleanor objected to Papani's interference, at first she did not dare to protest publicly. Papani is one of the oldest and most authoritative men in the community.

Aunty Eleanor's behaviour exemplifies the complex relationship between social responsibility and principles of seniority. Socially, it is wrong to intervene in other people's marriages without being called upon or at least if one does not live in the same compound. Seniority structures prevent younger members of a compound from directly opposing the decisions of the elders. At the same time, one's closest alliances lie with one's consanguine and lineal family members, and their authority is structured according to seniority, with older siblings standing over younger siblings. As the younger sister of Papani's wife (Aunty Kadie), Aunty Eleanor knows that the main alliance lies with Aunty Kadie rather than with her husband, Papani. But living under his roof, she must balance her loyalty to her older sister with her responsibilities to the head of the compound she inhabits.

Accusation of Infidelity

Eventually, Aunty Eleanor accused Papani of being unfaithful to his wife (her sister) by having an affair with Ester. Upon learning about the allegations, Papani asked to take an oath on the Quran that he and Ester were not 'there', meaning that they did not have a sexual relationship. Both Papani and Aunty Eleanor made public palaver, and each tried to garner support from the community. Papani accused Aunty Eleanor of '*kongosa* business' (spreading rumours) and of aiming to 'scatter the married house'. For her part, Aunty Eleanor accused Papani of infidelity and violence against his wife in the form of economic exploitation, because he ran his shop and bar with her money but did not share the income with her.

The next day, Papani's wife and elder sisters as well as his children arrived to preside over the case. Even though Aunty Beth, the oldest of the sisters, was not present when the case started out, she opened the conversation by asking Aunty Eleanor and Papani to explain one after the other what had happened and why she was asked to intervene. Aunty Kadie was not addressed and merely listened.

Interestingly, neither of the participants tried to establish whether Papani was in fact unfaithful or whether Aunty Eleanor had wrongly accused him. Instead, what was of key importance was the cause of disagreement between them. All agreed that there was a long-standing grudge: 'Something is underneath, and we have to find out what is under the issue and solve it at once', stated Mariama (19), Papani's youngest daughter. But while the younger family members thought that the underlying problems should be uncovered and resolved, Aunty Beth explained that she rather wanted these two elders of the house to realise their responsibilities to ensure the 'house functions'. This involved 'swallowing the grudges to clear the carpet' rather than examining and 'fixing' holes in its individual fabrics. Aunty Beth concluded that Aunty Eleanor needed to respect Papani as the elder and head of the house and as the husband of her older sister. To Papani, she said: 'Papani, listen, you are the elder, and you are not supposed to hold a grudge. You must swallow it'.

Ester, who was washing clothes just a stone's throw away from the porch where the negotiations took place, was never called. This was a family matter and therefore did not involve her.

The Death of Ester's Child and the Resulting Accusations

A few days later, during the night of 18–19 February, Ester's child, who had been sickly from birth, died. The next morning, straight after the burial, the family of the biological father accused Ester of neglect and child cruelty.

They held her responsible for causing the death of her child. Subsequently, Ester's husband asked for divorce and sole custody of the children. The case of the suspected infidelity alongside witness statements constituted the evidence considered by the community. The community decided that Ester was responsible for the child's death because of how she conceived the child and comported herself in the community. However, partial blame was also given to all the others implicated for failing to guide Ester properly.

After the burial, Ester's husband rejected the invitation to enter Ester's compound and did not agree to eat there. A few days later, he returned and explained to Ester's grandmother that he wanted the marriage to be dissolved and to take the two children with him. Otherwise, he would take the case to the police station and report Ester for child cruelty. While the divorce would certainly be granted, in Sierra Leone children until the age of 7 belong to the mother and can only be taken from her if she is unable to care for them or if they are in danger. After that, a father can take the children away from the mother. As the children were 5 and 3 years old, they still 'belonged' to the mother. Despite the legal situation, Ester's grandmother decided to allow Ester's husband to take the children and divorce her. She told me: 'A court case will take years, years where he does not provide, and everyone knows that her very husband is suing Ester. She would be finished, and her sisters would not find husbands or fiancés. Agreeing with him was my only option'. Within a few months, Ester lost her three children and her husband.

Preserving Relationships

This case shows that decisions were aimed at preserving the accepted status of the relationship even if they led to violence and hardship. It shows that relationships are a means to contrive and cultivate social relations (see also Porter 2013). Potential violence between intimate partners is therefore not a private but a social phenomenon. Unacceptable violence and transgressions provide a threat to the continuity of a relationship. They put at risk the social connections that the relationship holds together and so concern other members of the family and community involved. Mediation practices seek the most suitable resolution, not for the persons implicated in the case, but for the sake of re-establishing stability within a household and the community. It is not harmony in interpersonal relationships that such mediations strive for, but stability within households and in the community overall.

The processes are shaped by principles of seniority. It is Ester's grandmother who made the decisions, not those directly implicated. Moreover, age is not a numerical but a social category. Much as in other places across sub-Saharan Africa, life stages such as youth and adulthood in Sierra Leone are forms of social becoming that are based on social position (e.g. Honwana and De Boeck 2005; Christiansen, Utas, and Vigh 2006; Honwana 2014). Legally speaking, Ester was still a minor who was unable to consent to sex and should not be married. In a state court, her marriage would be considered a child marriage and therefore illegitimate. Her children would be treated as the product of sexual violence, irrespective of her consent. However, as a married woman and mother of three, the community evaluated her case differently. Her grandmother never considered her as a minor.[12] This case reveals some of the effects of the discrepancy between community perceptions of age, which are guided by an individual's social position and are measured in life stages, and numerical age, which is measured in time and which is important to state institutions.

Accusations of Temptation

When temptation is reported to a household or community, the accusation takes one of two forms. Either a man reports his partner for controlling his mind and shaping his behaviour, or the relatives or friends of a man report his partner after observing drastic changes in his behaviour within a short period of time. Let us consider two cases.

In the first case, which was relayed to me by Darren, Mimi (59), the mother of Said (31), from EAUC, reported Said's girlfriend. At the start of the first hearing, when Mimi had to officially 'bring the case' (that is, present the accusations and the scenarios surrounding them), she said:

> This woman has taken his mind. She is controlling him. I do not recognise my own son. He is handing over all his money, he is neglecting his family, and only taking care of her. He is doing woman's work in the house, and he plays with the children instead of going to work. All the while she works. Everyone is already laughing at him, and it is shameful. This woman is controlling him too much.

During the case, Said's girlfriend denied any involvement in the change in his behaviour, while Said explained that he was merely adhering to the demands of being a 'modern developed man'. This, he reiterated, entails sharing work, domestic chores, and caring responsibilities equally between partners. Because he was unsuccessful in obtaining gainful

---

[12] To a state court, the child's death would have been a case of infant mortality, whose rates are high in Sierra Leone and higher still among teenage mothers, a group to which Ester still legally belongs.

employment while his girlfriend had done so, they decided that he should stay home and be with the children.

Those attending the hearing finally decided that Said was indeed influenced, not by his girlfriend – or at least not solely – but by the teachings of development discourses promoted by NGOs. They further decided that while it was important for a man to take care of his mother and family, Mimi needed to give him the space to form his own household. As a big man, he should oversee his own decisions. The concluding statement went like this:

> Said, the decisions you make are surprising to us. We have human rights now, and many things are changing, but men should not become women. A difference must be maintained to uphold respect within your home, at work, and in society overall.
>
> Now, you are a big man and have decided to let your woman work and for you to stay at home. That is acceptable for now, but you must not stay at home forever. A real man should work.
>
> Still, you must visit and support your own family. Neglect, as you know, is violence. They rely on you.
>
> Madame Mimi must also respect your choices. She is not to question them, and she is to respect your woman. In turn, you must not stop supporting her.

In this case, Said was not denied his big man status. His actions were described as 'surprising', not as unacceptable. That he chose to stay at home was understood as a consequence of changing relationship dynamics. Said's girlfriend was not mentioned, because she denied the accusation and her influence in the matter could not be accepted without question.

The case gives interesting insights into current relationship dynamics and the way they are perceived by different generations. The elders who presided over the case believed in clear roles between women and men. Mimi's perspective can be illuminated by the argument of Deniz Kandiyoti, who, in her work on women's strategies and coping mechanisms in patriarchal systems, holds that 'older women have a vested interest in the suppression of romantic love between youngsters to keep the conjugal bond secondary and to claim sons' primary allegiance' (Kandiyoti 1988: 279).

Said and his girlfriend chose their roles based on what was practicable for the household as well as on what public discourse currently declared was worth striving for. Finally, while Said's girlfriend denied any responsibility for the change in his behaviour, she did not seek to rehabilitate the relationship between Said and his mother, and never encouraged him to visit or support her more. This is in line with Kandiyoti's observation that 'young women have an interest in circumventing and possibly evading their mother-in-law's control' (Kandiyoti 1988: 279). These different views on gender relations give rise to different relationship dynamics and may lead to friction between opposing camps. The concept of gender complementarity, which used to be predominant in society, has been joined and contested by various other ideals, which derive from international currents and the particularities of urban life.

In the second case, MSaw (of EAUC) reported his girlfriend for temptation. His accusation sounded like this: 'Lately my mind goes crazy. I cannot sleep or eat or do anything. All I want is to be with her, and all I see is her. That woman bewitched me, and I need it to stop. I am going crazy'. She was eventually convicted on the basis of several witness statements given by his friends that detailed his radically changed behaviour and because it could be established that 'she cooked daily for him and could easily have put something in his food'. Her sentence included an appointment with a traditional doctor, who was supposed to lift any spell she might have put on MSaw. Additionally, she had to pay a fine of SLL 200,000 (GBP 19.53).

After she had been to the traditional doctor and stopped cooking for him, the two continued their relationship. When asked what had changed, MSaw said: 'I still love her very much, but now I know that it is natural, and all spells have been lifted. Once she saw the traditional doctor, I felt free, and now I can love her without any problem'. When I asked him whether he was angry at her for having put a spell on him, he laughed and said: 'No. It just shows how much she wanted me. She would do anything to have me because I am irresistible. That I realised what she was doing just shows how smart I am'. As this perception illustrates, certain forms of violence can be acts of affection. MSaw understood the spell as a declaration of love on her part. He needed the case, though, to work through his own emotions and to regain a sense of control. While MSaw was still madly in love with his partner, the proceedings naturalised these affections.

When accused of temptation, women can either deny the accusation, as in Said's or MSaw's case. Here the defence will argue that they did not deliberately influence the change of behaviour and that whatever transformation happened occurred without coercion or violence. Women especially who are not in a relationship with the man whose change in behaviour is attributed to them, and who are not interested in commencing a relationship, argue that they themselves find his attention and courtship troubling and would benefit from its cessation. A third response entails admitting to capturing and controlling his mind. Here, Maria's case is exemplary. Maria (19), the third wife of Musa (57), was accused by her two co-wives (45 and 33) of tempting Musa so that he only focussed on her and neglected his other wives. When the elders asked her whether she used temptation in a violent way, she said: 'Yes, I put something in his food, and I reorganised his head, but you will be unable to break it or to punish me because he will do exactly as I ask, and if you try, I will ask him to kill himself'.

In this case, Maria was asked what her demands were in exchange for letting go of Musa's mind. Maria had recently married Musa. As his third wife, who was significantly younger than his first and second wives, she felt excluded from her new family. While the two other wives lived close to each other in the west of Freetown, Maria lived in the east. She demanded to be moved to the same community as her co-wives and that the three would share Musa's time equally.

This case was really one between the three wives. Capturing Musa's mind was intended to get their attention and force them to take Maria seriously. Musa was cautioned to be more attentive to the needs of his wives in the future and to prevent such incidents from happening. He reacted by apologising to Maria for treating her differently from his other wives and for neglecting to see that she was suffering, and he promised to move her to a place close to the other two. They, in turn, explained that they now understood that the reason Maria was spending so much time with Musa was not the result of bad intentions against them, but because she was lonely.

The Basis of Community Mediations

As these cases make clear, the deciding factor is not that violence occurs, but *why* it occurs. In the hearings, the actions of both partners are analysed to reach a conclusion about whether the violence present is justified. In examining who is at fault and how the case may be solved, these household and community mediations put people on trial, not acts.

The influence of those involved in deciding what constitutes the most favourable solution depends on their social standing, their level of seniority, their (kin) relation to the persons directly involved, their gender, and their character. The older a person and the closer their relationship to those involved, the more their voice counts. Closeness is differentiated by two categories: one is biological and relates to blood and affinal relations; the other is determined by the time spent together. A third factor is the duration of these conditions. A long-standing neighbour who is older has a considerable say, and so do (older) family members irrespective of cohabitation. What is important is social standing, not only as regards seniority and influence, but also as regards one's character. The most valued members of the community are usually persons who are reflective, socially minded, fair, and consistent. And it is these persons who are often asked to give character testimonies of others involved in various cases. Persons who are easily angered, engage in favouritism, have previously been found untruthful, or engage in gossip (*kongosa*) are not usually called upon when cases are mediated. Furthermore, when they give testimony, their statements are evaluated against the accounts of other, more trusted members. Lastly, because women are said to be more knowledgeable about social conflicts and relations within households, their voices count for more than those of men. Women often lead mediations, while men supply the 'muscle'. When, for instance, Ester's grandmother caused palaver, it was the men of the neighbouring compounds who came and physically forced Ester's boyfriend to retreat. However, it was Ester's grandmother who made the decisions all along.

Swallowing Grudges: Harmony as a Sociopolitical Strategy to Keep State Institutions at Bay

Scholars studying community mediations of violence have often explained these processes as forms of shared closure in which, guided by the overall aim to find and preserve social harmony, members of social groups seek to establish ways to restore the harm that was done and move forward (Porter 2017). For the upper Guinea coast, James Gibbs explained that the concern of community mediations among the Kpelle of Liberia is 'with maintaining harmony and the well-being of the group as a whole' (Gibbs 1963: 4; see also Pirie 2007; Porter 2013). In Sierra Leone, this internal striving for harmony is not a main aim. Not only is the term 'harmony' never used, but research collaborators also actively counter its very foundation. In fact, most explained that 'forgiveness' is not easily achievable. On 30 March 2017, for instance, I joined some of the EAUC members at 24. We watched an Indian movie about claims to village leadership. The rightful heir had been betrayed by his own family members. His uncle had killed his father. The uncle then made the protagonist believe that he had been adopted and had no claim to the throne. However, towards the end of the movie the truth came to light. There was a scene in which the uncle asked the rightful heir for forgiveness for ruining his life and being responsible for his father's death. At the end of the scene, both were in tears and hugged.

Gas blasted: 'Ah, *this na Indian man or white man but Africa man na slap* [this reaction may come from an Indian man or a white man, but an African man would slap]'. The others laughed but immediately agreed. There would be no way that they would just forgive such a situation. First, they said, they would curse and slap and fight, and, even after having been forced to swallow it, they would probably forever carry a grudge inside of them. Gas mocked: 'Here, he will be forced to swallow it, but it will give him an ulcer instead of peace'.

There was consensus that putting group interests before personal ones does not come naturally and is often achievable only through force. This notion of 'forever carrying the grudge' and having to 'swallow' it appeared again and again during my research. Swallowing is an important part of mediation proceedings. However, if those involved are asked to 'swallow' disagreements and anger, their relationship with each other may deteriorate. The aim of 'keeping people together' may not always provide the outcome with the least violence. The ritualised apology at the end of cases not only symbolises the consensual nature of the solution, as Gibbs (1963) highlights, but it also coerces participants into acceptance. Mabinti explained this in the following way: 'Hopefully, by the end of the case everything is solved. But if not, they make you eat your anger. You must put it back in yourself and live with it, deal with it inside you. If it comes back out, you are automatically in the wrong. But, you know, sometimes carrying a grudge inside of you can only make it stronger'.

The public offer and 'acceptance of tokens of apology' not only 'indicate that each party has no further grievances and that the settlement is satisfactory and mutually acceptable' (Gibbs 1963: 5)', but they also are non-negotiable and expensive, and can cause financial hardship. In the cases I observed, restoration was not always possible. Instead, there were often long-term ruptures, such as when Ester lost guardianship over her children. Younger people may be helped to deal with swallowing by informally discussing remaining grudges with elder female family members or designated community elders, who then advise them on how to master swallowing.

Generally, the higher a person's status in a given social order, the better that person should have mastered swallowing grudges. However, as Gas mentioned, this does not mean that the grievance dissolves. Superficial harmony tells us more about a person's self-control and the management of emotions, than about the existence or nature of these emotions. It does not say anything about possible feelings of hatred or revenge, nor can it capture whether people believe that justice was served. Another elder who presides over cases, Mammie Jusef (61), said to me:

> We have a very famous saying here, which goes like this: 'A man's white teeth cannot reveal his black heart'. That means that a man might smile, and you might see his teeth, but it can tell you nothing about what goes on in his heart. Maybe he is calm, maybe angry, maybe there is hate. Forgiveness is a difficult thing. Maybe it will happen, maybe not. We cannot know. What matters is that the community

continues to function and that the different opinions and feelings stay inside and do not boil over to the outside too much. It is about finding a solution which is the best for all, even if it might not be good for some people.

In *How Lifeworlds Work*, Michael Jackson states:

> Despite this emphasis on communitas ... Kuranko readily admit that neighbourliness is not sweet ... and that one can never know what is in another person's mind. As one adage puts it: 'People that are neighbors are the people that quarrel'. ... 'White teeth black heart', people say, pointing to a problem that is endemic to any close-knit community, where resentment, hate, envy, mean-spiritedness, and backbiting constantly undermine the ideal of amity. (Jackson 2017: 68)

Moreover, the ability to swallow was presented to me as not only increasing with experience and age, but also as being gendered. Sulaiman (in his fifties), a shop owner, said:

> Women know how to swallow too much. They always put their children first, and they must learn to be patient with their husbands and fathers and everyone: they must learn to bear others and not to make palaver all the time. But men, now, they do not learn that. Because women swallow, men air their grievances. They think of themselves, and they act very quickly. Only a very old and very wise man will have learnt swallowing and thus only those who have will be true role models and leaders, because the others will always make irrational and quick decisions.

This notion stresses the power of women as masters of the social world. But it also impacts on the ways in which sanctions are imposed. To resolve a case, women are often punished more severely than men because the main mediators – themselves women – feel that women are better able to swallow and that they are needed to preserve a household (Chapter 7). Women swallow, as we will see in the next chapter, partly to preserve the union and because they feel emotionally stronger, and partly because other means of reporting can leave them in even more precarious situations. Here, the metaphor of the teeth and the tongue comes into effect again. Swallowing is mainly facilitated by the tongue – the women – while the teeth remain unmoved.

Harmony is not understood as a social ideal or a belief system with intrinsic value, much less a practically achievable state This stands in contrast to, for instance, the Acholi of Northern Uganda, where, according to Holly Porter (2017), social harmony is the primary moral imperative after harm occurred. All in all, rather than reaching a completely harmonious situation, swallowing is a strategy that allows cases to be closed. It is also aimed at keeping state interference at a minimum and communities and households functional and self-sufficient. Mammie Zainab summarised the overall goal: 'It's not about happiness for everyone, not even for someone. It is about reaching an acceptable state for the group. You may be very unhappy with this today, I might be tomorrow, someone else next tomorrow, and so on ... but overall, it will do. Life is not about perfection. It is about finding working solutions'.

In her study of a Zapotec village in Mexico, Laura Nader describes how a 'harmony ideology' has been created by almost five hundred years of colonial influences, combined with a conscious strategy (Nader 1990). Her research collaborators used compromise to resolve internal conflicts to present a united but harmless front to outsiders as a strategy to evade colonial influence and a defence against foreign domination (Nader 1990; see also Pirie 2007).[13] Mammie Zainab reiterated that, in Freetown,

> it is like before in the war. The house may be in conflict, but if the walls seem quiet from the outside, the rebels will not go there. In here, the state only comes when we seem like we are not in control. So, the trick is to make them think everything is great no matter how big the problem is on the inside.

So long as communities and households appear to solve cases among themselves and accounts of excessive punishment do not become public, the criminal justice system tolerates, even endorses, these mediation systems. In that sense, community and household mediations can be understood as systems of normative 'non-state ordering' (Pirie 2014: 40), which are 'semi-autonomous'[14] from state institutions (Moore 1973) and have the ability to regulate aspects of social life effectively. They have their own *modus operandi*, and they generate rules, but they exist under the umbrella of state laws and are heavily influenced by them, even if they try to maintain their relative autonomy. In Sierra Leone's 'weak legal pluralism' (Griffiths 1986; Sezgin 2004; Foblets, Graziadei, and Renteln 2017)– where several legalistic systems exist hierarchically, fulfil different functions within society, and deal with different kinds of cases – community mediations play a crucial role. Their way of mediation addresses some aspects of relationships, whereas others are better dealt with by state institutions. Considering this difference helps people choose where to turn. In Freetown, on the one hand, relationships are characterised by experimentation, fluidity, and multiplicity. On the other hand, household and community mediations are firmly invested in preserving relationships and keeping people together. Ruptures are only accepted in the most extreme cases.

---

[13] Pirie describes similar tendencies among the Ladakhi of Tibet, where the village meeting 'was responsible for resolving all disputes' (Pirie 2014: 35). It also provided a 'strategy ... for distancing all ... outsiders from certain village affairs' and for the village to remain 'autonomous of any model of order that might be imposed through law, even internally-generated laws' (Pirie 2014: 35; see also Pirie 2007).

[14] These were later called 'social spheres' by Galligan (2007: ch. 6).

This is radically different from state institutions, where it is acts rather than personhood that are examined, and where only one party is found guilty; where punishment through imprisonment separates couples; and where the repercussions of police reporting and court cases usually rupture relationships. When people decide which system to employ, they must therefore weigh a multitude of factors against each other, as we will see in the next chapter, which concerns the reporting to police of unacceptable violence among adults.

7   Invoking the State
When Adults Report Violence in Their Relationships to the Police

Most mornings Ester (17, with three children, divorced), Zainab (17, with no children, no partner), Issa (33, with one son, separated, one boyfriend), Apsatu (34, with one son, divorced), Effe (25, with four children and several boyfriends), Fatu (39, with three children, married), and Brima (48, with four children, married) meet under the shade of the mango tree in front of Papani's house, where they braid hair, sell foodstuffs, and share the news of the night. They show injuries to each other, offer advice on their treatment, voice their opinion on the 'rights' and 'wrongs' of each other's behaviour, and share strategies to 'bear and change' their husbands and partners. Until recently, the only reporting considered was to friends, family, or community.[1] That changed once Apsatu joined the group a few months ago. Not only did she report her husband to the police and later divorce him, Apsatu is also a journalist who reports on domestic violence cases heard at the Magistrate's Court. Through her work and her own case, the new laws around domestic violence have become the topic of heated debates among these women.

Such debates, decisions, and consequences regarding police reporting are at the heart of this chapter.[2] Indeed, the questions of how, when, and in which circumstances adults turn to the state to report their partners for unacceptable violence are entwined with questions of risk, opportunity, social standing, and influence. This chapter builds on Apsatu's story. It depicts her case in her words, from its reporting and its passage through the courts to its dismissal. It then discusses what happens when men report their partners to the police (of which I did not see a single case during my time in Sierra Leone). In conversation with these accounts, the chapter reflects on the factors on which convictions depend and which distinguish successful cases (economic violence and violence

---
[1] See Ester's and Issa's cases in the previous chapter.
[2] This chapter draws on and expands on the arguments I made in my article 'Partners as possession' (Schneider 2019a).

against minors) from unsuccessful ones (sexual and physical violence against adults). It discusses the complex risks involved in reporting a partner to the police, which include loss of status, fines by family or community, and social exclusion. The risks of reporting are intersectional and are influenced by gender, socioeconomic background, and class. Those who consider reporting to the police consist of specific classes – usually those who work for the state or engage with state institutions frequently, as well as people who can support themselves if they lose their relationships or familial support. Such people therefore constitute a bridge between those who keep state institutions at a distance and instances where state institutions use citizens to report on other citizens' relationships (Chapter 8). The foundation for these dynamics lies in post-war legal developments around violence in relationships. Finally, this chapter builds on these findings to reflect on the notion of gender parallelism, which is a strong undercurrent of academic debates in the region. I show that gender parallelism is used as a tactic rather than accepted as an unquestioned fact – a tactic that helps Sierra Leoneans to navigate the crisis of gender relations that they are currently experiencing.

The Gender Justice Laws

After the civil war came to an end in Sierra Leone, response institutions and service providers were largely destroyed or became dysfunctional. Those that remained were confronted with the outcomes of war-time violence and were heavily influenced by IOs and NGOs, which demanded restructuring. The prevalence of sexual violence during the civil war made violence a principal concern after the conflict ended. Awareness of violence was increased by the findings of the Special Court for Sierra Leone (SCSL) and the Truth and Reconciliation Commission (TRC 2004a) as well as the research, advocacy, and awareness raising of local women's movements, NGOs, and IOs. Reports described women's and girls' exposure to violence in post-war Sierra Leone as endemic. Violence in relationships, which once had been a private matter, became a public and political concern, leading to intricate negotiations over its acceptability, repercussions, and response. As I have argued elsewhere (Schneider 2019a), five key issues were identified:

1. domestic violence.
2. the dispossession of property on the death of spouses.
3. disadvantages due to unregistered and customary marriages.

4. matrimonial cases.³
5. rape.

The Law Reform Agenda prioritised these issues,⁴ leading to the passing of the 'Gender Justice Laws', which included the Domestic Violence Act and the Devolution of Estates Act, which came into effect on 26 July 2007, and the Registration of Customary Marriage and Divorce Act, which came into effect on 22 January 2009. As a result of these laws, any behaviour within an intimate relationship that causes physical, psychological, economic, or sexual harm to those in the relationship constitutes a crime that can lead to conviction and imprisonment (Mills et al. 2015). Apart from criminalising all forms of violence in relationships, these laws encourage women to enter their traditional and religious marriages into the formal register. They also grant equal rights to spouses over all possessions, including property and land in the case of divorce.

As women increasingly engage with state courts through these laws, they begin to impact on women's choices. Ethnographic work can elucidate such changes and thus illuminate the relationship between policy, agency, and social change. My own study, which analyses how laws are experienced and what effects they have in practice, sets out to describe the multifaceted barriers women face in reporting. It examines how, when reporting increases, there are changes in norms as well. These not only generate new opportunities for those who feel they could not have reported previously, but also forge new constraints that prevent reporting, as we can see from the lives of the women of the Allentown community.

Apsatu: A Woman Who Reports

'I married my main love', said Apsatu, 'but he was a bad husband'. She continued:

He beat and raped me, and he stopped me from working and seeing friends. He always said: 'You are ugly'; 'You are worthless like a dog'; 'I will beat you like a plastic bag in the wind' ... Eight years it was like that until I went to the police. For us here, it goes like this. When you report to your family or community at first, they will try to settle you and tell you that you should 'bear', like with Issa ... you were there, so you understand what I am talking about. But then, when you report again and again, they become aware and they will also tell the man off.

---

³ For example, to lay claims regarding marriage, one must show a valid marriage certificate, which was not issued for customary marriages.

⁴ Jointly organised by the Parliamentary Human Rights Commission, the Law Reform Commission, the government, and partners.

If you then report again and again and show your injuries, they will allow you to divorce. Some think that you failed as a wife because you didn't control him very well, but they let you go.

But because I am a journalist and I always see these cases at court and believe in human rights, I went to the FSU. From there, I did a 'medical' at the Rainbo Centre. The paper said that I have bruises and marks. Because I am a mother, the broken hymen does not count. From there, I went to L.A.W.Y.E.R.S. [an NGO offering free legal representation to women and girls], and they gave me a free lawyer. When they called for my husband at the police station for his statement, luckily he beat me there, so they sent him to court. There, myself and the policewoman gave witness statements. My family did not come.

My case went on for three years. It was very difficult to go to court always, and my husband got so much worse, even beating our child. Can you imagine? But the worst thing was my family. You know, we Africans, we need the family. But they were ashamed of me. They hate me for going to the police. It is like a betrayal for them and a useless one. Because from the community they would have got money or work or something, but now ... nothing. One day, after six adjournments, the judge dismissed the case. They said the evidence was lacking.

Later, Apsatu divorced her husband. She moved away from the community, where she was no longer welcome, and relocated to Allentown, where she now rents a room.[5] She resumed her work as a journalist and is now self-sufficient, supporting both herself and her child. She is convinced that had she reported the case to her community, it would have led to a faster dissolution of the marriage and to recompense for herself and her family:

But with the law, there is huge stigma, and women are usually banned from everyone. Also, no one will marry you again. But I think that we still need to report so that one day it will become normal and women do not have to put up with this behaviour anymore. The change, I think, is in our hands, but it is slow, and there is much suffering on the way.

Apsatu's lawyer told me: 'If more women report, more women will be there to support others later on, so it becomes a norm, you see'. To understand the rationale behind Apsatu's actions, we must appreciate how she perceives violence, how she positions herself within a social world that places various conflicting demands on her, and why she decided to take the route of reporting to the police. Apsatu interprets her husband's violence differently in different scenarios. When she decided to report him for beating, raping, and cursing her, and for stopping her from working and seeing friends, she described the fact that he beat her at the police station as 'lucky'. It was 'lucky', she told me

---

[5] So far, she has had no contact with her parents, but her sisters recently started coming to visit her.

later, because it confirmed her testimony, and the case subsequently went to court. 'We women would never just be believed. But men's actions ... men have warm hearts; they cannot hide their true selves when they are challenged, so when he beat me, his true self came out and my words did not need believing', she said. Here, Apsatu interpreted the immediate beating by her husband as possibly preventing more long-term violence and as giving her report credibility. She built on the notion that women (the tongues) are flexible whereas men (the teeth) are rigid and can neither bend nor roll nor change their shape. This makes women better at controlling and strategically using words and emotions, but it also suggests that men show their true form more because they cannot do much else.[6] Apsatu felt that it was not her behaviour, her testimony, or the medical report that made her account credible and incontrovertible, but her ex-husband's beating of her in front of the police.

Apsatu was familiar with the structures of reporting to the police and to the household and community. She was deeply aware of the risks that accompany reporting to these different institutions for her and for women in general. She was conscious that turning to the police means turning her back on family and community and that she may subsequently lose their support. Having followed hundreds of similar cases as a journalist, she was informed about the low conviction rates and the time such cases take to move through the courts. Apsatu was one of many research collaborators who referred to 'human rights' as a contemporary universal norm. Her decision to report was rooted within her approach towards and her belief in human rights.[7]

Competing Ideals of Community and Human Rights

Building on Richard Rorty (1993) and Norberto Bobbio (1996), Jane Cowan demonstrates how today's 'human rights culture' shapes 'discourse' and structures 'how the world is apprehended' (Cowan 2006: 10; see Cowan, Dembour, and Wilson 2001). Human rights, she says, are 'defining a social and ideational space, one that entails certain ideas of "self" and "sociality", specific modes of agency, and particular rules of the game' (Cowan 2006: 10). In this book, we see how the gendered views underlying human rights interact with local concepts. In Sierra Leone, this issues in frequently uttered statements such as 'today we

---

[6] See Chapter 4 and the discussion about warm and cold hearts below.
[7] Ton Salman's discussion of how certain Bolivians in marginal positions take calculated risks, which place them under conditions of insecurity to achieve long-term security, shows interesting parallels (Salman 2010: 23–44).

believe in human rights', 'now there is human rights', or 'that was before we had human rights'. These mark a clear turn in behaviour and attitude towards certain practices today from a pre–human rights time. In *Stages on Life's Way*, Søren Kierkegaard (1940) describes the ethical as the expression of the universal, a stage in which all actions are undertaken publicly for the common good, and the betterment of the whole is prioritised over the self. Apsatu legitimises her decision to turn to the state as an attempt to improve the situation of women in general. This prioritisation of 'the greater good' allows her to neglect her moral obligations towards her family and community. Apsatu knows that she will probably not win a court case. However, as a standard-bearer in changing the future conditions for women in Sierra Leone, Apsatu not only decides against the needs or wishes of her family. She is also willing to sacrifice her own marriage and the moral support of her loved ones to further these human rights principles and pave the way for a future in which women will win their cases in court. Even after her divorce and after she was asked to leave her community, her belief in human rights remains unchanged.

The negotiation between accessing 'rights' that have been legally granted and transgressing community and household needs or norms complicates the clear boundaries between individualistic and sociocentric positionings. As previous chapters have shown, in Sierra Leone personal relationships and agency exist in a complicated liaison between individualistic and community-based wants and needs (e.g. Piot 1999; Jackson 2012). In *Between One and One Another*, Michael Jackson describes the 'oscillation between sociocentric and egocentric consciousness' as dialectic and therefore as presenting an inescapable ethical problem (Jackson 2012: 3). Through permanently reconfiguring their relationship to one another, these two facets of human existence engage in a dance between 'I' and 'we' whose steps are never similar but always relational in constantly changing choreographies. Building on Georg Simmel (1971), Cowan argues that 'in situations of contested ideologies/normative frameworks, methodologically individualist understanding of both rights and culture simply cannot grasp the complex, countervailing pressures, evolving situationally and historically, on individuals caught in the[se] dynamics' (Cowan 2006: 14). When deciding whether to report domestic violence to their household or community or to the police, adults in Sierra Leone must make distinct choices, balancing their individual needs and the needs of their families, partners, and social groups. If they report to their household or community, the needs of the social group will be put before theirs. But if they report to the police, they may, by following their own needs, risk the dissolution of the social group and a loss of support.

Whether adults can safely report violence to state institutions therefore depends not just on the existence of facilities to do so and on protective laws, but also on what is normative within their social setting. Social policy and interventions must therefore take into account the settings in which they operate, consider existing norms and rules, and, if possible, collaborate with those institutions and individuals – for example, households, community leaders, traditional or religious institutions – who decide upon such matters in a given context. Turning opposition into alliances and rejection into cooperation can go a long way in making reporting safe and in offering exit strategies.

In Sierra Leone, such cooperation between the criminal justice system and other actors is rare and infrequent. Reporting domestic violence to the police is associated with complicated processes of risk-taking. Not only are conviction rates low, but within households and communities reporting threatens the reputation of both partners and families. In the view of families and communities, a woman who reports is frequently assumed to be conducting a purely selfish vendetta focussed on satisfying her hunger for revenge, hindering her family from fulfilling its role as mediator, and preventing them from receiving support or remuneration. Keebet von Benda-Beckman's analysis of diverse dispute mediation systems in Sumatra is relevant here. She distinguishes between different but overlapping scales and reaches of mediation systems. She shows how people choose between them (what she calls 'forum shopping') and how the systems themselves seek to advance their own interests ('shopping forums'): 'I shall speak of "forum shopping" here, because disputants have a choice between different institutions and they base their choice on what they hope the outcome of the dispute will be, however vague or ill-founded their expectations may be,' she says (Benda-Beckman 1981: 117).

Not only do parties shop, but the forums involved use disputes for their own, mainly local political ends. These institutions and their individual functionaries usually have interests different from those of the parties, and they use the processing of dispute to pursue these interests. So besides forum-shopping disputants, there are also "shopping forums" engaged in trying to acquire and manipulate disputes from which they expect to gain political advantage, or to fend off disputes which they fear will threaten their interests. (Benda-Beckman 1981: 117)

In Freetown, personal, household and community interests compete. After Apsatu's case became known, the pros and cons of reporting to the police were discussed frequently during the morning sessions at Allentown.

Police Reporting: Betrayal or Ethical Duty?

Most of the women had very clear positions on reporting to the police. Effe, for instance, maintained: 'If you are reporting somebody to the police, then surely that is the end of you. Maybe you also have done something bad before. No ... police reporting: what's the use of it? There is no benefit for no one, but pain for all'. Eastina (37), a cook from Calaba Town, held a similar position:

> I cannot report somebody that is putting food on the table. It is a taboo to report my husband ... My whole family and the whole other family, they will see me as an enemy ... And my children will suffer because relatives who would have rendered help will not help if my husband is in jail. That would be the end of your marriage and of you being married to any other person because ... news fly (*laughs*). People will go and tell: 'Ah, that lady she took her husband to police station, and now he is spending time in prison'. In Sierra Leone, men don't want to take chances. They say: 'If I mistakenly beat her or I mistakenly slap her, she will do the same to me, so that lady is off marriage' (*laughs*). And for African ladies, you know, we want to get married or be committed to be completed. Definitely!

Men's positions were similar. Diamond stated: 'The whole problem of relationships is *kongosa* [gossip]. Men and women in relationships they don't discuss with each other ... But if you bring the police now, that is even worse. There is no way back from that. We all have fault, you know. If you start this nonsense, then we can all go to prison'.

For persons whose lives are lived within households and communities, seeking state intervention to address violence in intimate consensual relationships is perceived as an unwanted intrusion into privacy. This not only causes havoc for those directly involved, but also destabilises the mechanisms that are in place to curb such violence. If people start turning to the police, thereby assigning strangers to decide over matters occurring within households and communities, the strong social fabric of communities may be weakened, and community mediations may lose their power. People who report may therefore be fined by their social group. Subsequently, they may also face hardship and social exclusion. Kadie (31) commented: 'You go to police only if a stranger attacks you or maybe if you find that someone has tampered with your child. But your man? No. You can find ways to end your man, yes. ... But prison? What is the use? He is just rotting when he should make good to you'. Violence, these research collaborators said, should be reported when strangers are involved. Rape should also be targeted by the state. But state institutions should stay out of bedrooms and intimate relationships, and should refrain from deciding on how partnerships should be lived.

Others, like Apsatu, position themselves within a human rights discourse. This leads them to believe that, consequences and calamities notwithstanding, accessing these laws is a moral and ethical duty, paving the way for a future in which all matters will be decided on similar principles (see Kierkegaard 1940). For such people, those who keep the state at bay are selfish because they hinder the state's mission to advance and extend equal rights for all. What we see from Apsatu's case and the perspectives of the other women in the community is that the barriers to reporting to the police are lower for specific groups. Apsatu is a formally educated woman with a professional career in journalism that has her working in courtrooms. Knowing that if she lost the backing of her family and community, she could sustain herself and her child and relocate to another area of Freetown certainly influenced her decision to report.

She is also part of a group of people whose daily lives are intertwined with state institutions. After the incorporation of human rights principles into the legal and political apparatus, she secured a position as a journalist documenting cases related to human rights. Through her work, she came in contact with other women who hold positions as journalists, writers, activists, lawyers, and so on – women who firmly believe that the alignment of the political and legal arena with 'human rights principles' permits them to balance their roles as mothers, wives, and successful professionals within the formal sector. This signifies the presence of a 'human rights culture' as described by Cowan 'in the sense of an increasingly pervasive structuring discourse in the late 20th and 21st centuries that shapes how the world is apprehended. It also signals a Foucauldian alertness to the power and knowledge relations associated with this expanding legal and political apparatus' (Cowan 2006: 10).

In contrast, people like Eastina, Effe, Ester, and Brima, who are not part of these apparatuses and social circles, rely on their family and community as their source of income, social support, and behavioural reference point. These women are entrepreneurs in the informal sector, making a living by selling food, offering laundry services, or braiding hair. Although many of them have thriving businesses, their customer base and their social network overlap, and their financial success is contingent upon maintaining and nurturing these relationships (Chapter 3). Moreover, these women – and men like Papani or Diamond – only seldomly engage with state institutions. Their daily lives and businesses are organised around kin, neighbours, and community members. Even extraordinary events like childbirth, marriage, or sickness are managed largely 'at the margins of the state' (see, e.g. Ferme 2004), as they can call upon known and trusted midwives, community elders, and so on. When people like these seek support from law enforcement, it not only represents a significant departure from habitual behaviour, but also threatens the underlying pillars upon which their lives are built. Hence, gender laws and the possibility of accessing the rights they offer can exacerbate existing power imbalances across various intersecting identities.[8]

Phenomenologically, these different social positions – of alignment with family and community or with 'human rights' and thus state institutions – give rise to different life-worlds in which different institutions are imagined as comprising different values, possibilities, and constraints. This positioning, which determines outlook, alliances, and possible actions, also informs responses to unbearable violence. These positions create specific 'social pressures, leading to both constraint and compulsion' (Cowan 2006: 14), and shape lives irrevocably.

Both standpoints require determination as well as sacrifice. Cowan explains that 'engagement in social life entails being caught by, as much as caught up in, its reciprocities, such that opting out is often not an option. Speaking and not speaking, as well as taking up or not taking up particular identities, are acts framed by the imperatives of sociability' (Cowan 2006: 14). Both positions require setting more general needs over individualistic ones. If one positions oneself with the state, one may have to 'swallow' one's personal needs with regard to emotional and familial support and 'bear' losing loved ones in the process of fighting for what one believes is a 'just mission'. On the other hand, people who position themselves with their household or community must 'swallow' grievances and 'bear' whatever solution the household or community sees fit. For believers in the state, the advancement of human rights goals and laws is put before personal well-being, while for proponents of family and community it is these social groups whose needs come before their own. Hence, as Cowan recognises, the rights and duties of the two positions are 'both enabling and constraining' and 'productive (of subjectivities, of social relations, and even of the very identities and cultures they claim merely to recognize)' (Cowan 2006: 10).

Reporting Trajectories: Institutions Caught between Competing Ideals

On the side of the criminal justice institutions, these lines of alignment become blurred. State apparatuses and institutions recognise marriages

---

[8] This is exacerbated because private legal representation is too costly for most people. Lawyers who offer free services have heavy workloads, which makes it impossible to spend more than a few minutes before the first hearing with their clients. Mostly, legal representation is reduced to hearings at the High Court.

and households as personal spaces – personal in that they are integrated within relational notions of personhood that involve the families and trusted social networks of the partners, but not the wider public or the state. They should therefore only be interfered with if no other solution is possible. The institutions involved have created procedures that aim at resolving such matters before they reach court. Consequently, adult reporting of violence in relationships almost never leads to a court case. Most often, the outcome is dismissal or a so-called friendly settlement, which means that the parties are urged to withdraw the case and find a solution outside the courts. As a result, the gender justice laws have largely become ineffective in mediating violence between adults.

Resource scarcity adds an additional difficulty. During my time in Freetown, FSU staff handled up to 20 new reports each day, which made proper investigations impossible. The Center for Accountability and the Rule of Law (CARL) published an assessment of the FSU, which stated:

> Currently, ... there is an average of seven FSU personnel who work in two shifts per FSU station ... However, a minimum of 20 officers per station, i.e. ten officers per shift, are required to have sufficient staff to handle the work load. Consequently, FSU stations are currently understaffed so that people who come to report a crime may be sent away and asked to come again on a later date. This has serious consequences for the investigation and prosecution of crimes as well as for the welfare of the victims/survivors.[9] (Center for Accountability and the Rule of Law 2015)

After making their report, alleged victims are referred by police to the Rainbo Centre, where they are treated free of charge. After having been examined, they receive a medical certificate, which is a key source of evidence should the case go to court. Then all those implicated are called together to discuss the case and establish possible solutions. This process is strikingly like community proceedings, albeit with significantly less time accorded to the process. Grievances are supposed to be aired in the space of a single hearing and, if possible, the case closed. To provide emotional support, the MSWGCA should have a social worker at hand to suggest alternatives to reporting individuals who feel unsafe going back home or who are concerned for their loved ones.[10] However, resource scarcity makes offering such alternatives impossible. Christiana Davies-Cole, former lawyer at Legal Access through Women Yearning for Equality Rights and Social Justice (L.A.W.Y.E.R.S.) and FSU trainee, explains:

---

[9] As I will show in the next chapter, preference is given to cases involving minors.
[10] This is also the reason for the FSUs' close collaboration with NGOs, such as Don Bosco or Save the Children, which often have temporary shelters for children.

These women come here, hoping for change: they are battered and raped, and they fear for their lives, but almost always we have to send them back home. Shelters are only available for children. We try to send them to family members. But most people think that what goes on in a home is private. They will blame the women for going to the police, and they will never be involved in suing their own families, so these women have to go back home. It is very ... tough here.

In nearly every instance, women are sent back to the households where they lived when filing their reports. Furthermore, even if cases go to court, it can take years for them to navigate through the legal system, leaving the reporting women vulnerable to escalated violence during this period. Finally, most cases are eventually dismissed. There are several reasons for this. Because of resource scarcity and reluctance to interfere, no proper investigations are conducted. In the courts, persons are treated as spouses or partners. Their subject positions are not considered those of alleged perpetrator and victim (unlike when minors are involved; see Chapter 8). When questioning witnesses, the magistrate and police ask: 'So your husband came home and then he beat you, his wife?' rather than 'So the accused came to the house and then the accused beat you?', which would be the language used in cases involving minors.

In addition, family members often refuse to testify against their own relatives. If a case is adjourned three times, such as due to a missing witness, the defence lawyer can request that the case be dismissed. Since many Sierra Leoneans have dependants to care for and regularly lack the resources to attend court, and magistrates and judges have to juggle a large volume of cases, those who appear in court are typically given a weekday when a potential hearing may take place. Thus, people come to court every week where they wait for their case to be called until they are unable to come, upon which the case is dismissed for lack of claimants. Additionally, intervening family members may prevent witnesses from testifying. A High Court judge stated:

One of the biggest problems we have is witness tampering. In these family matters, sometimes an aunt or uncle will stop the victim or the alleged perpetrator from appearing in court. Then suddenly they 'visit family in the interior' or their 'child is sick' ... they are removed under some pretence so that we cannot get a hold of them, but if they don't appear in court, we have to discharge the case.

Thus, in Sierra Leone, accessing the 'rights' that the gender laws technically provide is impossible for most people, partly because of social conditions and partly because of the way such adult cases are handled in police stations and courts. Again, we see the effect of different and irreconcilable ideals of gender relations weighing on individuals who work in such institutions and on those who turn to them. Moreover, while men are excluded from the conversation, activists, international actors, and state institutions – those who are positioned within a human rights discourse – 'push women to access the criminal justice system' without offering long-term solutions and viable exit strategies (Porter 2013: 56). Such activists ignore the fact that 'a woman may choose to prioritize her social and economic wellbeing above the pursuit of a "just" punishment for the perpetrator' (Porter 2013: 56). They also fail to take account of the fact that the police and the courts are not able to deal effectively with such matters.

When Informal State Mediations Fail: Initiating a Downward Spiral

FSUs were strengthened in the course of the post-conflict 'human rights' processes to replace informal mediations, which were believed to be biased, with an effective, impartial, and equal treatment of cases (see TRC 2004a). But rather than establishing their services in dialogue with communities, they pushed mediation strategies to the periphery. FSU mediations mimic the format of community and household mediations in that participants are asked to present their respective positions and find a collective solution. However, the FSUs cannot spend significant amounts of time on such cases, as communities can, nor do they have the wealth of knowledge about the people involved that communities can draw on. Finally, they cannot offer reparations similar to those of communities in which people can be made to contribute. FSU mediations in their current form are an example of how ideals of universal human rights, governed through state legislation, can become counterproductive. Such processes lack consideration of context and take place without the resources necessary to provide alternative solutions to existing structures. Indeed, the police know that, because of resource scarcity and big case-loads, they cannot handle all cases effectively. What ends up happening is that the FSU encourages people to have their cases mediated within their communities, if possible.

However, if individuals are first encouraged to position themselves within a human rights discourse and asked to act in accordance with it – as Apsatu did – and then, after being put through a poor copy of what they would have faced at home, sent back to the communities and structures they were asked to turn their backs on, the risks women face increase disproportionately. If a report is made to the community first, support structures are in place (Chapter 6), but if they enter the realm of the state and then return to the community, the 'betrayal which occurred cannot go unsanctioned', Mamie K, another community elder from Allentown, said. These adverse effects and tremendous risks have led many to mistrust state authorities and, even more so, the police.

Reporting: A Phenomenon on the Rise and a Class Question

Notwithstanding these difficulties, more and more reports are made by adult women. I did not get to see any official statistics from before 2011 and was told that Sierra Leone did not digitally record offences statistics before then.[11] From 2011 to 2015, the reporting of domestic violence rose from 522 to 8,043 cases. In 2015, when outcomes were first recorded, 3,521 cases were investigated and 1,438 were charged (FSU crime statistics, which I was allowed to view).[12] In 2015, 43 per cent of reported cases were 'investigated', which means that they proceeded to a preliminary investigation at the Magistrate's Court. There, witness statements are heard, and the magistrate then decides whether there is sufficient evidence to send the case to the High Court. Only 17.8 per cent of cases were charged. To understand these rates better, we need to analyse 'what is being reported'. According to the Domestic Violence Act, domestic violence includes any of the following acts or threats of any such act:

(a) physical or sexual abuse;
(b) economic abuse;
(c) emotional, verbal or psychological abuse, including any conduct that makes another person feel constantly unhappy, humiliated, ridiculed, afraid or depressed or to feel inadequate or worthless;
(d) harassment, including sexual harassment and intimidation;
(e) conduct that in any way harms or may harm another person, including any omission that results in harm and either (i) endangers the safety, health or wellbeing of another person; (ii) undermines another person's privacy, integrity or security; or (iii) detracts or is likely to detract from another person's dignity or worth as a human being.
(3) An offence under subsection (1) shall be punishable by a fine not exceeding SLL 5,000,000 or by a term of imprisonment not exceeding 2 years or by both such fine and imprisonment. (Government of Sierra Leone 2007c)

---

[11] From 2011 to 2015, only the aggregate number of all reports made was made available to me. In 2011, 522 cases of domestic violence were reported; in 2012, 4,452; in 2013, 7,391; and in 2014, 9,157.
[12] Rape is a crime committed against non-partners and is therefore a different offence.

158   Invoking the State

Reports of economic violence – mostly concerning husbands not supporting their children – have risen starkly. Moreover, people are increasingly registering traditional marriages. Cases regarding the division of resources after a divorce or inheritance cases are common. Between adults, only cases where the physical or sexual violence is so severe that lasting injuries occur that can be unquestionably identified by doctors and described in a medical report (e.g. fractures, stab wounds, burns) have a high chance of leading to a court case. As regards emotional violence, mostly cases of *mami kɔs* are reported. The cases that have a high chance of leading to a conviction are those involving children, such as neglect or if physical violence is committed (child cruelty). The state's lenience changes drastically when minors are involved, and state resources are channelled to protect minors (Chapter 8).

Why Men Cannot Report

As I showed in Chapter 4, in conversations and interviews, both women and men explained how they 'fought' with each other using physical violence such as slapping or beating. However, when I asked if men ever report violence to the police, I was met with embarrassed responses such as 'Of course not, what kind of men would these be?' Not one of the people I spoke to in communities knew of a man who had reported his wife or girlfriend for violence to the police.

In the police stations, the same question met with laughter from the then chief of the East End Police Station, and professionals from the head office of the FSU at the CID in Freetown.[13] Except for one professional, whom I will call Dr Momo, none of them had ever encountered a case in which a man reported his wife or girlfriend for being violent to him. Dr Momo told me about this case when there was nobody else present. Leaning over from his side of the table, he spoke in whispers. He started his story with a disclaimer, referring to the universality of human rights: 'Well, you know that the Gender Acts are for equality, so anyone can report a case to us: men, women, children, everybody'. Dr Momo then continued, his voice a mixture of disbelief and sensationalism:

For men now, this is not easy. They report when something happens to their children or maybe inheritance cases or neighbours' quarrels. Many report *mami kɔs*, like when their wife curses their mother. Then they report to show their wives that they cannot do that and to respect their mother. But reporting 'Oh, my wife beats me', that is unheard of. Society expects them to be different. Let me tell you about the only 'yes', the only case when a man reported. Ah that man.

[13] I do not name them, because I want to protect their anonymity.

He reported his wife for battering. Yes, she was a fearful wife, strong woman, and that man was so weak, so small. When he reported, it was like he was crawling into the police station, you know, like with his penis in his hands, giving it to the investigating officer. He failed as a man not even being able to be respected in his own home. Not able to stop his wife, a woman ... can you imagine? In all the hearings at the police station, everybody was laughing, and if that gets out to his community, *eh bo* that man. Of course, he was advised to drop the case before he becomes the laughing stock of the entire nation. He would have never won.

To contextualise Dr Momo's story, I turn to Pierre Bourdieu (2001). In *Masculine Domination*, he describes the construction of gender as a project of opposites within an overall conceptual world of binaries (up/down, in/out, above/below, behind/in front). Here, the idea of sexual difference is normalised (MacCormack and Strathern 1982). Gender is therefore 'onto-formative' (Connell 2005) 'in the sense that it anchors one's existence ... one's sense of belonging to a community and to a world' (Mann 2014: 1). It is formative of sexual relationships between men and women. It shapes conceptions of affection, intimacy, and violence, and it generates possibilities for action. As Dr Momo's story and the metaphor of teeth and tongue show, the notion of a binary division of gender roles, responsibilities, and opportunities has led men and women to be positioned at opposite ends of the spectrum in Sierra Leone (Coulter 2009: 6). As Michael Jackson argued in his research on the Kuranko, it serves 'as one of the basic armatures for structuring all social relations' (Jackson 1977: 81 cited in Coulter 2009: 6). Indeed, notions of personhood in Sierra Leone continue to be highly gendered in a dialectic between normative assumptions and lived realities. Gendered agency is exhibited through particular ways of exercising power or producing effects that are unique to individuals based on their gender, either as women or men (Wardlow 2006). Many research collaborators based their ideas on nearly unquestioned gendered expectations, for example:

'Women and men are naturally different and have particular roles and responsibilities, with men dominating over women in all spheres of life'.
'Women have the weak and men the strong mind or that women are the weaker sex (God made Eve out of the rib of Adam)'.
'Husbands have control and rights over the bodies and sexualities of their wives. Wives need to be sexually available always'.
'Love and affection are accompanied by jealousy and social monitoring'.
'Physical and sexual violence can illustrate affection. Men who do not beat and monitor their wives may have stopped being jealous and have therefore ceased to love'.
'Wives are beaten if they have done something wrong'.
'A husband's behaviour is a wife's responsibility. Wives have the duty to "change" their husbands. A violent husband indicates a wife's failure to be a "good wife".' (Schneider 2019a)

Such perceptions are described as traditional. However, while gender parallelism has a long history in the region, the question arises whether gendered hierarchies may be the outcome of the colonial encounter and ongoing international influences.[14] It may be that it was these encounters that brought about a sense of starkly juxtaposed and clashing viewpoints and gave rise to diverging demands (see, e.g., Cooper and Stoler 1997; Comaroff and Comaroff 2021). When trying to comprehend the threat reporting can pose to masculinity as well as femininity, we must first understand the social positioning of adult men and women within households.

Gendered Expectations That Affect Reporting

Here, the popular concept of the weak mind (women) and the strong mind (men) is particularly helpful.[15] Explaining this notion to me, Tejan (35) from Goderich says: 'A woman's mind is like a piece of paper. It is crumbled and stretched by everyone she loves, who shape its form. It has no mind on its own'. Suge explains: 'Women make you crazy, really! Men have a strong and independent mind; they make their decisions for themselves, but women, ah, they are always connected. Everyone influences them: family, friends, children ... You have no say on your own'.

Suge's notion of women as the social connectors between people and as those who build their lives firmly on others recalls the metaphor of the teeth (men) and the tongue (women), where the tongue moves the food between different parts of the mouth. The concept of a weak mind, as articulated by Tejan, views women as confined to the house and emotionally reliant on their family and children. Despite their malleability and permanence, like tongues in the mouth, women are perceived to be 'the weaker sex' (Jackson 2017: 71) and hence in need of male protection. Sons are therefore required to defend and protect their mothers when they become adults and to prioritise their mothers' needs before the needs of their wives. Dr Momo's statement that men report when their wives curse their mothers is based upon this conviction. Papani explains: 'It is like a progression. As a wife, you have children and you do everything for them. Then later, they will be the ones who take care of

---

[14] This appears even more likely considering that while gender fluidity, multiple genders and queer relationships have a long history in Sierra Leone—evident in traditional sodalities and social formations—current public discourse blends them out. Other genders, relationships and sexual orientations are either carefully concealed behind the normative, heterosexual male-female binary or marginalized to the point that they exist beneath, rather than alongside, heteronormative arrangements.

[15] And it also relates to rigid teeth and flexible tongues.

you'. And his wife, Aunty Kadie, adds: 'As a wife, you expect your husband to put his mother first, just like you expect your sons to put you first. You know Josephus ... when Issa cursed me, he had to make a case out of that' (see Chapter 6). A man who does not protect his mother and ensure her well-being loses respect.

Men who report their wives for cursing or mistreating their mothers therefore act in accordance with their duties. 'When your wife curses your mother, either you beat her or abuse her, or you must report her for her to be told off and for everybody to see that you respect and cherish your mother and that nobody should dare to go near her', explained Lansana (38). However, in relation to their wives and girlfriends as well as their children, men are often characterised as self-centred, pursuing their desires and needs with greater independence than women. Men are considered unpredictable, not 'steady', and difficult to restrain; if someone tries to limit their freedom, they resist with great force, even if it means causing destruction in the process. From the perspective of the social union of the household, however, this means that women are regarded as the resilient foundations of their households, who prioritise the well-being of others over their own (Wardlow 2006; Wolputte 2016). In contrast, men are inflexible and egoistic. As a result, a family can withstand the absence of a man, but not of a woman, who is considered the nucleus of the home.

The Gender of the Heart

Within sexual relationships, men's actions concerning emotions and desires are often interpreted as responses to women's behaviour. The notion of warm and cold hearts plays into this as well. Common proverbs depict men as having warm hearts, which suggests that they are hot-tempered and prone to anger. Meanwhile, women have cool or washed hearts, which implies that they tend to approach situations thoughtfully and avoid impulsive actions based on affect. These notions further hold that the need to 'put their families first' has imparted to women the ability not to give in to their affects; to live with, not according to, their emotions. Because of their ability to control their emotions as well as to read the emotions of others and influence them, women's words are not easily believed (see Apsatu's case above and Chapters 4 and 6). Moreover, women are expected to 'control and change men', as men are viewed as being susceptible to the influence of strong women. As a result, women are held accountable for the actions of their partners or sons, both within and outside of the household. For instance, if a man engages in infidelity or if he is 'spoilt', the responsibility may fall on his female partner or mother. This means that when a woman reports her partner to the police for violence, it is akin to admitting her own failure to prevent such behaviour or accusing his mother for failing to raise him appropriately. Reporting, furthermore, provokes men's already warm hearts. During a broadcast of 'Love Talk' by Radio Galaxy, the presenter stated:

Women should not cause problems but encourage a man. They should be neither disrespectful nor harsh to the man. Men do not appreciate women with warm hearts and women who cause palaver and *wahala*. Women have the highest responsibility for changing the men. A man's character is naturally rough and loud, and women should make them calm and help them to change. If women do not encourage their men, then men cannot be stopped from beating them and from going to the streets. The woman is greatly responsible for male violence.

Teeth and Tongue: Of Multiple Gendered Ideologies

Pierre Bourdieu's crucial proposition is that 'masculine domination' (Bourdieu 2001), as he calls it, does not depend on demonstrations of physical power because it has become an accepted, internalised, symbolic construct for men and women alike. But the Sierra Leonean case is much more complicated than this. If one followed Bourdieu, violence due to a crisis of masculinity would mean that the subconscious agreement that men are in power has collapsed, making physical violence necessary for 'domination'. By contrast, however, the lived realities of my research collaborators in Sierra Leone subvert the prevailing gendered expectations of 'dominant masculine' and 'dominated feminine', just as authors criticise Bourdieu for lacking nuance, complexity, and historical depth (e.g. Mottier 2002: 353).

As we see in Sierra Leone, the idea of masculine domination is much more than a subconscious product of history. Instead, women and men consciously reflect upon their respective positions. Women are said to be stronger emotionally and socially and to be better able to put the needs of others before their own. In Freetown, women are often the main breadwinners, the heads of their households, and the mediators of violence within communities. This position is not a present-day phenomenon but was already described by various elders with whom I conducted research and by older ethnographies alike (Hoffer 1972; Rosaldo, Lamphere, and Bamberger 1974; White 1981; Alie 1990; Day 1994; Ojukutu-Macauley 1997: 92; Coulter 2009). Among the Kuranko, Michael Jackson discusses the paradox involved in the idea that women are 'the weaker sex' while in everyday life they often feed and provide for the household (Jackson 2017: 17, 37). Caroline Bledsoe (1980a) observes that, although men formally hold power, women maintain considerable personal autonomy through strategic manoeuvres, thereby securing significant political and economic influence for themselves. Mariane Ferme shows how 'the division of the world between brave men and senseless women masks a cultural strategy that tends to elide these distinctions when they most matter' (Ferme 2001: 61). In her work on the Mende of the Gola rainforest, Melissa Leach describes the 'covert strategies' used by single and married women alike to acquire resources 'partly on favours from lovers' and partly through obtaining and selling resources 'from their husbands and male kin without explicit authorisation' (Leach 1994: 198).

In trying to understand the role of dominant narratives and how they align with or collide with lived experiences, I turn to the distinction that Jean and John Comaroff made between ideology and hegemony, and thus to 'the two dominant forms in which power ... is entailed in culture' (Comaroff and Comaroff 1991: 22).[16] The way in which Bourdieu and those projecting such gendered expectations naturalise their argument seems to imply hegemony: static, taken for granted as universally true, seldom contested (see, e.g. Comaroff and Comaroff 1991: 23; Bakare Yusuf 2003: 7). Yet, because gender ideals must be articulated and argued for, they present ideologies rather than a static, taken-for-granted, and seldom-contested hegemony. As Bibi Bakare Yusuf states, this 'discursive framework seeks to legitimate and reproduce certain norms of power and privilege' (Bakare Yusuf 2003: 132). However, the idea of male dominance and its concomitant metaphors remain powerful. And not only men promote and recite them; women do too. Masculine domination is used as a conscious tactic that allows people to live with contradictions and negotiate a certain freedom within seemingly rigid structures. Rather than presenting an unquestioned and taken-for-granted hegemony, masculine domination should be understood as an ideology that has to be articulated and argued for to 'legitimate and reproduce certain norms of power and privilege' (Bakare Yusuf 2003: 132; see also Comaroff and Comaroff 1991: 22–3).

In Sierra Leone, state bodies and communities, for example, express different 'systems of meanings, values, and beliefs' around gender, relationships, violence and responses to it (Comaroff and Comaroff 1991: 24). Consequently, in the contested sociopolitical fields of Sierra Leone, different ideologies, which shape conceptions but which do not neatly

---

[16] This facilitates an analysis both of competing ideologies at a given moment and their developments.

align with lived realities, confront, challenge, and influence each other (Comaroff and Comaroff 1991: 24; see also Nader 1990). In urban Sierra Leone, there is no longer one hegemonic ideal of gender complementarity (cf. Ferme 2001). Instead, there are multiple gender ideologies that aim to establish hegemony. This is captured by the notion of the teeth and the tongue, and its various interpretations. At the core of these competing ideologies today is an abrasive relationship between men and women, in which complementarity is not given but must be constantly struggled for through conflict, compromise, and, often enough, violence. Relationships today are shaped and influenced by, and often torn between, such competing ideologies of households, community and state, and human rights and development discourses. The teeth and the tongue thus provide a novel lens through which to gauge contemporary gender relations in urban Sierra Leone as well as beyond. Indeed, in the contemporary globalised world gender relations and relationship dynamics are not forged in isolation from such ideologies, nor can they split from their own histories.

Reporting as a Threat to Successful Masculinity and Femininity

In present-day Sierra Leone, there is an unspoken recognition that women possess greater emotional, social, and economic strength than men. Women are more adept at shaping the behaviour of others and of directing and managing social groups. Nonetheless, it is important for both partners to maintain the appearance of male dominance and female subordination in order to preserve social capital and retain the respect of their families and communities. This illustrates the significant influence that such gendered concepts hold in day-to-day life. In this context, the popular notion that women must be controlled so they do not 'dance on the heads of men' or 'make men their marionettes' takes on a different connotation. They need to be 'kept low' or, more accurately, be put down because they are in fact stronger. Just as women are punished more severely because they are believed to be better able to 'swallow', women's oppression is justified by a notion of superior abilities that must be contained. The result is two different cognitive spheres – the physical and the imagined – which position women's and men's roles in relation to each other differently.

The covert acknowledgement of the strength of women simultaneously makes women responsible for male violence. Male violence becomes a symbol of women's failure to 'dominate in hiding'. Thus, while women are understood to be nominally weaker, in practice they are expected to govern seemingly free-wheeling male nature. And while everyday realities reveal women as more capable of directing and managing social groups, they must not openly demonstrate their superior capacities. If they do, they provoke men's retribution. Men are said to be 'cornered into' demonstrating their strong role within a household by using physical force. Failure to do so leads to their downfall, not only within the home but within society (Chapters 4–6). Men are therefore coerced into demonstrating a certain form of masculinity. Apsatu explains:

> Sierra Leonean society corners men and brands them as being used by their wives if they are not strong and dominant and if they contribute to the household chores and child-rearing duties. So, to be considered a real man, you have to stop that. If men want to be given authority or a job, they might be denied that if others know that they work in the household because this is considered as them being weak and unmanly. Public shaming and exclusion is common, and especially severe by men who themselves do not want to be emasculated. Men do whatever they can to keep their prestige and reputation in society. Their violence is just part of upkeeping that image.

Aunty Kadie, Papani's wife, told me: 'It is not natural for men to do these things [household chores]; we have women for that. If I want somebody to cook and clean ... I take a woman. What's the role of men, if they are not even real men anymore?' And Mr Mohamed further added: 'When you as a man do these things in the home, nobody will take you seriously anymore. You will be the laughing stock of everybody and you will never get a promotion in your job. Never ever. What kind of man can be trusted to run a business when he is not even able to run his wife?'

This recalls the literature on the 'crisis of masculinity in Africa' or the crisis of the self-made man in Europe, which interprets violence by men against women as a response to their diminishing economic and social 'domination' (see Morrell 2001; Xaba 2001; Whitehead 2002; Walker 2005; Morrell, Jewkes, and Lindegger 2012; Dunaiski 2013). This literature is valuable in understanding the complex pressures and circumstances under which men and boys negotiate their masculinity. However, it depicts these dynamics as new rather than showing their continuities. What must also be considered is the important role women play in these dynamics and the many ways in which women expect and execute violence themselves, react to violence from their (sexual) partners, and are in charge of mediating violence. A further major role is played by specific legal landscapes, institutional developments, and the discourses and interventions of activists, NGOs, and human rights organisations.

My research shows that gender parallelism is not a fact but is better understood as a tactic. To the observer, it may seem like a smooth blanket, but underneath the covert worlds of tactics obfuscate clear boundaries and challenge assigned roles within the social hierarchy. In Freetown, research collaborators' practices upset neat gender parallelism while still using it as a framework of reference. Moreover, as my analysis reveals, there is no longer one model of gender parallelism. Indeed, gender parallelisms or, rather, different gendered ideologies more accurately capture the current situation. In Freetown, household, community, and state ideas of gender relations are often at odds with each other, and interpersonal relationships are caught between these different dynamics. What is happening in Sierra Leone is not a crisis of masculinity but rather a crisis of gender dynamics in a gendered social and legal world. In Freetown, men and women negotiate their relationships between personal circumstances, (legal) developments, and various norms. It is through untangling these competing ideologies and irreconcilable notions of gendered personhood and gendered expectations that we can better grasp the extreme situation of men when they report domestic violence to the police.

In an earlier chapter, we came across a mother (Chapter 6) who reported her daughter-in-law for controlling her son because he changed diapers and conducted household chores. This situation was interpreted by her as the result of his having lost all control over his mind and being – an unnatural and fearful outcome of violence committed against him. In MSaw's case, the community approached it as one in which his dispositions had been muted owing to the violence committed by his girlfriend. Hence, his masculinity was suspended, and he could not be judged for his actions. Only once the woman was made to withdraw her hold over him was he believed to have acquired agency again.

Therefore, in Sierra Leone, gender and gendered practices are deeply ingrained in underlying assumptions that seek to justify and excuse behaviour and assign responsibility. Both men and women frequently described the gendered ideologies around appropriate behaviour as 'heavy'. Even though empirical reality and personal needs or desires may differ considerably from these expectations, transgressing them openly questions and threatens masculinity or femininity. Reporting is one way in which people's habits, tacit behaviours, and positioning challenge each other. And here we need to consider not only the discrepancies between world views and lived experiences, but also the possible disconnection between habits and positions consciously reflected upon. Referring to habit, to 'ordinary everyday forms of social exchange and reciprocity', Cowan shows that 'culture is more than intertwining, enduring, and contesting narratives; it also includes the very significant domain of the tacit and unspoken' (Cowan 2006: 17). 'Social symbolizations, hierarchies and exclusions', she says, 'are quietly and often unreflectively reproduced' and inscribed in 'the structures of fantasy of the individual unconscious' (Cowan 2006: 17).

Reporting to the police to further 'human rights' means breaking with the habitual way in which 'things are done', as Papani says. When men turn to the police to look for assistance with their relationships, they contradict ideologies that position women and men on opposite ends of emotional, affective, and intellectual traits. It makes them visible, questions them. When reporting, women risk the dissolution of the household and of their femininity, while men risk the disintegration of their masculinity. Women who report embody the fear of the feminine (discussed in Chapter 5), which threatens to make men obsolete. When they report, women may carry both the 'feminine' and 'masculine' simultaneously. On the one hand, they take charge over their decisions, thereby displaying 'masculine' independence and individualism; on the other, reporting may also be done in the interest of protecting one's children (the ultimate 'feminine' characteristic).

Men who report challenge their masculinity. They are seen as unmanly, as castrated. Bonnie Mann (2014), in her work on terrorism and masculinity in the United States, shows how many of the men she spoke to described as the ultimate horror, not the physical torture they endured, but their being stripped of their masculinity, becoming women. In Sierra Leone, however, men who report do not become women; rather, they are described as children: irresponsible, unable to take care of themselves, in need of the protection of another, of a stronger body or institution (Mann 2014). Consequently, men's turning to the police when experiencing violence, thereby acknowledging their lack of control and power, is interpreted not only as problematic, but also as the ultimate weakness. Pepemboy (52), a plumber from Allentown, said: 'That man might as well kill himself. He is weaker than a woman, that one. Imagine your wife beats you and you can't even handle it, so you run and report to the police, like a child. Oh Salone. What will happen to this country?' In many ways, reporting a woman for beating harms the masculine ideal more than enduring a public slapping (Chapter 5).

In Sierra Leone, the gender justice laws have failed to adequately consider the specific social situations and power dynamics that contribute to the subordination and responsibility of both men and women. By taking these factors into account, we can understand why women, who often bear the burden of carrying entire households on their shoulders, are hesitant to report their partners to the police. Such an action would result in the breakdown of the relationship and could lead to the loss of crucial familial support. They also explain why men do not feel able to report at all. Because there is little dialogue between the different ideals of gendered behaviour held by the state, the community, and the household, men and women caught between them are unable to turn to one without turning their back on the other. Hence, competing ideologies that overrule the hegemony of gender complementarity present advertisements for lived realities that are often unachievable for people whose daily lives are grounded in a different system.

In addition to the ideological and normative underpinnings, one also needs to consider the material and practical possibilities of reporting. If those who experience violence are urged to come forward and are tacitly, sometimes even openly, held responsible for further violence if they do not or cannot come forward, this adds additional burdens. The call to report must go hand in hand with political and social struggles to offer real possibilities for reporting securely and being safe thereafter. The success of efforts to prevent and respond to violence depends to a large extent on their ability to break down gendered expectations as well as their alignment with either state or community. Only if people from all backgrounds are able to report, and only if reporting no longer demands existential choices, can social policy really work to decrease violence and advance gender justice. The first prerequisite for such a development is dialogue and a thorough understanding of the local context.

The next chapter engages with the SOA and the school ban on pregnant girls and thus with regulations concerning minors. It thereby examines yet another set of gendered state ideologies that aims to overrule community principles.

8 Minors before the Law
Building Futures, Policing Sex

> Each month, hundreds of cases of rape and sexual assaults are being reported. These despicable crimes of sexual violence are being committed against our women, girls, and babies. On this note, I therefore declare rape and sexual violence as National Emergency. With this declaration, I have also directed the following ... With immediate effect, sexual penetration of Minors is punishable by LIFE IMPRISONMENT. (Maada Bio 2019)

What happens when state institutions and citizens have different views about what constitutes violence in relationships with and between minors and how it should be dealt with?[1] This chapter discusses the Sexual Offences Act (SOA) and the Sexual Offences Amendment Act (SOAA), and the school ban (SB) on visibly pregnant girls. It considers the ways in which the criminal justice system and its institutions treat violence in relationships involving minors. Here, the main (often only) focus lies on sexual relationships that are regarded as violent irrespective of the perspectives of those involved. The chapter commences with an analysis of the legal regulations of the SOA and how they are perceived among research collaborators. It shows how, based on the recommendations of the TRC (2004a) in post-war Sierra Leone, development agencies, lawmakers, and politicians discursively framed and justified the SOA by positioning the people implicated in sexual offences cases within an 'imagined otherness' (Carlbom 2003: 57; Sartre 2004; Ahmed 2014: 42–3). Thereafter, there is a discussion of the political aspects of this act and its amendment as well as the subsequent school ban (Mahtani 2016; Villa 2017). I also describe the structures of reporting and the trajectories of cases of sexual offence. To be effective, the criminal justice system renders persons and acts abstract. It constructs 'constitutive outsides' (Hall 1996: 3; Esposito 2011). When minors are involved, sentences are no longer relative and relational. The courts would not consider the

---

[1] To be clear, this chapter does not consider rape or assault. It focusses on sexual activities with or between minors in which consent applies but which are unlawful.

cases, for example, of Issa against Josephus or Apsatu against her husband. Rather, they examine whether there is a clear perpetrator–victim relationship between defendant and claimant. These abstractions seek to provide clarity without considering the complexity of social and emotional factors. The chapter also explains the role of age in public perception as a social factor and how this differs from the numerical certainty required by legal frameworks. It provides the reflections and criticisms of citizens and criminal justice personnel, and puts these in conversation with the analysis.

The Sexual Offences Act and the School Ban on Visibly Pregnant Girls

A Sexual Penetration Case

Principal Magistrate Binneh of Freetown Magistrate's Court No. 1 presides over 15–30 cases daily. If the power works, several rows of fans are turning on the wooden-tiled ceiling among two flickering light-bulbs, one in the front and one in the back of the room. If, as on most days, the power is interrupted, litigants, their families, journalists, and criminal justice personnel wave leaflets and fans in front of their faces to make the heat bearable. The large room is divided into several sections. On a raised podium in the front is the magistrate's seat facing the courtroom. A door to its left leads to the Magistrate's chambers, where he presides over particularly sensitive cases. A caged space to its right is the witness stand. In front of his podium, there is a small desk reserved for his two paralegals, women in their early twenties; on the table are piles and piles of case files. Then facing the judge's podium follow rows of comfortable leather seats and tables for the lawyers. On the left-hand side are three rows of benches and tables reserved for police officers and Rainbo Centre personnel. The second half of the room is divided as follows. Next to the entrance door, there are three rows of benches for 'journalists only', which is where I usually sit. In the very back, there are rows for litigants and family members. On the right and farthest away from the door is a small bench on which the accused are seated, handcuffed together in pairs of two. Finally, in the middle of the room is a fenced-in space where the accused must stand when their case is heard.

When I enter the court on 17 June 2016, Magistrate Binneh is just about to open another case dealing with sexual penetration. He calls the accused. After the police officer has uncuffed him, the young man is called to enter the fenced space in the middle of the courtroom. But because his hands are shaking so much, he is unable to open the small door to enter the stand without the help of the police officer. Magistrate Binneh reads the accusation, 'sexual penetration of a minor', and asks the young man how he pleads: *na so I bi or notto so I be?* ['how do you plead?']. When asked to speak, the accused starts shaking uncontrollably, and the silence of the courtroom lifts under the murmurs of those present. I can hear his teeth chattering. He looks no older than 15 or 16. His terror invokes sympathy and pity among those present: 'Sahr, this man is only a small boy', remarks one woman. 'Look at him, he is so afraid', states another. After Magistrate Binneh demands silence using his gavel, he says: 'You have been declared an adult at the police station. I will send you for age assessment, but I do not believe you to be under 18. If you have a lawyer, you want to ask for a birth certificate. For now, you are going back to prison'. He adjourns the case to the following Tuesday. The accused keeps looking at what may be his parents, tears running down his face. He never enters his plea. Upon returning to the accused's bench, the other accused persons hold him around the shoulder. It looks as though they are preventing him from falling off the bench, but it is unclear whether this is to comfort or threaten him.

The following week, the case is heard in chambers. The alleged victim is a 17-year-old girl [the same age as Ester in Chapter 6], who is seven months pregnant. The accused is asked to face the wall during her testimony. The accused has such severe stomach pain that he has trouble standing. He frequently drops on his knees until the police officer cautions him to stand up again. The accused then struggles to get back on his feet until his knees give in once more. The surveillance police officer says he has had this pain since being transferred to the remand block in Pademba Road Prison, to which a man says jokingly: 'This prison will kill you, just wait. First the soup is like water running down your arm and then it runs right back out of you.' Another lawyer also not involved in the case turns to the alleged victim and says: 'Ah Salone, na so you treat us men. First you seduce us, then you punish us?'

When testifying, the alleged victim explains that she had sex with the accused regularly between December 2015 and March 2016 because he was her boyfriend at that time. When she was asked how it made her feel, she said: 'I felt fine'. She explains that eventually she became pregnant and that once her pregnancy was visible, her teacher took her to the police station to report the matter. From there, they went to the hospital to obtain the medical report that stated that her hymen was broken and that she had been found to be pregnant. Subsequently, and in accordance with the 'school ban for pregnant girls', she was expelled from school.

The accused is from a poor family and cannot afford a lawyer. He has not yet been assigned a free lawyer from the Legal Aid Board because his case has not reached the High Court. Magistrate Binneh says that the accused should try to prove he is underage but that he has no time to do special things for him because he has far too many cases to preside over. Without proof, he cannot be tried as an offender in a juvenile court rather than as an accused in a regular court. Binneh asks the accused when he was born, and he replies: '8 September 1999'. A week later, after an informal age assessment that was unable to verify his age below 18, Binneh says that he has no choice but to send the matter to the High Court.

The case is called at the High Court about six months later and is concluded in three hearings. In all hearings, the girl and boy confirm that they are in a relationship. When I speak with her, the alleged victim consistently smiles and laughs when describing being with the accused. It is very clear that they are a couple who were together with the blessing of those family members living under the same roof. On 19 February 2017, the accused is convicted and sentenced to eight years in prison.

What Is the Sexual Offences Act and Why Was It Implemented?

This case is a consequence of the SOA. The SOA was the product of the recommendations of the TRC (2018) and the research of IOs, NGOs, and local women's movements, which pointed to large-scale sexual trafficking, sexual slavery, rape, and sexual assault during and after the civil war, particularly involving minors. The TRC report highlighted the high numbers of young girls being sexually abused by much older men (TRC 2004a; 2004b). It pointed to the difficulty girls experience when reporting such issues due to the prevalence of informal or 'friendly' settlements (Chapter 7). The report further made a strong recommendation to raise the age of maturity to 18. Jointly promoted by the Parliamentary Human Rights Commission, the Law Reform Commission, the government, and various partners, the SOA was ratified in 2012. It raised the age of sexual consent to 18, criminalised all sexual relationships with minors, and increased sentences to a maximum of 15 years. Marriage would no longer be a valid defence. In 2019, following the declaration of a national emergency on rape and teenage pregnancy, the SOA was amended and now includes the possibility of life sentences for perpetrators. It also lowers the age of criminal responsibility and now allows boys as young as 12 to be sentenced for sexual acts (Government of Sierra Leone 2019).

Prior to the ratification of the SOA, Sierra Leone regulated sexual violence against minors by the Prevention of Cruelty to Children Act (PCAA) of 1926. Section 6 of the PCAA defined unlawful carnal knowledge – penetration of the victim's vagina by the penis of the accused – of a girl below 13 as a crime that carried a punishment of 15 years of imprisonment, irrespective of her consent. Section 7 stated that if a girl was above 13 but under 14 years, the sentence should be reduced to two years of imprisonment. For any sexual crime committed against a person above 14 years, consent was a possible defence.

To bridge this gap between 14 and 18, section 1, part 1 of the SOA defines a child as any 'person under the age of 18'. Part 1, section 4 of the SOA states: 'a person below the age of 18 is not capable of giving consent ... it shall not be a defence to an offence under this Act to show that the child has consented to the act that forms the subject matter of the charge'. The Act describes sexual penetration (SP) as 'any act which causes the penetration ... of the vagina, anus or mouth of a person by the penis or any other part of the body of another person, or by an object'. SP is an offence 'liable on conviction to a term of imprisonment not less than five years and not exceeding fifteen years'. Moreover:

A person who –

(a) touches a child in a sexual manner; or
(b) compels a child to touch the accused person's own body in a sexual manner ...

is liable on conviction to a term of imprisonment not exceeding fifteen years. (Government of Sierra Leone 2012)

Consequently, as anyone under the age of 18 is legally regarded as a child, any sexual activity with them constitutes a criminal offence with a prison sentence of up to 15 years.

Political Developments That Influenced the SOA

The development and ratification of the SOA dovetailed with former president Ernest Bai Koroma's re-election platform (*The Agenda for Prosperity 2013–2018*).[2] In its attempt to address donor interests and development agendas, this strategy focussed inter alia on the girl child and on the 'fight against teenage pregnancy' that was formulated in the *National Strategy for the Reduction of Teenage Pregnancy (2013–2015)*

---

[2] See https://faolex.fao.org/docs/pdf/sie149110.pdf. Sierra Leone is highly dependent on foreign aid, which gives donors power to shape local agendas. Koroma aimed at aligning Sierra Leone's political strategy with the goals of international donors (e.g. UN agencies, governments and international NGOs) and local civil society organisations. These groups focus mainly on partnering against poverty and abuse, (girls') education, gender equality, and girls' empowerment, as well as protection from violence (e.g. Fofana 2009; UNICEF 2014; 2017).

(Government of Sierra Leone 2013).³ In the post-war era, Koroma's efforts to promote Sierra Leone as a nation in which development goals were a top priority and which was therefore deserving of development funding seemed to be undercut by young people's fluid relationships and their sexual experimentation. Consequently, young people's behaviours and diverse relationships were less and less appreciated. Young people were reconfigured as unruly subjects interfering with government attempts to demonstrate that in Sierra Leone sex was sufficiently policed.

In aligning some of the TRC recommendations for preventing violence with the concerns of donor bodies for educating girls and preventing early marriage and teenage pregnancy, the SOA was supposed to solve two problems at once. By criminalising all sexual relationships with minors and removing perpetrators from society, it was thought that teenage pregnancy and rape could be stopped. Koroma's successor, the current president Maada Bio, followed in his footsteps by declaring a national emergency on rape and sexual violence and by subsequently ratifying the SOAA.⁴ The SOAA makes further age-related distinctions. A 'child' – which, according to chapter 44 of the Children and Young Persons Act, 'means a person under the age of fourteen years' (Government of Sierra Leone 1945) – 'who engages in an act of sexual penetration on another child or rape commits an offence and is liable on conviction to a term of imprisonment of not less than five years (5) and not more than fifteen (15) years imprisonment' (Government of Sierra Leone 2019: section 4, no. 8). A 'young person', on the other hand, means 'a person who is fourteen years of age or upwards and under the age of seventeen years' (Government of Sierra Leone 1945). According to the SOAA, a young person 'who engages in an act of sexual penetration or rape on another person commits an offence and is liable on conviction to a term of imprisonment of not less than ten (10) years to life imprisonment' (Government of Sierra Leone 2019: section 4, no. 8). Finally, 'a person above the age of a youth who engages in sexual penetration or rape on another person commits an offence and is liable on conviction to a term of imprisonment of not less than fifteen (15) years to life imprisonment' (Government of Sierra Leone 2019: section 4, no. 8).

---

³ The strategy was later reviewed and reformulated into the *National Strategy for the Reduction of Adolescent Pregnancy and Child Marriage* (2018–22). See Government of Sierra Leone (2018).

⁴ The first Lady, Fatima Maada Bio, launched the *Hands Off Our Girls* campaign in December 2018, which aims to ban early child marriage, end gender-based violence and rape, and increase access to reproductive healthcare and treatment (Sambira 2024).

While both presidents were responding to the urgent need to address high levels of rape and sexual violence,[5] the resulting laws have tremendous implications for desire and for the consensual sexual relationships of young people as well. Indeed, as I have argued elsewhere, age-of-consent law creates multifaceted challenges. If the age is set too high, it undermines the agency of young people. Conversely, if the age is set too low, it does not provide adequate protection for vulnerable young people (Schneider 2019c).

By setting the minimum age of consent at 18 and, at the same time, passing laws that can convict people below that age for sexual acts, Sierra Leone has created a gendered paradox – even though the laws are technically gender-neutral. Young girls cannot consent to sexual relationships, yet young boys can be sentenced for them.

During Koroma's presidency, increased campaigning began around young girls' and boys' sexual behaviour. A poster by UN Women and the United Nations Population Fund (UNFPA) (see Figure 8.1), which was displayed in western Freetown, was addressed to men and boys and told them to abstain from having sex with girls legally unable to consent. Although she is depicted in the picture, the girl has no decision-making power. Her opinion and her possible desire do not matter. It is men who must decide how to act, while girls' sexuality is at the mercy of their decision. The poster does not show a girl in a school uniform or a man who is an elder. Rather, it depicts a young couple with a much smaller age difference. Interestingly, while the law is written in a gender-neutral manner, the kind of attitude displayed on the poster carries over into sentencing. What magistrates and judges consider is whether boys have committed a crime against girls who are unable to consent, not vice versa. To my knowledge and that of my research collaborators, no woman has ever been convicted for sleeping with an underage boy.

Another poster, produced by the Sierra Leonean Development and Media Agency, the government, and German partners (see Figure 8.2), depicted sex as a distraction and as destructive of girls' education and their futures.[6] The two posters taken together show that girls are addressed and warned about sex prior to puberty. Once they have entered puberty, they

---

[5] Maada Bio, for instance, declared a national emergency of rape and sexual violence as a response to 'intense pressure and protest by civil society groups after the rape and subsequent paralysis of a 5-year-old girl ... While such heinous crimes were not new, activists cited an increasing number of rapes ... and Sierra Leone's history of violence against women' (Afro Barometer 2021).

[6] See also Bledsoe's (1990b) work on school fees and the marriage process among the Mende in Sierra Leone or Lynn Thomas's (2003) discussion of state interests and their influence on women's bodies and reproductive capacities in Kenya.

176   Minors before the Law: Building Futures, Policing Sex

Figure 8.1 An example of the campaigning that accompanied the SOA. Poster by UN Women and UNFPA.

are silenced. The communication is not conducted with them, but about them. It seems that institutions find it easier to forbid men to engage in sexual activity than to address female desire. Moreover, these posters do not actually speak about rape. Rather, they refer to sexually active young people. However, the SOA, the SOAA, and the campaigning around them did not manage to end teenage pregnancies. This continues to be regarded as one of Sierra Leone's biggest problems.

The School Ban on Visibly Pregnant Girls

UNICEF Sierra Leone's main page on its website states:

In Sierra Leone, teenage pregnancy and child marriage are common. According to the country's 2013 Demographic and Health Survey, 13 per cent of girls are married by their 15th birthday and 39 per cent of girls before their 18th birthday ... Teenage pregnancy reduces a girl's chances in life, often interfering with schooling, limiting opportunities, and placing girls at increased risk of child marriage, HIV infections and domestic violence. According to the World Health Organization, teenage pregnancy is also a leading cause of death for mothers in

Figure 8.2 Poster framing early sex as destructive.

Sierra Leone. Data from 2015 show the country's maternal mortality rate is at 1,360 deaths per 100,000 live births. (UNICEF 2017)[7]

Sabrina Mahtani, writing for Amnesty International, states that 'even before Ebola broke out in late 2013, Sierra Leone had one of the highest teenage pregnancy rates in the world, with 28% of girls aged 15–19 years pregnant or having already given birth at least once' (Mahtani 2016). During the Ebola pandemic (2013–16), studies reported an increase in teenage pregnancy. According to one such study by the Secure Livelihoods Consortium, UNFPA surveys indicated that 18,119 teenage girls became pregnant during the Ebola outbreak (Mahtani 2016). These studies have been sharply contested by local health workers and by

---

[7] This is an example of the selective use of statistics, which are unable to say anything about the factual risks of teenage pregnancy because the data refer to all pregnancies and are not differentiated into age groups.

Rainbo Centre personnel who, in interviews with me, described these statistics as political fabrications. 'Before the Ebola outbreak, most institutions did not gather data', explained a former Rainbo Centre employee. 'We only had data from the war and the TRC. During Ebola, suddenly statistics became very important. But it seemed as if they showed a devastating trend, when really they showed nothing new'.

Nevertheless, government officials relied on these data and likened the 'teenage pregnancy epidemic' to the Ebola pandemic (Seema 2016; Whyte 2016). This second 'disease of social intimacy' (Richards et al. 2015: 1) was presented as threatening the prosperity and well-being of all Sierra Leoneans. Even before the pandemic, girls found to be pregnant were regularly banned from attending school and sitting exams. However, this practice had never been formalised. In April 2015, the Ministry of Education, Science and Technology published a statement that formally banned pregnant girls from mainstream education and from taking exams. The ban took effect immediately and was carried out by means of searches and physical examinations of girls. Although international donors proposed an alternative 'bridging system' (Mahtani 2016) in the form of special education for pregnant girls in different schools, this has never been fully realised.

How Is the Effectiveness of the SOA and the SB Ensured?

To function, the SB and the SOA require the participation of citizens. By themselves, state institutions would have been largely ineffective in policing young people's relationships. They are unable to enter communities or households without the assistance of citizens. They do not have the resources to do so and can only act if they are called upon. Furthermore, different mediation systems have their own jurisdictions. According to Sally Falk Moore, 'an inspection of semi-autonomous social fields strongly suggests that the various processes that make internally generated rules effective are often also the immediate forces that dictate the mode of compliance or noncompliance to state-made legal rules' (Moore 1973: 721). And, as we have seen in previous chapters, many citizens have ambivalent opinions about state institutions and take great care to keep the state at bay while informally and internally regulating disputes. State laws differ extensively from community procedures and point to different perceptions of gender, violence, and punishment. Compliance with them is therefore not a given.

Nevertheless, the reporting of sexual penetration cases has increased dramatically, from 95 reports in 2011 to over 2,398 in 2015 (FSU crime statistics). But how was it possible to mobilise enough citizens to render the laws effective? How could their reach encompass the different jurisdictions of households, communities, and the criminal justice institutions? To be effective, state institutions needed to persuade citizens that the laws were in their best interest. This required a discursive framing and subsequent calls to action. What needed to be created was the idea of an imaginary future Sierra Leone free of teenage pregnancy and rape. But such a future could only come about, it was claimed, by the smooth implementation of these laws. And their smooth implementation, in turn, was made the responsibility of citizens.

Sex as Pollution That Threatens Familial Control over Sexuality and Reproduction

Subsequently, state personnel adopted a language of pollution and described all sexual activity among young people, irrespective of consent or protection, as destructive. Consider the following statement by a politician whom I interviewed in September 2016:

We have a disease here in this country. All these young people go out and have sex without no consideration for nobody. They cannot stop that, and then they get pregnant even when still in school, and that is a hopeless situation for the parents and for the development of this country. So, we need laws which stop all that because only when there is fear, actual fear of a sentence, will people's actions change.

This politician's concern was not primarily for the two persons involved in potential sexual activity, but with the consequences for their families and for society. Hence, it taps into local notions of gender relations. Shanti Parikh has argued that the defilement law in Uganda, which also raised the age of consent to 18, is in effect an attempt to help fathers regain authority over their daughters' sexuality and sexual decision-making (Parikh 2012: 1779). 'It is plausible', says Deniz Kandiyoti in her work on patriarchal systems in Africa, that 'the emergence of the patriarchal extended family, which gives the senior man authority over everyone else … is bound up in the incorporation and control of the family by the state … and in the transition from kin-based to tributary modes of surplus control' (Kandiyoti 1988: 278).

The Sierra Leonean state thus sought to build its gendered ideals on those of communities and attempted to speak to them to mobilise their support. Subsequently, the president was urged to accept the role of guardian for all Sierra Leonean girls. This can be interpreted as an extension of the power of the paternal figure over the sexuality of those under his guard. The president, the father of all households, would

180   Minors before the Law: Building Futures, Policing Sex

Figure 8.3 Then president Ernest Bai Koroma's poster under the cotton tree.

become the ultimate guardian of young girls' sexuality and reproductive capacities (Figure 8.3).

The construction of the president as 'guardian of girls' was made possible by the TRC report, which stated:

316. Women and girls were the deliberate targets of sexual violence and rape by all the armed groups during the conflict. Women continue to be victims of gender-based violence. The Commission has noted the submissions made by women's groups, which point to the failure of successive governments to protect women and girls during the conflict and post-conflict periods.

317. The Commission recommends that the President, as the 'Father of the Nation' and as the Head of State, should acknowledge the harm suffered by women and girls during the conflict in Sierra Leone and offer an unequivocal apology to them ... This is an imperative recommendation. (TRC 2004b)

Thus, when Koroma claimed that 'violence against women is violence against the state' (see Figure 8.4), he was identifying with the subject

Figure 8.4 President Ernest Bai Koroma as the guardian.

position of guardian of women and girls. Simultaneously, he created an 'other' in the violent perpetrator, against whom the state could position itself and against whom it could unite to protect those under its guard. In a similar vein, President Maada Bio was quoted as stating:

On a sad note, thousands more cases of rape and sexual violence were unreported because some families and communities practise a culture of silence or indifference about sexual violence, leaving victims traumatised. He noted that alarmingly, the perpetrators were getting younger and their acts getting more violent and bestial ...

He said that government would engage communities and civil society in dialogues to eliminate the culture of compromise and silence around sexual violence, adding that the country must put an end to the scourge that was slowly wrecking the nation.

'On this note, I, therefore, declare rape and sexual violence as National Emergency'. (Statehouse of Sierra Leone 2019)

With the guardian installed, the next step was to pave the way for political action. To this end, ideas of safety, security, and prosperity were used to create the image of a future community free of violence and teenage pregnancy. Then a 'threat' to this wonderful future was conjured up by likening sex among young people to an infectious disease that polluted this possibility.[8] The issue here is not whether the threat is real and contagious. It may be entirely separate from the empirical reality. Rather, the threat is a 'structural function' that justifies the execution of violence against this 'other' (see Žižek 2008).[9] By being assigned a function, namely that of 'saving the girl child', groups of people could form a community. To enable this 'community of Sierra Leonean citizens' to act, the SOA was set up in such a way that anyone could report a case to the police. The official campaigns around the Act promoted the view that it was the duty of all Sierra Leoneans to ensure that sex did not take place with minors. By reporting pregnant girls and boys who have sex with girls to state institutions, communities made it possible for these institutions to extend their reach and effectively police young people's sexuality. The criminal justice system could now survey households and bedrooms, ban pregnant girls from school, and imprison boys who slept with these girls. Such actions seemingly expelled the 'threats' from the community and prevented them from re-entering and 'spreading' (Esposito 2011). By these means, state institutions helped form communities that would ensure the efficacy of its laws.

Responsible Citizens Report

However, not every Sierra Leonean started reporting. In the case described at the start of this chapter, those present were very sympathetic

---

[8] See Steinberg's (2013) work on the paradox between simultaneous openness about sexual activity and stigma and shame around sexual behaviour in South Africa.
[9] Yet this imagined 'other' is not a perpetrator of violence. While violence among adults is also illegal, it does not constitute a threat, as shown in the previous chapter.

towards the accused. People usually regard reporting others' 'private business' as *kongosa*, equivalent to 'name spoiling' and thus 'antisocial behaviour par excellence' (Szanto 2018). But in the eyes of the state, those who do not report, the 'families who practise a culture of silence' (in Maada Bio's words) and who thus obstruct the workings of the SOA, are separated out and made to form a 'them', as opposed to the 'respectable citizens' who do report (Comaroff and Comaroff 2016: x) – an imagined 'us'. It is not surprising therefore that most cases are not reported. After all, the victim is part of 'them', part of the persons who had sex.

For the family of the girl, reporting a case to the police is often a last resort. If, after a pregnancy occurs, negotiations with the family of the man or boy fails, or if the father of the child is deemed to be economically unable or socially unfit to care for the girl and her baby, they may turn to the police. An employee of the Rainbo Centre said:

> Most cases brought to us are statutory rape. Many only go once a pregnancy occurs and the family feels responsible to act. They need someone to take responsibility for the pregnancy to fend off shame from the family and ensure that the child will have a name. Many are frustrated if they paid for their daughter to go to school and then the daughter ends up pregnant and stops her education. They want someone to remunerate them for their expenses.

As I have shown, this remuneration usually takes place in informal settlements between the families involved. In the case of *ansa bɛlɛ*, it fends off shame for the pregnancy out of wedlock and assigns a father to the baby (Chapter 3).

The state's campaign to promote reporting has mainly been successful among those citizens who work for state institutions or interact with them frequently, such as teachers and pastors (Chapter 7). They tend to have faith in the ideas of human rights and the future of the nation-state, which are enshrined within this 'ideoscape' (Appadurai 1990: 296). State employees, moreover, frequently come in contact with human rights principles. Because they engage with large numbers of people, the state's campaign is effective even if it is unable to capture the masses. Reporting often takes place once a pregnancy occurs or if the relationship has become public. George (47), a middle-school teacher, told me: 'We the teachers are especially important. Whenever you see a pregnancy of a girl having sex and falling astray, you must report so for the greater good'. And Madame Conteh (34), a high-school teacher, said: 'We cannot rely on the girl or the parents to report. Maybe he is the boyfriend or maybe they will settle'.

These citizens who report act as a vanguard, helping build the ideological foundations of these laws, which then create their very subjectivities and shape their actions (Althusser 1972: 11). This allows them to report on sexual activity 'for the greater good'. In their practices of reporting on those who have sex, they doggedly attempt to create this world of tomorrow, thereby turning the destructive act of *kongosa* into an act of true faith (Kierkegaard 1983).[10]

Case Trajectories from the Police Station to the Magistrate's Court

After sexual penetration cases have been reported, the police and, later, the courts need to determine whether sex has taken place. At the police station, the alleged victim gives a first-person statement, which is included in the police report. Then the girl is sent to the Rainbo Centre, where a medical examination is conducted. Besides screening for diseases and injuries, this examination tries to establish whether the girl has a ruptured hymen. In the absence of forensic testing, it is the Rainbo Centre's medical report that plays a main role in determining an accused's fate. If the report says the hymen of the alleged victim has been broken, though it is unable to tell under which circumstances or when, a conviction is almost certain. This is so in the majority of cases. Then the accused is called to the station to make his statement. After that, he is usually sent to the remand block in Pademba Road Prison or, if he is very young, to Dems, the remand home for minors.

All sexual violence cases as well as matters involving minors are handled in chambers. Only the opening of cases is conducted in open court. All sexual penetration cases follow the same pattern. Those present in the chambers include the witness, the interrogating police officer of the FSU, the accused, sometimes journalists, and, if the accused has representation, his lawyers. The paralegal hands the case file to the magistrate. They then leave and close the door. During proceedings, the magistrate copies down the witness's statement word by word.

The police officer conducts the 'prosecution of the witness'. After the witness is sworn in, either with the Quran or the Bible, the witness is asked whether she recognises the accused person or persons. She is cautioned not to address them by their names but to refer to them by numbers (from one onwards). Then she is asked whether she remembers

---

[10] Kierkegaard interprets acts of true faith as the belief that one's 'God' (in this case 'the state') will deliver on a promise – here, a future free of sex with and among minors, thereby eradicating rape of minors and teenage pregnancy – which one knows well is too absurd to be possible (sex and desire cannot be eliminated), while one still maintains that it will happen – and believes that one must play one's part in this impossibility (Kierkegaard 1983: 47–50).

the date when the incident happened. After she confirms the date, she is asked to explain in detail the sequence of events: 'Tell us step by step what did happen'. The FSU officer has prepared the witness prior to her testimony.[11] They may ask follow-up or clarifying questions after or during the interview. After describing the incident, the alleged victim is asked: 'How did you feel after the incident?' and 'Did you witness anything on your body?'

Determining whether penetration has taken place is the prerequisite for a conviction. The length of the sentence is then determined by means of the last two questions: 'How did you feel?' and 'Did you witness anything on your body?' Here, alleged victims are asked to speak loudly and clearly not only about 'having sex' but also about the specific acts involved as well as how they felt about them. Witnesses usually either say 'I felt fine', 'I was enjoying', or 'I felt pain'. The first two replies may lead to a decreased sentence. A pregnancy counts as an aggravating factor. The second question, 'Did you witness anything on your body?', is answered with 'blood and white fluid', a variation of these, or 'no'. If the answer is no, a defence lawyer may contest her statement by saying that sex did not take place and that she had had sexual intercourse before, which might be accepted as a mitigating factor.

Chambers are supposed to create a safer and more private environment than open court. In effect, there are often up to ten people in the room, some of whom are not connected to the case. Journalists often answer phone calls or engage in unrelated casual conversations with each other. Lawyers may enter and discuss (confidential) cases at any moment. If a child cruelty matter or a matter of unlawful carnal knowledge is heard – thus cases where the alleged victim is under 14, often very young – the prosecutor and magistrate are patient, calm, and focussed. The alleged victim can take her time and is frequently given encouragement. However, in sexual penetration cases where the alleged victim is between 14 and 18, the situation is very different. Then, alleged victims are often shouted at if they do not speak loudly or clearly enough or if they add too much or too little detail. Furthermore, because the magistrate is personally responsible for taking notes, he often interrupts or halts the testimony by saying 'Move on, this is not relevant' or 'Only talk about the day of the act, how it happened, and what happened after'. The court is not interested in detailed accounts and urges the witness to speak only about the act in question and those performing the act. After

---

[11] Although the officer is not supposed to coach the witness, in the preparation sessions I heard that the witness was usually told what to say and how to say it.

testifying, the witness is asked to identify her medical report and to agree to its content.

While the alleged victim is speaking, the accused must turn away from her and face the wall. He is not allowed to speak until the witness has concluded and signed her statement. (I have never seen a witness reading her statement before signing it.) The accused is then allowed to turn around. If a lawyer is present, they will conduct the cross-examination, which usually includes questioning the alleged victim's age, virginity, and intentions, and confirming that the act took place ('I put it to you that you are not below 18'; 'I put it to you that you were not a virgin'; 'I put it to you that you never lay down with this man'). If no lawyer is present, the accused may cross-examine the witness. Accused persons are usually unable to counter the statements. Some claim that they were never there. Others say that what happened was 'different', without explaining how, or that the alleged victim begged them to do whatever it is they did. After gathering the statements by the police, the alleged victim, and the accused, the magistrate determines whether there are sufficient grounds for the case to be tried in the High Court or whether it should be dismissed.

Bail may be given only after the Magistrate's Court's investigation is complete and after the witness has given testimony. A magistrate who wishes to remain anonymous said:

People have the tendency to interfere with prosecution witnesses. That's why we are a bit hesitant to put accused persons on bail immediately after they are brought to court. So, we get the prosecution to come forth with their witnesses, principally the start witness, who is the victim. It is after the victim has testified that we can consider the question of bail.

Bail is often set at SLL 50 million (GBP 4,590.07), which means that accused persons can bail themselves out by paying SLL 500,000 (GBP 45.90) to the court clerk. In the unlikely event that a person is able to pay bail in full, the amount has to be paid to the National Revenue Authority (NRA). It is illegal to bribe magistrates or judges, but bribery in police stations and prisons and of clerks is common, even expected.[12] In many cases, the defendant needs to provide surety to be granted bail. In Sierra Leone, this is a person who signs on behalf of the defendant, accepting accountability for the charge in case the prisoner jumps bail. Finding such surety is difficult. John, a prison social worker at Don Bosco, told me of one case where the charged person ran away and the sentence was

---

[12] Magistrates, judges, and lawyers also receive bribes, though these transactions occur covertly.

transferred to the surety, who then spent eight years in prison. A judge explains: 'Because of pressure from human rights activists and civil society representatives and the media, most of us are always afraid to put accused persons on bail when such allegations are made against them even when the matters do come to court'. Many of the men and boys I spoke to at Pademba Road Prison had not been granted bail even though the investigations at the Magistrate's Court had been concluded. Since the implementation of the SOAA, cases can proceed directly to the High Court, and accused individuals are no longer eligible for bail.

Trial through Abstraction: Victims and Perpetrators

As we have seen, courts cannot consider contextual factors. Unlike communities, they cannot analyse a person's comportment or personality. They are strangers to the people they deal with. When writing about sexual violence, Steffen Jensen remarks that 'law to a large extent cannot work with unsettled categories; something needs to be held constant' (Jensen 2015: 101). For cases to be adjudicated, the law must construct as 'other' two subject positions that exist only in relation to each other: victim and perpetrator. One imagined 'other', the perpetrator, is fashioned as the subject who executed the violence. The victim, the second imagined 'other', is envisioned as the subject to whom violence was done.

The criminal justice system unhinges the act in question from its context. It considers it only in its abstract sense and tries to determine whether the litigants can be positioned in a clear victim–perpetrator relationship. If such a relationship is found, a conviction results (guilty); if not, the defendant is acquitted (not guilty). If it is not possible to determine this relationship, the case is dismissed (through lack of evidence or because the case cannot be concluded without reasonable doubt).

As in the case described above, in court proceedings the courts employ certain tactics that cement these categories of victim and perpetrator further. First, the fact that the accused must face the wall and may not speak does not allow us to imagine them as a person. Second, given that the prerequisite for a conviction is whether the alleged victim is below 18 and whether sex took place, not why and how, the accused is a priori regarded as a possible perpetrator rather than as innocent until proven guilty. Magistrate Binneh stated that 'with these cases, the law is too rigid, and the presumption is that the moment you are reported then you are guilty'. This is very much in line with the Comaroffs' reflections that in the postcolony today 'policing in the name of order frequently makes felons before-the-fact, punishing them prior to their breaches being legally established. Or even committed' (Comaroff and Comaroff 2016: preface). A High Court judge explains: 'The law says: innocent until proven guilty. But with sexual penetration, the second you are accused you are treated as guilty and you remain that *unless* you can prove that without any doubt you are innocent, and for that you need a good lawyer'. This shows that criminal justice personnel may be as critical of the Act as citizens are. And yet they were part of its creation, even though they now outsource this responsibility to 'strangers'.

Magistrate Binneh comments:

Anyone can make the report, and once the report is made, you are in big trouble because the human rights organisation, media, and activists are very much interested in such cases. When they are reported to the police, they give them the greatest of attention and they will write and publish about you, so even if you make it out, your image is ruined.

Although the victim does speak, she does not exist independent of the perpetrator and is labelled as a minor and hence unable to consent. What she says can change the severity of the sentence but not whether the act is considered as a form of violence or the dynamics of her or the perpetrator's positioning. In this regard, she is not heard. It is only others who can unleash her personhood from the subject position of the victim. In his work on female combatants in African wars, Mats Utas warns that 'by employing a perspective that makes a woman exclusively a victim, researchers risk creating a permanent state of what Kathleen Barry calls victimism ... i.e. a woman's victim status "creates a framework for others to know her not as a person but as a victim, someone to whom violence is done"' (Utas 2005: 407). In the case of the victim in court, this reductionism is the intended effect. The state cannot know her as a person; it must not become interested in her as a person. Its sole interest lies in establishing whether she is in fact a victim or not in relation to an 'other', whose position is dependent on hers.

Critical Voices

While the SOA is internationally celebrated as an important step towards countering sexual violence, its effects have been ambiguous. Research collaborators criticised the SOA for criminalising local norms of sexuality and consent. Mr Samura (73), a former teacher, referring to the campaigning around the SOA, told me:

What they are saying is that when you have sex, you will only think of sex and lose your mind somehow. Then that will lead you to drop in school and to lose attention for what is important. I think what they don't realise is that they themselves had sex when they were young, and they still built homes. We always say that in the village everyone saw you, so you could not just have sex. But people were also married when they came out from the initiation, so when they were between maybe 13 and 16, and then they had children. How is that different from the girls who have boyfriends in the city when they are in middle school?

A male sodality elder said:

It is natural for young people, for any people, to think of sex. Sexing and making new life is what makes us human and what makes us connect, especially for young people. If you forbid it, it will be even more distractive because they will think of it even more and will spend a lot of energy finding ways to do it. It is not about forbidding it but finding ways to do it in a responsible way. These NGOs, they are really not thinking.

In their criticism of how the development discourse has infiltrated sexual education and how sex is depicted as destructive, these statements expose the one-sidedness of this approach. They reveal the limitations of the intention to ban sexual activity, which does not hold up to critical enquiry. They show, too, how a dialectical approach could have led to a far more realistic and successful solution.

The clash lies, among other things, in different interpretations of age: numerical for the state, social for research collaborators. While the law requires numerical certainty, age in Sierra Leone is not understood as a number. It is in exchange with others that one's position within relational dynamics is determined (Bledsoe 1980a; Leach 1994; Ferme 2001; Jackson 2017). Depending upon whom one relates to, one can be older, younger, big, or small (Oyěwùmí 1997; Bakare Yusuf 2003). It is as common for men to be kept in the stage of youth until well into their forties as it is for young girls to fall pregnant and marry well below the age of 18. Not one of the 53 men whose stories I heard at Pademba Road Prison knew the age of the girl they allegedly penetrated. It was only at the police station that this number was revealed to them. Consider the explanation of a young man who was convicted: 'They [the police] asked me for her age. I told them that she is grown up, that she started having sex, that her breasts are developed and that she has given birth to a child. Then they told me she was 15 and I am 19'. Alusine (21), one of the men I interviewed in prison, told me that in accordance with social standards, these men rated the girl's age in terms of her physical appearance. As soon as a girl starts to develop breasts, she is 'ripe' and can be approached for intercourse (Jackson 2017: 42). With the first pregnancy she is a woman, and after breastfeeding, when her breasts begin to 'fall down', she 'has matured'.

The Act remains only marginally effective in protecting very young girls from sexual violence and harassment by much older men. At the same time, it has led to the incarceration of numerous young men and boys. Many research collaborators disapprove of the Act's execution because a teacher raping a 14-year-old student may receive the same prison sentence as a 19-year-old sleeping with his 17-year-old girlfriend. A lawyer from the Legal Aid Board – an institution established in 2012 to offer free legal representation to those who cannot afford a private lawyer – who represented most of the men I interviewed at Pademba Road Prison, explained: 'Sometimes I defend a teacher or pastor or neighbour who rapes a small girl or a child, but mostly it is youth. Some are fooling around, you know, some are maybe impregnating someone. Mostly I have boyfriends, lovers, I would say'. A High Court judge states:

> We have serious problems with rape in this country. But of 25 or maybe 30 cases I see, few are child cruelty, few are domestic violence, few are rapists, but mostly there are boyfriends here you know, lovers. Maybe almost 23 of them are lovers. But the law is so rigid that I have to convict no matter the circumstance.

Because the main burden of proof is to show that sex has taken place, it is cases involving girlfriends and boyfriends that are more easily convictable. Girlfriends often believe that they can help their accused partners by explaining their relationship in court. They rarely miss court hearings and enable a quick processing of cases. Yet, by confirming that sex took place while they were legally unable to consent, they usually ensure their partner's conviction. This situation was often described to me as 'the girlfriend trap'. Magistrate Binneh comments: '*If* she was a minor, *if* sex took place and *if* it took place between the litigants, we must convict'. Although people have become aware of this 'trap' and have increasingly developed tactics to avoid it (e.g. if girlfriends do not attend court hearings, the case will be dismissed), the law is still very recent. Owing to the Ebola pandemic, during which legal proceedings were often slowed down or interrupted, the Act has only been in operation uninterruptedly since mid-2016 and the SOAA has brought additional changes, the consequences of which are yet to be fully assessed.

Many Sierra Leoneans who were involved in ratifying or executing the SOA and the SB were equally critical of their workings. During one of the cases in chambers between a 19-year-old accused and a 16-year-old alleged victim, a current politician who was the defence lawyer of the accused interrupted the hearing in frustration. After we had listened to both parties stating that they were in a consenting relationship, the defence lawyer exclaimed:

> This makes no sense at all. What are we even doing here? There are real rape cases to attend to. In the UK, the age for consent is 16, and they are debating to

lower it to 14 even. This is ridiculous. These people want to have sex. You can't send them to prison for that. Look, this is her boyfriend!

Magistrate Binneh, who presided over the case, replied:

You say that now, but remember when we were making this law, you were one of the first to stand up and tell the commission that this is the best thing to do. Even back then I was against it, I knew that it would be a catastrophe and you would have all these boyfriends which you then need to convict. This is the difference between politicians and the lawyers and judges who deal with the law daily.

The defence lawyer replied with a sigh: 'Yes. I thought it would get us developed super-fast. No more rape or early marriage, girls in school and focussed on work ... but it is a disaster now, and I only know that because I am a lawyer'.

Others blamed the laws on the TRC and on development agencies. Even though they had ratified the law, they claimed that they had done so not on their own account but because they were 'told to do so'. By regarding themselves as influenced by the ideas of foreigners, they created a narrative of deferred responsibility that allowed them simultaneously to ratify the SOA and criticise it. This erased their culpability and created a position of exceptionalism in which they could carry out the law and yet wash their hands of any responsibility for its consequences. A lawyer and politician who was part of designing the SOA and is now carrying it out, explains:

I think someone out there, some of you white people, were thinking: 'OK, how do we stop this violence in Sierra Leone?' 'OK, we are just telling these Africans to stop having sex'. This is what happens all over Africa. But this is nonsense. You can never stop that. Then you can also send these young girls who have been raped to prison because they had sex. No, sex is not the problem. Violence is the problem. In your country is sex under 18 a crime?

That the foundations of the law are not believed – that it is sex rather than violence that is under consideration – is also evident among criminal justice personnel in chambers. It is very common for those present to tease a witness or laugh at the ways in which she describes acts. Mocking statements by lawyers and others present are common, such as: 'So here you are to put your man in prison?' or 'Oh baby, first you enjoy the sex and then you complain about the consequence'. These claims may be interpreted in two ways. First, they can serve as an extension of the punishment, a form of social punishment, for the alleged victim. Second, they may be a form of everyday resistance (Scott 1985), albeit a cruel one, to the law's attempt to criminalise young people's sexuality and strip girls of their sexual agency. By being recognised as sexual subjects who tempt men and boys, they are perceived and also criticised as actors with agency rather than as silenced victims.[13]

Another criticism concerns the ineffectiveness of the law in targeting rape. In rape cases or in cases involving children or teenagers who were assaulted by older men, victims often do not report, withdraw their statements, experience pressure to withdraw, do not attend court hearings, or are too young to give testimony (see Medie 2013 for Liberia). Thus, their cases tend to take much longer and are often dismissed. Furthermore, older men or the families of wealthier youth continue to be able to reach a 'friendly settlement', which is an out-of-court solution. Such people can pressure third parties to abstain from reporting. Rape cases that do not lead to pregnancy are rarely reported to the police because the parties involved find the out-of-court solution preferable. If a report is made, it is usually because the girl in question is extremely young, was gravely injured, or became pregnant. Consider what a teacher told me:

Now with the girl child agendas, you should report such cases to the police. But you yourself are struggling. If you report someone from a rich family to the police, they will come after you and it will be very difficult for you in your school from then onwards. If you just talk to them, there will be some remuneration for you. They will settle the matter otherwise and will reach an agreement, and you will benefit. If the case ever goes to court, they report something like larceny, never rape. Let them settle this case among themselves; otherwise, they will destroy you.

When everyday struggles and social realities are accounted for, this 'imagined image' of Sierra Leoneans who report no matter the circumstances collapses. Since it is often poorer and younger men and boys who are accused, the Act becomes yet another powerful reinforcement of the prison system that confines poor city-dwellers and disproportionately punishes the poor (Wacquant 2001). Moreover, reporting by third parties and bystanders has led many to believe that accusations of sexual violence are made out of vengeance, because of quarrels between families, to punish certain types of young men and to remove them from society.[14] Many understand the new laws as a Western attempt to make sexual relationships out of wedlock illegal and to regulate fertility. Concurrently, this has made it even more difficult for women and girls

---

[13] This also speaks to the gendered forms of violence depicted in Chapter 5 and women's resort to violence through temptation and revenge.

[14] Larry's and LB's cases described in the next chapter are exemplary here. They were reported by their girlfriends' families, who were unhappy with the relationship. In Larry's case, his relationship with the alleged victim was rejected entirely by her family and he was reported for rape.

who suffer violence to report safely. Moreover, although the SB has since been lifted, its effects continue to linger and the stigma surrounding teenage pregnancy makes attending school difficult.

This chapter has hopefully shown the strengths of detailed ethnographic work. In situations where the intentions of policy-makers to protect certain groups from violence differ substantially from the ways in which these targeted populations experience them, ethnography becomes practically relevant for law and policy. It uncovers the social world in which laws passed to combat violence and 'advance' gender justice take root. It demonstrates how people react to and feel about them, and how this in turn influences the application and impact of such laws. An ethnography that examines the interaction between law and lived experience can show the potential gaps between the intention of laws, their implementation, and their impact. When development experts and policy-makers try to promote safety, security, and justice through laws without careful consideration of the context in which they are passed and implemented, their effects may end up hindering instead of furthering the goals desired. Including the testimony of affected people as well as the insights of scholars can help avoid well-meant laws and interventions like the SOA(A) to produce adverse consequences.

9 Perpetrators?
The Consequence of the Sexual Offences Act for Young Men

The scope and implications of the SOA and its amendment cannot be understood without examining its consequences for those young men and boys who have been imprisoned for sleeping with their girlfriends. In this chapter, I therefore draw on two ethnographic cases: those of LoverBoy (LB), aged 19, convicted for sleeping with and impregnating his long-term girlfriend, and Larry, aged 14, convicted for raping his classmate. Both were in relationships with the alleged victims prior to the ratification of the SOA and continue to be so. Neither was reported by their alleged 'victims'. I describe how they negotiate their actions, attitudes, and experiences during the term of their sentences in Pademba Road, Freetown's central prison. Prisoners convicted of sexual offences under the SOA undergo a state performance of excessive punishment. After a 'rite of terror' (Whitehouse 1996), which attempts to separate prisoners totally from any pre-prison attachments and relationships, they end up at the lowest end of prison hierarchies. Applying Michel de Certeau's (1980) distinction between strategies and tactics, I analyse how Larry and LB experience and navigate their everyday lives, how they live with or against their 'criminalised' subjectivity, and how they negotiate their position within the prison.

Some of the people convicted under the SOA, such as LB, try to assimilate to prison life. They take on the role of docile prisoners (Foucault 1977) and eventually identify with the subject position of the criminal. Others, however, resist in ways closely related to the revolt that has come to be known as the 'dirty protest' (Aretxaga 1995; see also Feldman 1991). By neglecting personal hygiene and any form of activity, they try to destroy the state's goal of re-educating them and disciplining their bodies. But their protest goes even deeper than that of the Irish prisoners whom Allen Feldman describes: it extends beyond the body and into the mind. Some prisoners within Pademba Road reject mental sanity and human behaviour to escape the state's reach as well as any attempt to shape their social being. In this way, they create a space of freedom, albeit at great cost. In Sierra Leone, prisons are sites of contestation, revealing stark disparities between internationally inspired norms and values, which are embodied in recent laws, and local ways and principles.

Freetowns Central Prison: Pademba Road

In Sierra Leone, formal incarceration started during colonialism in 1787:[1] At that time, abandoned slave ships were reconfigured as makeshift prisons (Sesay 2014). After several relocations, British officials founded Freetown's central prison in Pademba Road in 1914 (Sesay 2014). Pademba Road, as this male correctional centre for adults is known, was originally designed for 200 prisoners, and its capacity was later extended to accommodate 324 prisoners. When the prison population rose above 1,000 in 2013, the government initiated plans for its relocation (Sierra News Media 2013), plans that have been on hold until today. On 17 May 2017, the prison population stood at over 2,000.

There are six cell blocks in which men and boys are held: Blyden, Wilberforce, Clarkson, Howard House, Remand, and the Condemned Block. Men and boys arrested or convicted under the SOA are assigned to one of these, apart from the Condemned Block, which houses imprisoned persons sentenced to life without the possibility of parole.[2] The cell blocks are hierarchically organised and differ significantly from each other in terms of prisoner numbers, size, and facilities. In most cells, there are a few sleeping mats provided for the occupants along with a bucket that serves as a toilet. The bucket can be emptied through a hole in the floor. Most prisoners are seldom allowed to leave their cell blocks. But to those who are, sharp instruments such as hammers and knives are readily available in the workshops. This led to an incident, famously known as the jailbreak of 2010, when a group of 19–30 imprisoned persons, who were convicted of murder and armed robbery, managed to escape through the main gate after firing a pistol that caused the guards to abandon their posts and seek shelter (BBC News Media 2010).

In the years after the civil war, several ex-combatants were imprisoned at Pademba Road. As a correctional centre for adults, it officially does not house minors, who are meant to serve their sentences at Dems, a juvenile detention facility. But men and boys who received sentences above seven years are brought to Pademba Road irrespective of the crime they have committed or their age. Because most sentences for sexual offences are severe – and an accused's age is not always known and can be wrongly

---

[1] Descriptions of imprisonment in Sierra Leone and Pademba Road Prison draw on my article 'Degrees of Permeability' (Schneider 2020b).
[2] This will change now that the SOAA has entered into force and those convicted may now receive life sentences.

assessed in court – many underage boys who are arrested under the SOA are eventually imprisoned at Pademba Road. Apart from convicted imprisoned persons, large numbers of prisoners are arrested for minor offences such as driving without a licence or stealing food or cheap items. Unable to pay their bail in full or produce surety, they are entirely at the mercy of a chaotic system and have to wait, often for years, to appear in court.

One of few organisations that offer frequent support to many imprisoned persons is Don Bosco. Don Bosco began its work at Pademba Road Prison in 2012. It oversees the distribution of food, ensuring its quality, and provides safe drinking water to imprisoned persons. In addition, Don Bosco has arranged for 75 prisoners from each block, except for the Condemned Block, to leave their cells from one to four in the afternoon, twice a week, in rotation, and gather in the library to pray. Afterwards they are given water and soap to wash themselves and their clothes. During this time, they are free to walk around the prison compound and interact with one another. Minor medical concerns are also looked after in the library, where injuries are dressed and medicines distributed. When I did my fieldwork, Don Bosco was building water tanks and showers so that prisoners can wash themselves more frequently. Because many men and boys are arrested without the knowledge of their families, one of Don Bosco's activities is to search for friends and relatives of imprisoned persons and inform them about the incarceration. John (in his thirties), the social worker in charge of these searches, told me: 'Mostly these families think the men have abandoned the family, gone on a temple run [the dangerous journey to Europe via Libya] or went to the city. Some live far or have children to watch, and many cannot afford to travel for only few minutes. If they come, maybe they are turned away. So mostly they leave it to God, you know'.

Levels of Totality: The Informal Prison Government

As I have argued elsewhere (Schneider 2020b), Pademba Road has a management style that blends a shared powers model and an imprisoned person control model (see Barak-Glantz 1981). The former provides imprisoned persons with certain rights to group association and a voice in administrative decision-making. In the latter, which is prevalent in Latin American prisons, imprisoned persons, frequently organised into gangs, assume control of the administration. At Pademba Road, there are inadequate resources allocated to the prison, making it challenging to hire sufficient staff to effectively manage the prison population. Consequently, the security regime has been constructed along the lines of social power, inclusion, and exclusion (Marcis 2017). Relations between prisoners and guards are drastically limited. As it is impossible to control the prison through policing, guards do not enter the cell blocks, which are secured with heavy metal gates. Instead, prisoners themselves are given the responsibility of overseeing their fellow imprisoned persons. These individuals, known as red bands, have complete control over the interior of the cell blocks with no external supervision and seemingly limitless authority. Red bands are commanders of a detachment of 'muscles', who carry out their instructions. Amadu (26), a close friend of Blush (in his thirties), who spent 11 years in and out of prison, explained: 'Every time they pick him up again, we are so afraid because the red bands are very fearful. Their muscles could just come any time and say "do this for me" or "I want you tonight", and then there is nothing you can do'. Ripper (23), a young man with multiple prison experiences, told me:

Many men, they know that their life is in there, and they think they can just run the place. The power is with the red band, you know; he can simply say: 'This guy needs to be raped, this guy needs to be beaten, this guy will sit in the shit-bucket today' ... and people are unable to refuse him and his will. He takes bribes for protection. If you don't pay ... you...eh. Each block has a red band. There are some blocks that go along and some that fight, and people can also be exchanged between blocks.

Scarrer (in his fifties), an ex-combatant and red band, said:

Red bands are untouchable. They rule. Because the officers are not many and very, very afraid of we the gangsters and murderers and hard criminals. No police will ever enter the cell blocks. The red bands have everything: money, cigarettes,[3] ties [marijuana]. Some can even leave the prison to go party or 'finish the job' if they just pay off a prison guard.[4]

Red bands are selected based on their social capital and their ability to mobilise, control, and evoke fear in other imprisoned persons. As a result, the most likely candidates are notorious gang leaders and imprisoned persons with life sentences. According to HungryBaller, a long-term imprisoned person in his forties, 'the guards and even the government fear them because they know that at any time they could be broken out. It is them who rule the prison, really, and they only stay inside because they want to'.

---

[3] One cigarette costs between SLL 500 and SLL 1,000 [GBP 0.046 and 0.09] in prison, while a whole pack can be bought for SLL 500 [GBP 0.046] in the city.

[4] This was regarded as one of the major problems during many interviews. John, one of Don Bosco's prison social workers, told me that especially imprisoned persons whose sentence is about to end or those with significant material or social resources can negotiate to be let out of prison at night so long as they are back in the morning.

In theory, Pademba Road is an example of a penitentiary combining a prison with workshops and a medical facility. Rather than housing prisoners, it is supposed to house delinquents (Foucault 1977). Yet, given the shared model of its management style, many imprisoned persons are confined exclusively to their cells while a small group control the kitchen, food distribution, the workshops, and all other social activities. Many prisoners spend their days in the darkness of their cells, where social exclusion is total, knowing that others not only hold authority over their lives, but also have an access key to the 'outside' in the form of information, money, or power.

Ethnographies of Confinement

I hear them praying next door. Maybe 70–75 men and boys, their malnourished bodies hunched on wooden benches, repeat in whispers what the Don Bosco social worker's confident voice declares. Due to the overcrowding and differences in status, some wear the clothes in which they were arrested, others wear garments provided by the prison.

The drunk uniformed officer in front of me performs intimidation, but his slurred voice swallows the threats of his shouting and replaces them with an aura of pitiful feebleness. 'Lady!' he exclaims, and reminds me once more of the things that I am under no circumstances allowed to do: ask imprisoned persons how they are doing or how they feel, engage in conversations beyond their cases, give them any information about life 'outside', or flirt. 'You ask them the questions then you leave. Understood. These are bad men. They are in here for women cases [cases involving sexual violence]. They kill women, they torture them, they rape them. They have not seen women in a long time. You don't talk to them. You don't encourage them'. His breath is right in my face.

I sit in the library that Don Bosco opened at Pademba Road Prison. Human rights posters are fading on the wall. 'Stop child labour. Send your child to school!' reads one. The Human Rights Commission of Sierra Leone announces: 'Making rights real. Let's join in the fight against torture and impunity'. The library comprises a few bookshelves spread around a rectangular room, several tables – there is a medical suitcase overflowing with pills and bottles on one of them – chairs around the tables, and a recliner in the corner, which is used to examine imprisoned persons who are ill and provide them with medicines.

Don Bosco workers are now discussing hygiene with the men next door. And, as always, the murmurs mix with my anxiety and carry my thoughts to the journey that brought me here. During many months of research on violence in relationships, the accused were absent from this study. Some of the men and boys I worked with across Freetown had been accused previously and had spent time in prison, but their cases occurred prior to the SOA and were eventually dismissed.

While following case trajectories, I witnessed hundreds of cases in front of the Magistrate's Court and some hearings at the High Court in Freetown, transcribed their sessions, adjournments, and witness statements. I followed the proceedings of the FSU, visited NGOs and IOs, journalists, legal practitioners, researchers, and experts, and traced statistics and case files on these matters. I talked to the women and girls about their cases outside court and spent time with those who had decided against reporting or had withdrawn their statements.

The accused, however, were beyond reach. They were present only as fists reaching out of police trucks, or men placed at the opposite end of the courtroom, handcuffed to their fellow imprisoned persons, guarded by police officers, their eyes fixed on the floor. They stood in silence while they were charged, being asked only one question: *na so I bi or notto si I bi?* ['how do you plead?']. During witness statements held in private chambers, shut away from the public gaze, the accused were warned to keep quiet and to face the wall. In the absence of lawyers, an accused person is granted the right to defend themselves and to question the witness. In 13 months, I did not hear a single accused cross-examining the witness, as they were largely unaware of their rights and their possible fates. Upon sentencing or dismissal of the case at the High Court, the judge usually allows the accused to say a sentence or two – an opportunity that largely passes in silence.

As a result, I strongly felt that without including the perceptions, attitudes, and experiences of those accused of committing sexual offences, any interpretation would be one-sided. For months, I tried to negotiate access to Pademba Road and met with unyielding faces, angry rejections, and doors slammed shut. Finally, Don Bosco agreed to facilitate access, and, with the organisation's influence, the iron gates opened, and, after a thorough screening, I came to be seated in the library and given a pen and paper to take notes.

At the outset of my work in prison, I introduced myself to each block, explained my research, and expressed my wish to hear from them about their cases. I clearly stated that talking to me was entirely optional, had no direct benefit, neither in prison nor in court, that I would not be able to reach out to family members or loved ones, was unable to take anything in or out of prison, and that I would not appear as a witness.

To my great surprise, 53 men and boys came to talk to me. I was permitted to spend one hour with a single prisoner at a given time, and I talked to most men several times. Others voiced an interest in participating, but after I objected to the guard's repeated romantic advances, my access to prison was revoked and I was told I was no longer welcome. I too had become someone who disappeared without a goodbye.

As the murmuring subsided and the officer approached the door, ready to let the first man in to talk to me, I sat up straight, tightened the scarf with which I had to 'tie' my head, and pulled the loose sweater over my wrist to leave only my hands exposed. These were further conditions attached to my presence in Pademba Road: no hair, no skin.

Larry: Embodied Sense of Prison Life or Radical Resistance

A tall, lanky malnourished teenager totters on bumpy legs through the small room and sinks into the chair opposite me. Larry is 14 years old. He was convicted of gang rape and received a sentence of 30 years.[5] Separated from my gaze and presence by the small table between us, he stares at the floor. The dirt on his skin is thick like a knife, and I see on his arm signs of craw-craw – 'an itching skin disease produced by the larvae of the filarial worm causing onchocerciasis migrating in the subcutaneous tissues' (Merriam Webster 2018). Others had told me about Larry long before I met him. Many prisoners said that he is not 'right in the head'. Larry believes that he died at the police station and as a result he treats his upper body like a corpse. He rarely moves or uses his hands and arms, and does not take care of his bodily hygiene. Rather than engaging in the fight against decay, he readily allows parasites, germs, and infections to take over his body.

Larry lives in the afterlife of a social death. He has never received a visitor and has no contact with his family. Larry's refusal to use his body, his constant demonstration of purposeless decay, and his giving in to his fate terrify his companions and simultaneously evoke pity. Despite the scarcity that is everyone's plight, they reserve portions of food and utensils for him – while usually engaging in fights over them. Larry is ignored by notorious gang members and exempt from struggles over power and control. Fearing transmission of the strange disease that is Larry's, people avoid close contact with him. Larry now has a quarter of a cell to himself in a crowded cell block. Having 'died' because of exclusion, he is left spending his days in the company of no one. Without

---

[5] The maximum sentence of 15 years was doubled in this case because it was an alleged gang activity. However, because he is a first offender his sentence will be halved, so he will leave prison after 15 years.

social or economic capital, without contacts, he is situated at the lowest rung of the prison's hierarchical structure.

The first 25 minutes of our meeting pass in silence. Larry does not look at me, does not initiate a conversation, and does not reply to my request for consent to pose questions. After letting the silence thicken, I tell him that this is his time and that he can decide how he wants to spend it. Even if he decides to remain silent, this hour is his. Too often, I have tried to penetrate silence that I perceived as uncomfortable in the past, not realising that in Sierra Leone keeping company does not require words. Suddenly, surprised and vivaciously lively eyes stare at me from under bushy eyebrows. With a raised chin, he orders the librarian – a young man (17) arrested for illegally renting out an apartment that belonged to his aunt overseas, who was thereafter named the Joker – to his side. The Joker hesitantly approaches, walks all the way round the table, and places himself halfway between me and Larry.

'This one', the Joker tells me, is from a village in Kailahun, the capital city of a district with the same name in the Eastern Province of Sierra Leone. Both of his parents are farmers, and he spent his time either in school or helping on their farm. After a classmate fell ill without recovering for a prolonged period, her father, the chief of the village, 'pointed' at Larry and three others, claiming that they had raped her. Larry was romantically involved with the girl, much to the dismay of her father, as Larry is from a poor family. 'But only *pikin biznɛs* [child's play]', the Joker remarks: the girl is still a virgin.

In view of its high profile and its occurrence outside Freetown, the case came to trial and conviction within a few weeks. After having been arrested in February 2016, Larry was sentenced to 30 years in prison in May 2016. Such 'interior cases' tend to be handled more quickly, with harsher sentences and less need for evidence. One person's word is often enough for a conviction. All four boys involved in the case are now in prison, each having received a sentence of 30 years. At the police station, the chief claimed that the accused were over 18 and should therefore be tried in a regular court.

In return for a bribe, the age of an accused can often be raised, or the age of the alleged victim lowered significantly at the time of reporting. While age tests are conducted in Magistrate's Courts and the High Court, they usually only take place when the authorities do not believe that an accused who claims to be a juvenile is below 18 (see Chapter 8). I have never seen an accused without a private lawyer being successful in showing that he is in fact younger or proving that an alleged victim is older. This was borne out by the case files I studied and by the testimony of expert research collaborators from the criminal justice sector. Age tests and birth certificates can be obtained by private lawyers, though they are costly. Nevertheless, in court what usually counts is the first police report rather than documents submitted later. The age of minors is also disguised by the fact that they should be at a different detention facility rather than at Pademba Road. Moreover, prison statistics, which routinely state that all imprisoned persons are above 18, deny the existence of minors within prison. Criminal justice personnel thus conjure minors out of existence.

In Larry's case, no medical examination was conducted on the girl and, upon appearing in court, she denied that she was the victim of any sexual violence. The Joker explains to me that Larry's family begged the mother of the girl to intervene – in fact, the whole village begged her – but she remained silent. Hierarchies of authority, age, and gender are difficult to transgress, and speaking out involves significant risks (Chapters 6 and 7).

As I got to know Larry better, it became painfully evident that he, like most men I talked to, was unaware of his legal rights. He did not have legal representation and did not know that he was entitled to ask for a lawyer. Free legal representation by the Legal Aid Board is available, if at all, once cases proceed to the Magistrate's Court or the High Court, at which stage new evidence is rarely admitted. Many imprisoned persons told me that it was in prison, after they were convicted, that they learnt from other prisoners what their crime and sentence entailed.

Especially in the beginning of my meetings with Larry, our conversation was dominated by non-verbal communication and gestures and aided by the Joker's explanations. Like many others, he was arrested without understanding what was happening. At the police station, he was beaten, intimidated, and exposed to a prolonged stay in a holding cell. He was told that he would be allowed to go home if he confessed to sexual penetration. He eventually did. And he did not see the statement that was written by the police officer in English, a language Larry does not understand.

Imprisonment as a 'Rite of Terror'

Young men held for sexual penetration are subjected to a state performance of exclusion and separation. As Larry's experience shows, many are entirely cut off from life outside prison and have no knowledge of occurrences beyond their cell blocks. Stories from outside become expensive items for trade, uncertain rumours, and mysterious phantoms. The logics of arrest, trial, and incarceration are based firmly on severance from social ties. The principle of restoration, in which punishment overcomes deviation to achieve reconciliation with norms, has been replaced by a 'paradigm of exclusion' (Bauman 2000). Through severing all ties with the outside world for marginalised prisoners, the 'prison complex' in Sierra Leone seeks to 'annihilate the individual as a social being' (Marcis 2017). Although goods, services, and communications are increasingly entering and leaving prisons as they become more integrated into a network of mutually influencing institutions, the majority of prisoners continue to be unable to participate in these exchanges.

Larry did not have legal representation or people to act as his advocate, and he had no way to prove his real age. His trial was held in the privacy of secluded chambers. He was one of 49 men (of the 53 I interviewed) who never received a visitor. Similar to many other prisoners, Larry is confined to his cell for six days in a row without any communication from the 'outside'. For Larry and others imprisoned for sexual offences, imprisonment is a 'rite of terror' (Whitehouse 1996). It is a performance with separation as its core: the separation of action from meaning, of the individual from the social, of internal from external control.

Larry's state is one of apathy. Larry sits in the same position for hours on end, staring straight ahead into the darkness that surrounds him in his cell. Many times, I left after the hour was up without either of us having spoken a word. Sometimes, I spoke a few words into the silence, probably to make it more bearable for me. What I learnt about him, I learnt from his fellow imprisoned persons. On only a few occasions, he suddenly turned towards me, facing me with full intensity and whispering never more than one or two sentences. What he repeated frequently were the following words: *R nɔ de du natin egen. Nɛva egen* ['I am not doing anything again. Never again'].

Resisting or Embodying Punishment

Larry's case provides a strong example of 'the creation of death-worlds' in which people are subjected to conditions that turn them into the living dead (Mbembé and Meintjes 2003: 39–40). Through the use of necropolitical practices, the criminal justice system of the state has transformed Larry into a criminal subject who serves a sentence proportionate to the severity of his crime. One of the essential elements of these practices is dehumanisation, which creates a divide that severs all connections between Larry and the various spheres of the world that he was once linked to. Larry's refusal to participate in prison life and to care for his bodily hygiene can be interpreted as his identification with the subject position of the wrongdoer who needs to be punished. He is embodying prison life. Larry thus assimilates himself to the necropolitics of the state, surrendering authority over his life and death and how his life should be lived.

At the same time, neglecting hygiene, as the dirty protest taught us (Feldman 1991; Aretxaga 1995), can also be a powerful form of resistance. Larry's non-actions may signify his withdrawal from the realm of the state's power and its attempt to discipline his body and mind. Rather than letting the state decide how he should live, he regains his agency by taking on the role of creator of his circumstances – which are circumstances of non-participation.

However, we must ask whether Larry's actions may just be a fulfilment of this oppression rather than a form of resistance to it. According to Achille Mbembé, 'under conditions of necropower, the lines between resistance and suicide, sacrifice and redemption, martyrdom and freedom are blurred' (Mbembé and Meintjes 2003: 40). Hence Larry's everyday forms of resistance, his submission and identification, are not mutually exclusive. Rather, Larry's subject positions are caught within the paradox they create.

LoverBoy: Fading Memories and Attempts at Self-Making

I met LoverBoy (LB) in 2012, when I first started research in Freetown. He then lived near Naimbana Street, and I knew his girlfriend, family, and social group well. After he met Lizzy in 2014, she became the main topic of his conversation. I heard LB's love story every time I met him. It is this story that gives him the strength and endurance to continue. Whenever he has the chance, he explains, with shining eyes, how he met Lizzy at one of his friend's club's *chillins* and 'started loving' her. LB was 19 years old, his girlfriend 16, when he was first arrested. They had been dating for about two years, when Lizzy accidentally got pregnant. Islam is very important to LB, and he firmly believes that terminating a pregnancy is a sin: 'You know, it is a gift from God, so you cannot just *pul di bele*'. LB explains that he went to the family of his girlfriend to 'show face', that he intended to start the proceedings of *ansa bele* to claim responsibility for the pregnancy (Chapter 3). He told me of his determination to become engaged to Lizzy and to provide a home for her and their child. But Lizzy's family objected to the union because LB was a poor young man who had not completed his education and did not have promising career prospects. Lizzy, on the other hand, went to the Annie Walsh Memorial School in Freetown, the most prestigious secondary school for girls in Sierra Leone. Angry that LB had 'spoiled' the girl's marriage prospects by impregnating her, but unable to separate the lovers and opposed to their continuing relationship, the family reported LB for sexually penetrating and impregnating Lizzy.

LB was first imprisoned during the Ebola crisis and therefore served the first part of his sentence with other new imprisoned persons in a separate building to reduce the risk of infection. Nevertheless, prison overcrowding became a major problem during the Ebola pandemic. Courts were locked, and cases were on hold. After the pandemic, some men and boys were released without completing trial, as it was said they had already completed the sentence they might have received. LB was one of these men. He described his experience as follows: 'One day when they took me to court, the judge said I should go'. 'Did you understand what happened?' I asked. 'Oh no, but he said I should go, so I went'.

LB shared a cell with two others who refused to talk to him. He often describes the isolation and pain he felt.[6] It was the daily prayers uniting voices across the cells that gave LB a sense of community and belonging, and made the seemingly endless days bearable.

After he was released, LB's friends and family described him as a 'changed man'. 'This man was not with us. Always in his own head. Only sitting and staring, but never talking. Like he was somewhere not here', explained his brother. Once the pandemic ceased, LB's case was re-evaluated, and he was re-arrested. After receiving his indictment papers, LB was transported to and from court weekly for several months without his case being called. 'My world was like covered by the dust of harmattan, you know. I could not see anywhere. Everything was just shadows', he told me.

Whether I talked to people inside or outside prison, almost nobody trusted the workings of the law or believed in official justice. The state law and its apparatuses, first introduced by the British colonisers and now governed by international standards, was often compared to a giant impossible to overpower, but easily angered; he would furiously attack and destroy everyone provoking him. The way of resistance and struggle often lies in non-cooperation (see Scott 1985). Many accused persons remain silent throughout their trials because 'the only thing we can do is not help them sentence us', the Joker said.

Because he had heard of the 'girlfriend trap' (Chapter 8), LB advised his girlfriend not to attend court. This strategy seemed to work. After six months and three adjournments, he was sent home. After returning from

---

[6] While researchers increasingly foreground the problems of overcrowding or overpopulation, we must take into account that for persons who are used to having many others around them at all times, being isolated may constitute a profound horror. Lisa Guenther, for example, writes about the breakdown of meaningful experience in situations of solitary confinement (Guenther 2013: xiv).

Pademba Road, his behaviour changed again. He was now loud and aggressive. T-Pain (22), his best friend from Kroo Bay, stated: 'He was super-violent now. And too much cursing, I am telling you. This man's language has completely changed from a gentleman to a gangster, you know. When you move with this crowd, you just lose it, you know'. LB could no longer sit still, and he started breaking promises and taking what was not his. This habit got him into trouble with his friends for whom honesty and sharing form the building blocks of their group. LB's family sent him on a course to prepare for an exam that, if passed, would qualify him for entry to college, but LB missed most of his sessions. Apart from praying five times a day, he abandoned most other commitments.

Among research collaborators, the prison was commonly understood as a place that breeds criminals, a place of rampant violence from which no one returns. According to them, experiences in prison lead to a reconfiguration of norms and an indoctrination of counter-values that harm society. 'Pademba Road is like Dante's inferno … the closest to hell. Once you enter you will never go out', said Fr. George, the director of Don Bosco. Unlike Karen Waltorp and Steffen Jensen's research collaborators who prepared each other for the possibility of imprisonment (Waltorp and Jensen 2017: 3), among those I interviewed there was an impenetrable silence around prison. It was as if those who had experienced confinement sealed off these experiences to stop the shadows of prison from encroaching on their daily lives. When prisoners return, they are violent, abusive and 'unable to feel pain with the pains of others', I was often told. Only with re-education and time can they be helped, and only if they have not been imprisoned for too long.

Notwithstanding the impressive work of NGOs and civil society institutions involved in gender-based violence in Freetown, their focus is on response rather than prevention, and on women and girls rather than men and boys. It is mostly church groups and activists that work to integrate men as champions of a new form of masculinity. To my knowledge, no organisation works specifically with men and boys who have been imprisoned under the SOA or with those who confess to be perpetrators of such violence.

After returning from Pademba Road, LB was arrested about two months later when Lizzy's family reported him anew, because he did not stop visiting her and their baby. This time, they brought Lizzy to court. There, she told the judge that LB was the father of her baby, that she was in love with him, visited him, and 'sent for him' whenever she could, and that they planned on doing *ansa bɛlɛ* as soon as he was finally allowed to return home. The judge, who called this case an example of 'the injustice this law brings', lectured the couple on the fact that she was legally unable to consent, that the intercourse was therefore a form of violence, and that LB must be sentenced. With a heavy heart, he committed LB to seven years in prison.

At Pademba Road, LB ended up in a cell block dominated by a red band whom he had known since childhood. This friend, who had been in and out of prison numerous times, offered to look after LB and helped him to receive the food and utensils his family sent for him.

In prison, LB began what he called 'strategising' to counter the arbitrariness of his arrest. 'Sister, where a cow is tied there it must graze', he told me. He promoted his superior education and reading and writing skills compared with those of the prison staff and the red bands. He behaved like a non-threatening person who might be a useful assistant. Combined with his friendship to the red band, these tactics enabled him to quickly become an important mediator between different areas of the prison and different kinds of people within it. He was appointed as an assistant to Don Bosco, charged with finding and calling imprisoned persons, documenting work, and so on. This meant that he was able to leave his cell block six days a week instead of the four hours once or twice a week permitted to many other prisoners. Consequently, other imprisoned persons would give him notices, letters, and questions to carry back and forth between places and people. Because he brings the happenings of the day into his cell, LB has become a cherished cell member. He is someone who brings 'life outside' and who can connect the prisoners with this world and carry their words and stories into it. But LB does not bear these 'gifts' for free. Giving and receiving information is exchanged for goods and services. While in prison, he strives to form connections and position himself in a manner that renders him indispensable to others.

However, LB misses his girlfriend and his daughter terribly. For the first few months, they continued to be his main topic of conversation: 'My woman and my baby girl. I miss am. I miss am too much', he told me whenever I saw him. After he was imprisoned, Lizzy had to move back to her family in Bo.[7] As the trip is long and expensive, she visits LB only infrequently. And when she does come, visitation time is limited to a few minutes. No matter how much LB tries to push against this process, the memory of his daughter and girlfriend fade more and more with time and everyday life in prison takes up more and more of his mind and energy.

---

[7] Bo is the largest city of the Southern Province and the capital of Bo District; it is about 147 miles from Freetown.

Living Relationships through Memory

In *The Imaginary*, Jean-Paul Sartre (2004) shows how it becomes increasingly difficult to keep a relationship alive when it can only be remembered, not lived. Then memory can only feed off the old – and never create new stimulants. Sartre says:

> In every person that we love, for the very reason of their inexhaustible richness, there is something that surpasses us, an independence, an impenetrability, that requires perpetually renewed efforts of approximation. The irreal object conserves nothing of this impenetrability: it is never more than what we know of it ... Thus, from the very fact of the extraordinary difference that separates the object as imaged from the real, two irreducible classes of feeling can be distinguished: genuine feelings and imaginary feelings. (Sartre 2004: 145)

LB's imprisonment has led to an annihilation of eros – erotic love or desire – and his relationship with his child and girlfriend is mainly nourished in his memory. LB has been stripped of his role as head of the household. During their short visits, he may occasionally listen to, but he is never able to influence or solve, the struggles and calamities facing his family. His failure to provide and his absence are public knowledge. The dissolution of his home serves as a symbol for the state's power to strip him of his subject positions as father, partner, and entrepreneur, replacing them with that of the destructive criminal. LB's only connection with his family is through visits that last for a few minutes every couple of months. LB's daughter is growing up in a world beyond the prison walls that he cannot access or imagine. She and Lizzy can temporarily enter part of his world while he is excluded from theirs and he needs to rely on hastily told anecdotes to create an 'imagined image' (Carlbom 2003: 57) of the lives of his loved ones. In relation to the world outside prison, he has been confined to his memory and to occasional speech acts: practical actions are impossible.

As a result of imprisonment, personal relationships transition from being based on actual presence to being imagined. They gradually dissipate and only persist in an imagined state of otherness. It is important to try to connect lives and worlds inside and outside prison, but this can only be partial because for those outside, the prison can only be imagined, never really experienced. For those inside the prison, the world outside is only alive in memory and imagination. While persons and things can cross the divide between the real and the imagined, they cannot carry the life world of the other side with them. In his relations with people outside Pademba Road, LB is in a process of social dying – a process that seems endless in its pain. It is not so much the aftermath of a social death (see Guenther 2013) that LB seems to experience; it is not a death; rather, it is a dying. It is constantly in the making, a companion (Dayan 2011: 39–70;

Guenther 2013). But LB also experiences a rebirth. As Whitehouse (1996) shows, rites of terror foster bonds between those who experience this terror together. This social bonding then leads to the creation of strong social relations that replace those that had existed previously. Every time I saw LB at Pademba Road, he had become more and more involved with the movement around his red band, and Lizzy and his baby were pushed further and further towards the back of his mind. Lizzy had become a story that was cherished but that was far removed from his new life in the prison.

Of Tactics and Strategies: A Power Bargain

Michel Foucault (1977) describes discipline as a creative toolkit that enables power to manifest itself – for example, the power of a state and its institutions over its citizens. By means of punishment (such as imprisonment, deprivation, forced separation, or labour), systems are established to promote the overall aim of creating specific citizens and, as a result, a specific state (Foucault 1977: 135–7). While the state and its laws operate with a 'strategy', criminal justice institutions are its instruments of 'will and power' (Certeau 1984: xix). Police stations, courts, and prisons are isolating environments that follow logics of subjugation. With their rules of contact (e.g. the 'perpetrator' stands against the wall; the victim sits and speaks only when asked and only in response to questions; the public is excluded; authority resides with the judge or magistrate), these strategies determine their relations with the public and everyday life – the 'exterior distinct from it' (Certeau 1984). This allows for the creation of 'wrongdoers', who are confined within these isolated spaces of prisons. Multiple subject positions, such as father, lover, son, and friend, are negated and reduced to that of offender and victim. Moreover, the degree of communication that people who are imprisoned have with the outside, and their ability to slowly recreate other subject positions than that of offender, depends on their compliance and willingness to be 'reintegrated'. At the same time, as my ethnography demonstrates, imprisoned persons do not passively acquiesce to these practices of oppression and discipline. Instead, they employ tactics to establish their own spaces of agency within the state's strategy.

Importantly, Sierra Leonean criminal justice institutions differ significantly from how similar institutions function in the West and are conceptualised in Western narratives. Police stations, state courts, and prisons in Sierra Leone are not simply arms of the state, and their system of governmentality does not operate in typical ways. Instead, they are much more informal, opaque, and messy. With their volatility, they further contribute to the 'weakness' of the Sierra Leone state and heighten fear in Sierra Leoneans, for one never knows what the outcome of engagement with them will be. We have seen how courts respond differently to adults and minors, how police treat women and men differently (see Chapters 7 and 8), and how much prison life depends on factors outside official laws and rules. Structural factors add to the unpredictability of institutions. Indeed, serious understaffing and lack of resources continue to hamper the proper functioning of the criminal justice system in Sierra Leone. The inability to conduct proper investigations, the lack of forensic testing equipment, and the large imbalances of wealth alongside unequal access to legal representation all create a situation in which existing laws often disproportionately target marginalised, impoverished people, while many wealthier perpetrators continue to escape justice. Furthermore, the likelihood that wrongful convictions will be made is strengthened by the fact that the SOA enables bystanders to report cases, that only directly implicated people and eyewitnesses can take the stand in court, that cases cannot be based on thorough investigations, and that a main piece of evidence continues to be hymen testing.

In public imaginaries, prisons are frequently regarded as distinct places that are characterised by specific rules, regulations, oversight, and a particular lived experience. These perceptions lead to assessments and judgements that can be positive or negative. Prominent prison scholars reveal that treating the prison as something given and pre-understood, as a fixed entity, assumes an ontological stability that may not exist and that should be critically scrutinised instead (Armstrong and Jefferson 2017). Such scrutiny allows one to examine volatility and chaos, and a lack of oversight and control. These features matter greatly for the role and place of such institutions in wider society as well as for their operations. Leaving power unconsolidated, absent, and nebulous may be a clever way to operate power, for it cannot be challenged or attacked properly. Certainly, criminal justice institutions can be shifting places where staff changes correspond to political tides, and oversight and continuity are short-lived. As Pademba Road shows, prisons can be extremely volatile places, where accidents and quicksand create worlds of their own. Such volatility needs to be investigated and understood not as a system of order but as a structure of mess.

Rather than acting as marionettes of this 'state strategy' of volatility, as 'objects' of the state's necropower, and of the manoeuvres of their girlfriends' families, Larry's and LB's reactions to their situation, though very different from each other, can both be understood as 'tactics'. Michel de Certeau (1984) describes tactics as isolated actions made possible because an opportunity arises within a specific setting. Hence tactics are reactions to environments and negotiations of subject positions within an environment rather than activities enabling the creation of new environments (Scott 1985). Rather than letting the state define their subjectivity, Larry and LB create counter-positions and counter-narratives (to negotiate their situation as well as their relationship to the state and its apparatuses). LB built a life within prison and has cultivated and expanded his social network there. Larry, on the other hand, retreated from the control of the prison into a state of privacy or absence that no one can penetrate. However, these platforms are built under the umbrella of the state's strategy. LB's and Larry's tactics do not dismantle the existing system, nor do they establish an alternative system. They are micro-tactics, practices that do not alter the status quo overall, but shape the individual experience of imprisonment and of being made a perpetrator.

But not only Larry and LB act tactically. In Chapter 8, I explained how research collaborators often criticise the SOA as enabling false accusations to break up relationships and remove certain persons from society. LB's and Larry's cases provide an example of this. They describe ways in which families may tactically manipulate the regulations of the SOA to pursue their own goals. LB's case is the classic example of a consensual relationship that was deemed wrong by the girlfriend's family and that was broken up by strategically employing the laws of the SOA. Once a pregnancy occurred, it could be proven without a doubt that sex had taken place, and LB could be made a perpetrator and separated from Lizzy. Larry's case is even more extreme. Together with others, he was accused of rape without having had sex with the girl. However, in view of the law's rigidity, even though Larry's girlfriend denied the accusations and no medical certificate was issued, he was still convicted. This illustrates how her father tactically used and manipulated the SOA to his own end. The question therefore remains whether the SOA has contributed to a significant change in attitudes towards violence in relationships or whether it provides a platform for pursuing personal goals. While 'swearing' enables families to force a person to accept responsibility for a pregnancy, and 'call name' allows lovers to be fined for infidelity, the SOA allows consensual relationships involving minors to be broken up and men and boys to be physically removed from any contact with their lovers.

Furthermore, these tactical manoeuvres show how people and institutions try to manipulate aspects of different systems to promote their ideas of gender relations, sexual behaviour, violence, and punishment. If we apply this to the metaphor of the teeth and tongue, we are able to understand not only how people tacitly transgress gendered ideals, but also that what is acceptable to one system may constitute a wrong to another and may lead to severe sanctions. In today's contested landscapes, persons can easily get caught between different ideals and can be severely punished as a result.

Conclusion

This book has offered an urban ethnography in which I analyse violence within intimate relationships in Freetown, Sierra Leone; its degree of acceptance or rejection; and the ways in which it is mediated at domestic, community, and state levels. If we seek to understand real people and real situations, we must, says Michael Jackson, elucidate 'the relationship between discursive notions of violence in relationships and the lived experiences of men and women who commit, expect, and suffer under such violence; who accuse one another and who confess' (Jackson 2019: 60). In doing so, this book has sought to make three broad contributions to the anthropology of (West) Africa. The first lies in deepening studies of violence in intimate and familial contexts in Africa by presenting a new lens for understanding gender relations and perceptions of violence in urban Sierra Leone (captured in the metaphor of the teeth and the tongue). The second contribution lies in advancing scholarship on law and rights by analysing how Sierra Leone's plural legal system mediates and regulates violence and intimacy. I show how contemporary laws are responses to past occurrences (in particular the civil war and the post-war processes), present-day local concerns, international influences, and global concerns, and how this multiplicity can cause friction and adverse effects despite concerted efforts to decrease violence. Third, the book adds fresh insights into the manifold works that engage with youths ('in crisis') by showing the ways in which young people in Freetown today negotiate their relationships. In particular, I emphasise how past and present are interwoven in continuous struggles to create a better future. Instead of a crisis of masculinity, what my research has uncovered is a crisis of gender relations and relationship trajectories that people try to mediate and that they help shape in the process.

Understanding Violence in Relationships

The terms 'violence' and 'Africa' have a problematic history that requires further enquiry. Local expressions of violence cannot be disconnected from the structural violence inherent in international political and economic arrangements, which marginalise countries like Sierra Leone. Moreover, as this book centrally argues, violence in intimate relationships cannot be understood solely as negative. Rather, it is at the heart of understanding how social relations are produced and reproduced. Indeed, it is attempts by the state and other institutions to regulate violence and loving relationships that can trigger complex and often negative consequences. To do justice to the multi-layered expressions and consequences of violence and to develop social policies that protect and empower, it is essential to deepen our understanding of how to interpret and respond to violence, and what we consider as violence and what we do not.

Love and Violence challenges prevalent victim–perpetrator narratives by demonstrating that, in Freetown, violence in contemporary relationships is a complex phenomenon with multiple purposes. It is neither solely positive nor negative and serves various functions, such as demonstrating love or punishing a partner. This interpersonal violence exists in a country that has experienced severe violence in its (recent) history. By placing the expression, execution, and negotiation of violence within historical and geopolitical contexts, this book does not seek to localise particularly visible forms of violence in an African context. Instead, it draws attention to the larger forces of structural violence in which these contexts are enmeshed.

This book also considers women's agency and analyses the ways in which women expect and carry out violence. Moreover, depicting how love and violence enter into a complicated relationship within the moral economy broadens our understanding of love as it is lived, enacted, and experienced in this particular context.

This book neither relativises nor vilifies violence but foregrounds the multifaceted nature of its manifestations. It highlights the pain violence causes, but also casts light on the social world in which it operates and the ways in which it animates that world. It examines empirically the consequences of how violence is enacted, experienced, and responded to for personal lives, for society, and for legal and political structures. This variety of experience and interpretation, based on the various actors' social positions, is crucial for understanding the effects of law and policy and for helping develop preventive and protective mechanisms.

The book demonstrates that Sierra Leoneans consider the acceptability or unacceptability of violent practices along intersectional lines of gender (men against women), age (elders against younger people), and hierarchy (those in power / dominant people against the powerless / subordinate people). Acts of violence are, furthermore, gendered in that women are said to use violence predominantly against minds and men against bodies. Men are said to use violence mainly to punish, and women to bind others to them.

While acceptable incidents of violence are resolved interpersonally, unacceptable violence may be reported to the authorities and may lead to a legal case. As I showed in Chapters 3 and 6, intimate relationships are a means to create and nurture social relations. Unacceptable violence between partners is therefore not a private matter. Instead, by rupturing the moral economy, such violence provides a threat to the continuity of a relationship and so concerns other social groups involved. Sierra Leone, a country where informal labour and social and group connections are deeply entrenched, presents a context where self-interest and opportunities for individual action are intricately linked to the interests of others. The prospect of fulfilling individual needs is therefore either amplified or restricted by interactions with others as these build a dynamic relationship (see Piot 1999: 18, 120; Ibrahim 2009; Jackson 2012: 3). Agency is therefore 'domesticated' (Nyamnjoh 2001: 29), and responsibility encompasses both egocentric and sociocentric personhood, enmeshing the two and involving not only the partners, but additional actors as well. Deciding how relationships should be lived, and what should happen when violence occurs, involves the family and the community. As Charles Piot showed for Togo, 'agency thus resides not within a singular identity (within the person) but in the relations people have with another' (Piot 1999: 120). In communities and households, this interdependence and interconnectedness shapes the actions of many people and also directs the manner in which violence is mediated.

As I pointed out in Chapter 6, people often report unacceptable violence to the patrons of their relationships, usually female consanguine elder family members, their church or mosque, or their community. In the last-mentioned instance, community members, led by female elders, discuss the case cooperatively and mete out punishment. It is interesting that households and communities can preside over both male and female forms of violence while criminal justice institutions are limited to predominantly male forms of violence (Chapter 7).

As we have learned, people risk losing family support and may be fined or asked to leave their community if they report their partners to the police. Moreover, reporting usually leads to separation. Only specific groups of people feel able to report, mainly economically independent women. As Chapter 7 highlighted, men are mostly unable to report because they risk having their masculinity diminished and being considered as children, while, in contrast, women may embody both masculine and feminine traits. Women who work for the state or engage with state institutions tend to have the resources to be able to start a new life if this becomes necessary. They are familiar with the proceedings of the police and the courts, and often align themselves with the human rights principles upon which these institutions are based. All these barriers to reporting have important implications for policy-makers and development agencies. Scholars of political economy and socio-legal dynamics thus need to focus not simply on individuals but on families and family dynamics. In this way, they can better grasp people's experiences and possibilities within the specific situations in which they find themselves (Collins 2000).

Under state law in Sierra Leone, sexual relationships involving minors are illegal. However, they are almost never reported by those implicated since they do not consider them as a form of violence. An essential finding of the book is that community mediations are not focussed on sex (unless it is withheld). State laws, on the other hand, are primarily concerned with sex. As I have shown, through the Sexual Offences Act and the school ban on visibly pregnant girls, sex became part of the national agenda in Sierra Leone, and reporting on other people's sexual activity became a civic duty for the realisation of national goals. However, mobilising citizens to report on one another proved mainly effective with state employees, while community members whose livelihoods are based on the informal economy continue to avoid state institutions. Hence, as we have seen, 'rights discourses' that attempt to empower marginalised groups may create divisions when they meet with different normative frameworks (Cowan et al. 2001; Cowan 2006; Foblets, Graziadei, and Renteln 2017). For instance, while the law is written in a gender-neutral manner and both boys and girls below 18 are unable to consent to sex, the criminal justice system perceives men and boys in terms of the SOA as perpetrators – those who penetrate – and girls as victims – those who are penetrated – and concerns itself only with this one dimension (Chapter 8). What constitutes violence in relationships and how it should be mediated are therefore deeply influenced by gendered expectations and by 'the interaction between international human rights theory and local cultures' (Burrill, Roberts, and Thornberry 2010: 3).

Chapters 8 and 9 brought to light the drastic consequences of these regulations for young people's sexual freedom, for the formation of households, for education, for making a future, and for social relations. The book thus adds a new dimension to the study of risk factors (e.g. García Moreno, Jewkes, and Sen 2002; Capaldi et al. 2012) by showing what happens when a state adopts the language of risk – here, teenage pregnancy and rape – to justify its interventions in citizens' private lives.

The book has also focussed on witnesses, on those people who complete David Riches's (1986) 'triangle of violence'. Indeed, reporting cases and informing on others are the mechanisms that keep the different mediation systems alive (Chapters 6–9). In community or household cases, what is reported and informed upon is the behaviour, social standing, and level of responsibility of those implicated. When, on the other hand, adults report a partner to the police, they inform on a specific act of violence. As for cases under the SOA, it is third parties who report on sexual activity involving minors.

When Is Someone Mature?

As I have revealed, one of the main differences between the approach of criminal justice institutions and that of households and communities to mediating violence in relationships concerns the notion of maturity. At the heart of the matter are questions about how and when a person becomes an adult, when and with whom a person should be able to have sex, and when a person can and should be held responsible for their actions.

Households and communities rely on gendered socialisation. In accordance with many feminist theorists (Butler 1993; Moore 1994; McNay 2000; 2004), most Sierra Leoneans do not understand gender as a given and stable category. Gender must be achieved and embodied with great and constant care. Therefore, it is, as Holly Wardlow says, 'an action, not an essence; a process not a category' (Wardlow 2006: n.p.; see MacCormack and Strathern 1982; Coulter 2009). As I have shown, Sierra Leoneans often speak with a sense of certainty about how women or men 'are', how they 'act', 'behave', 'feel', and so on. Women and men are said to see and interpret the world differently, to have differing needs and desires, different emotional, affective, and intellectual dispositions, and different modes of executing and reacting to violence. This delicate balance is frequently disrupted and must be reset anew. Furthermore, gendered subject positions place men in positions of power and privilege, while women occupy lower positions with fewer opportunities for authority and influence. However, everyday lives clearly differ, and gendered expectations are constantly and tacitly transgressed (Ferme 2001).

Violence in relationships, I have argued, can be better understood by observing lived realities in which prevailing masculine and feminine subject statuses are constantly overturned by the constraints of lived experiences and by struggles in relationships (Chapters 3–4). Relationships and gender dynamics are both firm and fluid. Changes in relationship practices, in labour, and in social organisation have led to new forms of relationships and new ideas about love. But masculinities and femininities continue to influence the ways in which individuals are categorised, evaluated, respected, or dismissed based on established norms and expectations. They are embedded in, dependent on, and reinforced by the existing material and social conditions of domination and subordination. These influence people's efforts to find a partner and the way relationships are lived as well as the way they are evaluated by friends, family, and society. Publicly transgressing expectations may lead to their breakdown, and this is therefore discouraged. As Caroline Bledsoe (1980a), Carol MacCormack and Marilyn Strathern (1982), Melissa Leach (1994), Mariane Ferme (2001), and others have emphasised, the complementarity of genders is not the underbelly but the true body of social relations in Sierra Leone. Gendered differences, as well as the need for cooperation, give birth to and sustain power structures, livelihood strategies, and social life.

However, as the metaphor of the teeth and the tongue shows, this complementarity does not necessarily make for a perfect fit. What occurs in Freetown today is not a performance where two different pieces – male and female – automatically build a completed puzzle (representing gender complementarity) if placed together. Rather, both parts are 'jammed together' and need to arrive at this complementarity. The road to achieving complementarity has become rocky and difficult to navigate. Underneath the neat performance was always a messier lived reality, but the deviations were carefully concealed and did not openly challenge the picture of complementarity. Today, relationships are often visibly spiked with violence and pain. The hegemony of one idea of complementarity has been upset, men and women can no longer be placed together according to expected patterns, and different ideologies vie to become hegemonic. In Freetown today, there is no longer one puzzle consisting of two pieces, but several puzzles that have been thrown together into one box. Institutions and communities struggle to advance their own ideals of gender relations and relationship dynamics against the opposing views of other systems. And partners in sexual relationships find themselves caught between these different views.

This book has thus offered a reworking of the classic theme of gender complementarity. It argues for an interpretation of gender relations that allows for an analysis of friction. It shows too how everyday practices differ from the prevailing gendered principles, but how the principles are nevertheless held in place because of the important role they play in shaping expectations and behaviours. The metaphor of the teeth and the tongue thus serves as a novel way to examine gendered identities and gender relations in contemporary Sierra Leone.

Scholars have shown the importance of social age across Africa (Christiansen, Utas, and Vigh 2006). Similarly in Sierra Leone, after a *rite de passage* that makes a person a big woman or a big man, they must assume the responsibility that comes with such a subject position. Here, the book builds further on the relational nature of 'youth' as a category, by showing its gendered foundation. Whereas a man in Freetown can remain a 'youth' until an advanced age, women's youth is ended by childbearing. In the event of a pregnancy, women and girls are expected to assume the role of mothers and thus of big women, irrespective of whether, numerically speaking, they are 15 or 35 years old (Chapter 6).

Responsibility grows with seniority. In analysing household and community mediations (Chapter 6), I have shown the importance that is placed on the perspective of female elders. In both case studies presented in Chapter 6, it was elders who decided the fates of their younger family and community members. Had Ester's grandmother been on trial, it would have been difficult to discipline her. As an elder, she is at the very centre of a broad web of social relations. In Freetown, people make their mark on the world through successfully mobilising their social networks (Bourdieu and Wacquant 1992). The communities I lived in were firmly based on shared responsibilities, shared labour, and mutual aid. The more senior someone was, the more weight was attached to their opinion in deciding cases.

The criminal justice institutions, on the other hand, have adopted a numerical understanding of age, maturity, and responsibility, which is seemingly separated from gendered practices. Adulthood and maturity are reached at the age of 18. Before then, people are assigned a guardian, who must ensure that they do not transgress age-related boundaries. This study has thus brought to light the consequences of two different perceptions of age in which neither system accepts the other.

Violence as Acts versus Violence as Relationships

For the criminal justice system to be effective, it must consider violence as acts: acts that can be observed and measured, in which right and wrong can be clearly assigned, and in which individuals can be constituted as perpetrators and victims. Communities and households, on the other hand, consider violence as a relationship not of physical acts but one between people. Here, individual acts of violence are almost meaningless. They are part of a much bigger relational dynamic of violence that must be uncovered. When engaged in mediation, communities and households therefore quickly move from looking at acts of violence, such as beating or neglect. Instead, they focus on the relationship between the people in question and on how they comport themselves towards each other and towards others, so as to determine who influences and manipulates whom.

After determining a victim–perpetrator relationship, state bodies put the burden of blame on the perpetrator and punish them. Communities, by contrast, never judge a single individual, whether right or wrong. For them, punishment is relational and different sanctions are given to those involved. Communities may say who was the main culprit, but, as Chapters 6 and 7 have shown, they do not believe in a sole culprit or in innocence. Moreover, the community immediately moves past the individual and considers the best solution for re-establishing stability within a household and the community. Sanctions are meant to reinforce and make secure the resolution that has been arrived at, while the punishment given by state institutions is aimed at transforming the transgressing individual and discouraging others from committing similar acts (Foucault 1977).

While the two models result in very different outcomes, both are shaped by power relations and unequal subject positions. Both have severe consequences. People are deeply aware of these differences and make conscious choices when deciding whether to report to the state or the community. Hence, as Keebet von Benda-Beckmann (1981) said, they shop between forums and the forums shop for them as well.

Whether institutions in Sierra Leone are rigid or pliable depends on who engages with them. The criminal justice system only intervenes in personal relationships when minors are involved. The SOA operates by decontextualising matters, considering only whether the alleged victim and accused can be inserted into a clear victim–perpetrator relationship and whether sex took place – not how and why. Here, intervention is justified as an effort to protect minors in the interest of national development. In all state cases, no out-of-court settlements are possible and no attempt to influence outcomes is tolerated.

Generally speaking, this abstraction, rigidity, and neutrality is not unusual. Globally, court procedures rely on this reductionism. However, in Sierra Leone, except for cases under the SOA, not only informal mediation systems, but also state legal institutions negotiate disputes through contextualisation. If adults are concerned, state institutions try to keep the privacy and inviolability of households and marriages intact. They seek to settle such matters and often refer them back to communities to be mediated informally. At times like these, law enforcement personnel act according to their gendered socialisation and not according to legislative prescriptions (Bierschenk and De Sardan 2014). This book therefore shows that the way in which institutions 'think' (Douglas 1986) is influenced by the perceptions of those who work in them.

Rights and Law after the TRC

Anthropologists have increasingly turned to studying 'human rights culture' in order to understand how rights and culture interact (Cowan et al. 2001; Hastrup 2003; Cowan 2006; Comaroff and Comaroff 2016). As a result of the seminal works on the Sierra Leonean Truth and Reconciliation Commission (TRC) by Kirsten Ainley, Rebekka Friedman, and Chris Mahony (2015) and by Rosalind Shaw, Lars Waldorf, and Pierre Hazan (2010), Sierra Leone has become a central case study for such analyses. Deborah Thomas (2012) shows how 'lawfare' – a term that Jean and John Comaroff applied to 'the use of legal means for political and economic ends' (Comaroff and Comaroff 2009: 56) – also encapsulates the aim of the TRC to promote ideals of development and empowerment by demanding legal changes. However, Kirsten Hastrup (2003) argues that lawfare, and the human rights ideals it is based upon, can have an essentialising and oversimplifying effect even if the aim is to protect minorities. Moreover, because such lawfare is mobilised 'within the realm of the transnational, its aims generally tend to target the more modest space of the nation-state' (Thomas 2012: 21). It thereby ignores historical forces by assuming that only a break from the old can help realise the desired goals.

This book has contributed in two ways to the study of law and rights. First, it focussed on domestic laws and legal reforms to prevent violence, which were largely based on the TRC's recommendations, and so it examined one of the effects of the TRC in Sierra Leone. Second, it analysed the impact of such lawfare on Sierra Leone's plural legal landscape.

In Freetown, the framing of laws around the idea of human rights succeeded in producing 'certain kinds of victims' (Ross 2003: 73), namely girls under 18, irrespective of how they perceive themselves. Additionally, it resulted in a construction of perpetrators, without whom no victims could exist. The lawfare of the violence prevention laws has therefore limited the agency of some of those citizens whom these laws tried to empower, and silenced others. In Freetown, the responsibility for such erasures is usually given to 'others'. The state blames the international community, prison guards blame the state, and lawyers and judges blame the international community.

But these human-rights-based laws did not radically reconfigure the relationship between state institutions and citizens. As Mariane Ferme (1998; 2004) has argued, laws are perceived as unfair and arbitrary by Sierra Leonean citizens because, since colonial times, their implementation has been shaped by foreign interests. After independence, reforms and legal changes continued to be based upon foreign concepts that rarely considered complex local realities. At the same time, they operated on the assumption that Sierra Leone was an independent state, which meant leaving their implementation and possible consequences to its institutions and its citizens. The Sierra Leonean state and its laws are thus regularly the object of others' influences. As I have demonstrated, within the country the blame for adverse effects can be shifted and reshifted until the source becomes impossible to pin down.

Antonio Gramsci (1971) described the make-up of society as consisting of two interrelated spheres: a political society that rules through force and a civil society that governs through consent. As this book has shown, in Sierra Leone the aims and objectives of development agendas and their legal enforcement lie within the sphere of the political society, while local norms, conceptions, and practices lie within that of civil society. Development and policy discourses shape public opinion to a certain extent – for example, through the languages of violence – but the contrast between such discourses, lived experiences and practical realities opens up contested spaces. The ways in which the SOA and its amendment rub against community practices bring to light differing understandings of violence, mediation, and punishment. With the power to regulate, enforce, and punish resting primarily on the side of the state, discrepancies between 'universal' concepts and local norms have significant consequences for the daily lives of Sierra Leoneans. People are governed by rules that do not reflect their norms and in which they do not uncritically believe. While communities and households are focussed on ensuring continuities through mediation, the criminal justice system enforces ruptures through punishment and imprisonment.

Like South Africa, as the Comaroffs showed, Sierra Leone has struggled in the post-war, post-Ebola era of reconstruction to 'build a democracy founded on the rule of law' (Comaroff and Comaroff 2016). In its aim to achieve human rights principles – freedom from violence, gender equality, high-quality and accessible education, and empowerment – the state has taken over the 'guardian function' for girls. This allows an individual's rights to be circumscribed in a bid to achieve human rights goals (see Foblets, Graziadei, and Renteln 2017, for similar trends in Europe). Transgressions of the rights to privacy, intimacy, and family life are justified by recourse to the language of universal human rights. This legitimises the state's claim to guardianship and the (partial) curtailment of the rights of citizenship for minors. The resulting form of sexualised citizenship has upset previous dynamics. Historically, the protective role and guardian function that the state has now adopted was held both by households and by the colonial state. While the guardian function has primarily been used by scholars to analyse attempts to restrict minority practices in Europe, in this book I have married the concept to studies of law, rights, and culture. The SOA and the SB have therefore provided a novel setting for a comprehensive analysis of the causes and effects of governmental interest in interpersonal affairs within the post-colonial setting of contemporary Sierra Leone.

The circumscription of personal autonomy and individual needs is not new in Sierra Leone. In relationships, persons are asked to submit to and subsume their needs under those of both their partner and of the relationship as a whole (Chapter 3). Within communities, personal autonomy is circumscribed as the elders – who mediate cases and issue sanctions – act as guardians of communities, thereby furthering the interests of communities over those of individuals (Chapter 6). However, we have seen that such authority must be earned. As Chapters 8 and 9 have shown, laws that do not reflect people's values complicate rather than improve the relationship between state institutions and citizens. The SOA has opened an arena in which competing ideas now struggle to gain the upper hand. Among the most prominent are questions around who should dictate notions of age, relationships, choice, consent, and violence. Which norms should govern sexuality? Who should be allowed to punish deviations, and which factors should determine punishment?

As we have seen, in Sierra Leone historical forms of punishment were centered on addressing the needs of those who were wronged rather than solely punishing and removing the wrongdoer. Chapters 6 and 7 revealed that many people believe that punishments should involve compensating the family and providing support to the victim. In contrast, prison sentences are viewed as exacerbating the harm that was caused, as they remove the individual from society and prevent them from contributing to society or providing compensation to the victim's family. Even after being released from prison, wrongdoers can only seldomly support a victim and their family since their sentence exacerbated their deprivation, confining their material and social possibilities and their futures (Jefferson 2014; 2016; Jefferson and Segal 2020).

The emphasis of official reporting and legal cases on only those directly involved prevent others from taking the stand and expressing their views. Because restorative justice and redistribution practices are of long standing in Sierra Leone, the state's practices of punishing through trial and conviction are not readily supported (Gibbs 1963; see also Gulliver 1979: 3–7; Pirie 2007). So far, the president has not 'earned' the position of guardian for teenage girls in the same way that households and community elders have done so. Rather, he has 'taken' guardianship because of his political position.

Indeed, when the SOA(A) and the SB are perceived as means to restrict young people's sexuality, rather than as an attempt to prevent the rape of teenage girls, the state – and the president as head of state – is imagined as a 'vehicle' of oppression. In Chapter 9, I showed how boys who have been imprisoned for sleeping with their girlfriends construct themselves as the imagined 'others' of a law that seeks to oppress the sexual relationships of marginalised youth. At the same time, understanding the law as an oppressive instrument hinders women and girls from reporting safely and becomes yet another silencing mechanism. Hence, it seems that women and girls are silenced whether they report or not.

Youth and Crisis: A History of Continuous Ruptures

In Freetown, just as Charles Piot showed for Togo, practices 'are enacted at the interstices, and amidst the jostle of contradictory forces' (Piot 1999: 42). As this book has demonstrated, historical and biographical trajectories are important not only in appreciating state–citizen relations, but also in understanding current issues relating to violence. Read in conversation with older works on Sierra Leone, this book reveals manifold parallels and continuities. As for the mediation of violence, we must understand the deep value that is placed on continuity by communities who have been confronted with intense and traumatic ruptures throughout a long history of violent intervention and conflict.

But current academic work also highlights important ruptures. As the literature on the crisis of youth and masculinity shows (Chapters 3 and 4), men's violence in relationships can be attributed to their struggle to cope with the pressure to uphold masculine ideals among changing relationship forms and labour patterns as well as amidst conditions of precarity. Gender dynamics have been upset by historical forces and urban influences, leading to intense negotiations about women's and men's roles and responsibilities that are fraught with conflict and violence. This disturbance of gender dynamics raises questions about what it means to be a man or a woman in Freetown today. And such questions lie at the heart of many forms of violence and the complicity of those who suffer it.

However, to understand these dynamics it is important to recognise generational tensions (see Richards 1998; Diggins 2014). This allows for an analysis, not only of the way things are, but also of how they were and how they came to be. While women have historically been described as men's subordinates, very often in practice they are the main breadwinners, they direct households and social groups, execute violence too, and mediate violence in relationships. Moreover, the practices of youth in

Freetown today are not unique to the present moment. Elders point to the existence of similar processes when they were young. Young people have always challenged elders. There have long been disputes, debates, and contestations around knowledge (Murphy 1980), power, and authority (Richards 1998). Romantic engagements have often transgressed accepted norms (Ferme 2001), and interpersonal violence has been an issue that has customarily required regulation. Focussing on the *longue durée* and on different age groups enables one to appreciate change as constantly in the making rather than as involving sudden ruptures, breakages, or endings. In this way, practices and regulations relating to violence in relationships can be analysed as historically shaped (Chapters 2–3 and 7–9). For instance, I depicted the inventiveness with which the category 'youth' is applied among young and sometimes not-so-young people in Sierra Leone as a kind of staged exceptionalism by means of which young people continually differentiate themselves from elders. This has shaped the country in the past (Richards 1998), but it has also adapted itself to contemporary issues.

Instead of being replaced, older and traditional practices are constantly reinvented as times change and new practices are introduced from elsewhere. Further, exposure to the new and previously unknown happens in the form of encounters, rather than impositions, creating a melting pot rather than an assemblage of distinct pieces. This kind of understanding allows for a historically grounded analysis of relationship practices, and the violence within them, that takes the notion of 'ruptures' seriously without giving them sole responsibility.

In Freetown, practices have undergone change in recent years. However, their foundation stones and ideals are still very much intact. Elders, for example, talk about agreement relationships (Chapter 3) and show how their own parents engaged in these, much as young people do now, though the latter explain them by reference to urbanity, modernity, consumption, and globalisation. These multi-layered incorporations, which are both self-asserting and differentiating, accompany the constant configuration and reconfiguration of agreement relationships (Piot 1999: 178). At the heart of intimate relationships and of the social bonds and alliances that they create is still the exchange of money, gifts, and goods.

During the civil war, the institution of marriage and the protective association of the family suffered. Their full rehabilitation and recovery are made difficult by contemporary economic struggles because many people continue to be unable to afford marriage. In Chapter 3, we have seen how other relationship forms have taken the upper hand. However, the later chapters have demonstrated that institutions responding to violence are still very much connected to marriage. It was usually spouses, or at least persons who underwent *ansa bele*, whose cases were dealt with. Furthermore, although marriage is decreasing, traditional notions of bride price and the union of two families reappear in the notion of *ansa bele*, which now regulates most pregnancies out of wedlock. *Ansa bele* became important when traditional pathways to marriage were blocked. It was a creative new way to keep the protective mechanisms of family ties alive, to continue kinship and alliance bonds, and to provide children with a father and a mother. Hence, while the protective association of the family has suffered, we have seen that it is still only committed relationships, formalised through monetary exchanges, that can rely on any continuous form of protection from the household or community.

As this book has demonstrated, gendered practices, relationships, and the violence within them cannot be understood merely as post-conflict phenomena, as results of modernity, globalisation, transnational flows, or new technologies and the media. Instead, Sierra Leoneans have creatively appropriated, reconfigured, and resignified rural practices of marriage, informal labour, and social organisation, and they have enmeshed them in global influences and practices in an urban setting. In this way, they have created a new relationship model that is based on heritage and on new ideas of loving and living. *Ansa bele* is not just the following practice in a long chronology of events, but an example of the way in which an innovative past has been critically reforged in the present. *Ansa bele* combines past and continuing demands with aspirations while at the same time being sensitive to the practical constraints of the present. It bridges the divide between social organisation in the villages and contemporary urban sociality. Through *ansa bele*, young people are able to conduct relationships outside wedlock but still become big men and big women.

The SOA and the SB were ratified in order to address problems like the rape of girls, teenage pregnancy, and interrupted schooling (see Chapter 8). They were responses to grassroots demands that the government take responsibility to prevent rape and severely punish rapists. They point to continuities as well because they were inspired by the problems of the civil war and the post-war moment. However, rather than offering additional solutions, they led to the breakdown of other mechanisms. For instance, they removed the protective mechanisms of *ansa bele* for implicated persons. The SOA and SB diminished the influence and power of girls within their families and simultaneously decreased family resources. As soon-to-be mothers, pregnant girls usually become 'big women' and have an important role within the family. Their relationships make possible the unification of two families and the exchange of bride price. With their practices criminalised and their partners in prison, the role of these girls within the household has changed dramatically. They are unable to show a father during their pregnancy or when the child is born, and they are faced with the task of raising and providing for their child independently. It is these unstable dynamics that expose the main point of friction between internationally inspired laws and local dynamics.

Additionally, it was often explained to me that children conceived by ex-combatants were one of the most consequential after-effects of the war. Already at that time, public schools did not allow pregnant girls to attend. Women and girls with 'rebel children' were often excluded from their families and communities, and were forced into a precarious existence. These trends of stigmatisation and exclusion may very well have been continued by the criminalisation of young people's sexual behaviour through the SOA and the SB. As this study has shown, perceptions of violence in relationships as well as its mediation, regulation, and punishment are all part of broader historical developments and must be understood as such.

Of Tactics and Strategies

Throughout the book, we have seen how people act tactically towards those above them in the social, legal, and political order, and strategically towards those below them. What is of direct relevance is de Certeau's (1980; 1984) distinction between tactics and strategies for understanding how persons and institutions act towards each other (see also Vigh 2006b for Guinea-Bissau). The Sierra Leonean state, for example, seems to be obliged to operate tactically when international development aid is made conditional on legal reform. It was also pressured by TRC recommendations for restructuring programmes, which would refashion the country's image in international eyes. Hence, the post-conflict, post-pandemic state, heavily dependent on foreign aid, tactically ratified laws that adhered to these demands. Turning to its citizens, the state then became a strategic player, establishing organisations and institutions – such as the FSU, and supporting non-governmental organisations – such as the Rainbo Centre – to enforce the legal regulations it had passed.

At the same time, it undertook a strategic but less visible reframing of citizenship. Poster campaigns and national strategies presented citizens with the prospect of a bright future based on their full compliance with the laws that were passed, including the SOA(A). However, young people's navigation strategies – through debts, favours, and various relationships by which they attempt to comply with the demands of the institutions of family and community and keep a certain freedom at the same time – involve transgressions of the SOA and the SOAA. We have also seen how communities navigate strategically to keep their members in line and tactically to keep state interference at a minimum. These strategies of doing favours and collecting debts, and the binding obligations and relations of compulsion they create, thus stretch from the very micro-level of interpersonal acts all the way to the president's decisions. In Sierra Leone's system of weak legal pluralism, all levels of society are affected by these webs.

Two practices are of key importance in this system of tactically navigating the demands of one's superiors and the strategic demands made of subordinates: the pretence of hegemony in the face of competing ideologies, and the resulting harmony ideology. Throughout my study, a 'harmony ideology' (Nader 1990) adopted towards outsiders was clearly observable, in which persons and institutions displayed a united front to the outside, while internally they might be conflicted. This resulted in an image of hegemony. Violence, as we have seen, intensifies when this performed hegemony is unmasked as an ideology and can thus be exposed to questioning and criticism. When family and community realise that in a relationship gendered ideals have been reversed to an unendurable extent, they intervene (Chapters 6 and 7). Individuals who are seen to transgress their expected gendered roles may lose respect and agency. If communities are unable to demonstrate harmony vis-à-vis the state, state institutions may no longer respect their autonomy but find a way to intrude upon community territory.

Ethnography for Society: The Importance of Working across Academic and Policy Silos

In their book, Jennifer Cole and Lynn Thomas reiterated the importance of 'historically situated words' (Cole and Thomas 2009: 3) in carrying meanings of love. Similarly, in this book I have shown how small terminological differences are used to distinguish between vastly different forms of relationships and violence in Freetown. Communities and laws have their own respective languages. People on the ground have combined historical metaphors, legal terms, and the language of risk and rights to create their own system of meaning. However, the terms they use differ from those of state institutions and non-state agencies. Consequently, they may not necessarily understand each other. Similarly, the numerous NGOs and IOs that shape the landscape of violence prevention are often unaware of appropriate local terminologies.

Consider poster campaigns for instance by UNICEF warning of imprisonment for 'sexual abuse'. However, sexual abuse, as we have seen, is not a term used by ordinary people and, on the basis of my

228 Conclusion

findings, I presume that not many people will feel this poster speaks to them. By contrast, while posters like the one depicting President Julius Maada Bio and First Lady Fatima Bio use the word 'abuse' as well (see Figure C.1), they pair such language with clear, unambiguous

Figure C.1 Poster in Freetown.

terminology. The poster communicates three messages – that they claim guardianship over all Sierra Leonean girls ('our girls') and will neither tolerate violence nor sexual activities involving minors ('hands off'). Another example is rape, which is an act executed with physical force against a stranger. Posters aiming to address sexual violence committed by known persons miss their target audience when they use the word 'rape' instead of *bambrusing* or 'forcing'.

Anthropologists are often criticised for being unable to generalise their results and make them meaningful to larger audiences. However, I believe that an important contribution anthropology can make is to bring to light the worlds of meaning assigned not only to the linguistic but also to the social life of particular words in specific contexts. I hope that my work will help do just that for terms referring to love and violence in Freetown.

For years, the SB has been widely criticised as discriminatory and as exacerbating risks and hardships associated with teenage pregnancy (see Amnesty International 2015; 2016). On behalf of the over ten thousand girls who had been banned from school, grassroots activists filed a case with the ECOWAS (Economic Community of West African States) Court. In December 2019, the court ruled that the ban is contrary to basic rights and must be abolished immediately. The court also criticised the government for failing to implement measures to reduce teenage pregnancy, as called for in the national strategies for the reduction of teenage pregnancies and child marriage (see Chapter 8). The government was also ordered to begin this work immediately, not in the form of bans or punishments, but through inclusive sensitisation, awareness raising, and sexual and reproductive health education. This is a landmark decision for West Africa and for Africa in general. It seems to achieve the goals of many teachers and grassroots organisations.

However, what remains unseen and unchallenged is the drastic effect of the consent laws for young couples, for adults, and for the relationship between communities and the state. What is more, the awareness of the plight of girls makes the invisibility of boys' fates even more worrying – an effect that points to a gender bias within human rights and development discourses more broadly. The actual consequences of the SOA and its amendment are unknown and invisible to international monitoring and evaluation programmes, because reporting statistics and conviction rates are age blind and do not record the relationship between alleged victim and perpetrator (whether he is a boyfriend or stranger). Additionally, because minors are not recorded in statistics for Pademba Road, organisations and agencies are largely unaware of their existence within Freetown's adult prison population. For those who *do* know, however, the conviction of young lovers as rapists seems to be accepted as a form of unavoidable collateral damage on the road to achieving a 'bigger' goal.

My research speaks to the important role academics can play in highlighting the actual effects of laws and policies. I hope that this qualitative study has helped to reveal not only what the laws are and what they are 'supposed to do', but also what they 'actually do'. And in fact, conflicting views of mediation and punishment are only one of many differences between dominant narratives, 'official government conceptions and the realities of local affairs' (Moore 1986: 319), that concern violence in relationships. This ethnography has considered what is known, revealed, or discussed, and then examined the multifaceted phenomena concerning love, gender, and law that are not readily seen or acknowledged, but which underlie what is visible.

This book has also shown the importance of working across academic and policy silos. Through an ethnographic exploration of the ways violence is mediated in Sierra Leone today, it exposes the dangers that exist when development and policy actors work to 'advance' gender justice through laws and policies like the SOA and its amendment. But it has also developed a road map for how such negative consequences can be avoided or overcome: by working in horizontal partnerships with affected people, and taking seriously their expertise, while also drawing on the insights of scholars who systematically analyse the consequences of such legal and policy work.

Living with Sierra Leoneans on their terms reveals a picture in which the apparently neat dichotomies of gender and generation and the different scales of mediation are blurred. This is a picture in which women are not simply oppressed, but also act on the world they inhabit, constantly rethinking, reinforcing, or reconfiguring norms and rules. It is a world in which men are not just violent perpetrators who are always in control, but people cognisant of their weaknesses and their limits vis-à-vis women who in many instances have significant power (Groes-Green 2013). It is a world in which violence is perceived on a spectrum from affective expectation to outright rejection. And it is a world with a diverse legal consciousness. In this book, I have shown the relationship between 'universal' and 'local' norms, values, and practices about masculinities and femininities, relationships, and the role of violence in them. Through analysing the multifarious interactions between the frontstage (that which is said to be, is performed, and is visible) and the backstage (that which is underneath), I have sought to complicate such binaries, shown how relationships are lived, and demonstrated how violence, responses to it, and the punishment it incurs are negotiated in Freetown.

Overall, by analysing violence and its mediation at interpersonal, domestic, and state levels, and by marrying studies of love, violence, and law, I have tried to uncover the complex and contradictory pressures and influences that impact on persons and institutions as they enact, experience, and respond to violence. It is necessary to recognise and examine the tensions between episteme and experience if we are to grasp the role and place of violence in intimate relationships and comprehend why interventions so often fail to achieve their goals. Violence, as I have shown, is far from a private matter that occurs between individuals. It is not solely the responsibility of communities or the state to regulate it. Instead, it is the complex interplay, dialogue, and the tensions between these different forces that structure perceptions of violence and responses to it, and that can be made intelligible through the metaphor of the teeth and the tongue.

References

Abdullah, I. 1998. 'Bush path to destruction: the origin and character of the Revolutionary United Front Sierra Leone', *Journal of Modern African Studies* 36 (2): 203–35.

Abdullah, J. H., and A. Fofana-Ibrahim. 2010. 'The meaning and practice of women's empowerment in post-conflict Sierra Leone', *Development* 53 (2): 259–66.

Abrahams, N., R. Jewkes, and R. Laubsher. 1999. '"I do not believe in democracy in the home": men's relationships with and abuse of women', CERSA Women's Health Medical Research Council, 1–27. http://196.21.144.194/gender/nodemocracy.pdf.

Abu-Lughod, L. 1991. 'Writing against culture' in R. Fox (ed.), *Recapturing Anthropology: working in the present*. Santa Fé NM: School of American Research Press.

Accomazzo, S. 2012. 'Anthropology of violence: historical and current theories, concepts, and debates in physical and socio-cultural anthropology', *Journal of Human Behavior in the Social Environment* 22 (5): 535–52. https://doi.org/10.1080/10911359.2011.598727.

Adichie, C. N. 2009. 'The danger of a single story'. TEDGlobal. www.ted.com/talks/chimamanda_ngozi_adichie_the_danger_of_a_single_story.

Afro Barometer. 2021. 'Most Sierra Leoneans approve of measures against sexual violence, want more to be done'. Amnesty International, 2 August. www.amnesty.org/en/documents/document/?indexNumber=afr51\%2F2695\%2F2015\&language=en.

Ahmed, S. 2014. *The Cultural Politics of Emotion*, 2nd ed. Edinburgh: Edinburgh University Press.

Ainley, K., R. Friedman, and C. Mahony. 2015. *Evaluating Transitional Justice: accountability and peacebuilding in post-conflict Sierra Leone*. London: Palgrave Macmillan.

Alie, J. A. D. 1990. *A New History of Sierra Leone*. London: Macmillan.

Althusser, L. 1972. *Ideology and Ideological State Apparatuses (Notes towards an Investigation)*. New York: Monthly Review Press.

Amnesty International. 2015. 'Sierra Leone: shamed and blamed; pregnant girls' rights at risk in Sierra Leone'. Amnesty International, 6 November. www.amnesty.org/en/documents/document/?indexNumber=afr51\%2F2695\%2F2015\&language=en.

2016. 'Sierra Leone submission to the UN Committee on the Rights of the Child', 73rd session, 13–30 September. https://tbinternet.ohchr.org/Treaties/CRC/Shared\%20Documents/SLE/INT_CRC_NGO_SLE_247 17_E.pdf.

Anderson, B. 1983. *Imagined Communities: reflections on the origin and spread of nationalism*. London: Verso.

Anthrobase. 2016. 'Mauss, Marcel-Israël (1872–1950)'. *Anthrobase*. www.anthrobase.com/Dic/eng/pers/mauss_marcel.htm.

Anzaldúa, G. E. 2015. *In Light in the Dark/Luz en lo oscuro: rewriting identity, spirituality, reality*, ed. A. Keating. Durham NC: Duke University Press.

Appadurai, A. 1990. 'Disjuncture and difference in the global cultural economy', *Theory, Culture and Society* 7 (2): 295–310. https://doi.org/10.1177/026327690007002017.

— 2006. *Fear of Small Numbers: an essay on the geography of anger*. Durham NC: Duke University Press.

Archambault, J. S. 2013. 'Cruising through uncertainty: cell phones and the politics of display and disguise in Inhambane, Mozambique', *American Ethnologist* 40 (1): 88–101. https://doi.org/10.1111/amet.12007.

— 2018. *Mobile Secrets: youth, intimacy, and the politics of pretense in Mozambique*. Chicago: University of Chicago Press.

Aretxaga, B. 1995. 'Dirty protest: symbolic overdetermination and gender in Northern Ireland ethnic violence', *Ethos* 23 (2): 123–48.

Armstrong, S., and A. M. Jefferson. 2017. 'Disavowing "the" Prison' in D. Moran, and A. Schliehe (eds), *Carceral Spatiality*. London: Palgrave Macmillan.

Autesserre, S. 2012. 'Dangerous tales: dominant narratives on the Congo and their unintended consequences', *African Affairs* 111 (443): 202–22.

Bakare Yusuf, B. 2003. '"Yorubas don't do gender": a critical review of Oyèrónkẹ́ Oyěwùmí's "The Invention of Women: making an African sense of Western gender discourses"', *African Identities* 1 (1): 121–43.

Banton, M. 1956. 'Adaption and integration in the social system of Temne immigrants in Freetown', *Africa: Journal of the International African Institute* 26 (4): 354–68.

— 1957. *West African City: a study of tribal life in Freetown*. London: University Press for the International African Institute.

Barak-Glantz, I. L. 1981. 'Toward a conceptual schema of prison management styles', *Prison Journal* 61 (2): 42–60. https://doi.org/10.1177/003288558106100206.

Baucom, I. 2001. 'Specters of the Atlantic', *South Atlantic Quarterly* 100 (1): 61–82. https://doi.org/10.1215/00382876-100-1-61.

Bauman, Z. 2000. 'Social uses of law and order' in D. Garland and R. Sparks (eds), *Criminology and Social Theory*. Oxford: Oxford University Press.

— 2001. *Community: seeking safety in an insecure world*. Cambridge: Polity Press.

BBC News Media. 2010. 'Sierra Leone: murderers escape in daytime jail break'. *BBC*, 6 December. www.bbc.co.uk/news/world-africa-11926329.

Benda-Beckmann, K. von. 1981. 'Forum shopping and shopping forums: dispute processing in a Minangkabau village in West Sumatra', *Journal of Legal Pluralism and Unofficial Law* 13 (19): 117–59. https://doi.org/10.1080/07329113.1981.10756260.

Berry, Maya J., Claudia Chávez Argüelles, Shanya Cordis, Sarah Ihmoud, and Elizabeth Velásquez Estrada. 2017. 'Toward a fugitive anthropology: gender, race, and violence in the field', *Cultural Anthropology* 32 (4): 537–65.

Berthomé, F., J. Bonhomme, and G. Delaplace. 2012. 'Preface: cultivating uncertainty', *HAU: Journal of Ethnographic Theory* 2 (2): 129–37. https://doi.org/10.14318/hau2.2.008.

Bierschenk, T., and J.-P. O. de Sardan. 2014. *States at Work: dynamics of African bureaucracies*. Boston: Brill.

Bledsoe, C. H. 1980a. *Women and Marriage in Kpelle Society*. Stanford CA: Stanford University Press.

1980b. 'The manipulation of Kpelle social fatherhood', *Ethnology* 19 (1): 29–45. https://doi.org/10.2307/3773318.

1990a. '"No success without struggle": social mobility and hardship for foster children in Sierra Leone', *Man* 25 (1): 70–88. https://doi.org/10.2307/2804110.

1990b. 'School fees and the marriage process for Mende girls in Sierra Leone' in P. R. Sanday and R. G. Goodenough (eds), *Beyond the Sex: new directions in the anthropology of gender*. Philadelphia: University of Pennsylvania Press.

Bobbio, N. 1996. *The Age of Rights*. Cambridge: Polity Press.

Bolten, C. 2012. *I Did It to Save My Life: love and survival in Sierra Leone*. Berkeley CA: University of California Press.

Bosire, O. T. 2012. 'The Bondo secret society: female circumcision and the Sierra Leonean state'. PhD thesis, University of Glasgow. http://encore.lib.gla.ac.uk/iii/encore/record/C__Rb2952211files/54/3506.html.

Bourdieu, P. 1977. *Outline of a Theory of Practice*. Cambridge: Cambridge University Press.

1986. 'The forms of capital' in John G. Richardson (ed.), *Handbook of Theory and Research for the Sociology of Education*, 241–58. New York: Greenwood Press.

2001. *Masculine Domination*. Translated by R. Nice. Cambridge: Polity Press.

Bourdieu, P., and L. J. D. Wacquant. 1992. *An Invitation to Reflexive Sociology*. Chicago: University of Chicago Press.

Bourgois, P. 2004. 'The continuum of violence in war and peace: post-Cold War lessons from El Salvador' in N. Scheper-Hughes and P. Bourgois (eds), *Violence in War and Peace*. Malden MA: Blackwell Publishing.

Boyce-Davies, C. 1994. *Black Women, Writing and Identity: migrations of the subject*. London: Routledge.

Browning, C. R. 2002. 'The span of collective efficacy: extending social disorganization theory to partner violence', *Journal of Marriage and Family* 64 (4): 833–50. https://doi.org/10.1111/j.1741-3737.2002.00833.x.

Burrill, E. 2007. 'Disputing wife abuse: tribunal narratives of the corporal punishment of wives in Colonial Sikasso, 1930s (La maltraitance des femmes mise en question: comptes rendus de tribunaux sur le châtiment corporel des femmes à Sikasso dans les années 1930)'. *Cahiers d'Études Africaines* 47 (187): 603–22.

Burrill, E., R. L. Roberts, and E. Thornberry. 2010. *Domestic Violence and the Law in Colonial and Postcolonial Africa*. Athens OH: Ohio University Press.

Butler, J. 1993. *Bodies That Matter: on the discursive limits of 'sex'*. New York: Routledge.

Campbell, A. 2017. 'Sierra Leone news: youth issues still not framed'. *Awoko*. https://awoko.org/2017/02/27/sierra-leone-news-youth-issues-still-not-framed/.

Campbell, C., and J. Mannell. 2016. 'Conceptualising the agency of highly marginalised women: intimate partner violence in extreme settings', *Global Public Health* 11 (1–2): 1–16.

Capaldi, D. M., N. B. Knoble, J. W. Shortt, and H. K. Kim. 2012. 'A systematic review of risk factors for intimate partner violence', *Partner Abuse* 3 (2): 231–80. https://doi.org/10.1891/1946-6560.3.2.231.

Carlbom, A. 2003. 'The imagined versus the real other: multiculturalism and the representation of Muslims in Sweden'. PhD thesis, Lund University, Sweden. https://lup.lub.lu.se/search/publication/20977.

Centre for Accountability and Rule of Law (CARL). 2015. 'Assessing the resource gap in the fight against sexual and gender-based violence: is the FSU hamstrung?' CARL. www.carl-sl.org/wp-content/uploads/2016/08/FSU\%20REPORT\%20PDF.pdf.

Certeau, M. de. 1980. 'On the oppositional practices of everyday life', *Social Text* 3: 3–43.

1984. *The Practice of Everyday Life*. Berkeley CA: University of California Press.

Chernoff, J. M. 2003. *Hustling Is Not Stealing: stories of an African bar girl*. Chicago: University of Chicago Press.

Christensen, M., and M. Utas. 2008. 'Mercenaries of democracy: the "politricks" of remobilized combatants in the 2007 general elections, Sierra Leone', *African Affairs* 107 (429): 515–39. https://doi.org/10.1093/afraf/adn057.

2010. *Jew-man business [Videorecording]: a documentary about Ice T, Bone Thugs and Junior*. Uppsala: Nordiska Afrikainstitutet.

Christiansen, C., M. Utas, and H. Vigh (eds). 2006. *Navigating Youth, Generating Adulthood: social becoming in an African context*. Uppsala: Nordiska Afrikainstitutet.

Cohen, A. 1981. *The Politics of Elite Culture: explorations in the dramaturgy of power in a modern African society*. Berkeley CA: University of California Press.

Cohen, D. K. 2013. 'Female combatants and the perpetration of violence: wartime rape in the Sierra Leone civil war', *World Politics* 65 (3): 383–415.

Cole, J., and L. M. Thomas. 2009. *Love in Africa*. Chicago: University of Chicago Press.

Collins, P. H. 2000. 'Gender, black feminism, and black political economy', *Annals of the American Academy of Political and Social Science* 568: 41–53.

Collins, P. H., and S. Bilge. 2016. *Intersectionality*. Malden MA: Polity Press.

Comaroff, J., and J. L. Comaroff. 1991. *Of Revelation and Revolution*, vol. 1. Chicago: University of Chicago Press.

2009. *Ethnicity, Inc*. Chicago: University of Chicago Press.

2016. *The Truth about Crime: sovereignty, knowledge, social order.* Chicago: University of Chicago Press.

2021. 'The colonization of consciousness' in M. Fredericks and D. Nagy (eds), *Critical Readings in the History of Christian Mission*, vol. 2. Leiden: Brill.

Comaroff, J. L., and S. Roberts. 1981. *Rules and Processes: the cultural logic of dispute in an African context.* Chicago: University of Chicago Press.

Connell, R. 2005. *Masculinities*, 2nd ed. Cambridge: Polity Press.

Cooper, E., and D. Pratten. 2015. *Ethnographies of Uncertainty in Africa.* Basingstoke: Palgrave Macmillan.

Cooper, F., and A. L. Stoler. 1997. *Tensions of Empire: colonial cultures in a bourgeois world.* Berkeley CA: University of California Press.

Coulter, C. 2005. *The Postwar Moment: female fighters in Sierra Leone.* Uppsala University, Department of Cultural Anthropology.

2009. *Bush Wives and Girl Soldiers: women's lives through war and peace in Sierra Leone.* Ithaca NY: Cornell University Press.

Cowan, J. K. 2006. 'Culture and rights after "culture and rights"', *American Anthropologist* 108 (1): 9–24.

Cowan, J. K., M.-B. Dembour, and R. Wilson. 2001. *Culture and Rights: anthropological perspectives.* Cambridge: Cambridge University Press.

Crapanzano, V. 2004. *Imaginative Horizons: an essay in literary-philosophical anthropology.* Chicago: University of Chicago Press.

Craps, S. 2010. 'Wor(l)ds of grief: traumatic memory and literary witnessing in cross-cultural perspective', *Textual Practice* 24: 51–68.

Crenshaw, K. W. 1991. 'Mapping the margins: intersectionality, identity politics, and violence against women of color'. *Stanford Law Review* 43 (6): 1241–99.

'Beyond racism and misogyny: black feminism and 2 Live Crew' in Mari J. Matsuda (ed.), *Words That Wound.* New York: Routledge.

Czarniawska, B. 2007. *Shadowing: and other techniques for doing fieldwork in modern societies.* Copenhagen: Copenhagen Business School Press.

Day, L. R. 1994. 'The evolution of female chiefship during the late nineteenth-century wars of the Mende', *International Journal of African Historical Studies* 27 (3): 481–503. https://doi.org/10.2307/220756.

Dayan, C. 2011. *The Law Is a White Dog: how legal rituals make and unmake persons.* Princeton NJ: Princeton University Press.

Deleuze, G., and F. Guattari. 2002. *A Thousand Plateaus: capitalism and schizophrenia.* London: Continuum.

Derrida, J. 1993. *Specters of Marx: the state of the debt, the work of mourning and the new international.* London: Routledge.

Diggins, J. 2014. 'Slippery fish, material words: the substance of subsistence in coastal Sierra Leone'. PhD thesis, University of Sussex.

2015. 'Economic runaways: patronage, poverty and the pursuit of freedom on Sierra Leone's maritime frontier', *Africa: Journal of the International African Institute* 85 (2): 312–32. https://doi.org/10.1017/S0001972014001041.

Douglas, M. 1986. *How Institutions Think.* Syracuse NY: Syracuse University Press.

Dunaiski, M. 2013. 'Gender-based violence in South Africa: a crisis of masculinity?' E-International Relations Students, 27 April 2013. www.e-ir.info/2013/04/27/gender-based-violence-in-south-africa-a-crisis-of-masculinity/.

Durham, D. 2000. 'Youth and the social imagination in Africa: introduction to parts 1 and 2', *Anthropological Quarterly* 73 (3): 113–20.

Durkheim, É. 1997. *The Division of Labor in Society.* New York: Free Press.

Eberl-Elber, R. 1936. *Westafrikas letztes Rätsel: Erlebnisbericht über die Forschungsreise 1935 durch Sierra Leone.* Salzburg: Das Bergland-Buch.

Ellis, S. 1999. *The Mask of Anarchy: the destruction of Liberia and the religious dimension of an African civil war.* London: Hurst.

Englund, H. 2006. *Prisoners of Freedom: human rights and the African poor.* Berkeley CA: University of California Press.

Enria, L. 2015. '"An idle mind is the devil's workshop"? The politics of work amongst Freetown's youth'. DPhil thesis, University of Oxford.

Epstein, A. L. 1981. *Urbanisation and Kinship: the domestic domain on the Copperbelt of Zambia, 1950–1956.* London: Academic Press.

Erikson, K. 1994. *A New Species of Trouble: explorations in disaster, trauma, and community.* New York: W. W. Norton.

Esposito, Roberto. 2011. *Immunitas: the protection and negation of life.* Cambridge: Polity Press.

Evans-Pritchard, E. E. 1940. 'The Nuer of the Southern Sudan'. eHRAF World Cultures. https://ehrafworldcultures.yale.edu/cultures/fj22/documents/010.

Farmer, P. 2004. 'On suffering and structural violence' in N. Scheper-Hughes and P. Bourgois (eds), *Violence in War and Peace.* Malden MA: Blackwell Publishing.

Feldman, A. 1991. *Formations of Violence: the narrative of the body and political terror in Northern Ireland.* Chicago: University of Chicago Press.

Ferme, M. 1998. 'The violence of numbers: consensus, competition, and the negotiation of disputes in Sierra Leone (La violence du dénombrement: consensus, compétition et résolution des conflits en Sierra Leone)', *Cahiers d'Études Africaines* 38 (150): 555–80.

——— 2001. *The Underneath of Things: violence, history and the everyday in Sierra Leone.* Berkeley CA: University of California Press.

——— 2004. 'Deterritorialized citizenship and the resonances of the Sierra Leonean state' in V. Das and D. Poole (eds), *Anthropology in the Margins of the State.* Santa Fe NM: School of American Research Press.

Fielding-Miller, R., and K. Dunkle. 2017. 'Constrained relationship agency as the risk factor for intimate partner violence in different models of transactional sex', *African Journal of AIDS Research* 16 (4): 283–9.

Foblets, M.-C., M. Graziadei, and A. D. Renteln. 2017. *Personal Autonomy in Plural Societies: a principle and its paradoxes,* 1st ed. London: Routledge.

Fofana, U. 2009. 'Partnering for girls' education in Sierra Leone'. UNICEF. www.unicef.org/infobycountry/sierraleone_51080.html.

Foucault, M. 1979. *Discipline and Punish: the birth of the prison.* London: Allen Lane.

Friedman Rudovsky, J. 2013. 'The women who bear the scars of Sierra Leone's civil war'. *The Telegraph,* 16 November. www.telegraph.co.uk/news/worldnews/africaandindianocean/sierraleone/10450619/The-women-who-bear-the-scars-of-Sierra-Leones-civil-war.html.

Fullagar, S., A. Pavlidis, A. Hickey-Moody, and J. Coffey. 2021. 'Embodied movement as method: attuning to affect as feminist experimentation', *Somatechnics* 11 (2): 174–90.

Galligan, D. J. 2007. *Law in Modern Society*. Oxford: Oxford University Press.

García Moreno, C., R. Jewkes, and P. Sen. 2002. 'World report on violence and health'. Geneva: World Health Organization. http://apps.who.int/iris/bitstream/handle/10665/42495/9241545615_eng.pdf;jsessionid=E3B3AE454CF6A81932B58547FAD00136?sequence=1.

Geertz, C. 1993. *The Interpretation of Cultures: selected essays*. London: Fontana Press.

―― 1998. 'Deep hanging out', *New York Review of Books*, 22 October. www.nybooks.com/articles/archives/1998/oct/22/deep-hanging-out/.

Geschiere, P., and S. Jackson. 2006. 'Autochthony and the crisis of citizenship: democratization, decentralization, and the politics of belonging', *African Studies Review* 49 (2): 1–7.

Gibbon, M. 1999. *Feminist Perspectives on Language*. London: Routledge.

Gibbs, J. L., Jr. 1963. 'The Kpelle moot: a therapeutic model for the informal settlement of disputes', *Africa: Journal of the International African Institute* 33 (1): 1–11. https://doi.org/10.2307/1157793.

Gilbert, J. 2016. 'The heart as a compass: preaching self-worth and success to single young women in a Nigerian Pentecostal church', *Journal of Religion in Africa: Journal of the International African Institute* 45 (3): 307–33.

Gluckman, M. 1963. *The Judicial Process among the Barotse of Northern Rhodesia*, 2nd ed. University of Zambia: Institute for Social Research.

Gobo, G. 2008. *Doing Ethnography*. Los Angeles: SAGE.

Goffmann, E. 1999. *Asylums: essays on the social situation of mental and other inmates*. New York: Garden Books.

Government of Sierra Leone. 1926. Prevention of Cruelty to Children Act: elimination of child labour, protection of children and young persons. www.justice.gov/sites/default/files/eoir/legacy/2013/11/08/prevention_of_cruelty_children.pdf.

Government of Sierra Leone. 1945. Chapter 44: Children and Young Persons Act. www.africanchildforum.org/clr/Legislation%20Per%20Country/sierra%20leone/sierraleone_childrenandyouth_1945_en.pdf.

―― 2007a. The Child Rights Act 2007: supplement to the Sierra Leone Gazette Extraordinary vol. CXXXVIII, no. 43 dated 3rd September, 2007. www.sierra-leone.org/Laws/2007-7p.pdf.

―― 2007b. The Devolution of Estates Act: enacted by the President and Members of Parliament. www.sierra-leone.org/Laws/2007-21p.pdf.

―― 2007c. The Domestic Violence Act: enacted by the President and Members of Parliament. www.sierra-leone.org/Laws/2007-20p.pdf.

―― 2009. The Registration of Customary Marriage and Divorce Act: enacted by the President and Members of Parliament. www.sierra-leone.org/Laws/2009-01.pdf.

―― 2012. The Sexual Offences Act. Act No. 12: enacted by the President and Members of Parliament. www.sierra-leone.org/Laws/2012-12.pdf.

2013. *Let Girls Be Girls, Not Mothers! National Strategy for the Reduction of Teenage Pregnancy (2013–2015)*. https://healtheducationresources.unesco.org/sites/default/files/resources/Sierra_Leone_National_Strategy_for_the_Reduction_of_Teenage_Pregnancy.pdf.

2018. *National Strategy for the Reduction of Adolescent Pregnancy and Child Marriage (2018–2022)*. https://sierraleone.unfpa.org/sites/default/files/pub-pdf/National%20Strategy%20for%20the%20reduction%20of%20Adolescent%20Pregnancy_final_Oct%202.pdf.

2019. The Sexual Offences (Amendment) Act, 2019. http://rogee.sl/docs/ROGEE-Sierra-Leone-Act-Sexual-Offences-2019.pdf.

Gramsci, A. 1971. *Selections from the Prison Notebooks of Antonio Gramsci*. New York: International.

Grant, M. 2006. '"I have been patient enough": gendered futures and mentors of female youth in urban Zimbabwe', *Social Dynamics* 31 (1): 21–46.

Griffiths, J. 1986. 'What is legal pluralism?', *Journal of Legal Pluralism and Unofficial Law* 18 (24): 1–55. https://doi.org/10.1080/07329113.1986.10756387.

Groes-Green, C. 2013. '"To put men in a bottle": eroticism, kinship, female power, and transactional sex in Maputo, Mozambique', *American Ethnologist* 40 (1): 102–17.

Guenther, L. 2013. *Solitary Confinement: social death and its afterlives*. Minneapolis MN: University of Minnesota Press.

Gulliver, P. H. 1979. *Disputes and Negotiations: a cross-cultural perspective*. New York: Academic Press.

Hall, S. 1996. 'Introduction: who needs identity?' in P. du Gay and S. Hall (eds), *Questions of Cultural Identity*. Thousand Oaks CA: SAGE Publications.

Harding, S. G. 1991. *Whose Science? Whose Knowledge? Thinking from women's lives*. Milton Keynes: Open University Press.

Hastrup, K. 2003. 'Violence, suffering and human rights: anthropological reflections', *Anthropological Theory* 3: 309–23.

Heise, L. L. 1998. 'Violence against women: an integrated, ecological framework', *Violence against Women* 4 (3): 262–90. https://doi.org/10.1177/1077801298004003002.

Hendriks, T. 2016. 'SIM cards of desire: sexual versatility and the male homoerotic economy in urban Congo', *American Ethnologist* 43 (2): 230–42.

Hoffer, C. P. 1972. 'Mende and Sherbro women in high office', *Canadian Journal of African Studies/La Revue Canadienne des Études Africaines* 6 (2): 151–64. https://doi.org/10.1080/00083968.1972.10803663.

Honwana, A. 2014. '2 "waithood": youth transitions and social change' in D. Foeken et al. (eds), *Development and Equity*. Leiden: Brill.

Honwana, A., and F. de Boeck. 2005. *Makers and Breakers: children and youth in postcolonial Africa*. Trenton NJ: Africa World Press.

hooks, B. 1983. *Ain't I a Woman: black women and feminism*, 3rd ed. Boston: South End Press.

Human Rights Watch. 1998. *Sierra Leone: sowing terror; atrocities against civilians in Sierra Leone*. New York: Human Rights Watch.

2003. *'We'll Kill You If You Cry': sexual violence in the Sierra Leone conflict.* New York: Human Rights Watch. https://hrw.org/reports/2003/sierraleone/sierleon0103.pdf.

Human Rights Watch, and C. Dufka. 1999. *Sierra Leone: getting away with murder, mutilation, and rape; new testimony from Sierra Leone.* New York: Human Rights Watch.

Hunter, M. 2010. *Love in the Time of AIDS: inequality, gender, and rights in South Africa.* Bloomington IN: Indiana University Press.

Ibrahim, A. F. 2009. 'Connecting testimony, trauma, and memory: the Sierra Leone experience', *Pacific Coast Philology* 44 (2): 249–71.

Jackson, M. 1977. *The Kuranko: dimensions of social reality in a West African society.* London: Hurst.

— 1996. *Things as They Are: new directions in phenomenological anthropology.* Bloomington IN: Indiana University Press.

— 2007. *Excursions.* Durham NC; London: Duke University Press.

— 2011. *Life within Limits: well-being in a world of want.* Durham NC: Duke University Press.

— 2012. *Between One and One Another.* Berkeley CA: University of California Press.

— 2017. *How Lifeworlds Work: emotionality, sociality, and the ambiguity of being.* Chicago: University of Chicago Press.

— 2019. *Critique of Identity Thinking.* New York: Berghahn Books.

James, W. 1904. 'A world of pure experience'. Classics in the History of Psychology. http://psychclassics.yorku.ca/James/experience.htm.

Jedrej, M. C. 1976. 'Medicine, fetish and secret society in a West African culture', *Africa: Journal of the International African Institute* 46 (3): 247–57. https://doi.org/10.2307/1159397.

— 1986. 'Cosmology and symbolism on the Central Guinea coast', *Anthropos: International Review of Anthropology and Linguistics* 81 (4): 497–515.

Jefferson, A. M. 2005. 'Reforming Nigerian prisons: rehabilitating a "deviant" state', *British Journal of Criminology* 45 (4): 487–503. https://doi.org/10.1093/bjc/azi034

— 2014. 'Conceptualizing confinement: prisons and poverty in Sierra Leone', *Criminology and Criminal Justice* 14 (1): 44–60. https://doi.org/10.1177/1748895812462593.

— 2016. 'Exacerbating deprivation: Trajectories of confinement in Sierra Leone', *Parole and beyond: international experiences of life after prison* 1(1): 243–69.

Jefferson, A. M., and L. B. Segal. 2020. 'The confines of time: on the ebbing away of futures in Sierra Leone and Palestine' in S. Turner and S. Jensen (eds), *Reflections on Life in Ghettos, Camps and Prisons.* London: Routledge.

Jenkins, R., H. Jessen, and V. Steffen. 2005. *Managing Uncertainty: ethnographic studies of illness, risk and the struggle for control.* Copenhagen: Museum Tusculanum Press.

Jensen, S. 2015. 'Corporealities of violence: rape and the shimmering of embodied and material categories in South Africa', *Critical African Studies* 7 (2): 99–117. https://doi.org/10.1080/21681392.2014.986707.

Jewkes, R., and R. Morrell. 2012. 'Sexuality and the limits of agency among South African teenage women: theorising femininities and their connections to HIV risk practices', *Social Science and Medicine* 74 (11): 1729–37.
Johnson, J. 2018. *In Search of Gender Justice: rights and relationships in matrilineal Malawi*. Cambridge: Cambridge University Press.
Johnson, M. P., and K. J. Ferraro. 2000. 'Research on domestic violence in the 1990s: making distinctions', *Journal of Marriage and Family* 62 (4): 948–63. https://doi.org/10.1111/j.1741-3737.2000.00948.x.
Kalish, R., and M. S. Kimmel. 2010. 'Suicide by mass murder: masculinity, aggrieved entitlement, and rampage school shootings', *Health Sociology Review* 19 (4): 451–64.
Kamara, P. J. 2011. 'Sierra Leone: Salone has 672 "ataya-base" spots'. *All Africa*, 5 December. https://allafrica.com/stories/201112060339.html.
Kandiyoti, D. 1988. 'Bargaining with patriarchy', *Gender and Society* 2 (3): 274–90. https://doi.org/10.1177/089124388002003004.
Karp, I. 1986. 'Review: "Agency and Social Theory": a review of Anthony Giddens', *American Ethnologist* 13 (1): 131–7.
Kaufman, G. 1980. *Shame: the power of caring*. Cambridge MA: Schenkman Books.
Kierkegaard, S. 1940. *Stages on Life's Way*. London: Oxford University Press.
    1983. *Fear and Trembling/Repetition*. Princeton NJ: Princeton University Press.
Kinsella, A. E. 2006. 'Hermeneutics and critical hermeneutics: exploring possibilities within the art of interpretation', *Forum: Qualitative Social Research* 7 (3). www.qualitative-research.net/index.php/fqs/article/view/145/319.
Kusenbach, M. 2003. 'Street phenomenology: the go-along as ethnographic research tool', *Ethnography* 4 (3): 455–85. https://doi.org/10.1177/146613810343007.
Lacey, M. 2004. 'A decade after massacres, Rwanda outlaws ethnicity'. *New York Times*, 9 April. www.nytimes.com/2004/04/09/world/a-decade-after-massacres-rwanda-outlaws-ethnicity.html.
Lascelles, L. C. A. 2020. 'Black feminism in a neoliberal world: resistance in contemporary black women's fiction'. PhD thesis, University of Leeds.
Last, M. 2000. 'Children and the experience of violence: contrasting cultures of punishment in Northern Nigeria', *Africa: Journal of the International African Institute* 70 (3): 359–93. https://doi.org/10.2307/1161066.
Leach, M. 1994. *Rainforest Relations: gender and resource use among the Mende of Gola, Sierra Leone*. Edinburgh: Edinburgh University Press for the International African Institute, London.
Lévi-Strauss, C. 1950. *Introduction to Marcel Mauss*. London: Routledge.
Lewinson, A. 2006. 'Love in the city: navigating multiple relationships in Dar es Salaam, Tanzania', *City and Society* 18 (1): 90–115. https://doi.org/10.1525/city.2006.18.1.90.
Little, K. 1965. 'The political function of the Poro, part I', *Africa: Journal of the International African Institute* 35 (4): 349–65.
    1966. 'The political function of the Poro, part II', *Africa: Journal of the International African Institute* 36 (1): 62–72.
Lorway, R. 2008. 'Defiant desire in Namibia: female sexual–gender transgression and the making of political being', *American Ethnologist* 35 (1): 20–33. https://doi.org/10.1111/j.1548-1425.2008.00003.x.

Lupick, T. 2012. 'Youths used as "pawns" in Sierra Leone polls: with elections two weeks away, pro-government youths are accused of receiving money to harass political rivals', *Al Jazeera*, 2 November. www.aljazeera.com/indepth/features/2012/11/201211182630194863.html.

Maada Bio, J. 2019. Statement for the Declaration of Rape and Sexual Violence as a National Emergency by His Excellency President Julius Maada Bio on Thursday, 7 December 2019, at State House, Freetown. www.sierra-leone.org/Speeches/bio-120718.pdf.

MacCormack, C. P., and M. Strathern. 1982. *Nature, Culture and Gender*. Cambridge: Cambridge University Press.

Mahmood, S. 2001. 'Feminist theory, embodiment, and the docile agent: some reflections on the Egyptian Islamic Revival', *Cultural Anthropology* 16 (2): 202–36.

Mahtani, S. 2016. 'Sierra Leone: continued pregnancy ban in schools and failure to protect rights is threatening teenage girls' futures', Amnesty International. www.amnesty.org/en/latest/news/2016/11/sierra-leone-continued-pregnancy-ban-in-schools-and-failure-to-protect-rights-is-threatening-teenage-girls-futures/.

Mahtani, S., and M. O'Gorman. 2018. 'Inside Sierra Leone's maximum security prison for women: the Freetown Female Correctional Centre houses about 90 women and their children', *Al Jazeera*, 25 March. www.aljazeera.com/indepth/inpictures/sierra-leone-maximum-security-prison-women-180320123948503.html.

Mann, B. 2014. *Sovereign Masculinity: gender lessons from the War on Terror*. New York: Oxford University Press.

Mannell, J., A. Umutoni, and S. Jackson. 2016. 'Women's responses to intimate partner violence in Rwanda: rethinking agency in constrained social contexts', *Global Public Health* 11 (1–2): 65–81. https://doi.org/10.1080/17441692.2015.1013050.

Marcis, F. le. 2017. 'The fiction of escape: in and out prison in Ivory Coast'. Conference presentation, Global Prisons Research Network and Security Roundtable Meeting, 3 November 2017, University of Amsterdam.

Marks, Z. 2014. 'Sexual violence in Sierra Leone's civil war: "virgination", rape, and marriage', *African Affairs* 113 (450): 67–87. https://doi.org/10.1093/afraf/adt070.

Masquelier, A. 2005. 'The scorpion's sting: youth, marriage and the struggle for social maturity in Niger', *Journal of the Royal Anthropological Institute* 11 (1): 59–83.

— 2009. *Women and Islamic Revival in a West African Town*. Bloomington IN: Indiana University Press.

— 2013. 'Teatime: boredom and the temporalities of young men in Niger', *Africa: Journal of the International African Institute* 83 (3): 470–91. https://doi.org/10.1017/S0001972013000272.

Mauss, M. 1970. *The Gift: forms and functions of exchange in archaic societies*. London: Cohen and West.

Mbembé, A. J., and L. Meintjes. 2003. 'Necropolitics', *Public Culture* 15 (1): 11–40.

McNay, L. 2000. *Gender and Agency: reconfiguring the subject in feminist and social theory*. Cambridge: Polity Press.

——— 2004. 'Agency and experience: gender as a lived relation', *Sociological Review* 52 (2): 175–90. https://doi.org/10.1111/j.1467-954X.2005.00530.x.

Mead, M. 1929. *Coming of Age in Samoa: a psychological study of primitive youth for Western civilisation*. London: Jonathan Cape.

Medie, P. A. 2013. 'Fighting gender-based violence" the women's movement and the enforcement of rape law in Liberia', *African Affairs* 112 (448): 377–97. https://doi.org/10.1093/afraf/adt040.

Mehlman, J. 1972. 'The "Floating Signifier": From Levi-Strauss to Lacan', *Yale French Studies*, 48(1): 10–77.

Merriam Webster. 2018. 'Medical definition of craw-craw'. www.merriam-webster.com/medical/craw-craw.

Meyer, B. 2004. 'Christianity in Africa: from African independence to Pentecostal-charismatic churches', *Annual Review of Anthropology* 33: 447–74.

Mills, E., J. Diggins, D. M. Tamba, and Z. Nesbitt-Ahmed. 2018. 'Gender-based violence in Sierra Leone'. Interactions: Empowerment of Women and Girls. http://interactions.eldis.org/gender-based-violence/country-profiles/sierra-leone.

Mills, E., Z. Nesbitt-Ahmed, J. Diggins, and T. Mackieu. 2015. '"They call me warrior": the legacy of conflict and the struggle to end sexual and gender-based violence in Sierra Leone'. Institute of Development Studies, Evidence report no. 154. www.ids.ac.uk/publications/they-call-me-warrior-the-legacy-of-conflict-and-the-struggle-to-end-sexual-and-gender-based-violence-in-sierra-leone/.

Mitton, K. 2018. 'Generation terrorists: the politics of youth and the gangs of Freetown'. Mats Utas blog. https://matsutas.wordpress.com/2018/02/26/generation-terrorists-the-politics-of-youth-and-the-gangs-of-freetown-by-kieran-mitton/.

Moore, H. L. 1994. *A Passion for Difference: essays in anthropology and gender*. Cambridge: Polity Press.

Moore, S. F. 1973. 'Law and social change: the semi-autonomous social field as an appropriate subject of study', *Law and Society Review* 7 (4): 719–46. https://doi.org/10.2307/3052967.

——— 1986. *Social Facts and Fabrications: 'customary' law on Kilimanjaro, 1880–1980*. Cambridge: Cambridge University Press.

Morrell, R. 2001. *Changing Men in Southern Africa*. Pietermaritzburg: University of Natal Press.

Morrell, R., R. Jewkes, and G. Lindegger. 2012. 'Hegemonic masculinity/masculinities in South Africa: culture, power, and gender politics', *Men and Masculinities* 15 (1): 11–30.

Morrison, T. 1987. *Beloved*. New York: Alfred A. Knopf.

Mottier, V. 2002. 'Masculine domination: gender and power in Bourdieu's writings', *Feminist Theory* 3 (3): 345–59. https://doi.org/10.1177/146470002762492042.

Moyi, P. 2013. 'An examination of primary school attendance and completion among secondary school age adolescents in post-conflict Sierra Leone',

Research in Comparative and International Education 8 (4): 524–39. https://doi.org/10.2304/rcie.2013.8.4.524.

Murphy, W. P. 1980. 'Secret knowledge as property and power in Kpelle society: elders versus youth', *Africa: Journal of the International African Institute* 50 (2): 193-207.

Nader, L. 1990. *Harmony Ideology: justice and control in a Zapotec mountain village*. Stanford CA: Stanford University Press.

Namy, S., C. Carlson, K. O'Hara, J. Nakuti, P. Bukuluki, J. Lwanyaaga, S. Namakula, et al. 2017. 'Towards a feminist understanding of intersecting violence against women and children in the family', *Social Science and Medicine* 184 (2): 40–8.

Newell, S. 2012. *The Modernity Bluff: crime, consumption, and citizenship in Côte d'Ivoire*. Chicago: University of Chicago Press.

Niehaus, I. 2013. 'Confronting uncertainty: anthropology and zones of the extraordinary', *American Ethnologist* 40 (4): 651–60. https://doi.org/10.1111/amet.12045.

Njogu, R. K. 2016. 'Decolonising sex: fifty shades of rape', *Southern African Journal of Policy and Development* 3 (1): 16–26.

Nkrumah, K. 1974. *Neo Colonialism: the last stage of imperialism*. London: Panaf Books.

Nunley, W. J. 1987. *Moving with the Face of the Devil: art and politics in urban West Africa*. Urbana IL: University of Illinois Press.

Nussbaum, M. C. 2004. *Upheavals of Thought: the intelligence of emotions*. New York: Cambridge University Press.

Nyamnjoh, F. B. 2001. 'Delusions of development and the enrichment of witchcraft discourses in Cameroon' in H. L. Moore and T. Sanders (eds), *Magical Interpretations, Material Realities: modernity, witchcraft and the occult in postcolonial Africa*. New York: Psychology Press.

O'Brian, C. D. 1996. 'Chapter five: a lost generation? Youth identity and state decay in West Africa' in R. Werbner and T. Ranger (eds), *Postcolonial Identities in Africa*. London: Zed Books.

Ofei-Aboagye, R. O. 1994. 'Altering the strands of the fabric: a preliminary look at domestic violence in Ghana', *Signs* 19 (4): 924–38.

Ojukutu-Macauley, S. 1997. 'Religion, gender, and education in northern Sierra Leone, 1896–1992' in A. Jalloh and D. E. Skinner (eds), *Islam and Trade in Sierra Leone*. Trenton NJ: Africa World Pres.

Ortner, S. B. 1984. 'Theory in anthropology since the sixties', *Comparative Studies in Society and History* 26 (1): 126–66. https://doi.org/10.1017/S0010417500010811.

1989. *High Religion: a cultural and political history of Sherpa Buddhism*. Princeton NJ: Princeton University Press.

Oyěwùmí, O. 1997. *The Invention of Women: making an African sense of Western gender discourses*. Minneapolis MN: University of Minnesota Press.

2005. *African Gender Studies: a reader*. New York: Palgrave Macmillan.

Parikh, S. 2004a. 'Sex, lies and love letters: rethinking condoms and female agency in Uganda', *Agenda* 18 (62): 12–20. https://doi.org/10.1080/10130950.2004.9676195.

2004b. 'Sugar daddies and sexual citizenship in Uganda: rethinking third wave feminism', *Black Renaissance* 6 (1): 82–106.

2012. '"They arrested me for loving a schoolgirl": ethnography, HIV, and a feminist assessment of the age of consent law as a gender-based structural intervention in Uganda', *Social Science and Medicine* 74 (11): 1774–82. https://doi.org/10.1016/j.socscimed.2011.06.037.

Parish, J. 2010. 'Circumventing uncertainty in the moral economy: West African shrines in Europe, witchcraft and secret gambling', *African Diaspora* 3 (1): 76–92. https://doi.org/10.1163/187254610X505664.

Pells, K., E. Wilson, and N. T. T. Hang. 2016. 'Negotiating agency in cases of intimate partner violence in Vietnam', *Global Public Health* 11 (1–2): 34–47.

Pessima, A., J. L. Massallay, P. O. Koroma, and D. J. Simbo. 2009. 'Education and women's employment: a study of their status and input in the informal sector in Sierra Leone'. International Household Survey Network. www.rocare.org/grants/2009/Education\%20and\%20Women\%200Employment\%20in\%20Sierra\%20Leone.pdf.

Peters, K. 2011. 'The crisis of youth in postwar Sierra Leone: problem solved?', *Africa Today* 58 (2): 129–53. https://doi.org/10.2979/africatoday.58.2.129.

Peters, K., and P. Richards. 1998. '"Why we fight": voices of youth combatants in Sierra Leone', *Africa: Journal of the International African Institute* 68 (2): 183–210.

Piot, C. 1999. *Remotely Global: village modernity in West Africa*. Chicago: University of Chicago Press.

Pirie, F. 2007. *Peace and Conflict in Ladakh: the construction of a fragile web of order*. Leiden: Brill.

2014. *The Anthropology of Law*. Oxford: Oxford University Press.

Porter, H. 2013. 'After rape: justice and social harmony in northern Uganda'. PhD thesis, London School of Economics. https://etheses.lse.ac.uk/717/.

2017. *After Rape: violence, justice, and social harmony in Uganda*. Cambridge: Cambridge University Press.

Potter, Hillary. 2006. 'An argument for black feminist criminology: understanding African American women's experiences with intimate partner abuse using an integrated approach', *Feminist Criminology* 1 (2): 106–24. https://doi.org/10.1177/1557085106286547.

Pratt, M. 2012. 'Youth rural–urban migration in Sierra Leone: Freetown – Western Area'. PhD thesis, Fourah Bay College, University of Sierra Leone. https://ir.lib.hiroshima-u.ac.jp/files/public/3/32537/20141016190800166662/ipshu_en_27_52.pdf.

Pratten, D. 2006. 'The politics of vigilance in southeastern Nigeria', *Development and Change* 37 (4): 707–34.

Radcliffe-Brown, A. R. 1950. 'Introduction' in A. R. Radcliffe-Brown and C. D. Forde (eds), *African Systems of Kinship and Marriage*. London: Oxford University Press for the International African Institute.

Rasmussen, S. J. 2001. 'Betrayal or affirmation? Transformations in witchcraft technologies of power, danger and agency among the Tuareg of Niger' in H. L. Moore and T. Sanders (eds), *Magical Interpretations, Material Realities: modernity, witchcraft and the occult in postcolonial Africa*. New York: Psychology Press.

Remoe, V. 2013. 'Sierra Leone psychiatrist warns "ataya" gunpowder tea induces psychosis'. *Switsalone*, 15 February. www.switsalone.com/19060_sierra-leone-psychiatrist-warn-ataya-gunpowder-tea-induces-psychosis/.

Restless Development Sierra Leone. 2012. 'Young people in Sierra Leone today: challenges, aspirations, experiences'. Restless Development. www.restlessdevelopment.org/file/state-youth-report-pdf.

Richards, P. 1998. *Fighting for the Rain Forest: war, youth and resources in Sierra Leone*. Oxford: James Currey.

— 2005. 'To fight or to farm? Agrarian dimensions of the Mano River conflicts (Liberia and Sierra Leone)', *African Affairs* 104 (417): 571–90. https://doi.org/10.1093/afraf/adi068.

Richards, P., J. Amara, M. C. Ferme, P. Kamara, E. Mokuwa, A. I. Sheriff, R. Suluku, and M. Voors. 2015. 'Social pathways for Ebola virus disease in rural Sierra Leone, and some implications for containment', *PLoS Neglected Tropical Diseases* 9 (4): 1–15. https://doi.org/10.1371/journal.pntd.0003567.

Riches, D. (ed.). 1986. *The Anthropology of Violence*. Oxford: Basil Blackwell.

Richter, H. 2016. 'Beyond the "other" as constitutive outside: the politics of immunity in Roberto Esposito and Niklas Luhmann', *European Journal of Political Theory* 18 (2): 216–37. https://doi.org/10.1177/1474885116658391.

Rorty, R. 1993. 'Human rights, sentimentality and universality' in S. Shute and S. Hurley (eds), *On Human Rights: the Oxford Amnesty Lectures*. New York: Basic Books.

Rosaldo, M. Z., L. Lamphere, and J. Bamberger. 1974. *Woman, Culture, and Society*. Stanford CA: Stanford University Press.

Ross, F. 2003. *Bearing Witness: women and the Truth and Reconciliation Commission in South Africa*. London: Pluto.

Rothberg, M. 2008. 'Decolonizing trauma studies: a response', *Studies in the Novel* 40 (1–2): 224–34.

Saleh-Hanna, V. 2015. 'Black feminist hauntology: rememory the ghosts of abolition?', *Champ Pénal/Penal Field* 12 (15). https://doi.org/10.4000/champpenal.9168.

Salman, T. 2010. 'Taking risks for security's sake: Bolivians resisting their state and its economic policies' in T. Hylland Eriksen, E. Bal, and O. Salemink (eds), *A World of Insecurity: anthropological perspectives on human security*. London: Pluto Press.

Sambira, J. 2024. 'Empowering change: safeguarding women in Sierra Leone – a discussion with the First Lady of Sierra Leone, Fatima Maada Bio', *Africa Renewal*, 7 March. www.un.org/africarenewal/magazine/march-2024/empowering-change-safeguarding-women-sierra-leone.

Sarró, R. 2005. 'The throat and the belly: Baga notions of morality and personhood', *Journal of the Anthropology Society of Oxford* 31 (2): 167–85.

— 2009. *The Politics of Religious Change on the Upper Guinea Coast: iconoclasm done and undone*. Edinburgh: Edinburgh University Press.

Sartre, Jean-Paul. 2004. *The Imaginary: a phenomenological psychology of the imagination*. London: Routledge.

Saveur editors. 2017. 'The secret of Senegal's ataya tea ceremony: this beloved ritual can take up to three hours, and it's worth every second'. *Saveur.* www.saveur.com/ataya-senegalese-tea-ceremony.

Schapera, I. 1994. *A Handbook of Tswana Law and Custom.* Münster: LIT with the IAI.

Scheper-Hughes, N. 2004. 'Dangerous and endangered youth social structures and determinants of violence', *Youth Violence: Scientific Approaches to Prevention* 1036: 13–46.

Scheper-Hughes, N., and P. Bourgois. 2004. 'Introduction: making sense of violence' in N. Scheper-Hughes and P. Bourgois (eds), *Violence in War and Peace.* Malden MA: Blackwell Publishing.

Scheper-Hughes, N., and A. Robben. 2008. 'Whose violence? Death in America: a California triptych', *Social Anthropology* 16 (1): 77–89.

Schindler, M. 2007. *Rumors in Financial Markets: insights into behavioral finance.* Chichester: Wiley.

Schlegel, A., and H. Barry. 1991. *Adolescence: an anthropological inquiry.* New York: Free Press.

Schneider, L. T. 2017. 'Concomitants of academic anthropology', *Paradigmata Zeitschrift für Menschen und Diskurse* 14 (1): 34–7.

2019a. 'Partners as possession: A qualitative exploration of intimate partner sexual violence in Freetown, Sierra Leone', *Journal of Aggression, Maltreatment and Trauma* 28 (2): 127–45. https://doi.org/10.1080/10926771.2018.1506854.

2019b. 'Sierra Leone takes welcome leap on rape but next steps are crucial'. The Conversation, Spring. https://theconversation.com/sierra-leone-takes-welcome-leap-on-rape-but-next-steps-are-crucial-112010.

2019c. 'Sierra Leone's laws to protect women have unintended consequences'. The Conversation, Autumn. https://theconversation.com/sierra-leones-laws-to-protect-women-have-unintended-consequences-109815.

2020a. 'Degrees of permeability: confinement, power and resistance in Freetown's Central Prison', *Cambridge Journal of Anthropology* 38 (1): 88–104.

2020b. 'Elders and transaction relationships in Sierra Leone: rethinking synchronic approaches', *Africa: Journal of the International African Institute* 90 (4): 701–20.

2020c. 'Sexual violence during research: how the unpredictability of fieldwork and the right to risk collides with academic bureaucracy and expectations', *Critique of Anthropology* 40 (2): 173–93.

2023a. 'Rape, ritual, rupture and repair: decentering Euro-American logics of trauma and healing in an analytic autoethnography of the five years after my rape in Sierra Leone', *Ethos* 51 (3) 255–70.

2023b. 'Time, Co-Creation and Collaborative Research: Moving from a Sympathetic Commonality towards Empathetic Distance', *Public Anthropologist*, 5 (2): 270–92.

Scott, James. 1985. *Weapons of the Weak: everyday forms of peasant resistance.* New Haven CT: Yale University Press.

Scubla, L. 2016. *Giving Life, Giving Death: psychoanalysis, anthropology, philosophy.* East Lansing MI: Michigan State University Press.

Seema, Y. 2016. 'The Ebola rape epidemic no one's talking about', *Foreign Policy*, 2 February. http://foreignpolicy.com/2016/02/02/the-ebola-rape-epidemic-west-africa-teenage-pregnancy/.
Sesay, A. 2014. 'Prisons Dept. to celebrate Pademba Road Prison centenary anniversary'. *Concord Times*. http://slconcordtimes.com/prisons-dept-to-celebrate-pademba-road-prison-centenary-anniversary/.
Sezgin, Y. 2004. 'Theorizing formal pluralism: quantification of legal pluralism for spatio-temporal analysis', *Journal of Legal Pluralism and Unofficial Law* 36 (50): 101–18. https://doi.org/10.1080/07329113.2004.10756580.
Shack Dwellers International. 1992. 'Kroo Bay settlement profile'. *SDInet*, April. https://sdinet.org/wp-content/uploads/2015/04/Kroo_Bay_Profile_21.pdf.
Shaw, R. 2007. 'Memory frictions: localizing the Truth and Reconciliation Commission in Sierra Leone', *International Journal of Transitional Justice* 1 (2): 183–207. https://doi.org/10.1093/ijtj/ijm008.
  2014. 'The TRC, the NGO and the child: young people and post-conflict futures in Sierra Leone', *Social Anthropology* 22 (3): 306–25. https://doi.org/10.1111/1469-8676.12081.
Shaw, R., L. Waldorf, and P. Hazan. 2010. *Localizing Transitional Justice: interventions and priorities after mass violence*. Stanford CA: Stanford University Press.
Shepler, S. 2004. 'The social and cultural context of child soldiering in Sierra Leone'. Paper for the PRIO Sponsored Workshop on Techniques of Violence in Civil War. August. www.researchgate.net/publication/235678865_The_Social_and_Cultural_Context_of_Child_Soldiering_in_Sierra_Leone.
  2010. 'Youth music and politics in post-war Sierra Leone', *Journal of Modern African Studies* 48 (4): 627–42. https://doi.org/10.1017/S0022278X10000509.
Sierra Leone, Statehouse of. 2019. 'President Julius Maada Bio declares rape and sexual violence as a national emergency in Sierra Leone'. Government of Sierra Leone, 7 February. https://statehouse.gov.sl/president-julius-maada-bio-declares-rape-and-sexual-violence-as-a-national-emergency-in-sierra-leone/.
Sierra News Media. 2013. 'Sierra Leone's Maximum Pademba Road Prison to be relocated: good news at last!' *Sierra Express Media*, 3 March. http://sierraexpressmedia.com/?p=54444.
Simmel, G. 1971. 'Sociability' in D. N. Levine (ed.), *On Individuality and Social Forms*. Chicago: University of Chicago Press.
Singerman, D. 2007. 'The economic imperatives of marriage: emerging practices and identities among youth in the Middle East', Middle East Youth Initiative Working Paper no. 6, 1–53. https://doi.org/10.2139/ssrn.1087433.
Smith, P. 1983. 'Hemingway's early manuscripts: the theory and practice of omission', *Journal of Modern Literature* 10 (2): 268–88.
Solomon, C., and J. Ginifer. 2008. 'Disarmament, demobilisation and reintegration in Sierra Leone case study', University of Bradford. https://au.int/sites/default/files/documents/39119-doc-85._disarmament_demobilisation_and_reintegration_in_sierra_leone.pdf.
Spivak, G. C. 2003. 'Can the subaltern speak?', *Die Philosophin* 14 (27): 42–58.
Statehouse of Sierra Leone. 2019. 'President Julius Maada Bio declares rape and sexual violence as a national emergency in Sierra Leone'. Government

of Sierra Leone, 7 February. https://statehouse.gov.sl/president julius-maada-biodeclares-rape-and-sexual-violence-as-a-national-emergency-in-sierra leone/.

Stasik, M. 2016. 'Real love versus real life: youth, music and utopia in Freetown, Sierra Leone', *Africa: Journal of the International African Institute* 86 (2): 215–36. https://doi.org/10.1017/S0001972016000024.

Steinberg, J. 2013. 'Working through a paradox about sexual culture in South Africa: tough sex in the twenty-first century', *Journal of Southern African Studies* 39 (3): 497–509. https://doi.org/10.1080/03057070.2013.818848.

Strathern, M. 1988. *The Gender of the Gift: problems with women and problems with society in Melanesia*. Berkeley CA: University of California Press.

Szanto, D. 2018. 'Congosa politics: rumours and elections in Sierra Leone'. Mats Utas blog, 28 May. https://matsutas.wordpress.com/2018/05/28/congosa-politics-rumours-and-elections-in-sierra-leone-by-diana-szanto/.

T. T. 2013. 'Tea in Sierra Leone: caffeine overload; Sierra Leone is worried that its young people are becoming addicted to tea', *The Economist*, 13 February. www.economist.com/baobab/2013/02/13/caffeine-overload.

Tamale, S. 2011. *African Sexualities: a reader*. Oxford: Pambazuka.

Temudo, M. 2019. 'Between "forced marriage" and "free choice": social transformations and perceptions of gender and sexuality among the Balanta in Guinea-Bissau', *Africa: Journal of the International African Institute* 89 (1): 1–20.

Thomas, A. R. 2016. 'Death penalty will not reform disenfranchised youths in Sierra Leone'. *Sierra Leone Telegraph*, 25 September. www.thesierraleonetelegraph.com/death-penalty-will-not-reform-disenfranchised-youths-in-sierra-leone/.

Thomas, D. 2012. 'Violence'. Oxford Bibliographies, 1 January. http://oxfordindex.oup.com/view/10.1093/obo/9780199766567-0027\#fullTextLinks.

Thomas, L. M. 2003. *Politics of the Womb: women, reproduction, and the state in Kenya*. Berkeley CA: University of California Press.

Thompson, R. F. 1979. *African Art in Motion: icon and act*. Berkeley CA: University of California Press.

Tirrell, L. 2017. 'Language and power' in A. M. Jaggar and I. M. Young (eds), *A Companion to Feminist Philosophy*. Malden MA: John Wiley & Sons.

Tonkin, E. 2000. 'Autonomous judges: African ordeals as dramas of power', *Ethnos: Journal of Anthropology* 65 (3): 366–86. https://doi.org/10.1080/00141840050198036.

TRC. 2004a. 'Report of the Sierra Leone Truth and Reconciliation Commission'. Freetown, Sierra Leone.

—— 2004b. 'Volume two, chapter three: recommendations'. Sierra Leone Truth and Reconciliation Commission. www.sierraleonetrc.org/index.php/view-report-text-vol-2/item/volume-two-chapter-three?category_id=20).

—— 2018. 'Sierra Leone. Truth and Reconciliation Commission. Recommendations matrix'. Sierra Leone Truth and Reconciliation Commission. www.sierraleonetrc.org/index.php/resources/recommendations-matrix.

Tuhiwai-Smith, Linda. 2012. *Decolonizing Methodologies: research and indigenous peoples*. London: Zed Books.

Ugelvik, T. 2014. 'Prison ethnography as lived experience: notes from the diaries of a beginner let loose in Oslo Prison', *Qualitative Inquiry* 20 (4): 471–80. https://doi.org/10.1177/1077800413516272.

UNICEF. 2014. 'Sierra Leone country programme document 2015–2018'. E/ICEF/2014/P/L.10. 2014. www.unicef.org/about/execboard/files/2014-PL10-Sierra_Leone_CPD-Final_approved-EN.pdf.

2017. 'Ending child marriage and teenage pregnancy in Sierra Leone'. UNFPA-UNICEF Global Programme to Accelerate Action to End Child Marriage, 19 September. www.unicef.org/infobycountry/sierraleone_100861.html.

Utas, M. 2005. 'Victimcy, girlfriending, soldiering: tactic agency in a young woman's social navigation of the Liberian war zone', *Anthropological Quarterly* 78 (2): 403–30.

Utas, M., and M. Christensen. 2016. 'The gift of violence: ex-militias and ambiguous debt relations during post-war elections in Sierra Leone', *African Conflict and Peacebuilding Review* 6 (2): 23–47. https://doi.org/10.2979/africonfpeacrevi.6.2.02.

Vaughan, M. 2011. 'The history of romantic love in sub-Saharan Africa: between interest and emotion', *Proceedings of the British Academy* 167: 1–23.

Vigh, H. 2006a. *Navigating Terrains of War: youth and soldiering in Guinea-Bissau*. New York: Berghahn Books.

2006b. 'Social death and violent life changes' in C. Christiansen, M. Utas, and H. Vigh (eds), *Navigating Youth, Generating Adulthood: social becoming in an African context*. Uppsala: Nordiska Afrika Institutet.

Villa, S. 2017. 'Sierra Leone news: girls should not be left out; education policy banning pregnant girls is discriminatory'. *Awoko*, 6 October 2017. https://awoko.org/2017/10/06/sierra-leone-news-girls-should-not-be-left-out-education-policy-banning-pregnant-girls-is-discriminatory/.

Wacquant, L. 2001. 'Deadly symbiosis: when ghetto and prison meet and mesh', *Punishment and Society* 31 (1): 95–133.

2002. 'Deadly symbiosis: rethinking race and imprisonment in twenty-first-century America', *Boston Review* 27 (2). http://search.proquest.com.ez.library.latrobe.edu.au/docview/1347838905/fulltext/6FA91C2EDEBE453EPQ/10?accountid=12001.

Walker, L. 2005. 'Men behaving differently: South African men since 1994', *Culture, Health and Sexuality* 7 (3): 225–38.

Waltorp, K., and S. Jensen. 2017. 'Awkward entanglements: kinship, morality and survival in Cape Town's prison–township circuit', *Ethnos* 84 (1): 41–55. https://doi.org/10.1080/00141844.2017.1321565.

Wardlow, H. 2006. *Wayward Women: sexuality and agency in a New Guinea society*. Berkeley CA: University of California Press.

White, E. F. 1981. 'Creole women traders in the nineteenth century', *International Journal of African Historical Studies* 14 (4): 626–42. https://doi.org/10.2307/218229.

White, L. 2008. *Speaking with Vampires: rumor and history in colonial Africa*. Berkeley CA: University of California Press.

Whitehead, N. 2004. 'Rethinking anthropology of violence', *Anthropology Today* 20 (5): 1–2.

2004b. *Violence*. Santa Fe NM: School of American Research Press.
Whitehead, S. M. 2002. *Men and Masculinities*. Cambridge: Polity Press.
Whitehouse, H. 1996. 'Rites of terror: emotion, metaphor and memory in Melanesian initiation cults', *Journal of the Royal Anthropological Institute* 2 (4): 703. https://doi.org/10.2307/3034304.
Whyte, L. 2016. 'The women battling the post-Ebola teen pregnancy epidemic'. Vice, 8 August. https://broadly.vice.com/en_us/article/vv55wa/sierra-leone-post-ebola-teen-pregnancy-epidemic.
Whyte, S. R. 1997. *Questioning Misfortune: the pragmatics of uncertainty in eastern Uganda*. Cambridge: Cambridge University Press.
Wilson, R., and J. P. Mitchell. 2003. *Human Rights in Global Perspective: anthropological studies of rights, claims and entitlements*. London: Routledge.
Winnebah, T. R. A., F. N. Brewah, and T. Francis. 2006. 'Republic of Sierra Leone population and household census: analytical report on poverty'. Statistics Sierra Leone. www.statistics.sl/images/StatisticsSL/Documents/Census/2004/2004_population_and_housing_census_report_on_poverty.pdf.
Wolputte, S. van. 2016. 'Sex in troubled times: moral panic, polyamory and freedom in north-west Namibia', *Anthropology Southern Africa* 39 (1): 31–45. https://doi.org/10.1080/23323256.2016.1147967.
World Bank. 2013. 'Understanding youth violence: cases from Liberia and Sierra Leone'. Washington DC: World Bank. http://documents.worldbank.org/curated/en/199821468151145997/pdf/864300WP0P1259260Box385179B000OUO0900ACS.pdf.
Xaba, T. 2001. 'Masculinity and its malcontents: the confrontation between "struggle masculinity" and "post-struggle masculinity" (1990–1997)' in R. Morrell (ed.), *Changing Men in Southern Africa*. London: Zed Books.
Zelizer, V. A. 2000. 'The purchase of intimacy', *Law and Social Inquiry* 25 (3): 817–48.
Zigon, J. 2009. 'Hope dies last: two aspects of hope in contemporary Moscow', *Anthropological Theory* 9 (3): 253–71. https://doi.org/10.1177/1463499609346986.
Žižek, S. 2008. *Violence: six sideways reflections*. London: Profile.

Index

Page numbers referring to figures are italicised. An 'n' after the page number indicates a note number to follow (example: '134n5' would mean note 5 on page 134).

Abacha Street, 28, 94, 96
abduction, 47–8, 51
abortion, 70n4, 104, 122, 126–7, 204
abstraction (in trials), 169, 187–8
acceptable violence, 6, 79, 89, 111
access, research, 19, 37–8, 40, 199–200
accommodation, 20, *21*, 39, 69, 195, *see also* compounds
accusations
　of child cruelty, 133
　false, 211
　in front of others, 64, 90
　of infidelity, 37, 124, 132–3
　of sexual offences, 36, 171, 192, 199, 211
　of temptation, 107, 135–8
adulthood. *See also* big men; big women
　blocked pathways to, 42, 45, 52, 54, 60
　and committed relationships, 70
　and criminal justice institutions, 218
　as a marriage prerequisite, 42–3
　and social position, 135
age
　coming of, 11, 43, 52
　of consent, 10, 172–3, 175, 179, 190
　groups, 11, 25, 224
　interpretations of, 129, 170, 189, 218
agency
　'domesticated', 214
　embedded nature of, 33, 77, 214
　embodied, 49, 77
　establishing spaces of, 148, 204, 209
　gendered, 7, 76, 159, 166, 213, 227
　limited, 220
　and sociocentricity, 149
　of young people, 10, 55, 175, 191–2
agreement relationships, 68–9, 224
aid, development, 14, 55, 226
Allentown (description), 1, 20, 23, 29
alliances, 11, 42–3, 45, 132, 150

analysis of friction, 13, 217
anger, 8, 116, 118, 140, 161
anonymity, 30, 36, 41, 56
ansa bɛlɛ (responsibility for pregnancy)
　importance, 206, 224–5
　initiation, 120, 204
　meaning, 53, 71, 106, 183
　problems, 73, 225
anthropology
　insights from, 7, 12, 33, 76, 109, 212
　language, 39
　literature, 1, 5
　methods, 3, 7, 39, 220, 228–9
arrest, 68, 195–6, 202, 205–6
ataya bases (coffee places), 28–9
authority, patriarchal, 107, 179, 186, 202, 216
autonomy
　community, 142, 178, 227
　personal, 16–17, 45n3, 117n6, 163, 222
availability (in relationships), 60, 65, 89, 122, 159

bambrusing (rough treatment), 48, 62, 90, 229, *see also* rape
beating
　acceptability of, 81, 97, 127
　children, 132, 147
　intervention, 122, 124, 132
　and masculinity, 48, 162, 167
　normalised violence, 48
　as prevention, 81, 131, 148
　reporting, 115–16, 148
　to show love, 82, 86, 88
　term, 96–7
Benda-Beckman, Keebet von, 150, 219
big men
　decisions of, 136
　expectations of, 54, 70, 129, 136

252

Index

process of becoming, 44, 225
responsibilities of, 56, 70, 73, 136, 218
big women
   expectations of, 129
   process of becoming, 44, 53, 70, 218, 225
   responsibilities of, 56, 70, 218
binary conceptions, 46n4, 46, 159, 230
biographical research, 32, 223
blame
   towards international community, 220
   for laws, 191, 221
   for male violence, 162
   within mediation, 119, 123, 126, 134
   for reporting to police, 155
   from state bodies, 219
Bledsoe, Caroline, 43, 45n3, 105, 120, 163, 217
Bourdieu, Pierre, 159, 162–3
bribery, 186, 197, 201
bride price, 44–5, 53, 71, 225
brothels, 22, 31, 67
Burrill, Emily, 77, 111
bush wives, 7, 47

Calaba Town, 23, 28, 30
'call name', 105, 211
campaigns
   official, 15, 110, 176, 182–3, 188
   poster, *176*, 226
   on protection for girls, 10
   against school bans, 16
case trajectories, 169, 184–7, 199
Center for Accountability and the Rule of Law (CARL), 154
Central Prison. *See* Pademba Road Prison
Certeau, Michel de, 194, 210, 226
child cruelty, 133–4, 158, 185, 190
child marriage, 135, 176
Christianity, 71, 102, 115, 117, 119, 125
CID (Criminal Investigation Department), 26, 30, 125, 158
citizens, responsible, 182–4
citizenship, 221, 226
civil society, 173n2, 175n5, 182, 187, 206, 221
civil war (1991–2002), 7, 14, 30, 46–52, 78, 145, *see also* Revolutionary United Front (RUF)
civil war, post (2002–)
   analysis, 9n3
   and coming of age, 44
   and 'crisis of youth', 52
   gangs, 30
   government work, 229
   imprisonment, 195

legal changes, 3, 9, 172, 225
marriage, 11, 42, 45–6, 60, 74, 224
club, social. *See* Eat as You Can (EAUC) club
cohabitation, 72, 85, 138
colonialism. *See also* neo-colonialism
   foreign influence, 17, 142, 220
   and incarceration, 195
   and masculinity, 84, 160
   and moral economy, 77
   patriarchal structures, 83
   and slavery, 14–15, 46, 78
   structural violence, 16
Comaroff, Jean and John, 163, 187, 220–1
combatants, 47, 51n7, 188, 195
committed relationships, 11–12, 43, 69–72, 74, 225
common good, 15, 129, 149, *see also* sociocentric positioning
community involvement, 130–2
community mediation
   basis of, 138–9, 142
   case proceedings, 125–7
   elders, 218
   power of, 151
   preserving relationships, 142
   and social context, 8, 215, 218
   social harmony, 112, 139
   structures, 118–21
community, ideals of, 148–50, *see also* common good
compensation, 71, 121, 222
competing ideals, 148, 153–6
complementarity, gender
   analysis of friction, 217
   gender parallelism, 13
   lived realities, 168, 217
   metaphor, 2
   relationship dynamics, 137, 164
compounds
   chores within, 122, 130
   descriptions of, *23–4*, 108, 124
   elders of, 121, 132
   and food, 130
   healing within, 19, 132
   neighbouring, 121, 125, 139
   prison, 196
   visitors to, 126, 131–2, 134
confinement, 38, 42, 160, 198, 207–9
Connell, Raewyn, 32, 81–3
consent
   age of, 173, 175, 179, 190, 207
   in civil society, 221
   global debate, 10
   laws, 10, 16, 173, 175, 229

254   Index

consent (cont.)
  to other romances, 102
  research on, 35–6, 41, 201
  sexual, 9–10, 90, 135, 175, 188, 215
  to terminate marriage, 67
  to touch, 100
contextualisation, 40, 127–9, 219
contract relationships, 59, 72, 121, 128
control of intimacy, 4, 11, 212
control, state, 14
controlling minds, 7, 135, 137, 166
corrective measures, 80, 82, 102
court hearings, 37, 190, 192
courts, state, 7, 18, 113, 135, 135n12, 146,
    see also High Court; Magistrate's Court
Cowan, Jane, 148–9, 152–3, 166
criminal justice institutions
  data, 8
  gendered forms of violence, 214
  and maturity, 216, 218
  overview, 209
  powers, 209–10
  reporting trajectories, 153
criminal justice system
  abstraction, 169, 187, 218
  access to the, 150, 156
  capacity, 11, 210
  enforcement, 203, 221
  intervention, 219
  jurisdiction, 15
  and mediation, 25, 142, 182
  perceptions, 215
  restrictions, 7–8
criminalisation
  of local norms, 188
  and prison life, 194, 203
  of sexual behaviour, 11–12, 191, 226
  of sexual relationships, 10–11, 172, 174, 225
  of violence in relationships, 146
crisis of masculinity, 13, 107, 162, 165, 212
'crisis of youth', 11, 52, 55n9, 223–6
cut and pass, 63–4, 90
cut and play, 63–4, 103

data collection, 31–41
  focus groups, 19, 24–6, 32–3
  informal discussions, 19, 34, 36, 39
  interviews. *See* interviews
  life histories, 19, 25, 27, 31–3, 38
  love histories, 27, 32, 38, 74, 110
  observation, 19–20, 26, 30, 34, 64
DDR (Disarmament, Demobilization, and
    Reintegration programme), 47n6,
    51n7, 51

debt
  economic constraints, 56
  power dynamics, 74
  reciprocity, 42, 57
  social navigation, 69, 226–7
  social networks, 57, 65
development aid, 14, 55, 226
development discourses, 1, 16, 110, 136, 189, 229
Devolution of Estates Act (2007), 9, 146
dialectical framework, 34
Diggins, Jennifer, 60–1, 106
disguise, 67, 85–6, 111
divorce
  with children, 134
  division of resources, 44n1, 158
  following domestic violence, 115, 144
  registered marriages, 9, 66–7, 146
  and shame, 147, 149
doctors, traditional, 102–3, 106, 137
domestic violence (DV)
  definitions, 78, 93n1, 166
  laws, 144–5
  reporting, 144, 149–50, 157
  sentencing for, 35
Domestic Violence Act (2007), 9, 146, 157
Don Bosco
  library, 198
  organisation, 26, 186, 196, 198–9, 206
  shelters, 35

Eat As You Can (EAUC) club
  accommodation, 20–2
  fieldwork with, 24–5, 31, 65, 102
  logo, *20*
  membership, 23–4
  social activities, 22, 30, 61, 87, 123, 139
Ebola pandemic, 177–8, 190, 205
Economic Community of West African
    States (ECOWAS), 16, 229
economic constraints, 13, 53–4, 56, 73, 103, 224
education
  access to, 10, 69, 175, 178, 183, 201
  formal, 152
  funding, 21
  sexual, 189, 229
  special, 178
  superior, 207
egocentric positioning, 75, 149, 214
elders
  community, 125–6, 129, 140
  control of, 44, 47, 52, 55
  expectations of, 12, 52, 54
  explanations of, 38, 140, 189, 224

Index

mediation judgements of, 112–13, 126–7, 129, 132, 136
as mediators, 117–21
punishment from, 80, 82, 214
responsibilities of, 45, 68, 71, 133, 218, 222
social status, 70, 127
emasculation, 48–9, 165, 167
emotional violence, 84–5, 158
emotions, communicating, 77, 82, 84, 86, 88
employment. *See also* unemployment
   formal, 21, 56
   gendered, 27, 54
   and social status, 70, 128
engagement, 71–3, 204
equal rights, 9, 72, 146, 152
equality, 57, 83, 158, 173n2, 221, *see also* inequality
ethical duty, 149, 151–2
ethics, research, 19, 34–7, 39–41
ethnographic accounts, 6, 121–38, 194, 198
ethnographic methods
   of analysis, 3, 10, 18, 33, 146
   and biographical research, 32
   overview, 19, 31
   for practical relevancy, 94, 193, 227, 230
   urban ethnography, 12, 212
ethnographic studies, 7, 43, 60, 85, 162
everyday interactions, 27, 29, 62, 103, 131, 166
everyday practices, 13, 19, 32, 61, 205, 217
exceptionalism, staged, 54, 56, 191, 224
exclusion, social, 10, 16, 151, 165, 198, 202–3
exploitation
   during the civil war, 51
   economic, 133
   gerontocratic, 47
   history of, 4, 17, 46–7
   mitigation in research, 40
   and moral economy, 77, 79
   in relationships, 64, 73

familial contexts, violence in, 6, 212
familial control, 179
familial support
   loss of, 74, 145, 148, 153, 167, 214
   neglect, 136
   without, 21
Family Support Units (FSUs)
   fieldwork, 26, 30, 35, 199
   investigations, 154
   mediations, 156
   visit, 147
family, extended, 21, 50, 56, 128, 179
fatherhood, 71, 105, 131

femininity, 99, 160, 164, 166
feminist perspectives, 2n1, 3, 16, 46, 216
Ferme, Mariane, 60–1, 85, 109, 163, 220
fighting (term), 96
fighting factions, 47–8
financial responsibility, 70–1, 105, 136
focus groups, 19, 24–33
food
   distribution, 196, 198, 207
   metaphor, 2, 160
   obtaining, 69, 130, 151
   preparation, 82
   refusal, 87, 96, 101–8
   selling, 28, 144
   sharing, 21, *101*, 120, 127, 200
   spells through, 106, 137–8
   during the war, 48, 50–1
foreign influences. *See* international influences
forgiveness, 87, 126–7, 139–40
'forum shopping', 150
Fourah Bay College (FBC), 29, 31, 40, 61, 66, 97
freedom
   cost of, 68, 194
   financial independence, 69
   of fluid relationship forms, 74
   irreconcilable desires for, 12
   and masculinity, 161, 163
   sexual, 215
   of young people, 69, 226
Freetown (locations)
   Abacha Street, 28, 94, 96
   Allentown, 23, 40, 121
   Calaba Town, 28
   Central District, 20
   Kroo Bay, 30
   Naimbana Street, 20, 22–3, 40, 204
   Western Freetown, 73, 175
friction, analysis of, 13, 217
friendship, 22, 61, 100, 207
future making, 13, 15, 17, 47, 55, 73

gangs, 23, 30, 67, 196–7, 200
garage, the, 27, 32, 51
gender complementarity. *See* complementarity, gender
gender dynamics, 12–13, 113, 166, 216, 223
gender justice
   advancement, 168, 230
   laws, 9, 26, 145–6, 154, 167, 193
gender parallelism
   definition, 43, 84
   and lived experiences, 13, 52
   in the region, 160

gender parallelism (cont.)
  as a strategy, 145, 165–6
gender relations
  crisis of, 13, 145, 212
  ideals of, 4, 155, 166, 211, 217
  interpretations of, 13, 179, 212
  and relationship dynamics, 137, 164
  transformation of, 52
gender-based violence, 9, 36, 84, 93n1, 180, 206
gendered agency, 7, 76, 159, 166, 213, 227
gendered expectations
  and agency, 77, 159
  and lived realities, 50, 162–3, 216
  and local cultures, 215
  and reporting, 160–1, 166, 168
gendered ideals
  of elders, 52
  hegemonic, 163–4, 227
  pressure of, 50, 84, 211
  of the state, 179
gendered ideologies, 11–13, 69, 162–4, 166
generational tensions, 6, 55, 78, 223, *see also* intergenerational dynamics
Gibbs, James, 112, 139–40
gift economies, 57, 69, 74
'girlfriend trap', 190, 205
global agendas, 3, 7, 16–17, 46
gossip (*kongosa*)
  punishment of men, 64, 101–2
  against stability, 23, 118, 123, 151
  and trust, 114, 139
government
  conceptions, 178, 230
  failures, 180, 229
  institutions, 127
  interests, 222
  plans, 174, 182, 195
  responsibilities, 225
  work, 51n7, 229
grabbing, 99–100
grievances
  airing, 8, 141, 154
  and harmony, 140
  managing, 116–17
  'swallowing', 8, 112–13, 119, 140, 153
guardianship
  of children, 140, 218
  choice of, 123
  of communities, 222
  president, 179–80, *181*, 222
  of rights, 117n6
  state, 221–2

'harmony ideology', 15, 142, 227
harmony, social, 8, 112–13, 134, 139–43, 227
health emergencies, 14, 16
hegemony, 163–4, 168, 217, 227
hierarchies
  gendered, 160
  household, 78, 202
  kin, 52, 70
  legalistic system, 142
  offence, 127
  prison, 194–5, 201
  social, 166
High Court
  age tests, 201
  cases, 30, 33, 172, 199
  judges, 155, 188, 190
  legal representation, 153n8, 202
  proceedings, 26
historical context
  civil war, 42, 46, 52
  colonialism, 14–17, 221
  of female political leadership, 7
  gender parallelism, 43, 160
  influencing relationships, 59, 78, 83
  and local lived experience, 4–5
  and research methods, 33, 38, 227
  ruptures, 8, 223–6
  structural violence, 48, 212–13
histories, life, 19, 25, 27, 31–3, 38
histories, love, 27, 32, 38, 74, 110
household chores, 60, 69, 73, 130, 165–6
household mediation, 8, 117–18, 142, 218
human rights
  activists, 187
  culture, 136, 148, 152–3, 167, 220
  discourse, 15, 152, 156, 198
  ideals, 148–9, 183, 220–1
  laws, 13, 15, 220, 229
  principles, 117n6, 147, 152, 183, 215, 221
  processes, 156, 188
  universality, 2, 17, 148, 156, 158, 215
  violations, 9n3, 11, 16, 81
Human Rights Commission of Sierra Leone, 172, 198
humiliation, 49, 87

ideals, gendered. *See* gendered ideals
ideals, opposing, 13, 75, 148–50, 153–6, 217
Imaginary, The (Sartre), 208
'imagined image', 192, 208
'imagined others', 13–14, 16, 182n9, 187, 223

Index

imprisoned people
  age of, 202
  communication between, 207
  control within prison, 196–8
  escape incident, 195
  interviews with, 35–6, 198
  legal representation, 35, 199, 202
  new, 205
  resources of, 196, 197n4
  spaces of agency, 209
imprisonment, 190, 195–6, 202–3
incidents, 124–5, 129–30
independence. *See* post-independence era
independence (personal)
  financial, 69, 122, 214, 226
  'masculine', 2, 160–1, 167
inequality, 1, 47, 73
infidelity
  accusations of, 37, 132–3
  'call name', 105
  contextualisation of, 128
  recompense for, 129, 211
  responsibility for, 161
  suspicion of, 125n10, 134
informal discussions, 19, 34, 36, 39
injuries
  examination of, 126, 184
  healing of, 19, 97
  lasting, 97, 158
  severity of, 46, 97, 114, 192
  showing, 108, 114, 144, 147
  treatment of, 114, 132, 196
intention (violent acts), 79–80
interdependence, 2, 78, 214
intergenerational dynamics, 11, 25, 42
international development, 5, 226
international influences
  defence against, 15, 142
  and deferred responsibility, 191
  on laws, 220–1, 226
  and local agendas, 4, 173n2
  ongoing, 14–15, 17, 160
international organisations (IOs), 145, 172, 227
intersectionality, 25, 38, 79, 81, 145, 213
interviews
  access to, 38
  analysis of, 59
  and ethics, 40
  methodology, 19, 32, 34, 39, 60
  overview of, 26, 30, 35–7
  themes from, 48, 50, 57, 117, 178, 206
intimacy
  contemporary, 13
  control of, 4, 10–11, 212
  and economic constraints, 54
  everyday, 7
  politics of, 4, 12, 178
  spaces of, 85
  and violence, 5–6, 32, 134, 212
  and vulnerabilities, 73
intimate relationships
  agreement relationships, 224
  conceptions of, 83
  conduct in, 9, 146
  mediation of, 15
  and state institutions, 151
  value of, 85
  violence in, 4–5, 7, 76, 213, 230
Islam, 71, 119, 125

Jackson, Michael
  economic constraints, 53, 103
  gender roles, 159, 162
  language, 109
  lived realities, 76, 212
  sociocentric consciousness, 141, 149
jealousy, 73, 81, 86–7, 99, 159
Jensen, Steffen, 187, 206

Kandiyoti, Deniz, 83, 136, 179
'keeping face', 65, 74
King George's old age home, 26–7, 29, 68
kinship
  hierarchies, 52, 179
  meetings, 111
  protective associations, 45, 113, 123, 225
  reciprocity, 56
Koroma, Ernest Bai, 110, 173–5, 173n2, 179–80, *180–1*
Kpelle, the, 105, 112, 120, 139
Kroo Bay, 30, 98, 104, 113, 121, 206
Kuranko, the, 141, 149, 159

language
  analysis, 109–11, 179, 215
  anthropological, 39
  change of, 206
  definition, 93
  and development discourses, 109–10, 221
  human rights, 17, 221
  legal, 95, 109–10
  terms, 94–5, 110, 155, 227
  understanding the, 202
Law Reform Commission, 172
law, state. *See* state law
lawmakers, 3, 10, 14, 169

258 Index

laws, new, 14, 18, 144, 192, *see also* Devolution of Estates Act (2007); Domestic Violence Act (2007); Registration of Customary Marriage and Divorce Act (2009); Sexual Offences Act (SOA) 2012; Sexual Offences Amendment Act (SOAA) 2019
learned behaviour, 82–3
Legal Aid Board, 35, 190
legal language, 95, 109–10
legal pluralism, 33, 113, 142, 220, 227
legal reform
 future making through, 13
 historical processes, 33–4
 international influences, 10, 226
 and legal pluralism, 220
 and relationships, 13, 94
 summary, 3
legal representation
 access to, 202–3, 210
 free, 35, 147, 171, 190, 202
 private, 153n8, 201
Liberia, 105, 112, 139
life histories, 19, 25, 27, 31–3, 38
lived realities, 159, 162, 164, 168, 216–17
local
 context, 5, 17, 33, 168, 215, 226
 groups, 25, 145, 172, 173n2
 importance, 109, 150, 195
 lived experience, 3, 5, 7, 93–4, 213, 221
 meanings, 2–3, 84, 212
 norms, 188, 221, 230
 people, 11, 15, 177
 perceptions, 76, 79, 109, 148, 179, 230
 practices, 79, 110
 terminologies, 59, 95, 110, 117, 227
love and violence relationship (context), 4–7
love histories, 27, 32, 38, 74, 110
love potions, 103, 106
lovers (definitions), 60–1, 72

Maada Bio (president of Sierra Leone), 10, 169, 174, 175n5, 181–2
Magistrate's Court
 age tests, 201
 cases, 33, 184, 199
 investigations, 157, 186–7
 legal representation, 202
 magistrate, 30
 proceedings, 26
main partners, 59–61, 65, 73, 102
malicing, 96, 107
mammie queens, 118, 120

manipulation, 74, 104, 150, 211, 219
Mann, Bonnie, 49, 53, 98–9, 167
marginalisation, 16, 42, 203, 210, 213, 223
market women, 25, 29, 96, 103
markets, 27–8, 31
marriage registration, 9, 44n1, 66, 146
marriage, child, 135, 176
marriage, traditional, 44n1, 67, 89, 158
marriages, religious, 44n1, 67, 146
'masculine domination', 25, 159, 162–3
masculine ideals, 53, 167, 223
masculinity, crisis of, 13, 107, 162, 165, 212, *see also* emasculation
maturity, 17, 172, 189, 216–18
Mauss, Marcel, 57–8, 74
mediation practices, 34, 134
mediation systems, 33, 129, 142, 150, 178, 216
mediation, community. *See* community mediation
mediation, household. *See* household mediation
mediation, state, 156–7
medicine, 103, 106, 196, 198, *see also* love potions
men reporting violence, 158–60
Mende, the, 44, 85, 104, 106, 109, 163
mess, 7, 210, 217
metaphorical usage
 and interpretation, 2n1
 'masculine domination', 163
 in speech, 110
 teeth and the tongue. *See* teeth and the tongue (metaphor)
methods, research, 19, 31–2, 34, 37, 39, *see also* data collection, ethics, research
monitoring practices, 85–6, 159
moral economy
 and gendered ideals, 84
 local lived experience, 213
 and pornography, 91–2
 reciprocity, 90
 of relationships, 52, 77–9, 78n1, 81, 93, 108
 ruptures, 7, 80, 111, 214
 of violence in relationships, 76, 83, 85, 88, 95, 109
music, 53, 63, 99, 106, 120

Nader, Laura, 15, 142
Naimbana Street. *See also* Eat As You Can (EAUC) club
 accommodation, 23, 31, 40
 description, 22
 fieldwork, 24, 31

Index

ghetto, 122
mosque, 50
narrative
 counter, 11, 211
 of deferred responsibility, 191
 dominant, 163, 230
 of interlocutors, 2, 5, 40
 interviews, 32
 simple, 3, 7
 victim–perpetrator, 6, 213
 Western, 209
national agendas, 10, 14, 215, 219, 226
national emergency, 10, 169, 172, 174, 175n5, 182
navigation, social, 58, 69, 226
neglect (in relationships), 76–88, 111, 133, 135–6, 138
neo-colonialism, 15, 17, 47
Newell, Sasha, 61, 67n2
NGOs (non-governmental organisations), 1, 13, 145, 189, 206, 227
nightclubs, 22n2, 22, 24, 31, 103
normalised violence, 11, 48, 51–2, 83
norms
 established, 217
 existing, 150
 internationally inspired, 195
 local, 15, 188, 221, 230
 reconfiguration of, 206, 230
 reproduction of, 163
 social, 16, 67, 127

oaths, 104–6, 126, 131, 133
observation, 19–20, 26, 30, 34, 64
oppression, 2, 93, 164, 204, 209, 223
otherness, 169, 208, *see also* 'imagined others'
'owning the story', 65, 74

Pademba Road Prison
 convictions, 36, 190
 description, 171, 184, 195–6, 198
 experiences, 206–7, 209–10
 leaving, 187, 206, 208
 legal representation, 35
 management style, 196
 minors in, 18, 189, 202, 229
 research in, 26, 33, 198, 200
 resources, 196
palaver (conflict)
 definition, 95, 118
 examples, 67, 119, 131–3
Parikh, Shanti, 34, 179
parties (gatherings), 22, 24, 81, 99, 115–16, 120

'passers-by', 62–4, 90, 103, 121
passion, 86
patriarchal systems, 47, 55, 83, 89, 136, 179
penetration, sexual. *See* sexual penetration (SP)
personhood
 construction, 2n1
 demands on, 12
 notions of, 69, 75, 154, 159, 166, 214
 position of victim, 188
phenomenological perspectives, 3, 76, 153
phones, 62, 85–6, 98, 127, 185
Piot, Charles, 214, 223
police stations. *See also* Family Support Units (FSUs)
 bribery, 186
 confession, 202
 giving statements at, 147, 184
 handling of cases, 155, 158, 200
 interpretations of age, 171, 189, 201
 interviews, 35
 reporting at, 134, 147, 151, 159, 171
policy
 actors, 230
 development of, 77, 93
 discourses, 13, 221
 effects of, 94, 213, 230
 ethnography, 193
 interventions, 14, 150
 silos, 230
 social, 5, 168, 213
 study of, 5, 7
policy-makers
 and ethnography, 3, 94
 implications for, 9, 215
 intentions of, 193
 language of, 3, 17
 notions of youth, 55
political developments, 173–5
politicians, 17, 26, 191
polygyny, 45, 47, 137
pornography, 90–1
positioning, researcher, 38, 40
possession, 44, 74, 89, 101, 106, 123
posters, *176–7, 180, 227–8*
post-independence era, 14, 47, 220
potions, love, 103, 106
poverty, 12, 53, 84, 173n2
power dynamics, 5, 43, 74, 153, 167, 219
powerlessness, 49, 107
precarity
 economic constraints, 12, 70
 and masculine ideals, 223
 from reporting, 141
 within research environments, 39

260 Index

precarity (cont.)
  and stigmatisation, 226
  vulnerability of research collaborators, 38
pregnancy (*get bele*). *See also* abortion; trapping
  acceptance, 71, 104–5, 129, 132
  big women, 70, 218, 225–6
  as proof, 211
  reporting, 182–3, 185, 192
  responsibilities, 53, 73, 104, 106, 204, 211
  school ban. *See* school ban (SB)
  shame, 183
  teenage. *See* teenage pregnancy
  violence during, 48, 115
President of Sierra Leone (role), 175, 179–80, 222, *see also* Koroma, Ernest Bai; Maada Bio (president of Sierra Leone)
pressures
  to abstain from reporting, 192
  from civil society groups, 175n5
  contradictory, 5, 149, 153, 231
  on court judges, 187
  economic constraints, 53
  to execute violence, 6, 84
  international influences, 5, 17, 226
  transitioning to adulthood, 70
  to uphold gendered ideals, 77, 84, 165, 223
prison government, 196–8, 209
prison hierarchies, 194–5, 201
prison life, 194, 200, 203, 210, *see also* Pademba Road Prison
prisoner(s). *See* imprisoned people
private forms of violence, 75, 88, 94n1
private matters, 14, 94–5, 151, 155, 183, 215
private spaces, 17, 108, 185, 199, 203, 211
protective association, 43, 224
protest, 55, 132, 175n5, 194–5, 204
punishment. *See also* corrective measures
  excessive, 142, 194, 211, 225
  through imprisonment, 8, 10, 143, 169, 173, 203–4
  from mediation, 8, 112, 116, 123, 219, 222
  of men, 64, 102, 104, 171, 192
  by partners, 83, 96, 98–9
  in plural legal systems, 3, 5, 80, 230
  state, 9, 80–1, 157, 187, 209, 222
  violence as, 83, 108, 122, 214
  of women, 113, 141

quarrelling, 73, 96, 105, 141, 192

Rainbo Centre, 26, 147, 154, 170, 178, 184

rape
  cases, 169, 190, 192
  during the conflict, 180
  definitions, 11, 151, 227–9, *228*
  eradication of, 15, 174, 179, 184n10
  and the law, 10, 174–5, 190, 192, 200
  national emergency on, 10, 169, 172, 174n5, 182
  prevention, 4, 10, 223, 225
  reporting, 182–3, 192n14, 211
  shared experiences, 39
rare gals (sex workers), 67–8, 67n2, 125
realities, lived, 159, 162, 164, 168, 216
reciprocity
  everyday, 166
  and gift economies, 58
  kinship, 56
  and moral economy, 83, 90–1
  and social alliances, 42
  and social pressure, 153
red bands, 197, 207, 209
reductionism, 188, 219
referrals, 17, 37–8
registered marriage, 9, 44n1, 66, 146
Registration of Customary Marriage and Divorce Act (2009), 9, 44n1, 146
relationship dynamics
  changing, 42, 136
  complex, 60
  contemporary, 5
  and gender relations, 137, 164, 217
  historical context, 42, 52
  laws and, 4, 94
relationship practices
  analysis of, 224
  changes in, 45n3, 52, 216
  diverse, 12–13, 42
  influences on, 69, 75
  post-war, 46, 52
  wartime, 47
relationships, agreement, 68–9, 224
relationships, committed, 11–12, 43, 69–72, 74, 225
relationships, contract, 59, 72, 121, 128
relationships, loving, 213
relationships, preserving, 84, 86, 134, 142
religious institutions, 21, 44n1, 115–17, 126, 206, 214
religious marriages, 44n1, 67, 146
reporting trajectories, 153–6
reporting violence, 113–21, 145, 147–8, 150–3, 158–60, 167
reputation, 59, 61, 64, 101, 150, 165
research collaborators (summary), 26, 31, 115

Index

research ethics, 19, 34–7, 39–41
research methods. *See* methods, research
research, sites of, 19, 25, 31, 39
resistance, 46, 161, 191, 200, 203–5
resolution, 127–9
resources
  ability to gain, 54, 57, 215, 225
  control of, 25, 52, 158, 163
  lack of, 59, 156, 178
  mobilising, 9, 57
  obtaining, 22, 163
  prison, 196, 210
  scarcity of, 154–6
  social, 56, 197n4
  state, 17, 158
responsibility, financial, 70–1, 105, 136
responsibility, social, 12, 15, 43, 76, 132
responsible citizens, 182–4
restoration, 83, 86, 120, 139, 202, 222
revenge, 64, 90, 102–3, 117, 140, 150
Revolutionary United Front (RUF), 9n3, 47n5, 47
'rites of terror', 194, 202–3
routines, daily, 22, 61, 85, 120, 137
rupture
  criminal justice system, 221
  historical context, 11, 223–4
  in intergenerational relations, 11
  long-term, 140
  of pathways to adulthood, 52
  prevention of, 119, 142
  in relationships, 8, 87, 113, 143
  state, 7, 9
  unacceptable violence, 80, 214
rural areas
  gender parallelism, 13
  marriage in, 73, 225
  relationships in, 42, 45n3, 60, 69

Saleh-Hanna, Viviane, 46n4, 46
salons, hair and beauty, 29
sanctions
  community, 58, 81, 89, 219
  by elders, 130
  gendered, 104, 141, 211
scholars (sex workers), 67–8
school ban (SB)
  consequences, 10, 14, 171, 223, 225–6
  criticisms, 190, 229
  discussion from, 222
  effectiveness, 178
  implementation, 178
  overview, 170, 176–8, 225
secrecy, 25, 44–5, 123–4, 128

security
  through community, 12, 75, 128, 219
  in daily life, 56
  financial, 32, 45, 54, 152
  of marriage, 43, 52, 123
  prison, 196
selling goods, 27
seniority, 27, 120, 132, 134, 138, 218
separation, relationship
  from children, 131
  without divorce, 66, 123
  equal rights, 72
  prevention of, 75, 116
  whilst in prison, 211
  after reporting, 214
sex as pollution, 179–93
sex work, 31, 63, 67n2, 67, 102
sex, withholding, 89–90
sexing, 62, 89, 98, 124, 189
sexual and gender-based violence (SGBV), 9, 36
sexual consent, 9–10, 172, 215, *see also* availability (in relationships)
sexual harassment, 9, 100, 157
sexual offences, 14, 34, 169, 195, 199, 203
Sexual Offences Act (SOA) 2012
  consequences, 183, 194, 211, 215, 225–6, 229
  convictions, 194–5, 210
  criticism of, 188–93, 211, 219
  discussion from, 215, 222
  effectiveness, 178, 211, 215–16, 219, 221
  implementation, 172, 178, 182, 227
  imprisonment under the, 10, 194, 196, 206
  overview, 169, 172–5, 215
Sexual Offences Amendment Act (SOAA) 2019, 10, 15, 95, 169, 174, 195n2
sexual penetration (SP)
  cases, 170–2, 178, 184–6
  definition, 173
  imprisonment, 10, 169, 174, 202
sexual practices (terms), 62–4
sexual violence (perceptions), 88, 90, 158–9, 189, 229
sexuality, control over, 175, 179–80, 182, 191, 223
shadowing, 34
shame
  economic constraints, 53
  pregnancy, 183
  and protective masculinity, 49
  public, 81, 97–8, 124, 165
  reporting to police, 147, 149
  around sexual behaviour, 182n8

262 Index

shame (cont.)
  unemployment, 135
'shopping forums', 150
'show face', 70, 73, 204
side-chick, 59–62, 65, 72
Sierra Leone (overview), 3, 221, 226
Sierra Leonean state, 44n1, 95, 179, 221, 226
slapping, 96–100, 127, 139–40, 167
slavery, 14–15, 17, 46–7, 78
snatching, 65, 74
social bonds, 8, 131, 209, 224
social capital, 69, 164, 197
social media, 26, 30, 62, 91, 123
social networks
  and debt, 57
  of elders, 218
  and pressures, 84
  in prison, 211
  and relationship separation, 65, 75
  trusted, 62, 154
  of women, 101, 152
social organisation, 11, 123, 225
social position, 3, 6, 64, 90, 134–5, 213
social relations
  analysis of, 111
  binary conceptions of gender, 159
  complementarity, 217
  cultivation of, 12, 107, 134, 209, 214
  of elders, 218
  around marriage, 45
  metaphor of, 59
  reproduction of, 42, 213
social responsibility, 12, 15, 43, 76, 132
social status, 70, 75, 85, 99, 107, 138
sociocentric positioning, 75, 141, 149, 184, 214
socioeconomic positions, 16, 21, 40, 42, 55, 107
sodality, 44–5, 52, 126, 189
songs, 63, 99, 106, 120
speech, 17n4, 81, 109–10, 208
spells, 102–4, 106–7, 137
stability
  community, 116, 134, 219
  financial, 42
  household, 118, 134
  long-term, 60
  ontological, 210
  relationship, 75, 86
Star Motors Garage, 27, 32, 51
Stasik, Michael, 53, 67, 85
state courts, 7, 18, 113, 135n12, 135, 146

state institutions
  and autonomy of communities, 139, 142, 145, 215, 227
  challenges for, 8, 14, 178, 227
  distance from, 152, 178
  human rights culture, 152, 183, 214
  implementation of laws, 179, 182, 220, 222
  mediation systems, 33, 219
  punishments, 80, 151, 219
  reporting to, 9, 15, 150, 182
  views of, 5, 135, 169
state intervention, 80, 113, 141, 151, 227
state law
  ambivalence towards, 14, 178, 205
  criminalisation of sexual behaviour, 12, 215
  historical context, 16, 205
  'weak legal pluralism', 33, 142
state mediation, 156–7
state strategy, 209–10
statistics
  crime, 157
  interpreting, 9, 33, 177–8, 177n7, 229
  prison, 202
status, social, 70, 75, 85, 99, 107, 138
stigmatisation, 10–11, 71, 147, 182n8, 226
strategy, state, 209–10
structural violence, 12, 16–17, 42, 48, 212–13
subject positions
  of the criminal, 194, 203
  gendered, 216
  of guardians, 181
  multiple, 38, 187, 208–9
  negotiation of, 40, 128, 155, 204, 209–10
  responsibilities with, 218
  unequal, 219
  of the victim, 188
subjectivity, 32, 38, 69, 194, 211
subordination, 83, 164, 167, 217, 223, 227
sub-Saharan Africa, 4, 7, 52, 135
support. See also DDR (Disarmament, Demobilization, and Reintegration programme); Family Support Units (FSUs)
  community, 74, 116, 133, 148–9, 179
  emotional, 38, 114, 147, 149, 154
  familial. See familial support
  financial, 67, 72, 103, 145, 222
  institutional, 9, 153
  organisational, 196
  outside the community, 15
  systems, 37, 136, 150, 156
survival, 48, 58, 60

Index

survivors of sexual violence, 26, 35, 154
'swallowing' grievances, 8, 112–13, 120, 133, 139–43, 153
'swearing', 71n5, 130, 211
symbolic violence, 84, 97, 164
symbolism, 44–5, 50, 71, 140, 208

teenage pregnancy
   data, 176–7
   development goals, 173
   eradication of, 15, 179, 182
   government failures, 229
   national emergency, 10, 172
   prevention, 4, 9
   school ban, 16, 229
   state language around, 178, 215
   stigmatisation, 11
teeth and the tongue (metaphor), 1–2, 141, 164, 217, 231
Temne, the, 30, 44, 48, 61n1
temptation, 106–8, 135–8, 192n13
terminologies, local, 59, 95, 110, 117, 227
traditional doctors, 102–3, 106, 137
traditional marriage, 44n1, 67, 89, 158
transactional relationships, 12, 42, 54, 67–8
trapping, 102, 104, 107–8
trauma
   long history of, 46, 223
   and research ethics, 35
   secondary, 39
   from sexual violence, 182
   wartime, 50–1
trust
   character witnesses, 119, 139
   during the civil war, 51
   food, 107
   and phones, 85
   of research collaborators, 40
   and sexual harassment, 100
   in the state, 154, 157, 205
   in young people, 15
Truth and Reconciliation Commission (TRC)
   aims, 9n3, 220
   blame towards the, 191
   data, 178
   following the, 9, 220
   recommendations, 169, 172, 174, 220, 226
   report, 145, 172, 180
24 (room), 22, 31, 87, 100, *101*, 139

Uganda, 14, 39, 179
unemployment, 29, 70, 122, 135
UNICEF, 176–7, 227, *227*
United Nations Population Fund (UNFPA), 175, *176*, 177
unity, 15, 22, 142, 227
university, 29–30, 68, 102, *see also* Fourah Bay College (FBC)
urban ethnography, 12, 212

victim–perpetrator relationship, 6, 8, 187, 213, 219
Vigh, Henrik, 24, 58
violence in relationships (conceptions), 4–7, 159
violence, acceptable, 6, 79, 89, 111
violence, acts of
   and affection, 75
   as communicating emotions, 84
   as corrective measures, 82
   gendered, 95, 213
   terms describing, 93, 95, 109–10, 218
violence, emotional, 84–5, 158
violence, gender-based, 9, 36, 84, 93n1, 180, 206
violence, normalised, 11, 48, 51–2, 83
violence, private forms of, 75, 88, 94n1
violence, sexual. *See* sexual violence (perceptions)
violence, unacceptable
   defining, 6, 79–81
   mediation, 112, 134
   and moral economy, 111
   neglect, 111
   reporting, 111, 113–21, 143–4, 214
violence, visible
   and acceptability, 97
   contemporary intimacy, 13
   and emotional support, 114
   and gender, 99, 109
   insulting, 96
   traceability, 7
violence, war-time, 7, 145
virginity, 14, 62, 79, 186, 201
visible violence. *See* violence, visible
vulnerabilities
   age of consent, 10, 175
   and emotional support, 38
   and intimacy, 73
   through reporting, 155
   within research, 31, 34, 39
   socioeconomic positions, 40

Wardlow, Holly, 32, 216
war-time violence, 7, 145, *see also* civil war (1991–2002)

weak legal pluralism, 142, 227
West Africa, 15–16, 212, 229
Western Freetown, 73, 175
witness statements
   in court, 147, 157, 199
   in mediation, 119, 134, 137

'women trouble', 45, 47, 69

youth, crisis of. *See* 'crisis of youth'
'youth' definition, 53
'youth', social construct of, 54–8
youthhood, 42–3, 52–3, 70, 189

TITLES IN THE SERIES (*continued from page ii*)

74. ANDREA MARIKO GRANT *Youth, Pentecostalism, and Popular Music in Rwanda*
73. LUISA T. SCHNEIDER *Love and Violence in Sierra Leone: Mediating Intimacy after Conflict*
72. MICHAEL STASIK *Bus Station Hustle: Transport Work in Urban Ghana*
71. LESLIE FESENMYER *Relative Distance: Kinship, Migration, and Christianity between Kenya and the United Kingdom*
70. KAREN TRANBERG HANSEN *Dress Cultures in Zambia: Interwoven Histories, Global Exchanges, and Everyday Life*
69. RAMON SARRÓ *Inventing an African Alphabet: Writing, Art and Kongo Culture in the DRC*
68. EMILY VAN HOUWELING *Water and Aid in Mozambique: Gendered Perspectives of Change*
67. KOREEN M. REECE *Pandemic Kinship: Families, Intervention, and Social Change in Botswana's Time of AIDS*
66. FERDINAND DE JONG *Decolonizing Heritage: Time to Repair in Senegal*
65. HANSJÖRG DILGER *Learning Morality, Inequalities, and Faith: Christian and Muslim Schools in Tanzania*
64. MARLOES JANSON *Crossing Religious Boundaries: Islam, Christianity and 'Yoruba Religion' in Lagos, Nigeria*
63. VAN ZYL-HERMANN *Privileged Precariat: White Workers and South Africa's Long Transition to Majority Rule*
62. BENEDIKT PONTZEN *Islam in a Zongo: Muslim Lifeworlds in Asante, Ghana*
61. LOUISA LOMBARD *Hunting Game: Raiding Politics in the Central African Republic*
60. MARK HUNTER *Race for Education: Gender, White Tone, and Schooling in South Africa*
59. LIZ GUNNER *Radio Soundings: South Africa and the Black Modern*
58. JESSICA JOHNSON *In Search of Gender Justice: Rights and Relationships in Matrilineal Malawi*
57. JASON SUMICH *The Middle Class in Mozambique: The State and the Politics of Transformation in Southern Africa*
56. JOSÉ-MARÍA MUÑOZ *Doing Business in Cameroon: An Anatomy of Economic Governance*
55. JENNIFER DIGGINS *Coastal Sierra Leone: Materiality and the Unseen in Maritime West Africa*
54. HANNAH HOECHNER *Quranic Schools in Northern Nigeria: Everyday Experiences of Youth, Faith, and Poverty*
53. HOLLY PORTER *After Rape: Violence, Justice, and Social Harmony in Uganda*
52. ALEXANDER THURSTON *Salafism in Nigeria: Islam, Preaching, and Politics*
51. ANDREW BANK *Pioneers of the Field: South Africa's Women Anthropologists*

50. MAXIM BOLT *Zimbabwe's Migrants and South Africa's Border Farms: The Roots of Impermanence*
49. MEERA VENKATACHALAM *Slavery, Memory and Religion in Southeastern Ghana, c. 1850–Present*
48. DEREK PETERSON, KODZO GAVUA, and CIRAJ RASSOOL (eds.) *The Politics of Heritage in Africa: Economies, Histories and Infrastructures*
47. ILANA VAN WYK *The Universal Church of the Kingdom of God in South Africa: A Church of Strangers*
46. JOEL CABRITA *Text and Authority in the South African Nazaretha Church*
45. MARLOES JANSON *Islam, Youth, and Modernity in the Gambia: The Tablighi Jama'at*
44. ANDREW BANK and LESLIE J. BANK (eds.) *Inside African Anthropology: Monica Wilson and Her Interpreters*
43. ISAK NIEHAUS *Witchcraft and a Life in the New South Africa*
42. FRASER G. MCNEILL *AIDS, Politics, and Music in South Africa*
41. KRIJN PETERS *War and the Crisis of Youth in Sierra Leone*
40. INSA NOLTE *Obafemi Awolowo and the Making of Remo: The Local Politics of a Nigerian Nationalist*
39. BEN JONES *Beyond the State in Rural Uganda*
38. RAMON SARRÓ *The Politics of Religious Change on the Upper Guinea Coast: Iconoclasm Done and Undone*
37. CHARLES GORE *Art, Performance and Ritual in Benin City*
36. FERDINAND DE JONG *Masquerades of Modernity: Power and Secrecy in Casamance, Senegal*
35. KAI KRESSE *Philosophising in Mombasa: Knowledge, Islam and Intellectual Practice on the Swahili Coast*
34. DAVID PRATTEN *The Man-Leopard Murders: History and Society in Colonial Nigeria*
33. CAROLA LENTZ *Ethnicity and the Making of History in Northern Ghana*
32. BENJAMIN F. SOARES *Islam and the Prayer Economy: History and Authority in a Malian Town*
31. COLIN MURRAY and PETER SANDERS *Medicine Murder in Colonial Lesotho: The Anatomy of a Moral Crisis*
30. R. M. DILLEY *Islamic and Caste Knowledge Practices among Haalpulaar'en in Senegal: Between Mosque and Termite Mound*
29. BELINDA BOZZOLI *Theatres of Struggle and the End of Apartheid*
28. ELISHA RENNE *Population and Progress in a Yoruba Town*
27. ANTHONY SIMPSON *'Half-London' in Zambia: Contested Identities in a Catholic Mission School*
26. HARRI ENGLUND *From War to Peace on the Mozambique–Malawi Borderland*
25. T. C. MCCASKIE *Asante Identities: History and Modernity in an African Village 1850–1950*
24. JANET BUJRA *Serving Class: Masculinity and the Feminisation of Domestic Service in Tanzania*
23. CHRISTOPHER O. DAVIS *Death in Abeyance: Illness and Therapy among the Tabwa of Central Africa*

22. DEBORAH JAMES *Songs of the Women Migrants: Performance and Identity in South Africa*
21. BIRGIT MEYER *Translating the Devil: Religion and Modernity among the Ewe in Ghana*
20. DAVID MAXWELL *Christians and Chiefs in Zimbabwe: A Social History of the Hwesa People c. 1870s–1990s*
19. FIONA D. MACKENZIE *Land, Ecology and Resistance in Kenya, 1880–1952*
18. JANE I. GUYER *An African Niche Economy: Farming to Feed Ibadan, 1968–88*
17. PHILIP BURNHAM *The Politics of Cultural Difference in Northern Cameroon*
16. GRAHAM FURNISS *Poetry, Prose and Popular Culture in Hausa*
15. C. BAWA YAMBA *Permanent Pilgrims: The Role of Pilgrimage in the Lives of West African Muslims in Sudan*
14. TOM FORREST *The Advance of African Capital: The Growth of Nigerian Private Enterprise*
13. MELISSA LEACH *Rainforest Relations: Gender and Resource Use among the Mende of Gola, Sierra Leone*
12. ISAAC NCUBE MAZONDE *Ranching and Enterprise in Eastern Botswana: A Case Study of Black and White Farmers*
11. G. S. EADES *Strangers and Traders: Yoruba Migrants, Markets and the State in Northern Ghana*
10. COLIN MURRAY *Black Mountain: Land, Class and Power in the Eastern Orange Free State, 1880s to 1980s*
9. RICHARD WERBNER *Tears of the Dead: The Social Biography of an African Family*
8. RICHARD FARDON *Between God, the Dead and the Wild: Chamba Interpretations of Religion and Ritual*
7. KARIN BARBER *I Could Speak Until Tomorrow: Oriki, Women and the Past in a Yoruba Town*
6. SUZETTE HEALD *Controlling Anger: The Sociology of Gisu Violence*
5. GÜNTHER SCHLEE *Identities on the Move: Clanship and Pastoralism in Northern Kenya*
4. JOHAN POTTIER *Migrants No More: Settlement and Survival in Mambwe Villages, Zambia*
3. PAUL SPENCER *The Maasai of Matapato: A Study of Rituals of Rebellion*
2. JANE I. GUYER (ed.) *Feeding African Cities: Essays in Social History*
1. SANDRA T. BARNES *Patrons and Power: Creating a Political Community in Metropolitan Lagos*

Printed by Integrated Books International,
United States of America